# The Handgun Story

*To the Usual Suspects*
*'A', 'A' and 'N' – and to Jack, who still doesn't believe*
*that the creative process takes precedence over throwing his ball . . .*

# The Handgun Story
## A Complete Illustrated History

*John Walter*

FRONTLINE BOOKS, LONDON

**The Handgun Story**

This edition published in 2008 by Frontline Books,
an imprint of Pen and Sword Books Ltd,
47 Church Street, Barnsley, S. Yorkshire, S70 2AS
www.frontline-books.com

ISBN: 978-1-84832-500-5

For more information on our books, please visit
www.frontline-books.com, email info@frontline-books.com
or write to us at the above address.

Printed and bound in Great Britain by Biddles Ltd, King's Lynn

# Contents

# *Illustrations*

**Plates**

## Line Drawings

# *Preface and Acknowledgements*

*The Handgun Story* has been written to accompany *The Rifle Story*, published in 2006, and takes much the same approach. It also plays on the same strengths and weaknesses in its attempt to provide a readable one-volume guide to the development of the pistol and the revolver.

Of course, any attempt to provide a 'broad canvas' – mentioning any and all of the 'one-hand guns' ever made – is hamstrung by the need to force a tremendous amount of information into a space that is inevitably restricted by publishing constraints. Yet even if thousands of pages and millions of words could be spared, coverage would still favour those guns that have been scrutinised in detail to the detriment of those that are still largely unremarked. The Borchardt-Luger (or 'Parabellum') and the FN Pistolet à Grande Puissance ('High Power') typify those that have been the object of intensive study: in the case of the former, in literally hundreds of books and articles. Against this, the amount of time devoted to the study of lesser (but sometimes more interesting) topics has often been minimal and there are still many extensive gaps in the story. My approach, therefore, seeks to provide an overview by concentrating on certain specifics.

I have, I admit, dealt too concisely with pre-cartridge handguns; this is partly because my personal interests lie more in the effects of nineteenth-century technological progress on gun design, and partly because research into the history of the oldest guns is best left to those whose expertise is far greater than mine. I'm also content to concentrate on the 'Suicide Special' revolvers or the Borchardt pistol, for example, instead of re-telling the story of the 'Luger' or the JSSAP trials of the 1970s. Hopefully, the Bibliography will point the reader interested in these topics towards more information.

No book is the work of its author alone, and so I would like to thank the many people who have helped. I hope that I have not misrepresented their trust. Information has come from a variety of sources, some more than thirty years old and others which have only recently appeared on the internet. I have also adapted a few articles that were published in periodicals such as *Guns Review*, *Guns Digest* and *Shooter's Bible*, and I remember with affection my association with the editors, principally Colin Greenwood, Chuck Hartigan, Ken Ramage and Bob Scott.

The photographs have been collected from a variety of sources, not all of which are obvious from the meagre amount of information on the individual prints. But I do know that the coverage would be poorer but for the assistance of the leading auction houses: Sothebys, Christies, Bonhams, Wallis & Wallis and Weller & Dufty. Individual illustrations were cheerfully provided by, among others, Beretta, Colt (in its many guises), FN Herstal SA, Glock, Hämmerli, SIG-Sauer, Steyr-Mannlicher, Sturm Ruger, Thompson/Center and Walther. Most of the line drawings were downloaded from the excellent websites of the US Government Patent Office and the UK Intellectual Property Office (formerly the Patent Office).

The Imperial War Museum, the Sotamuseo (the Finnish war museum in Helsinki), the Eidgenössische Waffenfabrik, the John M. Browning Museum and the Kungliga Armémuseum in Stockholm always responded to requests for information, as have friends and acquaintances – Joe Schroeder, Karl Schäfer, Henk Visser, Randall Gibson, Ferdi Hediger, Reinhard Kornmayer, Rolf Gminder, Jack Krcma, and Fred Wilkinson among them. But the passing of the years also reminds me of the loss of Ian Hogg and Joachim Görtz, who together did so very much to support me.

My colleagues at Fire-Power International, Christian Cranmer and Chris Fox, get my thanks for continuing to encourage my efforts, as do Lionel Leventhal; Michael Leventhal and Kate Baker at Frontline Books; editor Donald Sommerville; and reader Stephen Bull, who together excised errors of fact and the 'sleights of pen' which had escaped attention. I'm responsible for any that remain . . .

When all is said and done, the brunt of the pressure generated by the creative process falls on my family. The support of Alison, Adam and Nicky means more to me than, perhaps, I sometimes show; and the menagerie – Rosie, Harvey, Bowie, Tallulah and Jack – can be a welcome diversion from the computer!

*John Walter*

# I

# *Prologue:*
# *From a Burning Brand to the Cap-Lock*

The origins of handguns stretch back to the earliest days of gunpowder, but not until technology improved did they become viable weapons. The first guns were exceptionally clumsy, even after a 'tiller' – the forerunner of a stock – had been added to what had previously been an unsupported barrel, at first made by hammer-welding short strips of iron onto a mandrel that could subsequently be drilled out to provide a 'bore'. Later barrels were cast in a single piece, allowing them to be stronger and less likely to burst by unwinding along an inadequately welded seam.

Many small guns have been retrieved from the ruins of castles and fortifications, dating as early as the fourteenth century, but most of these were simply diminutions of the tiller-gun. They usually have sockets in the breech-end of the tube, and the smallness of their bore begs a question: were they weapons, or merely toys? It is hard to believe that they would have had much offensive threat, as the bores were very small and the capacity for the poor-quality gunpowder of the day was extremely limited. It seems more likely that they were the playthings of the nobility, or perhaps the sons of the nobility. There is no evidence that they were made in quantity. Indeed, guns of all types were in short supply prior to 1400.

The idea of a one-hand gun remained in limbo until the invention of the wheel-lock, attributed to a variety of men – including Leonardo da Vinci – but almost certainly a product of the south German clock-making industry in the early 1500s. The clockmakers were amongst the most skilled of the earliest mechanical engineers, used to working accurately in small scale.

To function efficiently, clocks needed to combine skill in design and great precision in the cutting of gears. It was a small step from a clock to the 'clockwork' mechanism of the wheel-lock, in which a small chain (often of only three or five links) connected a spring with a rotating wheel. To work the lock, a small key was used to 'span' the mechanism by winding the chain against the pressure of the spring onto a spindle fixed in the wheel. The other major part of the action was a piece of iron pyrites held in the jaws of a 'cock' that could be rotated until held against the serrated rim of the wheel by a small spring.

Pressure on the trigger or 'tricker' released the captive wheel, which was spun by the action of the spring pulling on the chain. A shower of sparks created from the contact of the pyrites and the serrated edge of the wheel cascaded into a pan of fine-grain priming powder and, after an infinitesimal delay, the main charge of gunpowder in the chamber also ignited.

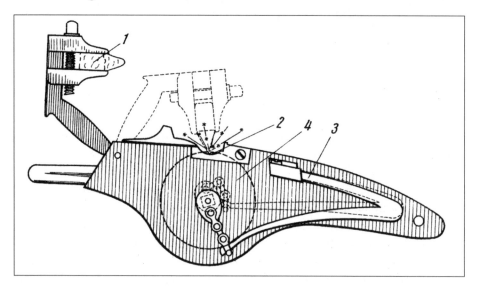

*The parts of a typical wheel lock. 1. Pyrites clamped in cock; 2. Priming powder in pan; 3. Mainspring; 4. Wheel.*

The advent of the wheel-lock had two important effects. It not only freed the firearm from the first, but essentially primitive method of ignition, the lighted match or tow, but also removed the need for two-hand use by providing a self-contained mechanism that worked automatically once released. In addition, by involving the highly-skilled clockmakers, it ensured that the status of gunmakers was rapidly elevated to a level that was jealously guarded for generation after generation. The recognition of gunmakers' guilds and the steadily increasing output allowed the small firearm to find military use, and the increase in use created an environment in which innovations – not always universally praised – could be promoted.

The wheel-lock was an efficient mechanism, but it also had several weaknesses. Production was limited by the need for skilled craftsmen and costs were therefore correspondingly high, even though considerable numbers of plain-looking guns were made for military service; the pyrites was comparatively weak, often disintegrating after a few shots had been fired; and the employment of a separate key or 'spanner' to wind the spindle was undesirable in combat. Something better was needed; something that could be used time and time again with a minimum of motion and a certainty of repetition.

The answer was the 'flinted lock', which was made in several forms. There has been much debate about the origins of these locks, and the differences between them. The most popular forms are the Spanish *miquelet*, the Dutch/German *snaphance*, and the French lock.[1] Though the principal difference between the *snaphance* and the French lock is often said to be the combination of the steel and pan cover in one component, it seems that the first French locks, introduced early in the seventeenth century (allegedly by the French gunmaker Marin le Bougeoys, Arquebusier du Roi), also had separate pan covers. The true difference will be found in the design of the sear, which works vertically to engage notches or 'bents' in the tumbler attached to the cock spindle. In the snaphance, the sear works laterally; in addition, notably in the miquelet, the nose of the sear projects through the lock plate to release the tail of the cock when the trigger is pressed.

The French lock gradually attained a position of supremacy by the end of the seventeenth century, which lasted until the advent of the percussion cap more than a hundred years later. The principle of the lock was simple: a specially shaped or 'knapped' flint, held in the jaws of a pivoting cock, was brought into contact with a rapidly-moving roughened surface so that a shower of sparks was diverted into a panful of priming powder. A true French-style flintlock, therefore, had the steel and the pan cover formed as a single part, and a sear that moved vertically to intercept a tumbler fixed to the axis-pin of the cock after it had passed through the lock plate. The dog lock, favoured in England, was simply a flintlock with a large safety catch or 'dog' on the outside tail of the lock plate to intercept the tail of the cock.

The flintlock offered no real economy of size compared with the preceding wheel-lock, but had the merits of simplicity and durability. Flint is much harder than pyrites, and gave more consistent ignition; and, excepting the relationship between the striking point of the flint and the steel, the parts of the flintlock were comparatively easy to make and easy to regulate. The ease with which the new lock could be made boosted production to a point where armies could issue firearms universally, at the expense of the bow and the pike. The guns were simple and sturdy, though often initially large, long-barrelled and cumbersome; as the years passed, however, even the regulation military weapons became more compact and better to handle.

---

1. The term 'snaphance' (or 'snaphaunce') is believed to derive from the Old German or Old Dutch words for 'hen thief', *schnapphahn* or *snaphaan*. The inspiration for the design undoubtedly came from the *miquelet*, as the Netherlands was then part of the Spanish empire. The genesis of the *miquelet* is, however, equally uncertain. The word may derive from the nickname given to Spanish bandits, *los miguelitos*, but the suspiciously early date ascribed in Jaroslav Lugs, *Handfeuerwaffen* (Berlin, 1962), to the invention of the lock – 1560 – is open to doubt. Credit is supposedly due to Simón Macuarte (Marckwart), a German-born gunmaker brought to Madrid by Charles V in 1530. Robert E. Gardner, in *Small Arms Makers*, suggests, more plausibly, that the lock was the invention of Simón Marcuarte the Younger (*fl.*1555–99) at the very end of the sixteenth century.

Flintlock pistols offered to the more discerning commercial purchaser came in far greater variety. The largest, the holster pistols intended to be carried on a saddle, were often very large indeed; travelling or carriage pistols, often cased and sometimes in pairs, were smaller and handier; and there were pistols, often based on a box-type lock,[2] which were small enough to be concealed in a gentleman's pocket or a lady's muffler.

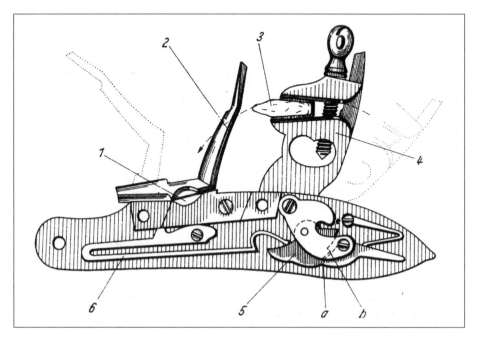

*The parts of a typical flintlock. 1. Pan; 2. Steel; 3. Flint; 4. Cock; 5. Tumbler; 6. Mainspring; a & b Half- and full-cock notches ('bents') on sear.*

Among the more specialist products were 'waterproof' flintlocks, not to be confused with the later waterproof-pan type; guns with more than one barrel, or which were capable of firing more than one shot through the same barrel (each type is considered in greater detail in the next chapter); and a few guns that could be loaded from the breech. The best-known of the breech-loading designs are the so-called 'turn off' pistols of the seventeenth and eighteenth centuries, with barrels which could be unscrewed from the standing breech with the assistance of a small spanner. Loading from the breech allowed a tight-fitting ball to be used, and the occasional provision of rifling improved accuracy. The best pistols of this type shot very well indeed, and there are records of marksmen hitting targets only a few feet wide at distances of fifty yards or more – which was good shooting by the standards of a muzzle-loaded smooth-bore.

---

2. A design in which the barrel and the breech were customarily made as a single piece.

The finest gun of this period was the duelling pistol, intended specifically for short-range accuracy. To minimise the effects of snatching a shot the pistols were often provided with a heavy barrel, often 'swamped' or swelling towards the muzzle; some guns had special hair triggers, others had refinements in their locks that included rollers between the steel and its spring, platinum-lined touch-holes (resistant to corrosion), and saw-handle grips. Though the guns were customarily plain finished, they could have the finest damascus barrels and woodwork of the best quality. Pairs were often provided – one for each protagonist! – in cases fitted for accessories including powder flasks and ammunition.

The pre-eminence of the flintlock endured for more than 200 years, until the realisation that the explosive properties of a group of chemical compounds known as the fulminates could be harnessed to provide a self-contained ignition system. Credited to a Scottish clergyman, Alexander Forsyth (though the potential use of fulminates as an igniter had been predicted by the Frenchman Claude-Louis Berthollet as early as 1786), the original percussion-ignition lock was patented in England in 1807. Known as the 'scent bottle', it relied on a rotating reservoir to deposit a small amount of fulminate powder alongside a touch-hole, where it could be struck and ignited by a hammer-driven pin. The fulminate lock was difficult to make, and prone to suffer the effects of corrosion. It was soon improved, however, and the effect it had on the sporting-gun market persuaded many enterprising gunmakers to produce alternatives: pill-locks, tube-locks, and a variety of other proprietary designs. These were soon all swept away by the cap, a pellet of mercuric fulminate contained within a small envelope – initially of board, later of tin and then copper, shellacked to be waterproof.

The genesis of the cap has always been in some doubt, though the consensus is to give the honour to John Shaw even though his claims are vigorously contested in France in particular. The percussion cap was the greatest step forward in firearms technology since the introduction of the flintlock. Though the mechanics of the cap lock differed from the flintlock only in the substitution of a nipple for the pan and steel, the means of ignition was far more efficient. Tests undertaken by the French Army in the 1830s suggested that the certainty of ignition improved by a factor of six once the cap had replaced the flint.

The cap-lock pistols were also near-duplicates of their immediate flintlock predecessors, sharing the same lines and construction. The changes were confined to the lock. Large, plain military pistols were accompanied by duellers, coach pistols, pocket pistols and all the other varieties of the flintlock handgun. Their heyday was comparatively short, however, owing to the advent first of the multi-shot pepperboxes and revolvers, and secondly the self-contained cartridge that the fulminate had made possible.

The cap-lock revolvers offered by Samuel Colt and his rivals in the middle of the nineteenth century (described in the next chapter) clearly held great advantages over any single-shot pistol. However, not only were revolvers expensive, but production was initially too small to dominate the market. The single-barrel pistol was so much easier to make that it co-existed with more sophisticated rivals until the American Civil War (1861–5).

The cap-locks made in Philadelphia from the 1840s onward by Henry Deringer were the most notorious of the earliest designs. Deringer's holster pistols had attained a certain amount of success in the Texarkana in the 1840s, but the guns with which his name is now associated could be hidden in a pocket or a hand. They were generally .41-calibre back-action cap-locks with rifled barrels as short as 2 inches, reducing overall length to just 4¼in. Genuine Philadelphia-made pistols were marked DERINGER over PHILADELA. or PHILA. on the lock. The barrel key was customarily retained by a pineapple-finial plate, barrels displayed a false damascus twist, and the locks were invariably case-hardened. The metalwork was usually blued, though nickel- and silver-plated trigger guards and barrel-key plates could be supplied to order.

The lasting success of the Deringer was due to the Gold Rush of 1849, which turned California from its Hispanic slumber to a rampaging boom economy. Limitations on Deringer's production capacity, which was too small to satisfy all but a fraction of the demand, persuaded many gunsmiths to copy the Philadelphia-made pocket pistol. Among the best-known copyists were Slotter & Company and A. J. Plate of San Francisco, and some guns were even given spurious authenticity by Philadelphia tailor Jacob Deringer, who granted appropriate 'licences' to several gunsmiths. The .38-calibre derringers[3] made by Jesse Butterfield of Philadelphia usually had a patented priming tube mounted vertically ahead of the hammer, where it could feed a pellet over the nipple each time the mechanism was cocked. Ingenuity of this type, however, was the exception to the simple-copy rule. After the death of Henry Deringer in 1867, his executors pursued many infringers through the Federal courts, but enforcement of the decisions was often impossible in areas which had not even been admitted to the Union. Transgressors simply continued to make their derringers until cartridge pistols appeared in quantity.

The derringer was the ideal covert weapon, acting as a back-up for larger guns. The .41-calibre ball was effective at close range – if a large enough gunpowder charge was used – and the tiny pistol could be tucked in the top of a boot or a garter.

Excepting the Deringer, its facsimiles and a few underhammer 'boot guns', single-barrel cap-lock pocket pistols were uncommon in North America. The smallest of the several Lindsay Young America guns was broadly comparable, though its barrel contained two superimposed charges. These were fired separately by two individual hammers; however, unless the charges were separated by properly greased wads, ignition of the first (front) charge was apt to fire the second (rear) charge at the same time.

---

3. The generic term 'derringer' usually features an 'rr' misspelling of Deringer's name.

# 2

# *The First Multi-Shot Guns*

The idea of guns that could fire more than a single shot was old, almost as old as the gun itself. The earliest efforts had simply clustered several barrels around a central spine, igniting each in turn with a lighted brand or 'slow match', but the second half of the nineteenth century was an inventor's paradise.

The search for an efficient self-contained cartridge was an important catalyst; so, too, was burgeoning technological advance. However, the improvements were patchy and often uncertain. Improvements in the manufacture of steels or moves towards standardised measurements were sometimes easy to see, but could take many years to step from promising ideas to profitable reality. One result was that virtually anything could be promoted, from sophisticated idea to gimcrack scheme, and a widespread ignorance of mechanical principles allowed even the science and engineering magazines of the nineteenth century to feature ideas that had no real merit.

The chaos that ensued largely bypassed the armies of the day, often simply because the innately conservative commanders and ordnance bureaux answered submissions by rejecting anything that showed ingenuity – simultaneously protecting their armies from the worst effects of the design boom, but also acting as a dead hand on progress.

A few multi-barrelled matchlocks had been made in the early years of firearms history, but the first multi-shot guns to be successful were two-barrel wheel-locks. These came in several forms. The most idiosyncratic had two barrels above each other ('super[im]posed'), two locks and two triggers, giving the appearance of two guns that had been joined together at the barrel. A straight-line butt, which enabled either barrel to be uppermost, completed the odd-looking package. Other pistols were more conventional, with two barrels, two locks – one usually placed behind and above the other – and a conventional stock with a downward-curving butt. A large pommel, often in the form of a hefty ball or a mace, enabled the gun to double as a clubbing weapon after the shots had been fired. The triggers were generally separate, within a single enveloping iron-strap guard, but some of the finest guns were made with triggers that fired the barrels sequentially and others incorporated setting levers to give a very precise let-off. Safety catches were also surprisingly common.

Typical of the wheel-locks that combined side-by-side double barrels with plain military-style finish was a gun made in the Netherlands or more probably in Germany in the middle of the seventeenth century by the gunmaker using the mark of 'IS' beneath a molet.[1] Sold by the London auction house Christie's in the spring of 2006, the pistol is 24.1 inches long and has two plain mirror-image locks, with sparing decoration on the cock and the small claw-like bracket retaining the external wheel. The left-hand lock has a safety catch, the pans have sliding covers, and the plain wooden stock ends in an ovoid or 'lemon' pommel. The trigger guard is a plain iron strap, and the single ramrod pipe is also iron.

Double-barrelled flintlock guns were also made in superimposed and side-by-side form. The latter retained popularity for many years, flintlocks giving way first to cap locks and then to metal-case ammunition. Typical of the seventeenth-century products was a two-barrelled gun sold at auction in 2006.[2] This particular pistol, dated to about 1670 and said to have Dutch or German origins, has full-length barrels with a wooden insert carrying a rammer on the right side in moulded pipes. The lightly engraved lock is a back-action pattern, carrying only the swan-neck cock; each of the barrels carries its own pan and steel, indexing with a spring-latch beneath the action ahead of the trigger guard. The butt cap is plain, with elongated straps and a single circumferential flute, and a mark on the butt was probably applied by the armoury of August-Frederick von Holstein-Gottorp, prince-bishop of Lübeck from 1666 until 1706.

The last pistols of this particular genre were really little more than diminutives of the sporting guns of their day, embodying the refinements made during the third quarter of the nineteenth century. Some of the many improvements in shotgun and sporting-rifle design chronicled in *The Rifle Story*, including the multi-bite breech, the doll's head and the box lock, apply equally to handguns.

Double-barrel break open pistols retained some popularity in the British colonies (India, for example) until the beginning of the First World War, largely because they could be chambered for cartridges which were much more powerful than any of the revolvers of the day could handle in safety. 'Howdah pistols' of .577 calibre, firing the Snider carbine cartridge, were particularly favoured.

The cluster-barrel design favoured by some of the earliest of all medieval proto-handguns reappeared in the eighteenth century, in the form of the duck's foot pistol – usually a flintlock with individual barrels splayed horizontally – and the pocket pistols promoted by John Waters of Birmingham and others, which had barrels in blocks, often in two rows orientated vertically. Some guns, known as 'volley guns', fired all the barrels as once, but others relied on a selector mechanism to fire individual barrels.

---

1. 'Molet' is an heraldic term for a straight-rayed star, derived from the rowel of a spur; the 'stars of heaven' or *estoiles* have wavy rays. The gunmaker's mark (Neue Støckel 6145) is accompanied by a shield bearing what appears to be an eagle displayed. This may indicate the place of manufacture to be Nürnberg.

2. Christie's, London: *Fine Antique Arms and Armour Including the Collection of Dr. Robert Amalric...* , 24 May 2006, Lot 146.

A particularly fine example of the key-selector genre was sold by the British auctioneers Bonhams in 2006 as an 'historic gold-inlaid 120-bore three-barrelled flintlock box-lock tap-action pocket pistol presented in 1802 by Lieutenant-Colonel Thomas Thornton to Napoleon Bonaparte as First Consul'. The tiny gun, only 5.1 inches long with 3.1-inch barrels, was the work of the renowned London gunmaker Durs Egg. The sales catalogue records that it had

'... blued turn-off barrels, each inlaid with an engraved gold foliate band around the muzzle and breech, and numbered from "1" to "3", the top barrel in gold, blued border engraved breech-block signed in gold beneath and inlaid with three gold stars and a gold starburst on each side, blued tap inlaid en suite, blued border engraved action inlaid in gold with Thornton's engraved coat-of-arms and motto on one side, and with a scroll engraved with the battle honour "Marengo" against a martial trophy on the other, blued gold-inlaid cock engraved with a dolphin highlighted in gold on each side, blued thumbpiece safety-catch also locking the blued steel and each inlaid with gold foliage, blued border engraved trigger guard inlaid with an engraved gold martial trophy on the bow, figured flat-sided butt inlaid with gold wire scrollwork and engraved gold foliage...'

Thomas Thornton (1757–1823) was celebrated as a sportsman and shot, owning a variety of air guns and multi-barrelled firearms including a fourteen-barrel volley gun. He is also remembered for *A Sporting Tour Through Various Parts of France*, published in 1802.

Compact multi-barrel pistols survived the transition to self-contained cartridges. The Marston and the Sharps designs had both appeared in the USA prior to the American Civil War, and the Remington Double Derringer, a fixed-barrel over/under design, not only remained in uninterrupted production until 1936 but has also enjoyed an exceptionally successful revival since the 1960s. These are considered in more detail in the next chapter.

The geometry of the wheel-lock virtually precluded the use of barrels revolving around a horizontal axis unless entirely separate locks were used, adding unacceptable penalties in the form of excessive weight and complexity. The flintlock was not only much simpler to make, but the functions of the cock and the steel were also easily separated; by fitting a single cock on the action body and a steel and a pan on each individual barrel, therefore, a loaded barrel could be revolved into place as soon as the first shot had been fired. Guns of this type could have as many as four barrels, sometimes with a single cock and four separate steels or, alternatively, as a 'double-barrelled turnover' with two cocks and four steels. Excessive weight usually restricted multi-shot handguns of this type to two barrels in 'over/under' form, either fixed or capable of rotating.[3]

---

3. The rotating-barrel type is now often known as 'Wenders' after Ignaz Wender, a gunmaker working in Kutná Hora in Bohemia, now part of the Czech Republic. Wenger was hailed as the inventor of the superimposed gun, but the evidence is sketchy and the claims are undermined by the existence of earlier guns of the same general type.

## Revolving Pistols

The first of these were flintlocks, relying either on barrels that revolved or a single fixed barrel ahead of a short multi-chamber revolving block. The actions were almost always achieved manually, but attempts had been made to automate the process long before the first patent was granted to the self-promotional entrepreneurial 'Colonel' Samuel Colt.

In 2004, the London auction house Sotheby's sold a fine pair of three-barrel guns made by William Jover the Elder, of 83 Long Acre in London, at about the time of the American War of Independence.[4] The manually-rotated barrels were full length, with small panels of flowers and a line of beadwork at the breech. The action – a single flintlock – was made of brass, with rounded contours and a rearward strap running down the underside of the butt almost to the cap. The decoration is rococo in style, with flower springs and decorative borders, and Jover's signature appear on top of the breech in a triple scroll. The steel trigger guard slides to act as a safety catch. The steel breech tang has acanthus engraving, and is set in a decorative foliate apron with a scallop tip. A silver side plate and escutcheon are cast and chased into trophies of arms, and the silver butt cap with beaded straps ends in a grotesque mask. The auction catalogue does not record the calibre, but the guns were each 13.1 inches long.

The best-known of the claimants to the invention of the first mechanically-actuated revolving cylinder was Elisha Collier, an American citizen whose English patent dated from 1818.[5] In the USA, the brothers Benjamin and Barton Darling also claimed to have pre-empted Samuel Colt, though the arguments over the grant of a patent – and, more importantly, the date on which models may have been deposited – have been compromised by the destruction in December 1836 of the US Patent Office, occupying Blodgett's Hotel in Washington, DC, with the loss of all the specifications, drawings and models that had been submitted to that date.

The bare facts show that Colt received his patent first: No. 9430X, dated 25 February 1836, whereas the Darlings' No. 9591X was not granted by the US Patent Office until 13 April 1836. But whatever its genesis, the revolver and its near-relation, the pepperbox (with a rotating barrel cluster instead of a separate cylinder), was an astounding success.

Colt laboured for many years to perfect his revolver, though his claimed inspiration – the spokes of a ship's wheel – is widely thought to be just a good story. The first wooden model is said to have dated from the beginning of the 1830s, when Colt sailed to India as an ordinary seaman on the brig *Corvo*, but there are those who suspect that Colt saw a Collier or similar revolver when the ship tied up in London in 1831. Development work continued until working prototypes were made in Baltimore, Maryland, by mechanic

---

4. Howard Blackmore, in *A Dictionary of London Gunmakers* (1986), records that this particular Jover worked in Long Acre only until 1777, when he moved to 337 Oxford Street.
5. Most Collier-type revolvers were made *without* the components required to rotate the cylinder mechanically, but this was not true of some of the earliest guns nor of the design shown in the patent specification. In addition, a handful of much earlier European-made flintlock revolvers reportedly have cylinders that are revolved by pawls operated by the cock.

John Pearson. The guns proved to be good enough to encourage Colt to apply for patents in Britain, France and the USA, which he successfully undertook in 1835–6. English Patent 6909 was the first to be granted, on 22 October 1835. The principal claims to novelty lay in the ease of loading and rapidity of fire, achieved by connecting the hammer and the cylinder-rotating pawl.

A factory was opened in the small New Jersey town of Paterson, and the 'Patent Arms Manufacturing Company' began assembly of revolvers and revolver rifles, the latter undergoing extensive tests with the military authorities without ever encountering success. The five-shot handguns ranged from a .28-calibre Pocket Model No. 1 to the large .36-calibre Texas or Holster Pistol No. 5, all with triggers which sprang down out of the frame when the hammer was thumbed back. The independent State of Texas purchased 180 of the No. 5 'Paterson Colts' in 1839–41, which served until the Texas Navy was disbanded. Unfortunately, the Texas purchase was a rarity. Colt's fortunes did not grow in step with his unbounded enthusiasm, and the Patent Arms Company was liquidated in 1842.

Production is estimated to have been about 2,250–350 true Paterson revolvers, plus about 500 sold by the one-time secretary and treasurer of the Patent Arms Manufacturing Company, John Ehlers, after the business had failed. Ehlers was also a major shareholder, allowing him to seize incomplete guns to compensate for the loss of his investment. Though the Paterson venture was a costly failure, the patent granted to Colt in the USA not only effectively conferred a monopoly to make guns with mechanically-rotated cylinders, but was also upheld in several landmark court cases. However, it was not as effective in Britain or France – and not effective at all in countries such as Spain, where patent legislation was not recognised.

By the start of the Crimean War in the mid-1850s, revolvers were already attaining popularity; they had seen service in the wars between Texas and the Mexicans, in the Seminole Wars, and in the confrontations between the USA and Mexico. They had been officially adopted by the US Dragoons, and pin-fire versions were being touted throughout Europe by Lefaucheux and his many imitators. Colts had been copied in Austria, Britain and Russia, with benefit of licence; and in Belgium and Spain, with no such acknowledgement. (The quality of the copies ranged from poor to as good – possibly even better – than the originals.)

And there were the many rivals. Though legislation delayed the appearance of mechanically-rotated cylinders in the USA, many inventors strove to provide guns with cylinders that were either rotated manually or, better, by something other than direct linkage with the hammer: a second cylinder-rotating trigger, for example, proved to be one method of circumventing Colt's patent.

One drawback of all the Colt revolvers introduced prior to 1873, with the exception of the so-called 'Colt–Root' of 1855, was the open-top frame that relied on a wedge running through the barrel-lug and the cylinder axis pin to hold the components together. Another feature that attracted criticism was the lock-work, which relied on manual retraction of the hammer to index the chamber and cock the trigger mechanism (a method now generally categorised as 'single action'). Inventors such as Robert Adams in Britain provided 'double-action' systems in which merely pressing the trigger cocked the hammer, revolved and then indexed the cylinder, and released the hammer to strike the cap on the nipple of the chamber directly in line with the bore.

Though substantial numbers of pepperboxes had been made in Britain in the 1840s, comparatively little interest was taken in the revolver until the 'Great Exhibition of All Nations' was held in the Crystal Palace, London, in 1851. An impressive display of machine-made Colts was upstaged by a solid-frame self-cocking revolver on the stand of Deane, Adams & Deane. Made to Robert Adams's English Patent No. 13,527 of 1851, one of those all-embracing specifications that also protected breech-loading sporting rifles, the revolver may even have been exhibited as an afterthought. However, though accorded no prominence in the catalogues of the Great Exhibition, it was to be the cornerstone of Adams's success – particularly when Deane, Adams & Deane received a prize medal for its 'double & single guns & pistols properly finished'. Colt received nothing.

The Times reported on 27 June 1851 that 25 Colts had been purchased by officers of the 12th Lancers, ordered to Cape Colony, and a Select Committee assembled at Woolwich in September to test the six-shot .44-calibre Dragoon Colt against a lighter .53-calibre (32-bore) five-shot Adams. The tests were repeated at the Royal Manufactory, Enfield, and again at Woolwich under the supervision of Lieutenant-Colonel Chalmers of the Royal Artillery. The Colt was judged to be clumsier; the Adams was easier to use, owing to the self-cocking lock, but was more delicate.

When the Crimean War began at the end of 1853, a letter appeared in The Times drawing attention to a 'decision' of the Russian Navy to arm its men with Colt copies made in Tula. It has been suggested that the letter was written by a Colt stooge, attempting to steal a march on Adams, but the case (if case there was) has never been proved. Had the intention been to force the issue, the letter succeeded admirably; the British Admiralty, acting decisively, asked Colt to supply 4,000 1851 or Navy-pattern .36-calibre revolvers in March 1854. More were ordered in the summer of 1854, followed within a year by an Army order for 14,000.

The British Commander-in-Chief, Lord Raglan, then refused to allow cavalrymen to use revolvers – apparently on the grounds that they would endanger men on horseback – and the guns were issued to infantry officers, serjeants-major, and irregulars. Combat experience suggested that the .36-calibre 'Navy Colt' was accurate, but not powerful enough; the 54-bore (.442-in) Adams fired a heavier and more effective bullet. Both guns were as efficient as could be expected from any that relied on external priming, and both were sufficiently well made to withstand the rigours of combat. Consequently, each revolver was purchased in quantity not only privately, generally by individual officers, but also by the British Board of Ordnance and its 1855-vintage successor, the War Department. Yet the revolvers were rapidly withdrawn after the fighting had stopped, testifying to the low esteem in which they were held by the authorities (if not the fighting men). Inventories compiled at the beginning of 1859 revealed that 17,344 Colt revolvers were 'in store at home' and only 713 remained 'on issue abroad'.

The original self-cocking Adams revolver, though its one-piece frame was extremely sturdy, had two important disadvantages: it lacked a hammer spur, preventing thumb-cocking, and the absence of a rammer hindered loading. The bullet had to be seated in the chamber by thumb pressure alone, and sometimes jarred forward to leave a gap between its base and the powder. In addition, as the chamber diameter was greater than the bore, the bullet needed to accelerate very rapidly to engage the rifling satisfactorily. Adams's guns worked perfectly when properly loaded, but attempts to use coarsely grained or slow-burning powder were often disastrous.

The Colt, conversely, had a powerful rammer that seated each bullet firmly onto the powder charge, preventing excessive pressures and fostering a reputation for excellent accuracy. Experience in the Crimea, however, showed that the .36-calibre Colt bullet was a poor man-stopper compared with the appreciably larger Adams patterns. The drawbacks became even more worrying during the Indian Mutiny of 1857–9, when many men lost their lives unnecessarily.

Robert Adams soon made substantial improvements to his basic design, chiefly the addition of a rammer. Designs patented in 1854–5 by John Rigby, Adams himself and James Kerr were all tried. The original Rigby rammer is rarely seen, and is habitually confused with the Adams rammer. This lay on the left side of the frame above the trigger guard. The efficient Colt-like Kerr rammer protected by British Patent No. 1722 of 1855 (most commonly encountered on the military-issue revolvers) was mounted on the left side of the barrel, but the best of them was probably the subject of British Patent 760/55 granted to Joseph Brazier in April 1855. However, this particular rammer was confined to guns sold by Brazier, Wilkinson and a few other gunsmiths, and only appears on a few of the British service revolvers that had been purchased privately by the officers.

Lock-work credited to Lieutenant Frederick Beaumont of the Royal Engineers proved to be the difference between commercial obscurity and military approval. Adding a spur to the hammer, enabling the Adams (or 'Beaumont-Adams' as it soon became) to be thumb-cocked at will, provided Colt with an efficient competitor.[6] Duly impressed, the War Department substituted the .442 Adams for the .36 Colt in British service and the first orders were placed in October 1855. However, the war in the Crimea ended before many of the new revolvers could be delivered, and only 19,123 Adams revolvers had been acquired by the end of 1860.

The merits of the Colt and the Adams, and its Beaumont-Adams successor, were the subject of acrimonious public debate throughout the 1850s. Colt had been enraged by the award of prize medals to Adams by the jury of the Great Exhibition of 1851; Adams

---

6. Another rival was the Cooper revolver, made during the Civil War in Pittsburgh and in Frankford, Philadelphia, in accordance with US Patents 29684 and 40021 granted to James Maslin Cooper in September 1860 and September 1863 respectively. The design was very similar to the Colt, with the same basic construction in all respects other than the addition of a double-action trigger system.

was irked by the preference for the Colt shown by many high-ranking officials during the Crimean War, which he believed was the result of undue influence brought to bear by his American rival. In the end, the early failure of Colt's London factory (though trade representation continued until 1913) handed the laurels to his arch-rival.

## The American Civil War

The Crimean War was followed within a few years by civil war in the USA, which provided the revolver with its greatest single impetus. When the fighting began in 1861, a prospective purchaser was faced with a surprisingly wide choice of revolvers: from the popular Colts and the more recent Remington, to the British Beaumont-Adams being promoted by the Massachusetts Arms Company[7] and a horde of lesser guns. As the war ran its course, more and more designs were offered, especially in the first surge of recruitment and then after fire destroyed much of the Colt factory in Hartford, Connecticut, in 1864. Some of these were extremely efficient, but a few of them owed their introduction more to money-making than to their claims of novelty or efficiency.

It has often been claimed that the personal-defence needs of individual soldiers during the American Civil War were satisfied with large cap-and-ball revolvers, and guns of this type were undoubtedly acquired in huge numbers. The Federal government bought more than 330,000 in .36 and .44 calibre, but even these were far from sufficient to meet the needs of armies that mustered hundreds of thousands of men.[8] Private purchases may have doubled this total, as soldiers often acquired secondary or 'back-up' guns in the form of gifts from their family, wives or sweethearts. These included cap-and-ball revolvers with calibres of .28 or .31, though these suffered exactly the same drawbacks as the larger military-issue versions with few of their advantages as combat weapons.

The shocking Civil War death toll provides mute testimony to the numbers of men that were involved[9] and the efficiency of their weapons. The most successful revolvers in quantitative terms were the elegant open-frame Colts and the sturdy, solid frame

---

7. A licence to make the Beaumont-Adams revolver was granted to the Massachusetts Arms Company in the late 1850s, resulting from an acrimonious dispute with Colt that had prevented the Massachusetts Arms Co. making its own design. Small numbers of .36 Belt and .31 Pocket Model Beaumont-Adams revolvers were made by the American licensee in 1857–8, but production, never large, had ceased prior to the Civil War. The Federal authorities purchased 623 assorted Adams revolvers from Schuyler, Hartley & Graham of New York (11 November 1861–23 April 1862), and it is assumed that these came from old Massachusetts Arms Company stocks.

8. The unexpected advance of the Confederate forces on Washington, DC, at the beginning of the war, repulsed only at the last moment, panicked the Federal government to order the raising of the Army of the Potomac – 500,000 men strong – in an unbelievably short time. It was unsurprising, given the limited production capabilities of the firearms industry, that guns were initially in very short supply.

9. The Civil War casualty figures are still disputed, and lack of information will doubtless allow the challenges to continue for many years. The *Encyclopaedia Britannica* credits the Federal armies with the use of 1,556,000 men, suffering 359,528 dead and 275,175 wounded. Though the casualty figures are probably accurate, there is less certainty about the total muster: not everyone enlisted through 'proper' channels, and the employment of volunteers and militiamen was not always recorded with precision. Record-keeping in the Confederate States was far sketchier than in the North, but the total muster, deaths and injuries are customarily estimated at about 800,000, 258,000 and 225,000 respectively.

Remingtons; many books have laid their history bare in meticulous detail. Among the lesser designs, however, were several that deserve scrutiny. The purchases ranged from guns that harked back to an earlier era, such as the Butterfield that resembled no more than a cap-lock pistol fitted with a cylindrical magazine, to some odd looking guns that contained some interesting features. These included the striker-fired Pettengill; the double-trigger 'Figure 8' Savage; and the Starr, statistically the third most popular of the Federal acquisitions, which was initially made with a double-action trigger system.

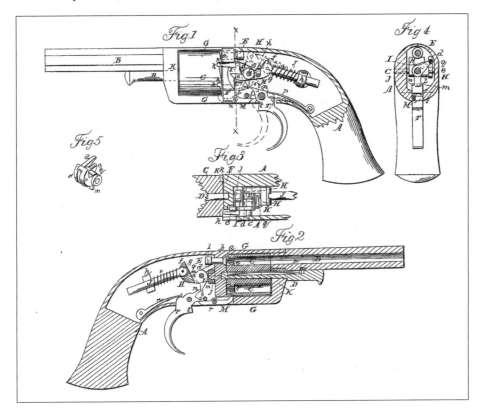

*The revolver designed by Charles Pettengill (US Patent 22511 of 1859) embodied an internal hammer and a small striker pin.*

Protected by patents granted in the USA to Charles S. Pettengill of New Haven, Connecticut, No. 15388 of 22 July 1856 and 22511 of 4 January 1859, and Edward Raymond & Charles Robitaille of Brooklyn, No. 21054 of 27 July 1858, the Pettengill revolver was made in small numbers by Rogers & Spencer of Willowvale, New York State. Federal purchasing records reveal that 2,001 guns were acquired in 1861–6 at a cost of $20.13 each, but guns have been seen with numbers in excess of 3,300 and it is evident that the commercial market took practically as many during the Civil War as the military authorities had done.

The pseudo-hammerless double-action Pettengill, with a hammer concealed within the frame and the butt running down from the frame in a continuous curve, was excessively clumsy: the .44-calibre Army Model was 14 inches long and weighed 3lb, though the smaller .36-calibre Navy Model was only 10.5 inches long and weighed about 1lb 9oz. A removable screw on the left side of the frame allowed the cylinder, the cylinder pin and the loading lever to be detached. The .44 barrel was octagonal, 7.5 inches long, and had six-groove rifling; the finish was generally blue, though the iron frame was sometimes browned. Experience soon showed that the guns were not particularly combat worthy, and, for all their interesting design features, they were never regarded among the pick of Civil War weaponry.

The Savage was an extraordinary-looking gun, in both its original 'Figure 8' and later 'Heart Guard' guise. The basis of the design was US Patent No. 15144, granted on 17 June 1856 to Henry North of Middletown, Connecticut, to protect a revolver in which an adjustable toggle-like linkage was used to move the cylinder forward far enough to effect a gas-seal between projecting rims on each chamber mouth and the suitably chamfered inner lip of the barrel. A ring-like lever was used to index and then slide the cylinder forward, before cocking the hammer. Pressure on a small blade-like trigger set into the front edge of the ring lever fired the gun.

The perfected form, protected by US Patent 28331 (May 1860), with chamfered chambers and a bevelled barrel-lip, had a distinctive operating lever in the form of the number '8' with a finger-ring in the base to move the cylinder and a trigger set in the upper section. Pulling the finger-ring backward pulled the cylinder away from the barrel before rotating to bring a new chamber into position; the movement also cocked the hammer. Releasing the ring allowed the cylinder to move back into its forward position, locked by the toggle, and the gun was ready to fire.

Savage revolvers had bronze frames, with a spurred back strap and walnut grips. Made only in 'Navy Caliber', .36, they were long and heavy: 14 inches, 3lb 7oz. The hammer was offset slightly from the centreline, to allow sighting to be taken, and a powerful camming rammer was fitted beneath the blued barrel. The barrel and the cylinder were usually blued, but the hammer and the rammer were case-hardened.

Several hundred guns were made in Middletown in 1856–9 by Edward Savage, many surviving to see combat during the Civil War, but the 'Figure 8' design was superseded by the so-called 'Heart Guard' type some time before hostilities began. A refined version of the earlier Savage, the Heart Guard guns were distinguished by an extraordinary trigger guard that ran almost to the base of the grip strap. This enclosed the ring lever, to operate the cylinder and cock the hammer, beneath a conventional trigger to fire the gun. The frame was iron instead of bronze, generally blued, and the rammer, the hammer, the ring lever and the trigger were all colour case-hardened. The .36-calibre gun was otherwise much the same as its predecessor, measuring about 14.2 inches overall and weighing, on average, 3lb 6oz. The barrel bore the markings of the Savage Revolving Fire Arms Co. (SAVAGE R.F.A. CO.) and,

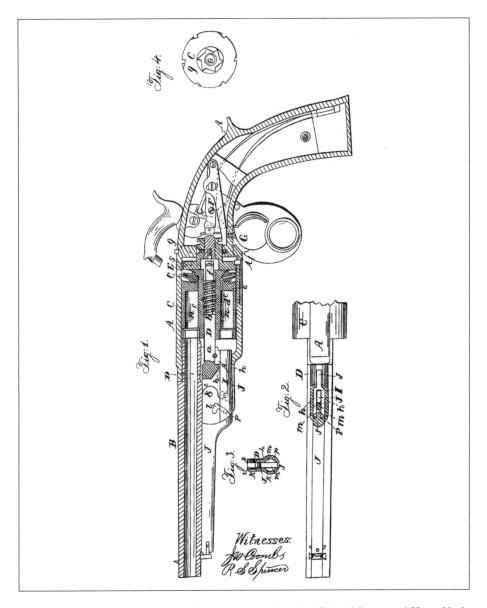

*The first Savage revolver, the so-called 'Figure 8', was designed by Edward Savage and Henry North. These drawings, taken from US Patent 28331 of 15 May 1860, show the unique configuration of the actuating lever and the trigger that gained the gun its name.*

unlike the earlier pattern, the Heart Guard guns almost always bear the marks of Federal Army inspectors: WCT and IT on the grips. The revolvers were much more successful than their bizarre appearance suggests, Federal purchases amounting to 11,284 of them from April 1861 onward at a cost to the Treasury of $19.62 apiece.

Work seems to have slowed considerably after 1863, when Savage began making revolver components under sub-contract from Starr.

The Starr revolver looked much more conventional than either the Pettengill or the Savage, but differed in many ways from accepted practice. Protected by US Patent No. 30843, granted on 4 December 1860 to Eben Townsend Starr of New York, the revolver had a lock relying on a cocking lever and a separate trigger to give the firer a choice of action. The key was a small sliding catch on the back of what appears to be the conventional trigger lever, in the centre of the guard, but is actually the cocking lever. If the catch was slid uppermost, a projecting lip caught the frame before the gun could fire; releasing the cocking lever left the hammer cocked, but the firer then had to press the small blade-like trigger projecting into the rear of the guard. If the slider was moved downward, however, the cocking lever moved back far enough to press the trigger lever, and the gun fired immediately.

The pivoting barrel was another unusual feature. Removing the large thumbscrew projecting from the right rear of the frame, above the recoil shield, allowed the barrel and cylinder assembly to swing forward. The cylinder was retained only by a cone-tipped axis pin entering a seat in the barrel lug, and could easily be replaced. Raising the frame and re-inserting the locking pin allowed the Starr to be reloaded much more rapidly than most other Civil War cap-locks, as long as additional cylinders were available.

The guns were originally made in two patterns. .36 (Navy) and .44 (Army), sharing similar construction but differing in size: the .36 pattern was 12 inches long and weighed 3lb 3oz, whereas the .44 was 11.6 inches long and weighed 2lb 15oz. The barrel, frame and cylinder were blued, and the hammer, rammer, cocking lever and trigger were all colour case-hardened. The walnut one-piece grip usually bore the mark of inspector A. D. King: ADK in a cartouche. An acknowledgement of the patent appeared on the lower right side of the frame, with the mark of the Starr Arms Company on the left. Some guns were made in Yonkers, New York, and others in nearby Binghamton.

Government purchases amounted to 47,952 Starr revolvers. Many of these, however, were of a simplified .44-calibre single-action pattern; the original .36-calibre Navy revolver is now particularly scarce. The single-action gun, which is about 13.7 inches long, had an 8-inch barrel (instead of 6 inches) and weighed a little over 3lb. It is believed to have been introduced to simplify and accelerate production, probably when the destruction of the Colt factory in Hartford (1864) put a premium on rapid delivery. Starr revolvers cost the Federal government only $15.39 apiece. Precise delivery figures for each of the three patterns are not available, but it has been estimated that total production (military and commercial) amounted to 3,000 .36-calibre double-action, 23,000 .44-calibre double-action and 32,000 .44-calibre single-action revolvers.

Some Civil War guns had proved to be better than others, though the advantages of magazine-feed rifles and carbines (for example the Henry and the Spencer) were often overlooked in post-war analysis that was calculated to protect the Treasury from

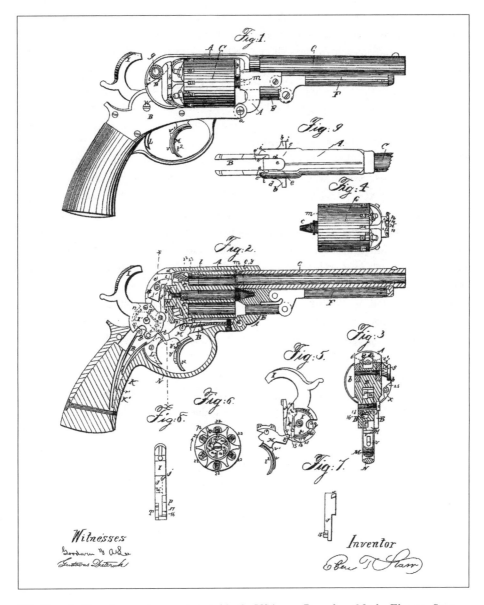

*The Starr double-action revolver was patented in the USA on 4 December 1860 by Ebenezer Starr (No. 30843).*

potentially expensive re-equipment. Judged as a combat weapon, the cap-lock revolver had shown several major failings. There was always a chance that a percussion cap would be dislodged from the nipple as the cylinder rotated, particularly as the manufacturing standards of wartime guns (excepting the output of Colt and possibly also Remington) were prone to fluctuate.

Cap-locks could also chain-fire if the bullets were not sealed satisfactorily in the chambers, allowing the flash from the ignition of the chamber immediately behind the barrel to flow radially across the cylinder face and into the remaining chambers. An incident of this type was potentially very serious; at the very least, it would wreck the gun. And, of course, loading powder and ball and then capping the nipples was a time-consuming process. In combat, it could be the difference between life and death.

## Turret Guns and Magazine Repeaters

The turret gun was a close relation of the cap-lock revolver, though not one that ever saw much combat. A disc was substituted for the cylinder, with the chambers bored radially, and rotated – sometimes manually, sometimes mechanically – around an axis in the frame. The axis could be horizontal, but the vertical axis (which allowed the disc to be orientated horizontally) was more popular. Turret guns are almost always cap-locks, as the design of the breech was not suited to conventional metal-case ammunition. Some proposals were made to chamber tapered-case ammunition with annular primers, others would have accepted pinfire rounds; and the Turbiaux Protector (patented in 1888 and a success commercially) accepted low-power rim- or centre-fire cartridges. But these remained the exceptions to the rule, and the best known of the turrets, the Belgian Genhart 'Monitor'[10] and the French Noël & Guéry pattern, both made use of external ignition.

The concept of a cap-lock turret gun was seriously flawed. As noted above, conventional cap-lock revolvers occasionally chain-fired. This was particularly likely if the projectiles had been loaded without a sealing plug of grease ahead of them. Near-simultaneous ignition of several chambers that were not directly aligned with the bore wrecked the gun and also often injured the firer. Yet reports speak of few serious injuries and even fewer fatalities, largely owing to the direction in which all of the chambers pointed – forward, away from the firer. Turret guns had chambers disposed radially. If the number of chambers was odd, it was likely that two of them pointed backward if the disc was horizontal, one either side of the frame, or back directly at the firer if the disc was vertical. If a gun of this type chain-fired, there was more than a chance that the firer would be killed. Not surprisingly, turret repeaters enjoyed a very short period in vogue...

Though the turret gun could not provide an effectual single-barrel firearm, many people regarded the revolver as clumsy and inefficient and were determined to pursue another goal. The magazine repeater also had a lengthy pedigree – as the Danish gunmaker Kalthoff and the Florentine gunmaker Michele Lorenzoni had developed surprisingly efficient designs in the seventeenth century. Working in the 1640s, Kalthoff used a swivelling trigger guard to transfer powder and ball from magazines in the stock,

---

10. This horizontal-disc design was patented in Belgium in 1853 by Heinrich Genhart of Liége. It was also protected by US Patent 16477 of 27 January 1857.

but his flintlocks were almost always long arms; the Lorenzoni-type disc-breech gun, devised in the last quarter of the seventeenth century, relying on movement of the disc to collect powder from a magazine in the butt and a ball from a reservoir, was made as a long arm or a handgun.

Lorenzoni guns were made in some numbers, by gunmakers including the Englishman John Cookson and Domenico Berselli of Bologna. A typical Berselli pistol had the disc placed vertically on a transverse axis pin, and a long slightly curving handle extending backward alongside the breech. A spring-loaded cap could be opened to reveal two chambers cut into the butt, the upper one to hold the balls and the lower one for the powder. The breech-disc was also bored-out to contain one small chamber – little more than the diameter of the ball – and a long powder chamber that ran back more than half the width of the disc. The chambers were set at about 75 degrees to each other, so that, when the disc was rotated backward, by moving the breech lever down, they each aligned with the butt chambers. As long as the muzzle was being pointed up, the powder chamber passed the ball chamber without incident. The muzzle was then tipped downward to allow a ball to roll into the small chamber and powder to fill the other. Returning the handle first allowed the ball to roll into the breech and then brought the powder chamber directly behind it. The gun could then be fired by the external flintlock. A pawl ensured that the breech-disc could only be rotated in the right direction, and some guns had priming magazines that automatically replenished the pan when the steel and cock were set.

The Lorenzoni system was greatly admired in its day, but the problems of sealing the potentially leaky interfaces between the periphery of the disc and the magazine throats were far too great for the technology of the time to solve. The consequences of flash-over in a gun that might contain a buttful of powder were horrendous, yet similar ideas continued to appear throughout the flintlock and cap-lock eras. They included a variety of rifles and shotguns described in *The Rifle Story*. However, the cap-and-ball repeater, patented in the USA in July 1850 by Orville Percival of East Haddam, Connecticut, and Asa Smith of New York, was made not only as the rifle illustrated in the patent specifications but also as a handgun. The Percival & Smith system had a large multi-chamber cylinder containing the balls, a propellant chamber and a small priming magazine all formed as part of a sleeve that could be rotated around the longitudinal axis of the gun. Reloading was simply a matter of placing the gun on half cock and rotating the sleeve, held by a detent, upward through 180 degrees. This allowed a ball to drop into the chamber, a charge of powder to fall behind the ball, and some priming to fall ahead of the hammer. Retracting the hammer to full cock and pressing the trigger fired the gun – hopefully without flash-over igniting the propellant magazine!

Paul Boynton of Canton, New York, was another enthusiast for cap-and-ball repeaters, filing US Patents to protect pistols (No. 23226 of March 1859 and No. 26646 of January 1860) at a time when the cap-lock revolver was nearing perfection. The earlier Boynton design had a powder magazine in the butt and a ball-tube beneath the

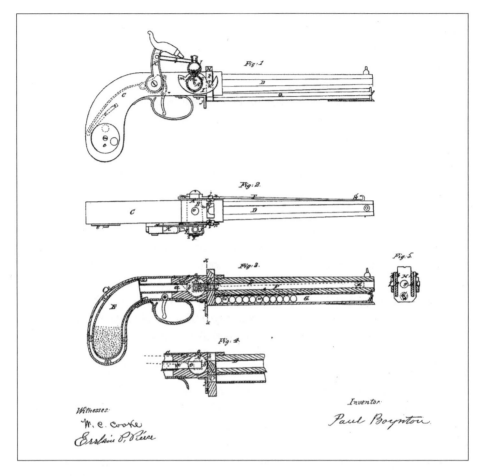

*Cap-and-ball magazine pistols were still being designed long after efficient revolvers had appeared. These drawings come from a US Patent granted to Paul Boynton on 15 March 1859 (No. 23226).*

barrel; the second type had the powder chamber between the barrel and the ball-tube. Both guns were fired with the assistance of automatic priming systems that released a small quantity of fulminate powder each time the hammer was drawn back to full cock. Neither encountered any tangible success.

Another old idea was to load more than one charge in a single barrel, as the 'Roman Candle' or *espignole* had originated in medieval times. The difficulties of igniting individual charges were well known: most of the earliest guns were designed to fire the entire barrel-load of projectiles sequentially, without attempting to stop the process until the last charge had been fired. Some are even known in which a series of charges, loaded from the breech, were fired sequentially by igniting the front one conventionally (usually with a flintlock) and then allowing each successive shot to be fired with the assistance of a fuse running back through all the projectiles and charges. The recoil of the gun must have been excessive, and the strength of the breech mechanism may not always have been great enough to ensure the firer's safety. Comparatively few of these weapons survive.

Attempts were made by many inventors to provide sliding locks and a series of touch-holes, each protected by a pivoting cover. A patent of this general class was granted in England in 1780 (No. 12700) to a surgeon, John Aitken, who proposed multiple touch-holes and 'intermedia or colfings' – wads of leather or suitable substitute – to separate each charge. Better known was the work of Joseph Belton of Philadelphia, who had petitioned the US Congress to test his gun and had been authorised to make 100 eight-shot muskets on 3 May 1777. There is no evidence that these guns were made, as Belton eventually departed for London. There the Master-General of the Ordnance granted his gun an official trial, which was undertaken at Woolwich on 28 July 1784. This particular Belton gun was a musket with a detachable 11-inch chamber holding seven charges, operated by two triggers. Though the Woolwich exhibition had failed to attract the interest of the Army, Belton entered into partnership with the London gunmaker William Jover and approached the Commissioners of the East India Company with his plans. The submission was welcomed, as the multiple charges were believed to give cavalrymen a great advantage in skirmishes where they were greatly outnumbered. The Company subsequently paid Jover & Belton £2,292 8s. 0d. for muskets and, presumably, some pistols.[11]

Multiple-charge guns were predictably long, clumsy, and prone to chain-firing unless the seals between each successive charge/projectile combination were exceptionally good. Superimposed loads, therefore, were another evolutionary dead-end even though attempts were made from time to time to increase firepower by combining turnover barrels and superimposed charges.

The brief heyday of the cap-and-ball repeater was over by the early 1860s, brought to a rapid close by the development of self-contained ammunition. Few of the designs, interesting though they may have been, had any long-term effects on the development of the handgun.

---

11. Howard L. Blackmore, *British Military Firearms 1650–1850*, p. 249, records that one surviving EIC musket dated 1786 also bears the number '124'. This and the payment, a large sum in its day, both suggest that substantial quantities were involved.

# 3
# *The Metallic Cartridge*

The self-contained cartridge had a lengthy pedigree that could be traced back to the separate loading chambers employed on some of the earliest cannon. Breech-loading and poor metallurgy proved to be bad bedfellows, and the idea of a separate chamber lay dormant for centuries. Occasional bursts of enthusiasm failed to overcome the technological drawbacks until the great advances made in iron-making in the middle of the eighteenth century and the beneficial effects of the industrial revolution on engineering combined to free designers from the previous constraints. The emergence of the pin-fire cartridge in France was the first step forward; acceptably waterproof, easy to make, and easily stored as long as care was taken not to strike the exposed igniter pin, ammunition of this type, and guns to fire it, were made in huge numbers from the middle of the nineteenth century into the 1920s.

Essentially European, the classic pin-fire handgun was usually (if not exclusively) a multi-shot pattern. However, uncertainty over the desirability of the revolver as a military weapon, common in many European armies in the 1860s and 1870s, allowed the centre-fire single-shot pistol to soldier on for some years.

The perfection of the centre-fire revolver then speedily ended the heyday of the single-shot military cartridge pistols exemplified by the rolling-block US Army and US Navy Remingtons or the Bavarian Army's Werder. More durable were the target-shooting adaptations of the Remington and others, which lasted into the twentieth century. The revival of the Olympic Games in 1896, and the increasing popularity of international target shooting, gave the development of the single-shot cartridge pistol a great boost. Great effort was expended on the development of firing-lock and trigger systems, the refinement of grips and the disposition of weights. The result was the Free Pistol, an essentially European creation. Invariably built on a dropping or pivoting-block action, such as the Martini or interminable variations of the Aydt, the best of the guns were capable of hair-splitting accuracy at the regulation 50-metre range. Descendants of these guns are still being made in quantity.

At the other end of the handgun spectrum, the tiny personal-defence pistols exemplified by the cap-lock Deringer also had their metallic-cartridge equivalents.

Patented on 19 February 1861 (US No. 31473) by Daniel Moore of Brooklyn, New York, the .41-calibre rim-fire National Model No. 1 derringer-type pistol was made in quantity by Moore's Patent Fire Arms Company and a successor, the National Arms Company of Brooklyn. It had a sheath trigger and a barrel which pivoted laterally to expose the breech. The No. 1 was undeniably clumsy, but it was exceptionally simple and strong enough to be used as a knuckle-duster.

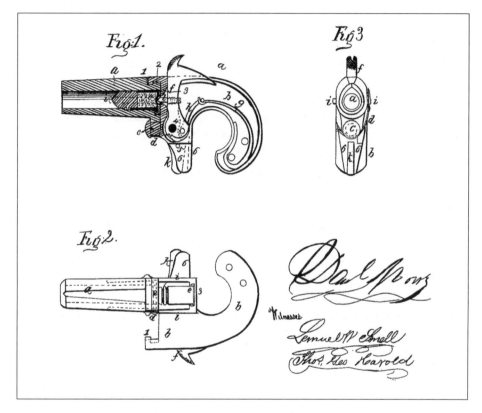

*The Moore or National twist-open derringer was patented by Daniel Moore on 19 February 1861. These drawings are taken from the appropriate US Patent, No. 31473.*

Production of the Moore derringers began before the patent had been granted; the first guns, therefore, lack the patent-date markings. Later examples had different hammers and a better breech catch; some guns had extractors, but others did not. The National Model No. 2 was similar to the No. 1, but the gap between the trigger and the grip was increased. The grips were made of walnut or rosewood. The National Arms Company was acquired by Colt in 1870, and production of the No. 1 and No. 2 derringers was immediately shifted from Brooklyn to Hartford, Connecticut. Only the manufacturer's marks were changed. Colt is said to have made about 15,000 Moore-type derringers, many of which were sold as matched pairs. Hand-cut scroll engraving was common.

The No. 3 Colt derringer, designed by F. Alexander Thuer of East Hartford, Connecticut, was protected by US Patent No. 105388 of 12 July 1870. Rights to the design were assigned to Colt's Patent Fire Arms Mfg Co. The barrel pivoted sideways to load, spent cases being ejected automatically as the breech opened. Most of the 45,000 guns made by 1912 fired .41-calibre centre-fire ammunition, though alternative chamberings could be supplied to special order; 2.6in barrels were standard. Finished in plain blue or nickel plate, the No. 3 had bird's-head grips of walnut, rosewood, or mother-of-pearl. The earliest guns had a bolster on the frame beneath the barrel; later examples are straight.

The simplicity of the Thuer-type derringers made them popular with copyists. Consequently, the Marlin 'O.K.' and 'Victor' pistols were essentially similar, as were 'XL' patterns made by Hopkins & Allen and Forehand & Wadsworth until 1889. However, the cartridge pistol lost much of its popularity to the revolver in the 1870s, particularly to small pin-fires in Europe and the 'Suicide Specials' in North America. Single-shot designs made in the twentieth century, excepting those made for collectors or the nostalgia market, have been restricted almost exclusively to game-hunting or target shooting.

### The Pin-Fire Cartridge

If the rise of the self-contained cartridge in Europe had only a limited effect on the design and distribution of single-shot pistols, it was a great catalyst in the development of the modern revolver. Many of the advances were due to a handful of French gunmakers, culminating in the patenting and eventual introduction of the pin-fire. Most of the credit is generally given to Casimir and Eugène Lefaucheux of Paris.

Pin-fire cartridges consist of a near-cylindrical tube, usually made of copper, with a hole in the circumference close to the base. A small pin passed through the hole to rest on a pellet of priming located either in a suitable seat or against the body diametrically opposite the pin-hole. The cartridges were loaded into the cylinder from the rear, allowing the pins to project radially. The nose of the hammer fell on to the pin, almost vertically at the moment of impact, and drove the pin into the primer to fire the main charge. The design worked well enough and was reasonably water-tight as long as a seal of lacquer or something similar was applied at the point where the pin passed through the case. But the drawbacks were serious. The pins were vulnerable to accidental blows, and there are instances of unwanted explosions occurring, for example, in gunsmiths' premises when packages of pin-fire ammunition were accidentally crushed. The position of the priming pellet and the direction of ignition were not ideal, as neither was linear, but the worst problem was simply the lack of power.

This drawback was common to most early forms of cartridge, as the first .22-calibre Smith & Wesson rim-fires would testify, but the centre-fire design soon overcame the restriction in a way in which the others did not. Consequently, while the manufacturing simplicity of the rim-fire found universal favour for low-power sporting use, the pin-fire disappeared into obscurity. Some manufacturers offered ammunition of this type as late as 1939, but this merely reflected the after-effects of the spectacular distribution of cheap pin-fire revolvers in the last few decades of the nineteenth century.

A great many pin-fire revolvers were made in Belgium, in the districts centred on Liége; substantial quantities were made in Saint-Étienne in France and around the town of Eibar in Spain. However, the general design was never favoured in Britain, and even the post-1871 German unification failed to encourage the large-scale production of pin-fire handguns in the gunmaking centres in and around Suhl. The French origin of the pin-fire system was probably responsible for the centre of focus on Liége, in the French-speaking part of Belgium… and possibly also for the lack of enthusiasm in Britain and the USA. For differing reasons, such as the impact of colonial service in Britain and the effect of the Wild West, the weakly loaded pin-fires could not hope to compete with the Webleys, the Colts and the Smith & Wessons.

The French had been among the first to accept pin-fire revolvers for service, when their Navy adopted the M1858, but had soon realised that the limitations of power overcame the advantages of waterproofing. By 1870, the search was under way to find a new centre-fire revolver for the French services. Once again, the Navy led with the M1870 and the Army followed with the M1873, Chamelot-Delvigne designs chambering 11mm centre-fire rounds. The weakness of the new cartridge loading merely reflected the low status accorded the revolver in European military circles.

However, though the military authorities rapidly discarded pin-fire ammunition across Europe, the commercial market had radically differing goals. Here, concealment often overrode the need for power; and compact dimensions were attained with calibres as small as 6mm. A typical Belgian-made pin-fire revolver of the 1880s had an open-top frame, a short barrel, and often also a trigger blade that could be folded forward along the underside of the frame. Guns could be fitted within purses or tins or books. The best of them were made of surprisingly good material, and had Liége proof marks to prove it. They could be highly decorated, with deeply carved grips and damascened metalwork. Others, including the largest, were fitted with blades beneath the barrel (some folding, others fixed), and a few had multi-row cylinders of the most outlandish dimensions. True freaks, they appealed more to uncritical export markets than the average European purchaser.

The exceptionally low power of the smallest pin-fire rounds (6mm, 7mm, 9mm) limited the application of the guns to close-range personal defence, but their perceived desirability provided a ready market for the first semi-automatic pocket pistols. But though the first of these (possibly the Bergmann No. 2) appeared in the mid-1890s, not until the commercial introduction of the FN-Browning blowback in 1906 did the heyday of the inexpensive European pin-fire revolver truly end.

## Rim-Fire and Centre-Fire Cartridges

The preferred alternatives to the pin-fires in Britain and North America were the rim- and centre-fire rounds. The rim-fire had been developed by Daniel Wesson and his partner Horace Smith, of Springfield, Massachusetts, and was protected by US Patent 27933 granted on 17 April 1860. The basis of the invention was a thin layer of priming compound spun into the rim of the cartridge case. The firing pin was offset to strike towards the rim of the case-head instead of the centre, and ignition of the main charge ensued. Though the earliest rim-fire cartridges were tiny and offered no real power, they were waterproof. They functioned much more effectively than the pin-fire equivalents. In addition, the rim-fire was made in the USA, rapidly becoming the most mass-production conscious of nations in the middle of the nineteenth century, and was available in large numbers during the American Civil War.

The Smith & Wesson revolvers, small and frail, were poor military weapons; but they were a popular 'back up' weapon, often purchased by wives and sweethearts to ensure that their men would not be defenceless if supplies of ammunition for the service-pattern handguns were unavailable. The certainty of ignition conferred by the sealed metal case was a great comfort to the men who carried them, and the tiny lead bullet could be lethal at close range. The first .22-calibre revolver was rapidly joined by a .32-calibre derivative, enhancing its appeal greatly. The Smith & Wesson revolvers were so successful that development stagnated for some time, a crucial inhibitor to progress being the acquisition of US Patent 12649 of 3 April 1855, granted to Rollin White of Hartford, Connecticut, to protect chambers which had been bored entirely through the cylinder. Just as Colt's master patent had given that company a monopoly for many years, so Smith & Wesson was able to defend its rights against a variety of transgressions. (Including, ironically, the Rollin White Arms Company of Lowell, Massachusetts, in which White himself had no stake.)

Though inventors tried to perfect a variety of alternative loading systems, including the teat fire and the Slocum sliding side-gate, none of them was capable of mounting a long-term challenge to the rim-fire revolvers and virtually all were swept away in the immediate aftermath of the Civil War when a financial depression, the result of a glut of war-surplus weapons, hit the New England gunmaking industry. But when the Rollin White patent finally lapsed in 1869, the floodgates opened and every revolver maker from Colt downwards began to make guns with bored-through cylinders. These were chambered for a variety of rim- and then centre-fire cartridges, and came in virtually every conceivable pattern from the very cheapest to deluxe cased sets.

The myth that virtually every Westerner carried a Colt Peacemaker has been demolished many times, but there can be very little doubt that the opening of the West – no mere five-year wonder, but a continuous process that lasted almost to 1914 – did have a beneficial effect on the production of revolvers. The Colts included a double-action design, the .38 Lightning and the .41 Thunderer (names bestowed by a distributor, Kittredge of Cincinnati); and there were many break-open Smith & Wessons ranging in size from .32 to .45. However, these have been well documented (*see Bibliography*) and there are other designs that merit attention here.

One of the most interesting was the Merwin & Hulbert, a quirky auto-extracting design with a barrel unit that could be rotated out of engagement with a transverse lug on the back of the top strap, immediately ahead of the hammer, and then pulled forward to leave spent cases attached to a star-plate in the standing frame. Guns of this type were also made in a variety of chamberings. These were unsuccessful militarily, as extraction proved to be unreliable under arduous conditions, but they were popular with those who needed a compact and powerful defence. The short-barrel 'Barkeep Guns', usually chambered for the .44-40 Winchester centre-fire rifle cartridge, could be kept butt-upward in a beer glass beneath the counter, ready for instant action if required. A cartridge of this size packed a fearful punch at short range, much more deadly than the initially ubiquitous .32 rim-fire.

Interest in the revolver had been sharpened by the Civil War, and many attempts were made in the immediate aftermath to 'improve' the tip-up Smith & Wesson and similar small-calibre metallic-cartridge guns. Patent records show many of these designs, some more practical than others. Typical were US No. 137043, granted to David Williamson in March 1873; 140516, to John Marlin in July 1873; and 175180, to Ebenezer Starr in March 1876.

## The Road to Mass Production

Many enterprising gunmakers could see that the ever-expanding 'Wild West' and the burgeoning population of the eastern seaboard, each often equally lawless, were clamouring for inexpensive revolvers. Realising that technology would help to increase output, particularly the advent of cheap sources of power and highly efficient machine tools, they sought to make large numbers of identical guns at highly competitive prices. The discovery that gutta-percha could be moulded under the right combination of temperature and pressure allowed highly decorative grips to be fitted to otherwise unsophisticated guns, and aggressive marketing was increasingly used to camouflage deficiencies in design or construction.

The most basic type of inexpensive revolvers came to be characterised by a short-barrel solid framed gun, chambering rim- or centre-fire ammunition up to a calibre of .41 (still a comparatively weak loading), with a sheathed trigger and a single-action trigger system. Some guns had rod-type ejectors, but most were reloaded simply by removing the cylinder axis pin and dropping the cylinder into the palm of the hand.

The term 'Suicide Special' was coined for this class of revolver by the late Duncan McConnell, writing in the *American Rifleman* in 1948. Intended as a term of disparagement, it has since become a useful, if a little misleading, label for these particular guns. In fact, the general description applies as much to some well-made guns, including a few of the smallest Colts, Remingtons and Smith & Wessons of the 1870s, as it does to the products of the 'Acme Machine Works'.

Among the first of the patents to protect a recognisable Suicide Special was US No. 174731 granted on 14 March 1876 to Freeman Hood of Norwich, Connecticut, and assigned to the Hood Firearms Company. The success of the genre soon attracted much more widespread interest. During the 1880s, therefore, the designers of the inexpensive revolvers filed far more specifications than the men employed by Colt and Smith & Wesson. Their names are now largely forgotten, but several of the most important designers deserve to be remembered; their contributions have lasted, in the form of some Harrington & Richardson and Iver Johnson revolvers, almost until the present day.

Virtually any gunmaker could (and often did) make Suicide Specials, but among the best known were:

| | |
|---|---|
| Bacon Manufacturing Company | Marlin Firearms Company |
| Colt's Patent Fire Arms Manufacturing Company | Meriden Arms Company |
| Crescent Arms Company | Norwich Arms Company and the Norwich Falls Pistol Company |
| Edward Dickinson | Prescott Pistol Company |
| Ely & Wray | Remington Arms Company |
| Forehand & Wadsworth Arms Company | Rome Revolver & Novelty Works |
| Harrington & Richardson Arms Company | J. Rupertus Patent Pistol Manufacturing Company |
| Hood Firearms Company | Ryan Pistol Company |
| Hopkins & Allen Arms Company | C. S. Shatuck |
| Johnson, Bye & Company (and its successors, Iver Johnson) | Otis Smith |
| Lee Arms Company | William Uhlinger |
| Maltby, Curtiss & Company (and successors Maltby, Henley & Co.) | Wesson & Harrington |
| | Whitney Arms Company. |

However, true series production was confined to companies such as Hood or the Hopkins & Allen Arms Company of Norwich, Connecticut, who made thousands of guns under a whole range of names and marks. The process of selling the cheap revolvers became one of who could tell the tallest tales, or devise the sharpest and most topical brand names. Consequently, the Suicide Specials offered by the Hopkins & Allen range from 'Acme' and 'Alex' to 'X-Pert' and 'You Bet'.

The criteria by which successful names could be judged were as valid in the 1880s as they are today, and followed similar lines. Names that made the purchaser feel at home ('Kentucky', 'Lone Star', 'Old Hickory'), inspired by patriotism ('American', 'Eagle', 'Southron'), or associate a cheap revolver with military or police service ('Metropolitan Police') all stood the test of time. So did those that harked back to childhood ('Boy's Choice'); those associated with royalty, aristocracy or power ('Duchess', 'Governor', 'King', 'Senator'); those that promised effectual defence ('Tramps Terror'); and those that suggested qualities that were not always as obvious in the gun as they were intended to be to the purchaser ('Dead Shot', 'Excelsior', 'Faultless', 'Invincible', 'Never Miss').

There were also more than a few oddities among the brand names, which may not have had the beneficial effects on sales that their promoters desired: 'Half-Breed' was used as a term of disparagement in nineteenth-century North America, and scarcely commended the product to an educated New Englander. Neither does 'Parole' seem appropriate, until it is realised that the original meaning was simply to give one's word. 'Bang-Up' meant to lock criminals away, which was what the promoters, Ely & Wray of Springfield, hoped that their product would help to do; 'Hard Pan' was a mining term, suggesting the discovery of gold or similar precious metal among the valueless dross.

New England, on the north-eastern seaboard of the USA, was the cradle not only of the gunmaking industry but also of precision engineering. The line drawn between the two professions has always been fine, and there have been many instances, in Europe as well as North America, where the two have blurred. Ferdinand von Mannlicher and Adolphe Berthier both started their careers as railway engineers; in the USA, Rollin White made a second fortune from the White Steam Car, and Sylvester Roper (whose modern reputation as a firearms inventor is possibly higher than can be justified) made his from the Roper Hot Air Engine.

Perhaps the most successful of the gunmaker-engineers were Elisha Root, to whom the efficient mechanisation of the Colt factory in Hartford, Connecticut, was largely due; and Christopher Spencer, designer of the magazine carbine used in quantity during the Civil War, who subsequently developed the first truly successful automatic turret lathe – a tool that transformed manufacturing techniques. It is scarcely surprising that the developers of the Suicide Special should also come from this background.

In Connecticut, Colt was based in Hartford and Marlin in neighbouring New Haven. Prescott and Shatuck traded in Hatfield. Otis Smith worked first in Middlefield and then in Rock Fall, and Meriden worked in the town of the same name. Whitney's factory was in Whitneyville, while Bacon, Crescent, Hood, Hopkins & Allen, Norwich Arms, the Norwich Falls Pistol Co. and Ryan all worked in Norwich. In neighbouring Massachusetts, Forehand & Wadsworth, Harrington & Richardson, Johnson, Bye & Co., and Wesson & Harrington were to be found in Worcester, and Dickinson and Ely & Wray in Springfield.[1]

In addition to these gunmaking businesses, sometime identifiable only by their brand names or trade marks, guns will also be found with the name of other organisations, largely spurious, applied more to hide the true identity of the manufacturer than impress the purchaser (though a few are probably legitimate distributors' markings). Marks of this type include 'Aetna Arms Co.' on guns made by Harrington & Richardson; 'Mohawk Mfg. Co.' on some by Otis Smith; 'Toledo Arms Co.', used by Hopkins & Allen; and 'US Arms Co.' on a few of the products of Hood.

---

1. Among the few makers of Suicide Specials working outside Connecticut and Massachusetts were the Lee Arms Company (in Wilkes-Barre, Pennsylvania); Maltby, Curtiss & Co. (New York City); Remington (Ilion, New York State); the Rome Revolver & Novelty Works (Rome, New York State); Jacob Rupertus and William Uhlinger (Philadelphia).

The popularity of the original first or primitive form of the Suicide Special soon showed signs of decline. The principal reason for this, though small numbers of technically superior guns were being imported from Europe, was the widespread distribution of the small-calibre break-open auto-ejecting Smith & Wessons. These were expensive compared with their simple sheath-trigger rivals, but were well made and very efficient once initial teething troubles had been overcome.

The success of the Smith & Wessons posed a real problem for the manufacturers of Suicide Specials. The market had been so competitive that margins had been pared to the bone; so far, indeed, that few of the gunmakers could afford to make large-scale changes. Only a handful of them had access to large-scale production facilities, forcing many to rely on machine tools that were becoming more primitive as the years passed. Competing with large, well-established gunmaking businesses such as Colt and Smith & Wesson was out of the question.

Yet there was still considerable inventive flair among the designers of the inexpensive guns, and a new phase in the US firearms industry soon began. The results could, perhaps, be called the 'Super Suicide Specials' – still cheaply made, often comparatively crude, but incorporating many of the refinements that the purchasers were demanding. The sheath trigger was potentially dangerous if a loaded-and-cocked gun was carried in a pocket, and a source of unwanted accidents when the trigger was pressed while adjusting grip or aim. The result was the universal introduction of a trigger guard, which the finger could enter only after a grip had been taken; the fingers could be rested on the front of the guard while the gun was being handled.

Some of the new guns retained the most basic form of ejection, relying on removal of an axis pin to let the cylinder fall free of the frame; this was ideally suited to ultra-short-barrel guns, and kept costs to a minimum. More sophisticated products were fitted with sliding rod ejectors, and the best of the Super Suicide Specials incorporated auto-ejecting systems. Some of the features could be a little quirky, often due to a desire to provide 'something different' (or avoid infringing patents), but the guns sold in huge numbers.

The sheer volume of output is difficult to comprehend. The production of Colt and Smith & Wesson revolvers, by comparison, was slow: when production of the Colt Model P, the 'Peacemaker' of 1873, finished for the first time in 1940, only a little over 310,000 guns had been made in 67 years. By comparison, Harrington & Richardson, the 1876 outgrowth of Wesson & Harrington, had made 3 million inexpensive revolvers by 1908 – an average of about 100,000 annually.

The poor reputation of the Suicide Specials has tended to obscure their fascinating history. This is partly because of the universal enthusiasm for the Colts and Smith & Wessons. In addition, the quality of material, strength of construction and widespread acceptance for military and police use has assured the survival of large numbers of Colt Peacemakers and Smith & Wesson Military Models. And, of course, both manu-facturers have continued in business to the present day – assuring not only that the production of revolvers has continued, but also that sales and marketing departments (including official historians) keep interest in the history of the guns alive.

The Suicide Specials have no such advantages, and, apart from a few well-researched articles in periodicals such as *Guns Digest*, have never been subjected to the same levels of scrutiny. Identifying them is complicated by either the absence of marks or a proliferation of still-unidentifiable brand names. Yet, perhaps more than any of the Colts or Smith & Wessons that were available in the last quarter of the nineteenth century, the Suicide Special was the true reflection of the basic public need for self protection.

They were exceptionally cheap, putting even comparatively sophisticated auto-ejecting designs, such as the Harrington & Richardson or the Iver Johnson, within the reach of even the most impoverished worker. In addition, the best of them were scarcely inferior in design to their better-known peers. Only in construction was the reduction in quality apparent: the material was rarely as good, the gauge of some components was reduced to save weight or money, and the finish lacked the depth of the best blueing.

## Ever-Increasing Sophistication

Though Harrington & Richardson claims the longest pedigree, with the formation of Wesson & Harrington in 1874, the exploits of Iver Johnson probably had the greatest effects on the development of the Suicide Special in the formative period. Johnson, a second-generation immigrant from Norway, had begun his gunmaking career in Worcester, Massachusetts, almost as soon as the Civil War had ended. In collusion with another of his countrymen, Martin Bye, Johnson was granted several relevant patents in 1878.

The success of the earliest Iver Johnson revolvers, which were made under a variety of brand names and will also found bearing the names of distributors instead of the manufacturer, encouraged an enlargement of operations to include bicycles, but the production of revolvers continued unabated until the First World War. The most famous of them was the so-called 'Hammer-the-Hammer' model.

The Safety Automatic Hammerless revolver had been introduced in its first incarnation in 1894, on the basis of a patent eventually granted to Homer Caldwell of Worcester, Massachusetts, on 16 June 1896[2] and assigned to 'Mary E. Johnson, of Fitchburg, Massachusetts'. Mary Elizabeth Johnson was the wife of Iver Johnson. The break-open revolver had a short spurless hammer concealed within a light machined-steel shroud pinned into the top of the frame above the grip, which simplified manufacture of concealed-hammer guns. The essence of the system was the bifurcated hammer, which allowed the tip of the inertia-type firing pin to protrude in the intervening space without being stuck – until the final stages of firing, when the trigger

---

2. The application was made on 2 May 1895, and there is evidence to suggest that manufacture of trial batches of revolvers (if nothing more) had already begun. Any gun made prior to the summer of 1896 would have displayed PATENT APPLIED FOR markings.

raised the tip of a transfer bar between the hammer and the firing pin. The Caldwell design also had a small blade inset in the face of the trigger lever, which prevented the components moving unless the trigger was pressed.

The advertising slogan is said to have arisen from a meeting convened in the summer of 1904 by the son of Iver, Frederic Johnson, with William Johns, representing the George Batten Company. The assistance of a marketing agency was being sought to ensure Iver Johnson products regained some of the ground that had been lost to Harrington & Richardson and others. The Iver Johnson Safety Automatic revolver had been promoted with the claim 'Accidental Discharge Impossible', and Johns made the mistake of questioning if such a misleading statement was defensible.

Johns subsequently claimed that Johnson had been outraged. He had sent for a revolver, loaded it, and thrown it against the office safe; he had kicked it around, then, with the muzzle pointing at his leg, struck the hammer as hard as he could with an iron bar. Johns finally calmed Johnson, and the discussion continued. But the advertising executive had been very impressed, realising that safety was indeed a defining characteristic of the Iver Johnson revolvers. The result was 'Hammer-the-Hammer', usually accompanied by a graphic representation of a claw hammer striking the firing hammer of the gun. The US patent protecting the perfected hammer-blocking mechanism (No. 933188) was granted on 7 September 1909 to Edward Leggett of Brooklyn, New York, and the catchy slogan was used successfully for 70 years.

Iver Johnson and his successors employed many designers, including Andrew Fyrberg and Reinhard Torkelson. In addition, his one-time partner Martin Bye continued to design handguns for some time after the split – which must have been friendly, as Iver Johnson made revolvers embodying elements of a patent (US No. 375799) granted to Bye in January 1888.

Andrew Fyrberg was responsible for a revolver protected by a patent granted in the USA in February 1892 (No. 469387). The drawings show a simple solid-frame gun, with the cylinder-axis pin held by a conventional pivoting latch in the front of the frame and an equally conventionally spurred hammer. The principal claim to novelty lay in the combination of the sear and rebounder in a single blade-like component. It is believed that revolvers of this particular form were made in small numbers, as the lock work, by Fyrberg standards, was simple and surprisingly robust. They can be recognised by the protrusion of the sear/rebounder blade into the trigger guard immediately behind the heel of the trigger lever.

Fyrberg was also granted a patent (US 642688 of 6 February 1900) to protect an interesting enclosed-hammer 'safety revolver' with a loose firing pin constrained by a lateral pin and a leaf spring in the top of the frame. When the parts were at rest, spring pressure ensured that the pin was tipped backward away from the primer of a chambered round. As the trigger was pressed, however, the hammer-lifting pawl pushed the firing pin up against the resistance of the leaf spring until it could be struck by the tip of the falling hammer. Releasing the trigger allowed the hammer-lifting pawl to

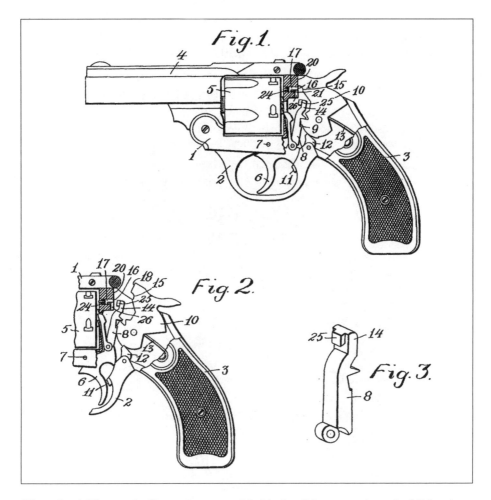

*The perfected 'Hammer-the-Hammer' system exploited by Iver Johnson was the work of Edward Leggett, who received US Patent 933188 on 7 September 1909.*

return to its rest or lowermost position and the firing pin was once again tipped back from the breech. The concept was an intriguing variation on the transfer-bar type, but was too fragile to be successful.

Among other overlooked inventors were the Smiths, Otis and John, of Middlefield and then Rock Fall, Connecticut. The relationship between these two is still the subject of debate. Some writers have suggested they were brothers or cousins, but the dates of the patents suggest that they were father and son – Otis was active in 1872–84, initially patenting variations of the tip-barrel Smith & Wesson design, whereas John Smith was active for several years from 1885 onward.

John T. Smith's first US patent, No. 311383, was granted in January 1885 to protect a double-action-only trigger mechanism with a spurless hammer rotating within upward

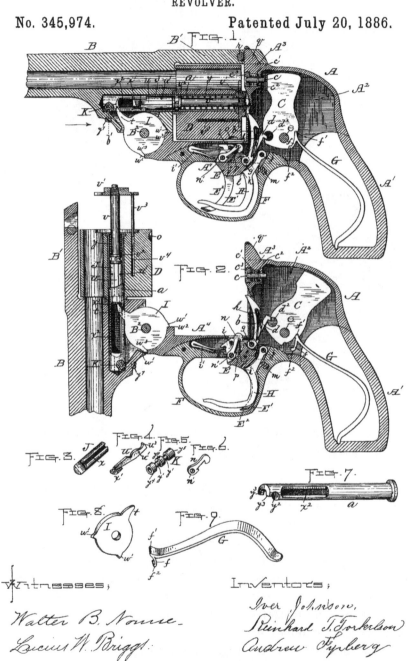

(No Model.)　　　　　　　　　　　　　　2 Sheets—Sheet 1.

## I. JOHNSON, R. T. TORKELSON & A. FYRBERG.

### REVOLVER.

No. 345,974.　　　　　　　　　Patented July 20, 1886.

Fig. 1.

Fig. 2.

Fig. 3.　Fig. 4.　Fig. 5.　Fig. 6.

Fig. 7.

Fig. 8.　Fig. 9.

Witnesses;
Walter B. Nonne.
Lucius W. Briggs.

Inventors;
Iver Johnson,
Reinhard T. Torkelson
Andrew Fyrberg

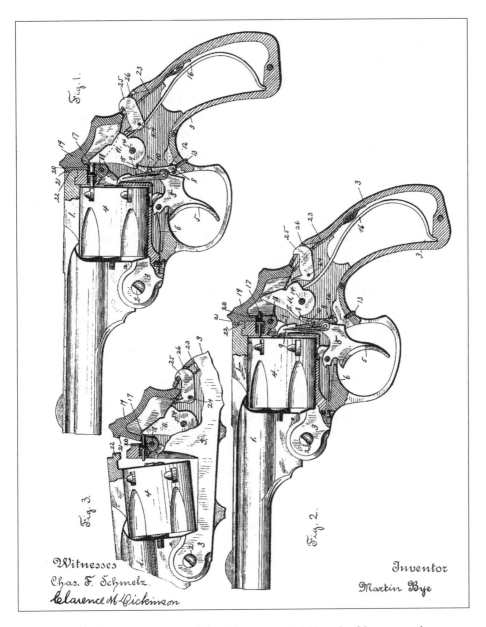

Above: *Martin Bye, once the partner of Iver Johnson, patented this enclosed-hammer revolver on 3 January 1888 (US No. 375799).*

Left: *Typical of the complexity of some of the designs of the 1880s was this break-open 'Super Suicide Special', the work of Johnson, Torkelson & Fyrberg (US Patent No. 345974 of 20 July 1886). Note the 'finger safety' that must be disengaged before the trigger can rotate the cylinder and the hammer.*

extensions of the frame behind the cylinder. Smith continued to develop revolvers until US Patent 413975 was granted on 29 October 1889 to protect, in the words of the specification,

'... an improvement in that class of revolvers in which the hammer is concealed within the frame and cocked and discharged under the pull of the trigger. The object of the invention is to provide a lock for the hammer in either the cocked or uncocked position as a means of safety; also, to prevent the possibility of the hammer striking the firing pin, except upon a pull of the trigger; also, to indicate to the person operating the revolver when the hammer has been brought to the full cock position... '

Guns of this type, with the hammer within an upwards extension of the frame behind the cylinder, had a small blade-like safety catch/cocking indicator set in the back strap. Though there is no evidence that any of the patents were assigned to other better-known manufacturers, the revolvers are rarely encountered under the Smith name (though they generally acknowledge the patent dates to comply with US laws). Most seem to have been sold through distributors, principally Maltby, Henley & Company of New York.

Henry Goodman of St Louis, Missouri, received US Patent 352185 on 9 November 1886. This protected a Smith & Wesson-type break-open revolver altered so that the main spring bore on an additional lever with a finger or 'push piece' to bear against the hammer-cocking and cylinder-indexing pawls simultaneously. The goal was simplification – the elimination of two small and potentially fragile springs – but there is no evidence that the design was ever exploited.

Gilbert H. Harrington and William A. Richardson, partners in Harrington & Richardson of Worcester, Massachusetts, were among the pioneers of the guns that are now classed as 'Suicide Specials'. The success of the earliest examples under the Wesson & Harrington name laid the foundations for a surprisingly successful business that lasted into comparatively recent times. Some H&R-type revolvers are still being made by two successors in the New England area.

On 5 April 1887, Harrington and Richardson received US Patent 360686 to protect a simple solid-frame double-action revolver with a special hammer, knurled at the tip to facilitate cocking but otherwise lacking a spur. This was intended to enhance safety, a common preoccupation among the designers of revolvers at this time. The gun shown in the patent drawings had a short octagonal barrel and a cylinder that could be removed simply by pressing a latch set into the front of the frame to release the cylinder axis pin. Guns of this general class, often with short barrels, provided the mainstay of the Harrington & Richardson product range until the early 1990s.

The partners were also assigned patents granted to Homer Caldwell of Worcester, Massachusetts, who is believed to have been a freelance designer working for Harrington & Richardson at this time. US Patents 395119 of December 1888 and 408457 of August 1889 showed similar break-open auto-ejecting designs. The claims to novelty centred on the design of the cylinder-rotating pawl, its associated spring, and its

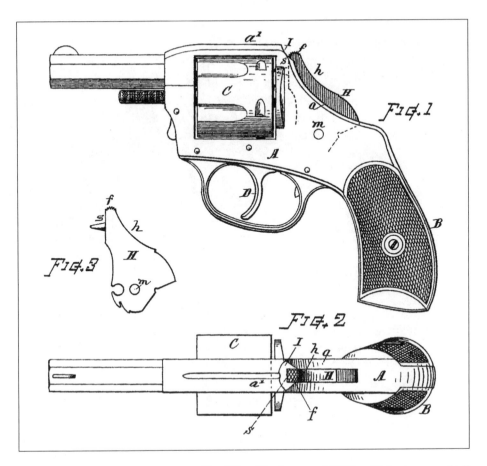

*Drawings of the 'safety hammer' patented by Gilbert Harrington and William Richardson on 5 April 1887. From US Patent No.360686.*

relationship with the remainder of the trigger mechanism. Caldwell was also the recipient of US Patent 425979 (April 1890), protecting improvements in the sear and the 'rebounder' – which ensured that the hammer was held back from the breech at all times excepting as it fell to strike the primer of the chambered round. Changes were also made in the auto-ejecting system with the dual intentions of improving performance and simplifying manufacture.

Caldwell's later patents suggest an initial return to his own affairs. US Patent 511406 of December 1893, protecting an H&R-type break-open revolver in which the sear additionally served the functions of a rebounder, mentions no assignees; 561963 of June 1896, protecting a transfer-bar safety system, was assigned to the widow of Iver Johnson and has been described previously.

Another patentee to serve Harrington & Richardson was George F. Brooks. Also giving his domicile as Worcester, Massachusetts, Brooks received US Patent 466952 on

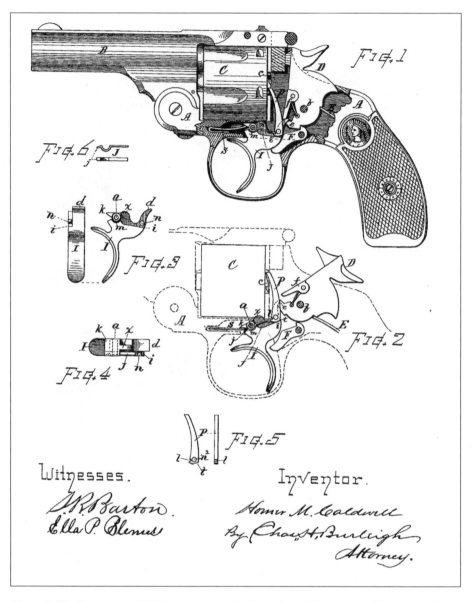

*Homer Caldwell was granted US Patent 395119 (25 December 1888) to protect this type of lock work.*

19 January 1892. The drawings accompanying the printed specification show a typical break-open H&R revolver – excepting a 'GFB' monogram drawn on the grip! – with the latch set in the top strap. The claim to novelty lay in the design of the sear and the rebound catch, which, by the standards of this particular class of revolver, was simple and sturdy.

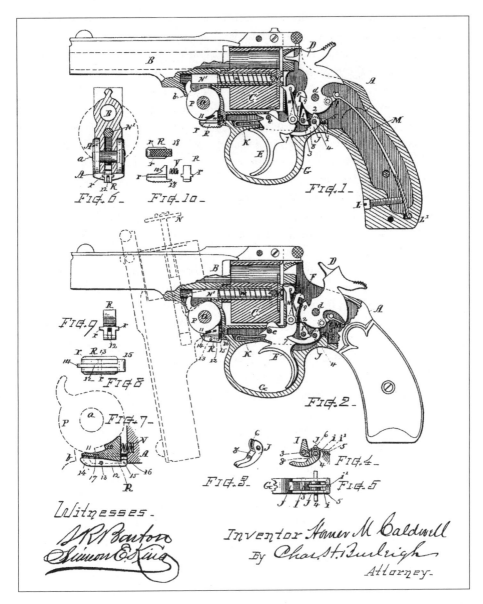

*The drawings accompanying US Patent No. 425979, granted on 22 April 1890 to Homer Caldwell, show a tip-barrel auto-ejecting revolver.*

The Foehl & Weeks Mfg Co. of Philadelphia made inexpensive revolvers protected by patents issued to the principals of the business, Charles Foehl and Charles Weeks, singly or together. US Patent 417672, accepted on 17 December 1889, protected a simple solid-frame revolver with a detachable cylinder axis pin. The frame was built up at the rear to enclose the hammer, and a safety blade was set into the front strap of the grip.

Another novelty concerned the firing pin, which was held in the hammer by a transverse pivot-pin set in annular bushes. A later design, Patent No. 447219 of February 1891, introduced a greatly simplified trigger system which included a leaf spring (anchored in the top front part of the grip) which snaked around the hammer pivot to ensure that the firing pin was held clear of the chambered cartridge unless struck by the hammer.

Foehl and Weeks also received US Patent 488243 (2 February 1892) to protect a simple, elegant, but possibly not particularly effective rebounder. The camming action of a pivoting blade set in the back of the enclosed hammer, pressed by the tail of the mainspring, forced the hammer back slightly after the gun had fired to release pressure on the free-floating firing pin.

George H. Fox and Henry F. Wheeler of Boston, Massachusetts, were the driving forces behind the American Arms Company.[3] Together, in March 1890, they were granted US Patent 422930 to protect the lock work of a double-action revolver. Wheeler then received No. 430243 on 17 June 1890, to protect a distinctive revolver with a selectable action (single or double), a locking snap to hold the barrel and frame together securely at the instant of firing, and a rocking blade-like safety lever set into the back strap immediately behind the tail of the hammer.

Elsewhere, Oscar Mossberg of Chicopee Falls, Massachusetts, received Patents 778500 and 778501 (27 December 1904) to protect double-action lock work and a safety lever, let into the back strap, that prevented the hammer moving back from its rest position. The patents were assigned to the J. Stevens Arms & Tool Company, but there is no evidence that they were ever exploited commercially. The same seems to have been true of a sophisticated folding-trigger pocket revolver (comparable in its basic conception to the European Velo-Dog or the 'Auto-Revolvers' popular prior to 1914) protected by US Patent No. 1007709, granted in November 1911 to Edward Leggett and Thomas Appleyard of New York.[4]

In Europe, in addition to the large rim- and centre-fire revolvers, huge quantities of small-calibre 'personal defence' patterns were made for the commercial market. They included a variety of pin-fires, commonly made in Liége or Saint-Étienne (more rarely in Birmingham or Eibar), which ranged from tiny open-frame guns chambering 6mm-calibre cartridges to much larger examples derived from the Lefaucheux revolvers issued by the French and the Spaniards for military service. The rim-fires had been pioneered by Smith & Wesson in the late 1850s, creating a market that was soon usurped not only by gunmakers in North America (whose exploits prior to 1870 were customarily stopped by lawsuits that upheld the primacy of the Rollin White patents) but also those in the principal European manufacturing centres. They were rapidly joined by the centre-fire

---

3. The American Arms Company was formed in Boston in 1871 to make Wheeler-patent derringers. Production of shotguns began in the mid-1870s, followed by revolvers in the 1880s, and a move to Milwaukee, Wisconsin, occurred in 1893. The assets, including shotguns and revolvers, were acquired by Marlin in 1901 – apparently shortly after George Fox died – and trading ceased.
4. The printed specification reveals that the rights were assigned to Loren M. Cowdrey and Frederick Winkhaus of New York, who are assumed to have been the financiers.

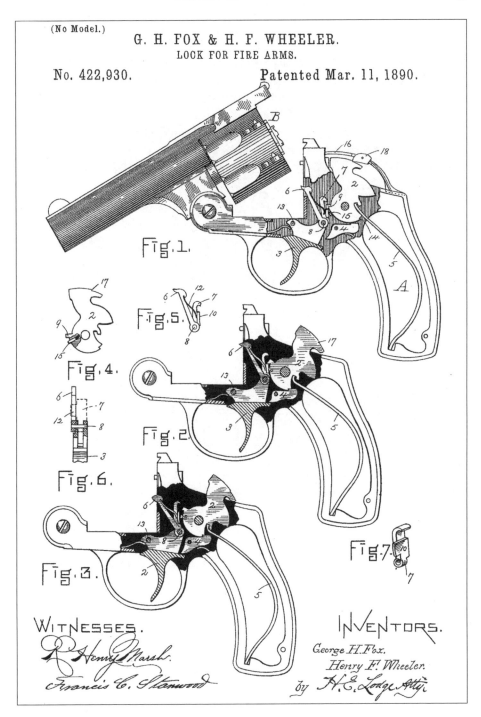

(No Model.)

# G. H. FOX & H. F. WHEELER.
## LOCK FOR FIRE ARMS.

No. 422,930. Patented Mar. 11, 1890.

Fig. 1.

Fig. 5.

Fig. 4.

Fig. 2.

Fig. 6.

Fig. 3.

Fig. 7.

WITNESSES.
Henry Marsh.
Francis C. Stanwood.

INVENTORS.
George H. Fox.
Henry F. Wheeler.
by H. E. Lodge. Atty.

*US Patent 422930 was granted on 11 March 1890 to George Fox and Henry Wheeler, to protect the trigger mechanism of a break-open revolver with a shrouded hammer.*

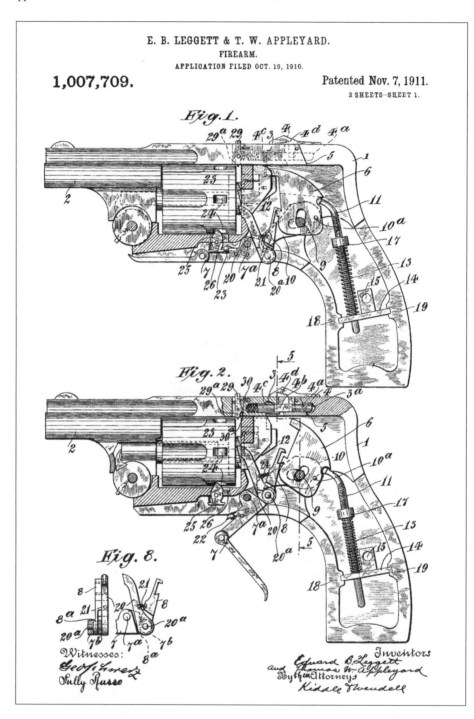

*Edward Leggett and Thomas Appleyard were responsible for this folding-trigger enclosed hammer break-open pocket revolver, patented in the USA on 7 November 1911 (No. 1007709).*

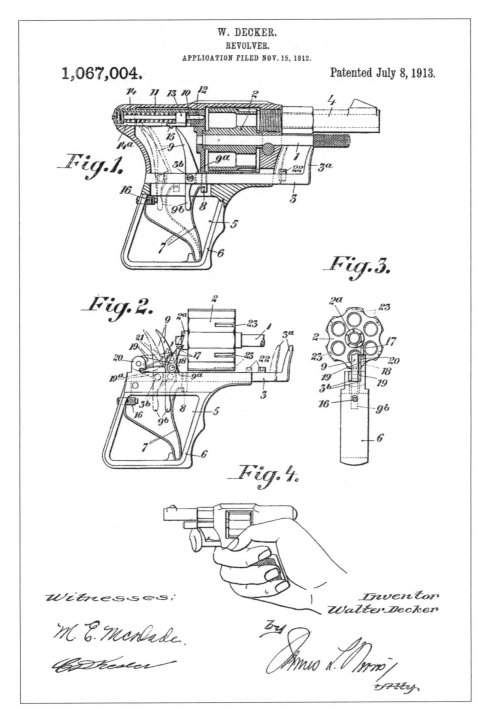

W. DECKER.
REVOLVER.
APPLICATION FILED NOV. 15, 1912.

1,067,004.

Patented July 8, 1913.

*Fig.1.*

*Fig.2.*

*Fig.3.*

*Fig.4.*

Witnesses:

Inventor
Walter Decker

*The compact revolver patented in the USA on 8 July 1913 by the German Walter Decker (Patent No. 1067004) had a distinctive sliding trigger beneath the barrel.*

guns, firing the most efficient ammunition; these, too, ranged from small personal-defence weapons to the largest and most efficient types based on military patterns.

The European equivalent of the Suicide Special came in several distinctive categories. Constabulary revolvers were generally chambered for centre-fire ammunition (.38, 9mm, .44 were common calibres); Bulldogs were sturdy short-barrelled guns, intended for personal defence and chambered accordingly; and there was a tremendous range of lesser designs, including the 'Velo-Dogs'. Made in huge numbers in Liége and Eibar, these revolvers were probably the nearest in design to the Suicide Specials; they were small, short-barrelled, and often had folding triggers. Some had open frames, others were more substantial; and almost all of them were chambered for the .22 Long or 6mm long-case 'Type Française' rim-fire rounds (and also, in later days, the 6.35mm Auto/.25 ACP).

Guns of this type owed their origins – and the stem of the distinctive name – to the rise of the bicycle, *vélocipède* in French, and to the universal fear of wild dogs carrying the rabies virus. The enthusiasm for bicycling was tempered by the knowledge that rabies had no known cure, and that, therefore, the fears were by no means groundless. One immediate result was the introduction of blank-firing guns and others that fired a

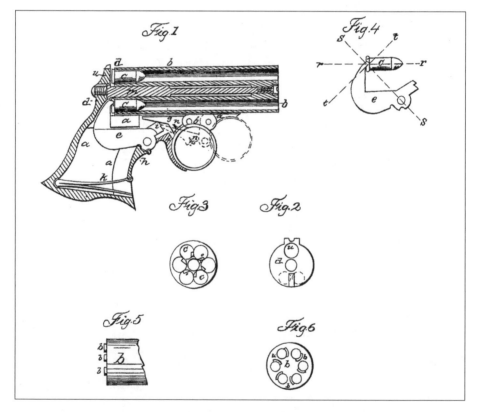

*The work of William Elliot, the Remington Zig-Zag derringer had a rotating barrel cluster and a ring trigger that was pulled forward before the firing cycle could begin.*

charge of pepper. These provided a humane but uncertain defence; cartridge weapons offered much greater protection.

The military heyday of the revolver, which had begun in the middle of the nineteenth century, had ended by the 1920s, excepting in the USSR and Britain where the Nagant and the Webley respectively remained in service for many years. Commercially, however, the story was very different. Total output of revolvers grew prodigiously. Variations of calibre, size and decoration are impossible to paraphrase adequately, such was their great diversity. Some later designs are considered in greater detail in later chapters, but their origins almost always lie in the guns of the nineteenth century.

One of the earliest attempts to miniaturise the revolver could be seen in the .22 rim-fire six-shot Zig-Zag derringers, patented in 1858–60 by William Elliot and made by E. Remington & Sons before the Civil War began. Only about a thousand had been made before hostilities commenced, however, and Remington abandoned the project to concentrate on the large-calibre cap-lock revolvers.

Another oddity was the Little All Right, the subject of US Patent No. 172243, granted on 18 January 1876 by Edward Boardman and Andrew Peavey, and made in Lawrence, Massachusetts, by the Little All Right Fire Arms Company. The tiny five-shot .22 rim-fire revolver had a sliding trigger bar above the barrel housing. It was held with the vestigial butt against the ball of the thumb, with the muzzle peeping through between the index and first fingers. The index finger retracted the trigger-bar, cocking the hammer, rotating the cylinder, and then releasing the hammer to fire the gun.

## Magazine Pistols: The First Steps

The revolver was the first single-barrel repeater to be made in quantity. However, though they could be fired very quickly, the cap-lock types were slow to load. The earliest rim-fire cartridges were too weak and pin-fire rivals were often deemed to be unsafe.

The first magazine repeater to demonstrate its potential, in the form of a carbine and a handgun, was the Volcanic. Its radical design was based on entirely self-contained ammunition, dispensing with a cartridge case, patented by Walter Hunt of New York on 10 August 1848 (US No. 5701) and assigned to financier George Arrowsmith of New York. Hunt's 'Volition Ball' was basically a lead envelope containing a larger than normal charge of priming compound. This allowed the projectile to be entirely self-contained, though it notably lacked power and accuracy was seriously degraded by the consumption of propellant and changes in projectile weight in flight. In addition, the propellant was highly corrosive and the metal parts of the gun – particularly the bore – suffered unduly.

Protected by an English Patent granted on 10 December 1847 and a comparable US Patent, No. 6663, dating from 21 August 1849, the Hunt rifle was far too cumbersome to succeed. Its backers, led by the railroad magnate Courtlandt Palmer, speedily commissioned gunsmith Lewis Jennings to make improvements. An appropriate patent (No. 6973) was obtained on 27 December 1849, and a few hundred rifles were subsequently made in Hartford, Connecticut, by Robbins & Lawrence. When the partners

realised that the project could not prosper, the patents were licensed to Horace Smith and
Daniel Wesson, and, in June 1854, Smith & Wesson opened a small workshop in Norwich,
Connecticut, to make handgun adaptations of the Jennings rifle. An improved design had
also been patented (the subject of US No. 10535 of 14 February 1854), and series
production began immediately.

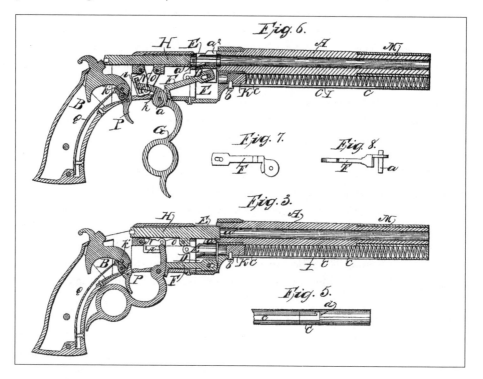

*The repeating pistol patented by Horace Smith and Daniel Wesson (US No. 10535 of 14 February
1854) was an improvement on the Hunt and Jennings patents of 1848–50.*

The lever-action pistols were loaded through a port cut near the muzzle in the
underside of the magazine tube. The projectiles were .31, .36 and .44-calibre Rocket
Balls. Guns were made in several sizes, with magazine capacities of 8–10 projectiles, but
rocket balls were too small to be effective, accuracy was poor and, as mercuric fulminate
was exceptionally corrosive, the bores deteriorated rapidly unless cleaned regularly.

Keener to exploit a revolver patented by Rollin White than wrestle with the repeating
pistol, Smith & Wesson sold the appropriate patents to a syndicate of clockmakers,
bakers, grocers, carriage makers and entrepreneurs in the summer of 1855. In August,
the tools, gauges and existing components were shipped to New Haven, Connecticut, to
equip the Volcanic Repeating Fire Arms Company. True Volcanics, made before the sale
of the company to Winchester, were invariably .40-calibre pistols with ring-tipped
operating levers and carbines whose appearance foreshadowed the Henry rifle.

By mid-summer 1857, the business was struggling once again. Sales had never been brisk, and the unstable fulminate powder, which sometimes blew the magazine tube off the breech, was proving to be a particular handicap. Charges of black powder cured the fault only at the expense of loss of power. The promise that lay in lever action and a tube magazine still lay hidden in the deficiencies of the Volcanic system. As Hunt, Palmer, and Smith & Wesson had all failed, so the Volcanic company also collapsed. Its assets were sold to Oliver Winchester, who presided over the incorporation of the New Haven Arms Company on 1 May 1857. The guns continued to be known as 'Volcanic Repeating Fire Arms'. A broadsheet published in 1859 advertised, in addition to carbines and long-barrel .40 'Navy' pistols, a .31 pocket pistol with a 4-inch barrel and a 6-ball magazine.

When the Civil War began in 1861, the New Haven Arms Company was still facing catastrophe. Salvation was found in a lever-operated .44 rifle developed by Benjamin Henry and work on the repeating pistols ceased. They had some good features, but among their greatest weaknesses was the necessity to use both hands – to hold the butt and the breech lever – placing the pistol at an obvious disadvantage against the revolver.

Other attempts were made in the mid-nineteenth century to provide a repeating pistol, including the 'harmonica gun' patented in France in 1859 by Joseph Jarre, which had a cartridge-chamber block capable of sliding laterally through an aperture in the breech. Protection for an improved version of the harmonica gun, with a block that could be carried vertically on the frame ahead of the trigger, was granted to Alphonse-Étienne and Pierre-Joseph Jarre in France in 1872.[5] Both guns were made in pistol form, though they were never widely distributed.

Guns embodying an endless chain of cartridge chambers were tried, but all were destined to fail. To be successful, a repeating pistol would have to incorporate a means of operation that allowed the gun to be cycled continuously or a one-hand cocking system, usually in the form of levers linking a reciprocating bolt with the trigger.

There were many inventors keen to produce a satisfactory alternative to the Volcanic. Among the earliest designs was that of William Marston of New York City, who received US Patent 17386 on 26 May 1857 to protect a break-open derringer with a monoblock containing three rifled barrels. The earliest experimental guns had a double-action trigger, which was replaced by a simpler single-action version before series production began. About 1,400 first-pattern .22 rim-fire Marston pistols were made in 1858–64; they were 5½in long and had 3-inch barrels. A few even had short knife blades on the left side of the barrel block. The hammer body was set into the frame, and a combination safety catch/selector lay on the right side of the frame ahead of the hammer. A travelling striker fired the barrels sequentially from the bottom upward.

An improved Marston, introduced in 1864, chambered .32 rim-fire cartridges in a bid to improve performance. An extractor was set into the right side of the frame; the selector was numbered '0', '1', '2' and '3'; and the body of the hammer projected from

5. The relevant US Patents are No. 35685 of 24 June 1862, with drawings showing a rifle, and No. 137927 of 15 April 1873, depicting a pistol.

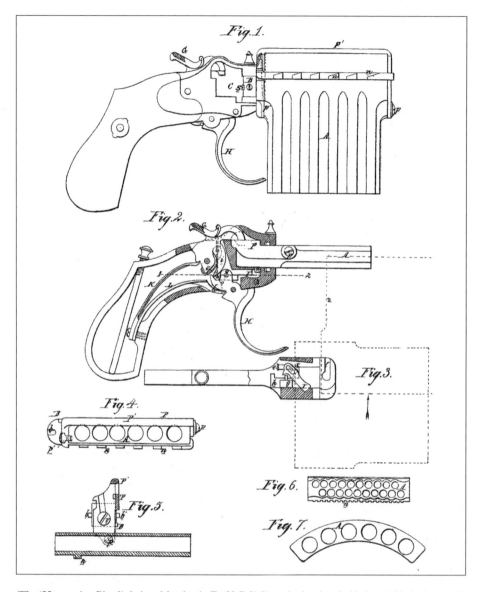

*The 'Harmonica Pistol' designed by the A. E. & P. J. Jarre had a detachable barrel block that could be carried vertically but replaced in the frame horizontally to fire. From the drawings accompanying US Patent 137927 of 15 April 1873.*

the frame-back. Work continued until 1874 in short and long versions, with 3-inch and 4-inch barrels respectively.

 The Sharps derringer offered an alternative approach. Christian Sharps originally patented a four-barrel cluster derringer with a rotating striker in December 1849 (US No. 6960), but had never exploited the design. After the inventor severed his links with

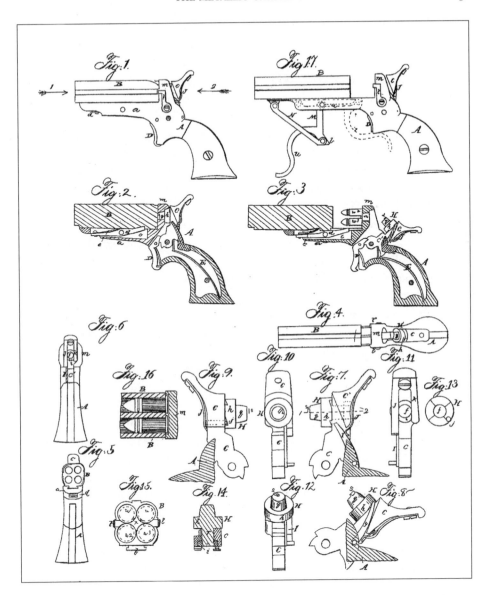

*Patented in the USA on 25 January 1859 (No. 22753), the cluster derringer designed by Christian Sharps had barrels that were drawn forward to load and a rotating striker on the hammer nose.*

the Sharps Rifle Mfg Co., in 1853, he continued to make firearms in collusion with Ira Eddy and, later, Nathan Bolles. After buying out his partners in 1858, he sought protection for an improved metallic-cartridge version of the 1849-patent gun with a sliding barrel block; US Patent 22753 was duly granted on 25 January 1859. The barrels were arranged as two rows of two, sliding forward to give access to the breech after a catch had been released. A rotating striker-plate, ensuring that the chambers were fired in the correct order, was generally fitted on the hammer but lay in the frame of some Sharps & Hankins guns.

Production began early in 1859, and almost immediately, the retaining pins of the original guns gave way to screws. Work continued under a 'C. Sharps & Co.' trading style until the partnership of Sharps & Hankins was formed in 1862. The original derringers had been made in .22 and .30 Short rim-fire chamberings, with brass frames and blued iron barrels measuring 2½–3¼ inches. Some were plated with nickel or silver, and the grips could be walnut, gutta-percha, ivory or mother-of-pearl. The chambers were customarily recessed to envelop the cartridge-case rims, and a few guns were made with safety catches mounted on the hammer. The standard Sharps & Hankins version, in .32 Short rim-fire, had an iron barrel and an iron frame. The standing breech was noticeably rounded instead of the original angular shape. Some guns were fitted with extractors, and most had the barrel-release catch transversely through the mid-frame area instead of under the front of the frame.

William Hankins left the business at the end of 1867, allowing Christian Sharps to continue operations until his death in 1874. Though work on the earlier patterns continued, a new variation of the .32-calibre derringer appeared. This had bird's-head grips, but was otherwise similar to the Sharps & Hankins type. Guns made after 1868 were marked as the products of the Sharps Rifle Company. Production has been estimated as about 150,000, with the original .22-calibre pattern contributing more than half the total.[6]

Patented in 1860–1 by William Elliot of Plattsburg, New York State, the Remington-Elliot derringer was made in two differing forms protected by the same group of US patents: No. 21188 of 17 August 1858, 28460 and 28461 of 29 May 1860, and 33362 of 1 October 1861. One type of gun – made as a five-shot .22 or a four-shot .32 – had a multi-barrel cluster which tipped down to load, and was fired sequentially by a revolving striker actuated by a ring trigger. The other, the so-called 'Zig-Zag' was comparable externally to the fixed-barrel version, with a ring trigger and a similar grip, but was a six-shot .22 revolver. The trigger could slide longitudinally, revolving the barrel cluster and cocking the internal hammer on the forward stroke. As it was pulled back again, the trigger then locked the barrels and released the hammer. The guns were generally blued, but the frames or the entire gun could be nickel-plated to order. Grips could be gutta-percha, mother-of-pearl or ivory. About 25,000 cluster derringers were made in 1863–88, and only about a thousand Zig-Zags in 1860–1.

The origins of the 'turnover' two-barrel cluster dated back to the days of the matchlock, and wheel- and flint- and cap-lock versions had been made in surprising numbers. Interest in guns of this type was renewed by the metal-case cartridge, which encouraged production of pistols which were simpler and easier to make than

---

6. Frank M. Sellers, 'A documentary review of Christian Sharps' 4-Barrel Pistols' in *Gun Collector's Digest* (1974), pp. 194–9. It has also been suggested that the production machinery was sold to Tipping & Lawden in Britain, where work may have continued until the late 1870s.

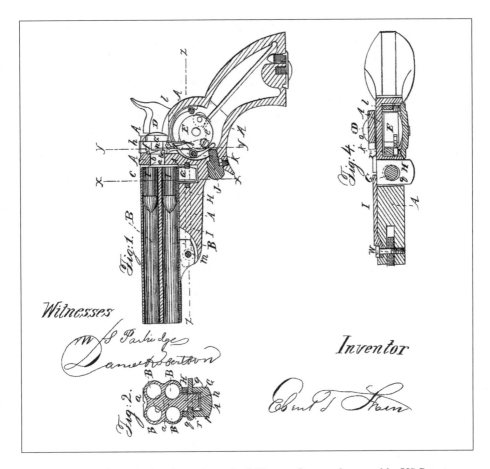

*This four-barrel 'cluster derringer' was the work of Ebenezer Starr, and protected by US Patent No. 42698 of 10 May 1864.*

pepperboxes or revolvers. A typical two-barrel design was registered in Britain in February 1863 by Woodward of Birmingham. It was a simple sheath-trigger design with a sliding hammer-locking catch on the back strap of the frame. After the first shot had been fired, the barrel cluster was rotated through 180 degrees to fire the second round. The hammer was then retracted to half-cock and the barrels were turned through ninety degrees to give access to the chambers.

A typical Woodward derringer, chambered for a .240 rim-fire cartridge, was about 4¾in long and had a 2¼in barrel. Similar guns were made by Philip Webley & Son in the late 1860s. However, these were larger and more powerful than their predecessors, chambering a selection of cartridges from 6mm rim-fire to .44 rim-fire or .450 centre-fire.

The turnover derringer patented in the USA on 31 October 1865 (No. 50760) and 19 June 1866 (No. 55752) by Henry Wheeler of Boston, Massachusetts, was a simple sheath-trigger design with a two-barrel monoblock that rotated through ninety degrees to give access to the breech once a small spring-loaded latch on the underside of the frame had been released. Turning the barrels through thirty degrees conferred a measure of safety. Made from 1867 by the American Nut & Tool Company of Boston, Massachusetts ('American Arms Company' from 1871), the Wheeler pistol was initially offered in .32 Short and .41 rim-fire, and then also in a .22/.32 combination. The barrel lengths of the three patterns were 2½in, 2⅝in and 3in respectively. Some guns were browned, but others were plated with nickel. The factory moved from Boston to Milwaukee in 1893, where work continued until the business was acquired by Marlin in 1901.

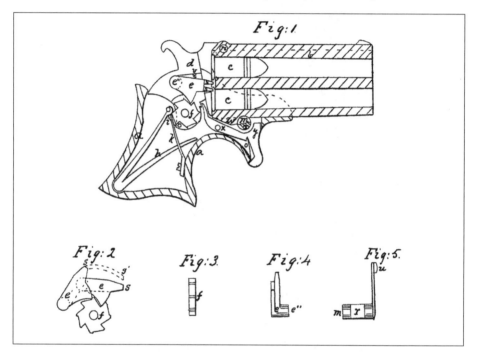

*This drawing shows the 'double derringer' invented by William Elliot, patented in the USA on 12 December 1865 (No. 51440), and made in quantity by E. Remington & Sons.*

The Remington Repeating Double Deringer (*sic*), designed by William Elliot, was patented in the USA on 12 December 1865 (No. 51440) and introduced commercially in 1866. Sales were amazingly good; when work finally ceased in the mid-1930s, about 150,000 had been made. The essential feature was a pair of superimposed 3-inch .41 rim-fire barrels in a monoblock hinged to the frame. The barrel block swung upward around a pivot at the top rear of the frame when the lever on the right side of the frame was pressed downward, allowing the gun to be reloaded. The firing pin fired the top barrel first, being re-set each time the frame was opened. Few changes were made to the design during its long life, excepting that an extractor was added in the early 1870s.

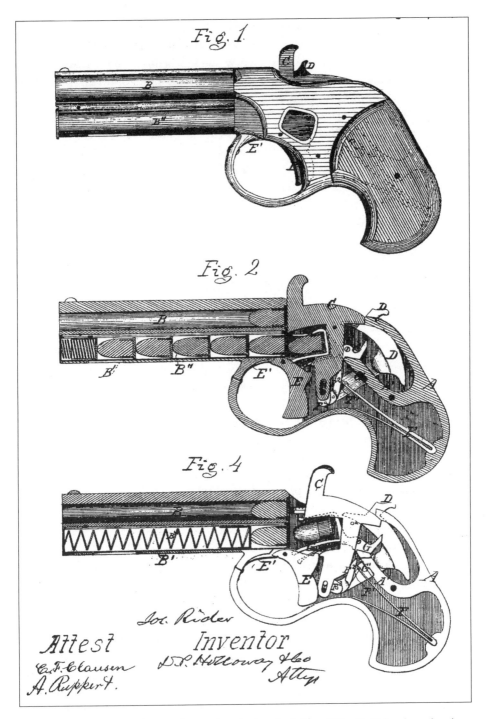

*E. Remington & Sons made a small magazine pistol to the designs of Joseph Rider, shown here in drawings taken from US Patent 118152 of 15 August 1871.*

Most of the guns were nickel-plated, although blued examples were produced in small numbers. Their grips may be walnut, rosewood, chequered gutta-percha, mother-of-pearl or ivory. The guns were about 4¾in long and weighed 11oz empty. About 150,000 were made before work stopped in 1935. The manufacturer's mark gives a clue to date: 'E. Remington & Sons' was used until 1888, 'Remington Arms Co.' from 1888 until 1910, and 'Remington Arms–U.M.C. Co.' from 1910 until the end of production.

Remington tried a different simpler approach to the repeating firearm with the 'Magazine Repeating Pistol', 15,000 being made in 1872–88 on the basis of US Patent 118152, granted on 15 August 1871 to Joseph Rider of Newark, Ohio. The sheath-trigger design had a tube magazine beneath the barrel for four .32 Extra Short rim-fire cartridges. A fifth round could be loaded directly into the chamber. Rider's design relied on a variant of the proven rolling-block action and an elevator to convey cartridges to the breech. Most guns had 3-inch barrels and weighed 10oz. Some had colour case-hardened frames, whilst others were nickel plated. The standard varnished walnut grips could be replaced to order with ivory or mother-of-pearl.

### The Later Mechanical Repeaters

The success of the small-calibre derringer-type repeaters in the USA eclipsed attempts to market repeating pistols that were closer in concept to the Volcanic. A ring-trigger design by Albert Ball of Worcester, Massachusetts, protected by a patent granted in June 1863 (No. 38935), relied on a breech-block that tipped and moved back to accept a cartridge from the under-barrel tube magazine. Henry Wheeler of Boston, Massachusetts, contributed a gun – US Patent 66110 of 25 June 1867 – with a ring-lever that moved the barrel forward from the standing breech to extract, eject and allow a new cartridge into the chamber. And Louis Rodier and Francis Bates of Springfield, Massachusetts, developed a dropping-block pistol with a ring lever and a separate trigger in the rear of the ring. Protected by US Patent 138439 of 29 April 1873, the Rodier & Bates pistol was remarkable for the insertion of an amazingly modern-looking box magazine in the rear of the bulky grip.

Work on large mechanical repeaters continued in the USA for many years, later contributions including that of William Kimball of Washington, DC, who received US Patent 513237 of 23 January 1894 to protect a straight-line bolt operated by rack-and-pinion and locked by a vertically moving block in the top of the frame. Perhaps more impressive, though too late to be successful, was the pistol patented in June 1900 (US No. 651577) by Oscar Mossberg of Hatfield, Massachusetts. Mossberg was an excellent draftsman, and the three pages of drawings accompanying the patent specification show in great detail what appears to be a superimposed-barrel pistol with the trigger at the front of an elongated guard. When the trigger is pulled rearward, a combination of a sliding barrel and a vertically-operating cartridge depressor extract a spent case, eject the case through a port in the right side of the frame, and feed a new round into the chamber from the tube magazine above the barrel.

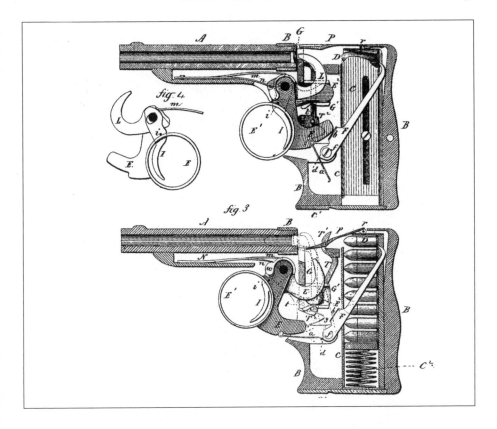

*The repeating pistol designed by Louis Rodier and Francis Bates incorporated a surprisingly modern-looking box magazine, shown here in drawings taken from US Patent 138439 of 29 April 1873.*

Though several small-calibre designs had proved to be exceptionally successful in the USA, the idea of the mechanically-operated repeating pistol was developed to its ultimate form in Europe. Though comparatively little is known in detail about the history of the 'Bohemian School', named after the area of Austria-Hungary where many of the inventors worked, there is little doubt that most of the developments took place in central Europe.

Most of these repeaters were locked by rotary bolts, operated by a ring-lever enveloping the trigger, but the relationships between them have yet to be resolved and even the chronology is now difficult to determine. Though a pin-fire turret pistol was patented in Germany as late as 1881 by Franz Drevenstedt of Klein Ammensleben bei Magdeburg, chambering a strange proprietary cartridge with the pin placed directly behind the bullet, most of the European mechanical repeaters followed the patterns that had been established in the USA by the Volcanic. They included the tilting-block pistols patented in France in 1877 by Jean Berger of Saint-Étienne (also protected by US Patent No. 233466 of October 1880) and in Germany in 1886 by Rudolf Österreich of Berlin.

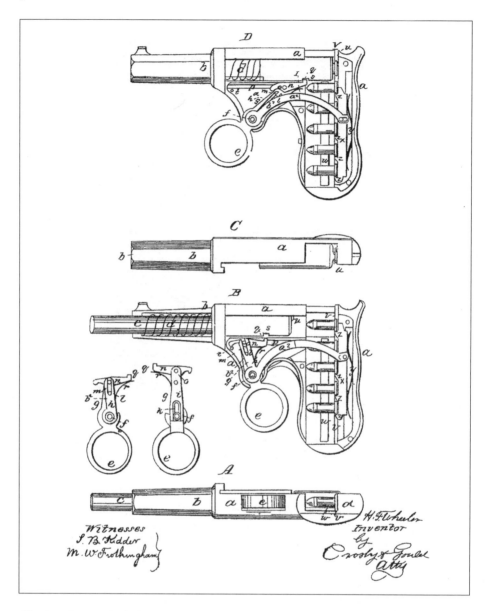

*The ring-trigger mechanical repeater patented on 25 June 1867 by Henry Wheeler (US No. 66110).*

Both guns were operated by ring levers and had tube magazines beneath the barrel, though the French design – made commercially in small numbers – had a hammer and the German pattern relied on a striker.

More popular, at least with the gunmakers, was a rotating-bolt lock, generally relying on a peg on the bolt engaging a camming slot in the ring-lever to rotate locking lugs out of engagement with the frame. A forward movement of the finger lever generally

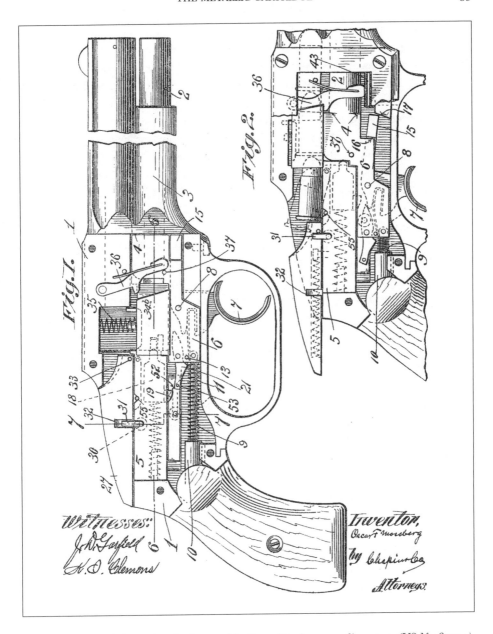

*The manually-operated repeating pistol patented by Oscar Mossberg on 12 June 1900 (US No. 651377) was among the most sophisticated of its type.*

unlocked the bolt and moved it backward. Pulling the lever back returned the bolt, stripping a round from the magazine into the breech, then re-locked the mechanism for the next shot. The final backward movement of the finger lever sometimes tripped the firing pin automatically.

The earliest representative of this class has yet to be satisfactorily identified, probably because the principle of the bolt action was far too well established to be patentable. Josef Schulhof patented a pistol in Germany in 1884 with a multi-column butt magazine, but the reciprocating bolt seems to have been locked with a toggle-link; more typical was the pistol developed by Karel Krnka,[7] first patented in Austria-Hungary in 1886, which embodied the rotating bolt. Like most of the promoters of large-calibre mechanical repeaters, Krnka was more concerned with the loading system. His British Patent 14088/88, granted on 1 October 1888, shows a six-round spool magazine beneath a sliding cover on the right side of the frame. This loading system was retained on the perfected form of the gun, the 5.1mm-calibre Krnka-Říha of 1892, which also had a ring lever that could be locked to allow single shots to be fired.

Where Krnka led, others followed. The Passler & Seidl pistol, patented in 1887,[8] had a clip-loaded magazine with a cartridge-lifting arm and associated spring stretching forward beneath the barrel; Erwin Reiger, grantee of British Patent 6360/89 of 13 April 1889, claimed novelty only in improvements in the magazine; and Gustav Bittner claimed in 1893 to have improved the bolt and safety mechanism of the Passler & Seidl design. Josef Laumann of Vienna was another enterprising gunmaker, best known (owing to modern publicity) for the Schönberger automatic pistol described in greater detail in the next chapter. However, the Schönberger is little more than an automated form of Laumann's mechanical repeaters of 1890–2.[9]

Though the repeaters were impossibly complicated, they were often very well made and could fire quite rapidly if they were kept clean. Their worst features were usually their clumsiness and, undoubtedly, a lack of primary extraction. Francotte of Liége made a compact pistol with a ring trigger and a detachable box magazine in the butt; and the Belgian Counet pattern is also reasonably compact, but they are the exceptions to the rule.

The heyday of the big European mechanical repeaters – and a very limited heyday it was – was 1885–95. Few of the few guns were made in large numbers, possibly excepting the Bittner. However, few surviving Bittners bear proof marks dated earlier than 1897; this places the attempt to exploit the design commercially as contemporaneous with the Borchardt and the Bergmann self-loading pistols, much more efficient handguns, and indicates why the large centre-fire mechanical repeaters were swept away almost as soon as they had been perfected.

---

7. Karel Krnka (1858–1926) was the son of the well-known Bohemian gunmaker/inventor Sylvestr Krnka. While serving in the Austro-Hungarian Army, he developed the first of a long line of firearms. His magazine rifle performed surprisingly well in the 1887–8 trials, but was rejected in favour of the Mannlicher. Krnka became chief engineer of the Gatling Arms & Ammunition Co. Ltd (1887–91) and then a patent agent, before working for Georg Roth, the Hirtenberg ammunition-making business, Zbrojovka Praga, and lastly Česká Zbrojovka.

8. Franz Passler, often in collusion with Ferdinand Seidl, received several patents in the 1880s. Typical is US Patent 385875 of 10 July 1888, granted to 'Franz Passler, of Ottakring, near Vienna, Austria-Hungary'. The application had been filed in October 1887.

9. Protected by, among others, British Patent No. 3790/90 of 10 March 1890, British Patent 2984/91 of 1891, US Patent 479284 of 19 July 1892, and US Patent 508228 of 7 November 1893.

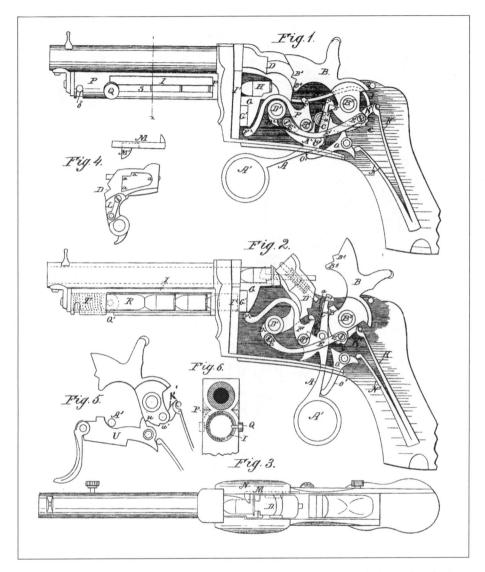

*These drawings from US Patent 233466 (19 October 1880) show the mechanical repeating pistol designed by the Frenchman Jean Berger.*

Conversely, some of the smaller repeaters fared surprisingly well. An oddity among them was the turret-type palm pistol patented by Frenchman Jacques-Edmond Turbiaux in 1882–3 (for example US Patent 273644 of 6 March 1883). A short barrel protruded between the firer's fingers from the frame or receiver, which contained a flat disc-like magazine. The gun was fired by pressing a spring-loaded plate at the back of the frame against the base of the firer's palm. Several finger spurs on the front surface of the frame, alongside the barrel, helped to improve the handgrip.

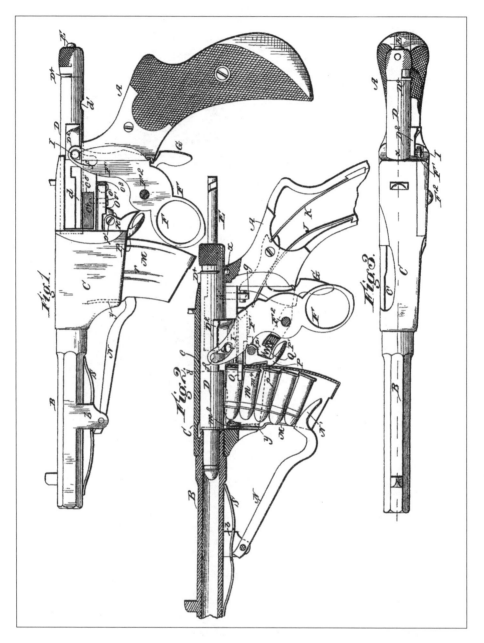

*Drawings of the mechanical repeater designed by Franz Passler, patented in the USA on 10 July 1888 (No. 385875). Note how the magazine follower was pivoted on a lug beneath the barrel.*

Large numbers of these guns, known as 'Le Protecteur', were made in France for an underpowered but no less distinctive short-case 8mm centre-fire cartridge. Others enjoyed a short vogue in North America under the brand name 'Protector', often

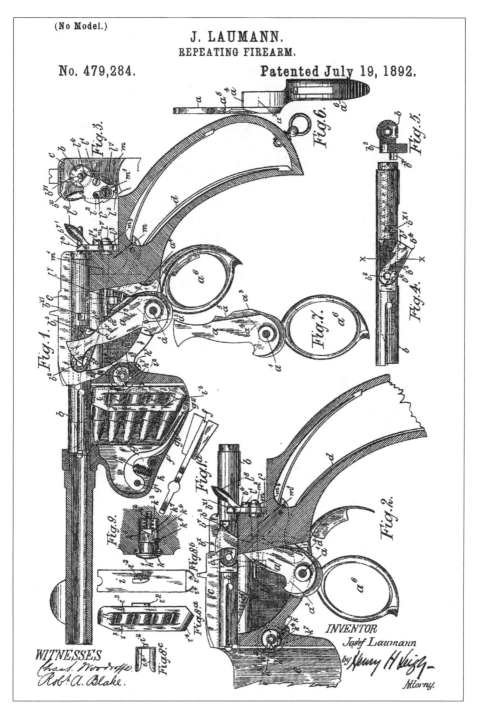

*This page of drawings from US Patent No. 479284, granted on 19 July 1892 to Josef Laumann, illustrates the complexity of the most sophisticated of the European mechanical repeaters.*

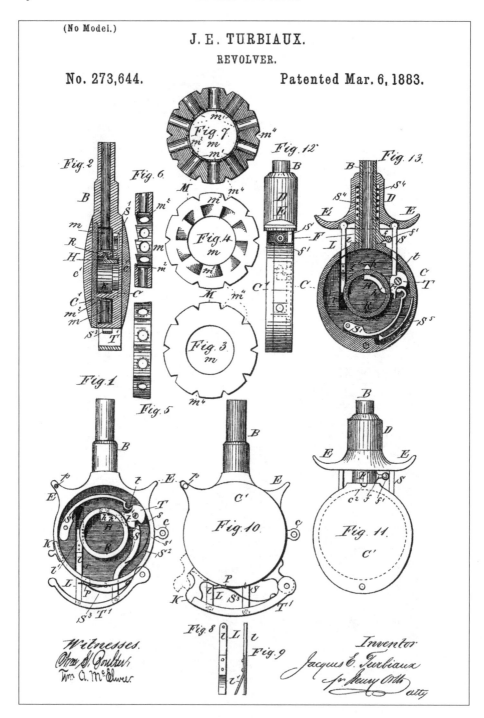

*The Protector repeating pistol, the work of the Frenchman Jacques Turbiaux, was patented in the USA on 6 March 1883. These drawings are taken from this patent, No. 273644.*

embodying improvements made by Peter Finnegan of Austin, Illinois, and patented in the USA on 29 August 1893 (No. 504154). Made by the Ames Sword Company of Chicopee Falls in Massachusetts, the seven-shot .32 Short rim-fire Protector was marketed initially by the Minneapolis Fire-Arms Company and then by the Chicago Fire Arms Company. Catalogues issued by Hartley & Graham in 1892 suggest that the Minneapolis Protector was made in three patterns: nickel-plated or blued, with rubber or pearl 'sides'.

Most Minneapolis-made guns had manual safety levers, whereas the Chicago examples relied on squeezing the trigger lever to disengage an automatic safety on the finger spur. The guns were loaded by removing the side plate. Some Chicago-made Protectors also have a distinctive double-ring finger guard designed about 1900 by John Norris of Springfield, Ohio; the guard prevented painful accidents by keeping the fingers away from the muzzle of the ultra-short barrel. Le Protecteur and its US-made cousin achieved limited distribution commercially, but were unable to compete with the popular pocket revolvers.

Much more successful were the repeaters with box magazines, particularly the 'Mitrailleuse à Poche' patented in France in August 1892 by Étienne Mimard and Pierre Blachon. Manufacture Française d'Armes et Cycles de Saint-Étienne began production of the Mitrailleuse in 1893 and continued work for almost twenty years.[10] The gun consisted of a box-like frame with a barrel at the front and a sliding grip at the back. The magazine held five 8mm Le Protecteur-type cartridges. The firer squeezed with the heel of his thumb, sliding the grip inward to strip a round from the magazine into the chamber, cock the striker, lock the breech, and then release the striker to fire the gun. When the spring-loaded grip was released, the spent case was automatically withdrawn from the chamber and thrown clear.

The Mitrailleuse worked surprisingly well and, as a result, enjoyed considerable popularity. The cartridge had to be very weak to allow the locking system to work properly, but the bullet was seated in the chamber at the moment of discharge to avoid the gas leaks customary in revolvers. A defective cartridge could be ejected mechanically without interrupting the operating sequence.

Originally marked MITRAILLEUSE on top of the barrel rib, the repeaters were renamed 'Gaulois' in 1896 and marked appropriately. Production may have been surprisingly large, though claims in excess of 1 million should be treated with extreme caution in view of the scarcity of survivors. Manufrance may simply have numbered *all* its firearms in a single sequence.

---

10. The term *mitrailleuse* was first associated with the proto-machine-guns designed by Montigny and de Reffye. The latter had seen service with the French Army during the Franco-Prussian War of 1870–1. Though it had proved to be a failure, largely owing to ignorance of its value as an infantry-support weapon, the gun was held in such great esteem by the public that its name was subsequently appropriated for virtually any small calibre rapid-firing weapon. Automatic rifles and machine-guns are still known as '*fusils mitrailleur*' and '*mitrailleuses*' in French service.

In 1900, four types of Gaulois were being offered, ranging from the Model 1 – polished and browned, with an ebonite grip – to the de luxe Model 4, which was chiselled, damascened and had a grip of ivory. Markings generally included the manufacturer's name, GAULOIS and an 'MF' monogram trademark. The pistols were very compact, only about 14mm thick, and were often hidden in what on first glance appeared to be a leather cigar case.

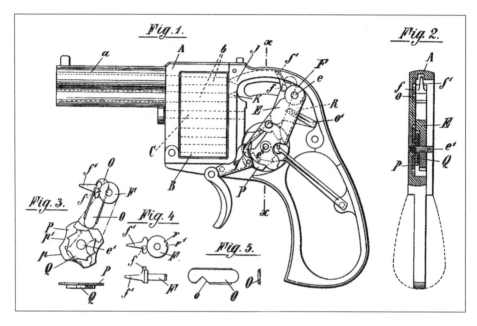

*US Patent 630478 of 8 August 1899 protected the Bär-Pistole – the design of a Swiss-domiciled Russian, Burkhard Behr.*

The Lampo was another of the 'squeezers' to achieve success. Patented by Catello Tribuzio of Turin in the early 1890s, it had a distinctive ring trigger protruding from the lower front edge of its sculptured frame. Sliding the trigger backward with the second finger of the firing hand operated the action in much the same way as the Gaulois, though the motion was somewhat easier. The 8mm Le Protecteur cartridge was retained.

The 8mm Rouchouse was another French design. The name is often said to have been an erroneous version of 'Rough-house', but the guns were made by J. Rouchouse & Cie of Saint-Étienne, successors to Manufacture d'Armes Escoffier in the 1880s. The pistol was a variant of the Gaulois principle with the grip unit sliding backward into the frame. It would have been easier to shoot than its rival, owing to backward movement, towards the palm, and the addition of a shaped pad on the back of the frame. However, it was never popular and very little is known about its history; the Rouchouse may simply have appeared too late to exert influence commercially.

Made by J. P. Sauer & Sohn of Suhl in the first few years of the twentieth century, the Bär-Pistole was patented by Burkhard Behr of Zürich in March 1898.[11] Its claims to fame included a folding trigger, two superimposed barrels, and a '2 x 2' breech-block. The two upper chambers were fired sequentially, then the block was rotated laterally through 180 degrees to allow the third and fourth shots to be fired. Reloading was simply a matter of rotating the breech-block to its intermediate ninety-degree position and punching the spent cases out of the chambers with a suitable tool. The first guns were chambered for a special 7mm cartridge, but post-1906 examples accept 6.35mm Auto rounds instead.

Among the most interesting of all repeating pistols was the 'Reform', patented in 1905 by August Schuler of Suhl. About 4,000 are said to have been made by 1914. It had a distinctive four-barrel block, raised vertically in the frame, shot-by-shot, by a double-action trigger mechanism. Each shot was fired by a single hammer and striker at the height of the first or uppermost barrel when the barrel-block was in its lowest position. Spent cases were expelled by residual propellant gas bled from the firing barrel through connecting ports. The fourth, or lowest, case had to be extracted manually after the barrel block was removed for loading. A safety lever lay on the left side of the frame beneath the hammer.

The earliest Reform had a flat-sided frame and BRÉVETÉ/D.R.P./177023 on the left side of the barrel block. A later type – possibly made by another contractor – had flat-sided barrels and a frame with prominent curved-bottom fairings. These guns were marked REFORM-PISTOLE, arched over D.R.PAT./D.R.G.M./AUSLANDS-PAT. Grips were marked REFORM-PISTOLE and BRÉVETÉ in a roundel, together with an 'SR' ('Schuler Reform') monogram.

The subject of a patent granted to Oscar Mossberg of Chicopee Falls, Massachusetts, on 4 December 1906 (No. 837867), the 'Unique' was made for a few years by C. S. Shatuck of Hatfield, Massachusetts. A four-barrel block, fired by a slider-actuated rotary striker, could be tipped down in the blued or nickel-plated iron frame to load. Unique pistols accepted .22 or .32 rim-fire cartridges. Sales were not particularly inspiring, but interest was strong enough to persuade Cornelius Vanderbilt Jr to patent an improvement in March 1916.

In Europe, a 6.35mm gun with a four-barrel block, sold under the brand name 'Regnum', was made by August Menz of Suhl from 1910 until the beginning of the First World War. Production is believed to have totalled a thousand. The barrels were locked by a sliding catch on the left side of the frame, immediately ahead of the safety catch, and were fired sequentially. A four-hammer disc on a central spindle struck each of four separate firing pins set in the standing breech. Spent cases were ejected automatically as the breech was opened.

---

11. See US Patents, No. 627966 of 4 July 1899 (granted to 'Burkhard Behr, of Bendlikon, Switzerland') and 630478 of 8 August 1899 (to 'Burkhard Behr, of Zurich, Switzerland'). Both specifications reveal that Behr was a 'citizen of the Russian Empire'.

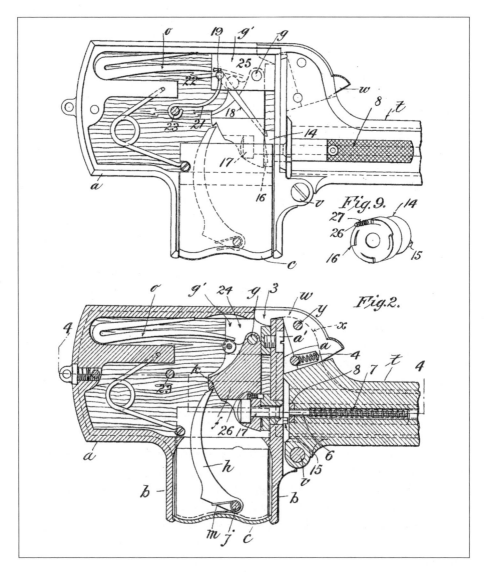

*The Mossberg 'Unique' was a compact four-shot pistol with a fixed barrel block and a rotating striker. From US Patent 837867 of 4 December 1906.*

The Tomma was similar to the Menz Regnum, with a tipping four-barrel block, but had a noticeably rounder appearance, a shorter grip, and a simple push-button barrel catch instead of a slider. Though a few 7.65mm examples have been reported, most of the guns accept 6.35mm Auto cartridges. About 3,000 were made in Germany and 2,500 by Manufacture d'Armes 'HDH' in Liége. Proof marks are the most obvious distinguishing feature, but the Belgian-made guns are longer (95mm compared with 87mm) and cruder.

When the First World War began, even the small mechanically-operated repeating pistols had been eclipsed by minuscule FN-Browning and similar auto-loading designs after enjoying a period in vogue of no more than a decade.

## Multi-Threat Weapons

Combining a handgun and a blade to provide a second line of defence was another long-lived idea that made its last stand immediately prior to the First World War. Comparatively few were made with the intention of keeping the presence of a firearm secret, as they were customarily to provide an alternative or supplementary means of defence. The pistol component is usually easy to detect; the direction of fire is customarily towards the blade-tip. Less obvious are the guns in which the pistol barrel forms the hilt. Many of these are designed to fire backward, away from the blade tip, and the triggers may be hidden.

The impetus for one of the periodic bursts of enthusiasm for these combination weapons was provided by the American Civil War, when a revolver-sabre was patented in March 1862 by Robert Colvin of Lancaster, Pennsylvania. Just one of many strange weapons being promoted enthusiastically across the USA, the Colvin sabre-revolver at least made the transition from patent-specification drawing to hardware. Unfortunately, the manufacturer has never been satisfactorily identified, though there were many in the Lancaster area – the original home of the American or Pennsylvania Long Rifle – who could have been responsible. The 'gun part' of the weapon was a five-shot cap-lock revolver rotated by a double-acting trigger within the crossguard of the sword.

The earliest sword and knife pistols were customarily single-shot, which enabled them to be kept as compact as possible, though a few double-barrel examples were made. A patent protecting a cap-lock revolver-sabre was granted in Britain in 1864 to Isaiah Williams, acting for an Italian designer named Micheloni, and Walter Davis of Bristol was granted protection for a combination weapon similar to Colvin's revolver-sabre as late as December 1877. Additional novelty lay in the sectional construction of the scabbard, which could be folded to act as a shoulder stock. A few European pistol-swords will even incorporate small-calibre pin-fire revolvers; usually made in Belgium, they date from 1870–1914.

Knife pistols are far more common than true sword pistols, as their compact dimensions made them so much easier to conceal. In addition, they were considered less as weapons of war and more as a way of providing hunters, trappers and similar woodsmen with an additional defence. Proof marks may occasionally identify nationality, but many pistol-knives pre-date the establishment of mandatory proof. This is notably true of pre-1891 German examples, as well as those made in the USA (where there is still no national proof system).

Samuel Colt made a double-action Paterson-type revolver with a sturdy blade beneath the muzzle, and substantial quantities of pin-fire examples were made in Europe in a range of sizes. Most of the pin-fires will prove to have been made in Liége, but some are Spanish and a few were doubtless made in Birmingham. One otherwise anonymous German-made example has a short barrel and a combination hammer-bar/breech block released by a small folding lever beneath the grip; another, unmarked, has two barrels flanking a central two-edged dagger and fired by a laterally-moving hammer forming the crossguard.

The disguises adopted by knife-pistols were usually much better than those of the bladed revolvers. From the 1850s onwards, the British sword-cutlers Unwin & Rodgers of Sheffield made a variety of knives, often multi-bladed, with a small pistol in the grips. Later examples (possibly made after 1867) were marked by Joseph Rodgers or, from about 1888 onward, Joseph Rodgers & Sons. These companies all used a distinctive trademark in the form of a six-point linear star and a cross patée. Joseph Rodgers also sometimes simply used ACME, METEOR, STAR AND CROSS, the German-language version STERNENKREUZ, the misleading UQS, or '6 Norfolk Street, Sheffield' instead of his name.

The earliest Unwin & Rodgers knife-pistols were single-barrel cap-locks with two folding knife blades beneath the handgrip; later ones were rim- or centre-fire, often with the barrel (which no longer required external priming) set partially within the grip. Some grips were wood, others were staghorn and a few were chequered gutta-percha. The barrel of these pistol-knives lay along the top of the grip, where it was clearly visible, and the trigger folded up beneath the grip to prevent snagging inside a pocket. Cap-lock models often carried a small scissors-type ball mould and a rammer in the slots in the grip, where they were held by friction. Most guns had a small hinged-lid trap in the butt to carry bullets or (later) spare .22 Short cartridges.

Unwin & Rodgers also made a few twin-barrel pistol-knives, marked SELF PROTECTOR, with as many as four blades. These generally had twin triggers. A few guns had a distinctive false breech, which had to be lifted before the extractor could be activated.

Among the most heavily disguised of all pistol-knives were the pen- or clasp-knife patterns. Andrew Peavey of South Montville, Maine, patented a cap-lock version in the USA in September 1865, and a rim-fire adaptation followed in March 1866. The Peavey pistol-knife had a single folding blade, offset to one side to allow a barrel to run the length of the grip beneath the elongated hammer bar. The gun was fired by pulling up on the rear of the hammer against the pressure of the leaf spring, until it was held by a serpentine catch doubling as the trigger lever. Pressing the tail of the catch released the hammer, which flew shut to strike either a cap on the nipple or the rim of a cartridge.

# 4
# *The Pre-1900 Automatic Pistols*

The realisation that power accompanied the discharge of a gun – the force of recoil, or of blast from the muzzle – intrigued many early scientists and military engineers, particularly from the seventeenth century onward, but their achievements were limited by the primitive technology of the day. One of the earliest pioneers of auto-loading operation was Martin Regul[us?] Pilon, described in his British patents 1911/1858 and 2113/1860 as a 'Citizen of the United States, residing in Aguascalientes, Mexico, and actually in Brussels, in the Kingdom of Belgium, merchant... ' A subsequent patent, 2998/1863, was also granted to protect his ideas; however, by virtue of exploiting his ideas in Europe, Pilon is still all but unknown in the USA. But his goals were extraordinary for the day.

Several Belgian-made pistols and rifles survive, embodying a barrel and breech which were designed to slide backwards in a frame, reducing the recoil sensation, and had thumb triggers designed to minimise disturbance of aim. Some were also configured so that they cocked automatically, though a reliance on externally-primed ammunition (in the form of a small separately capped chamber) restricted them to single shots. One two-barrel shotgun survives, but all the other representatives are single-barrelled.

The Spanish gun museum in Eibar possesses a gas-operated revolver allegedly made by Ignacio Orbea in 1863, but credit for developing efficient automatic operation is really due to Hiram Stevens Maxim (1840–1916). Maxim's considerable genius spanned many fields other than firearms, but it is for his machine-gun that he is best remembered. Though Maxim was not the first person to suggest harnessing recoil forces to ensure that a gun fired automatically, he was the first to transform vague theory into practicable reality.

Born in 1840 in the remote township of Sangerville, in the New England state of Maine in the USA, Hiram Maxim was of French Huguenot descent. His family had settled in the United States after a brief stay in England, and Maxim was always aware of his 'English connection'. Raised in a remote pioneering community, he was self-assured – some said on the verge of arrogance – as well as physically strong and a master of everything that interested his exceptionally adroit mind. He neither smoked nor drank, but enjoyed a fight and undoubtedly had a keen sense of humour.

Maxim first came to Europe to attend the 1881 Paris Exposition Universelle, and had come to Britain, or so he thought, to investigate the state of the electrical industry before returning across the Atlantic. He subsequently claimed to have made the 'first drawing of an automatic gun' in Paris and to have stayed in England to continue his experiments after an acquaintance persuaded him that there was nothing more likely to make a fortune than a successful weapon.

Maxim made the first machine-gun drawings in the premises of the Maxim-Weston Company in Cannon Street, London, but subsequently moved to a small workshop in Hatton Garden, the centre of the city's diamond trade. A Winchester lever-action rifle was altered so that recoil operated the action through a spring-loaded butt-plate and a series of levers. The gun worked well enough to convince Maxim that the forces could be put to good use, and a working machine-gun was developed out of the Winchester conversion.

Patents were sought in Britain, and The Maxim Gun Company Limited was incorporated on 5 November 1884 with the assistance of capital provided partly by the Vickers family.[1] Albert Vickers became the first chairman, and a comparatively new factory in Crayford, Kent, was acquired to allow the assembly of machine-guns to begin. The company – subsequently Vickers, Sons & Maxim Ltd – was also destined to enjoy a close association with first Ludwig Loewe and then Deutsche Waffen- und Munitionsfabriken.

No sooner had Maxim completed his machine-gun[2] than his expectations of success were dashed by the British press and government authorities, who, aware that Gatling, Gardner and Nordenfelt 'machine-guns' were all hand-cranked, refused to believe that any gun could fire 500 rounds per minute automatically. It scarcely mattered that one of the first guns was exhibited to great acclaim at the Institution of Mechanical Engineers in 1885 nor that it had been awarded a gold medal at the International Inventions Exhibition held in Paris in the same year; British official reaction was apathetic. But the same could not be said of the aristocracy, as the Duke of Cambridge, the Duke of Devonshire, the Prince of Wales and many others visited Hatton Garden to fire the new gun. Finally, the British Army acquired its first two Maxims in March 1887 and, from that point, there was to be no turning back. The first large contract for the Maxim gun, for a hundred 8mm-calibre guns, was placed on behalf of the Austro-Hungarian government on 23 July 1888.

---

1. The capital was £35,000, raised from £10,000 is cash and the issue of 1,250 £20 shares – 416 to Maxim, 417 to Randolph Symons (some time President of the Mexican Central Railway), and 417 to Albert Vickers.
2. The first machine-guns were crude and ungainly, and scarcely resembled the modern ideas of such weapons. But they incorporated several advanced features, including a variable firerate system, belying their bizarre appearance. The hook-type locking mechanism was quickly replaced by a toggle system, and perfected designs had appeared within a year of the founding of The Maxim Gun Company.

The absence of suitable ammunition and the ignorance of the underlying principles of automatic operation allowed many alternative systems to be touted. In addition to the revolver, the manually-operated repeater had been perfected, relying on the trigger or a combination trigger/operating lever to complete the loading and locking cycle. As the previous chapter shows, the products of the fertile (if often backward-looking) minds of inventors and gunmakers such as Bittner, Krnka, Kromar, Laumann, Passler & Seidl, Reiger and Schulhof were interesting concepts. But the Borchardt and the other early automatics swept away the large military-style mechanical repeaters virtually overnight.

### The First Auto-Loading Pistols

None of the earliest attempts to perfect the self-loading pistol could have succeeded without the development of a satisfactory smokeless small-arms cartridge, the pioneering design being introduced with the French Lebel rifle in 1887. Credit is usually given to a French military chemist, Paul Vieille,[3] but the rudiments of smokeless propellant had been appreciated for many years[4] and the German-made Schultze Powder, based on nitrated wood fibre, had been available commercially for some time. By 1885, therefore, the scene had been set for the arrival of the automatic pistol: Vieille had produced an effective smokeless propellant for small-arms cartridges, and Maxim had eloquently demonstrated the application of recoil operation to small-arms.

Though Maxim claimed to have invented a pistol in the 1880s, the most plausible claimants are the French Clair brothers, Benoît, Jean-Baptiste and Victor. Their pistol was an unwieldy diminutive of the 'Clair-Éclair' gas-operated shotgun dating, so the French claim, from 1885–9. Naturally, this has been strongly disputed and the only relevant British patent, 15833/93 of 21 August 1893, is often cited to discredit the Clairs' claim; however, a pistol had been submitted to the French Army in 1888 along with a semi-automatic rifle.[5] As the French introduced the first military small-bore cartridge loaded with semi-smokeless propellant, and as the Clair-Éclair shotgun was being marketed commercially by 1890–1, the brothers Clair *may* deserve the lion's share of the credit.

---

3. Paul-Marie-Eugène Vieille (1854–1934): army officer and professor of physics at the French Army École Polytechnique (Polytechnic School) 1882–1916, the author of many pamphlets and books on the combustion of explosive substances, and co-originator of the bomb calorimeter. Appointed Inspecteur Général des poudres et salpêtres (second class) in 1904, and then Inspecteur Général (first class) in 1911. He was also successively honoured as a chevalier, officier, commandeur and grand officier of the Légion d'Honneur, and finally – in December 1928 – awarded the grand croix.

4. Braccono (1832) and Pélouze (1838) discovered that some fibrous substances became highly combustible when treated with nitric acid, but xyloïdine, as the explosive was initially known, had proved too dangerous to use. In 1846, however, Schönbein discovered guncotton by soaking cotton wool in nitric acid and then carefully washing the residual acid away. Guncotton burned with practically no smoke and left no residue, but proved too dangerous to handle until a British chemist, Frederick Abel, found that compressed wet guncotton made of the finest particles was safer to handle. The final breakthrough came with the discovery that fibrous cotton could be transformed to a crystalline texture, giving a hard horn-like material that was far less sensitive than guncotton (even when dry), burned appreciably slower and could be moulded, chopped or flaked.

5. Colonel en retraite Jean Martin, *Armes à Feu de l'Armée Française 1860 à 1940* (1974), p. 369.

All that can be said with certainty is that Clair pistols were made some time between 1889 and the British patent of 1893. The Clair was gas-operated, tapping gaseous propellant from a port at the muzzle to act on the rotating bolt mechanism. It was very large and appears to have chambered the standard Mle 92 revolver cartridge. The choice of cartridge has been used to discredit claims that the pistol had been perfected prior to 1892, but it had existed experimentally since 1887. A curious tubular magazine emerged from the bottom of the pistol butt, curving forward and upward to meet the receiver ahead of the trigger. Of course, there is no evidence that the Clair design was made in quantity, as its size, complexity and strange feed would all have inhibited commercial success.

Other early failures included an obscure long-recoil design by the Hungarian Otto Brauswetter, acquired by Theodor Bergmann to be transformed into the delayed blowback Bergmann-Schmeisser and then into a simple blowback. A more popular 'first successful automatic' claimant is Josef Laumann. The relevant pistol was developed by (or perhaps for) the Schönberger brothers from the patents of Josef Laumann. A few guns were made by Österreichische Waffenfabriks-Gesellschaft in Steyr, but it is not known exactly when this occurred. Even the operating system of the Schönberger has sometimes remained in dispute; the renowned authority Lt.-Col. R. K. Wilson claimed in his book *Automatic Pistols* (1943) and a variety of articles published in the 1950s and 1960s that it was a delayed blowback, but other authorities have identified rarely encountered primer actuation – strangely, as the patent specifications, though sometimes vague in their description of the action, make no claims of novelty in the ammunition. The need to seat special primers deeply in the case, to allow their backward movement to begin the unlocking action, would undoubtedly have been highlighted by Laumann if this had been his intention.

The beautifully made Schönberger was comparatively simple compared with the mechanical repeaters, but its breech-lock would have been marginal and the internal magazine was inferior to the detachable box of the Borchardt. Dating it is less easy. There can be little doubt that too much reliance has been placed on Wilson's statement that the Schönberger was the first self-loader to be a commercial proposition. However, he did not claim that it *was* commercially marketed and his commentary may simply suggest that the gun could have been manufactured in quantity had the promoters chosen to do so. However, as the highest known serial number is only 10, and no cartridges are known, the Schönberger may be nothing but an Austro-Hungarian military trial-piece dating from the mid-1890s. The inflated modern reputation rests entirely on the claims made by Colonel Wilson forty years after its heyday had passed, and it is possible that more credit should be given to the Salvator-Dormus and Kromar pistols – two of the Schönberger's most likely rivals.

A patent was granted in 1892 to Theodor Bergmann (on behalf of Eisenwerke Gaggenau) and Otto Brauswetter, a watchmaker of Szegedin in Hungary, to protect auto-loading pistols and shotguns operated by long recoil. The illustrations included a

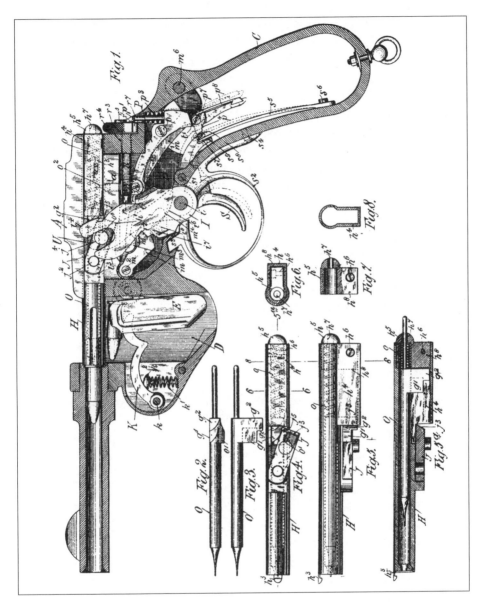

*The Schönberger pistol was the work of Josef Laumann. These drawings are taken from US Patent 534894, granted to Laumann on 26 February 1895.*

pistol with a typically revolver-type trigger mechanism and a clip-loaded magazine with a detachable side plate. These typified all Bergmann pistols made prior to the introduction in 1897 of the No. 5 or Military Model. The locking system of the Brauswetter-patent pistol, a bolt displaced laterally into the wall of the receiver, was subsequently resurrected for the No. 5. The similarity of the triggers and magazines of the Brauswetter and the later Bergmann-Schmeisser pistol of 1893 suggests that only the locking unit owed anything to the Hungarian designer. The remainder of the gun was almost certainly the work of Louis Schmeisser.

## The Borchardt Pistol

On the heels of the Schönberger and the Bergmann-Brauswetter came better designs, some of whose origins may eventually prove to pre-date Laumann's final patent by several years. The Borchardt pistol – patented in Germany in 1893 – probably deserves to be recognised as the first truly successful semi-automatic pistol, though all too soon overshadowed by the Mauser C/96 and the perfected Borchardt-Luger.

Hugo Borchardt was born in Magdeburg on 6 June 1844 but left Saxony for the USA at the age of sixteen. In 1865, soon after the Civil War had ended, he was appointed Superintendent of Works for the short-lived Pioneer Breech-Loading Arms Company of Trenton, Massachusetts. Pioneer made breech-loading rifles and five-shot .32 rim-fire revolvers, but operations soon failed. Shortly afterwards, therefore, Borchardt accepted a foremanship with the Singer Sewing Machine Company before moving for a few months to Colt's Patent Fire Arms Manufacturing Company in Hartford, Connecticut. From Hartford he moved a few miles to New Haven, Connecticut, to work for the Winchester Repeating Arms Company. His first patent sought in his new employment, US No. 153310 of July 1874, protected a method of machining lubricating grooves into hard lead bullets.

Borchardt's name has been linked with experimental revolvers exhibited by Winchester at the Centennial Exposition in Philadelphia in 1876. Eleven of these guns survive, and it has been claimed, on shaky evidence, that Borchardt played a major role in their development. There is no doubt that he played some part – for many years, the Winchester museum had a small box labelled 'Extractor for Model '76 pistol' in Borchardt's handwriting – but the basis of the guns is generally believed to have been the American patents granted to Stephen W. Wood.[6] One type has a solid frame with a special radial-lever extractor on the right rear of the frame beneath the hammer; another has a cylinder mounted on a yoke or crane, which swings out to the right once a sleeve around the cylinder axis-pin has been pulled forward. The latter foreshadowed similar efforts made by Smith & Wesson, but was never taken seriously even though Winchester submitted a gun for trials with the US Army on 5 December 1876.

The principal goal of Winchester's revolver-designing exploits was to compete with Colt, who had built a lucrative trade in Model P (Peacemaker) revolvers chambered for the .44-40 Winchester Central Fire cartridge. The handgun became a popular companion for the Winchester lever-action rifles, benefiting both manufacturers. When the Colt-Burgess lever-action rifle appeared in 1883, however, the situation changed dramatically. Winchester then revealed a solid-frame rod-ejector revolver designed

---

6. Specifically, those granted in June 1876 (No. 178824) and January 1877 (No. 186445). But a study of these begs more questions than it answers, and there is still scope to admit Borchardt's participation.

largely by William Mason, who had previously worked for Colt. The Winchester-Mason revolver (not the Winchester-Borchardt or the Winchester-Wood patterns) was shown to Colt by T. G. Bennett, Oliver Winchester's son-in-law, ostensibly to seek Colt's views on marketing – but mainly to demonstrate that Winchester could compete with the Colt Peacemaker if promotion of the Colt-Burgess continued. The ploy worked very successfully; in 1884, Colt abandoned the Burgess-pattern rifle.

Some claims have been made that this marketing agreement disenchanted Borchardt so greatly that he left Winchester for Sharps, but the chronology is inaccurate. Borchardt was appointed Factory Superintendent of the Sharps factory on 1 June 1876; if he was disenchanted, it was by the failure of Winchester's management to promote his designs in the mid-1870s – not by 1883, by which time he had returned to Europe.

At Sharps, Hugo Borchardt at last achieved a great success: on 26 September 1876, whilst living in Bridgeport, Connecticut, he was granted protection (US Patent 185721) for a hammerless dropping-block breech-loader derived from the familiar Sharps system of 1848. A patent of addition followed on 23 July 1878 (No. 206217), both being assigned to the Sharps Rifle Company.

Unfortunately, Sharps collapsed before the Sharps-Borchardt rifle could attain its full potential. In addition, many Westerners were reluctant to accept the hammerless action. The external-hammer Sharps was widely preferred, as the state of cocking could be seen at a glance. Even though the Sharps-Borchardt had a safety catch behind the trigger which applied automatically each time the breech opened, the position of the striker could not be seen instantly.

Once work on the Sharps-Borchardt had been completed, Borchardt turned his attention to a bolt-action rifle developed by James P. Lee, which Sharps had agreed to manufacture. Borchardt was responsible for the development of tooling, but only a handful of prototypes (sporting and military) had been made when the rickety Sharps Rifle Company collapsed in the autumn of 1880. Liquidation was concluded in 1881.

Borchardt, then residing in Peekskill in New York State, found himself out of work. His last US Patent, No. 273448, was granted on 6 March 1883 to protect a detachable magazine for machine-guns. As Borchardt had already returned to Europe, after failing to find work elsewhere in New England, the patent was assigned to Joseph W. Frazier – who in turn patented a magazine firearm in December 1883 (US Patent No. 290636).

Hugo Borchardt had joined the staff of the Hungarian government firearms factory in Budapest, Fegyver és Gépgyár Részventársáság; by 1889, it is claimed, he had risen to the position of managing director. During this period, Borchardt had attended demonstrations of the Maxim machine-gun to the Austro-Hungarian Army and it can be surmised that he was impressed by the strength and efficiency of the toggle-lock breech mechanism embodied in the machine-gun, and decided to adapt the principles to create not only the Borchardt pistol but also an automatic rifle.

Few details of Borchardt's sojourn in Hungary have become public knowledge, though, while living in Budapest in the mid-1880s, he married Aranka Herczog –

possibly his second wife. In 1891, Borchardt returned to North America to advise Remington on the development of the Lee rifle to compete in the contemporaneous US Army trials. However, as the Krag-Jørgensen was accepted instead, Borchardt retraced his steps to Europe to perfect his semi-automatic pistol.

The lack of reliable information makes it possible to offer only a conjectural development history. Owing to the rapidity with which the Borchardt was supplanted by better guns, few commentators writing at the turn of the century paid it much attention. What little we know with certainty generally comes from military test reports; regrettably, these pay little heed to history.

The oldest surviving pistol appears to be No. 19, which is claimed to have been presented to Eley Brothers in the mid-1890s. Gun number 27, owned by a member of the Browning family in Ogden, Utah, also has an interesting – if somewhat apocryphal – story. According to Val Browning, son of John M., it was left in the Fabrique Nationale factory in Herstal-lèz-Liége by Borchardt himself. The gun bears the marks of Ludwig Loewe & Co., but is largely in the white. The inventor allegedly threw it on the boardroom table after the Fabrique Nationale directors refused to make the gun in quantity. The date of this event, a tantalising piece of information, has been placed as early as the summer of 1893, but FN records are infuriatingly silent.

Confronting Fabrique Nationale with a Loewe-made pistol begs a question: if, as has been assumed, Loewe was committed to the project, why should the inventor approach someone else? The most obvious explanation is that Borchardt, knowing that Loewe was about to transfer exploitation of his pistol to DWM (as described below), was keen to regain control. But this would place the meeting with the FN management in the autumn of 1896 instead of three years earlier.

German patent 75837 was granted on 9 September 1893, and a patent of addition protecting the method of breaking the toggle, D.R.P. 77748, followed on 18 March 1894. The crucial question is whether Borchardt, having returned from Hungary, was actually working for Loewe at this time. It seems likely that Borchardt had developed the pistol on his own account as a speculative project, using his proven skill as a machinist to make (or at least supervise the construction of) the prototype from which the patent specification drawings were prepared. Perhaps seeking a partner, he approached one of Germany's leading precision machinists, Ludwig Loewe. This assumption is partly supported by the way in which the patents were granted, as they are in Borchardt's name alone. If Borchardt had been an employee of Loewe, it is much more likely that the gun would have been patented in the name of Loewe.[7]

Growing out of a partnership formed in the mid-1860s by brothers Ludwig (1837–96) and Isidor (1848–1910), Ludwig Loewe & Companie was established in 1870 to make

---

7. This was common at a time when employees did not enjoy the rights they have done in more liberal times, when the name of the inventor as well as the patentee has had to be noted. Filing patents in the company name has probably obscured the identity of many people to whom credit would otherwise be due; for example, the Mauser C/96 was designed by the Feederle brothers rather than Mauser himself.

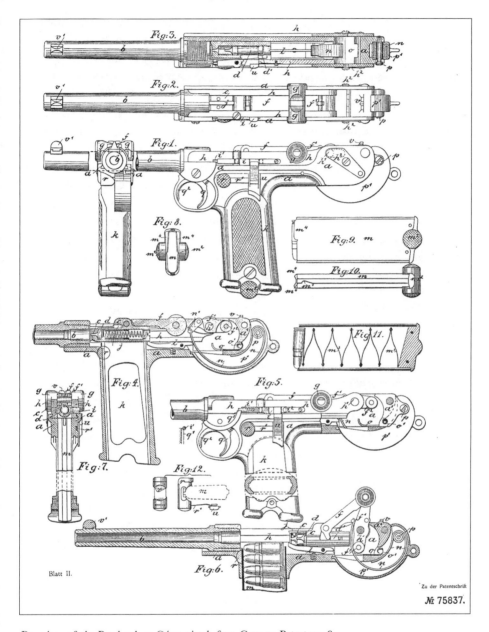

*Drawings of the Borchardt or C/93 pistol, from German Patent 75387.*

machine-tools and sewing machines. Thousands of back sights were made for the single-shot Mauser service rifle in the early 1870s, the success subsequently encouraging a tender to make 70,000 Smith & Wesson-type revolvers for the Russian government. By the end of the 1880s, Loewe had diversified so greatly that the company had become Germany's leading manufacturer of machine tools.

In December 1887, Loewe had purchased the Württembergische Vereinsbank in a straightforward transaction which disguised that the bank had loaned money secured against shares to several leading firearms makers; principal amongst these was Waffenfabrik Mauser of Oberndorf. Loewe thus gained a controlling shareholding in Mauser. When a huge rifle order was obtained from Turkey in 1887, the intention had been to divide production between Oberndorf and Charlottenburg. Before work began, however, the German authorities offered Mauser a contract to make 425,000 of the new 1888-pattern Army rifles. Mauser was not keen to promote a gun designed by an Army commission, incorporating features developed by his arch-rival Mannlicher, so a compromise was arranged: the Turkish guns would all be made in Oberndorf, and the 'Commission Rifles' would be made in Berlin by Loewe. A suitable arms-making plant was then built in Martinikenfelde in the Moabit district to fulfil the German order. The original factory in Hollmanstrasse, Charlottenburg, was subsequently re-equipped to make Maxim machine-guns.

The links between Loewe and Mauser were to have far-reaching repercussions on the story of the Borchardt pistol, and it may be no coincidence that Loewe had become involved in the promotion of the Maxim in Germany. The principles governing the machine-gun and the pistol were essentially similar.

Loewe may have initially accepted an order for nothing but a batch of experimental pistols, though doubtless retaining an option on large-scale exploitation. Though there is no direct confirmation of this particular claim, there is some circumstantial evidence: even the oldest surviving Borchardt pistol bears Loewe markings. Work on the first Borchardts was certainly under way in June 1893, when an American military attaché, Lieutenant Robert Evans of the US Army, visited the Charlottenburg factory. But the exact state of progress at this time is unclear.

In the *American Machinist* of 6 April 1899, amongst 'Random Notes from Germany on Things Mechanical and Otherwise', Harold E. Hess reported a claim by Max Kosegarten (a director of Ludwig Loewe & Co.) that the series-made Borchardt pistol was 'in every respect like the first pilot model' submitted by the inventor. This has been questioned, but comparison of the patent drawings, engravings accompanying sales literature and photographs in pre-1900 periodicals supports the claim; the differences are largely insignificant.

The patent-specification drawings suggest that the front sight was originally rounded; the sear spring was once retained by a small screw; and a small coil spring powered the trigger lever instead of the later leaf. The drawings accompanying the *Reports of the* [US] *Chief of Ordnance* in 1894 show both the rounded front sight, dovetailed into a seat forged integrally with the barrel, and the later collar type; they also share a single-leaf return spring with the gun drawn in the patent specifications. The two-leaf pattern is universal on surviving guns. The earliest magazines had flat undersides, grasping knobs with a concentric-circle design, and the follower spring was made from several short leaves riveted together. The flat-sided toggle-grip grip shown on the patent specification, with circumferentially milled grooves, was soon replaced by an improved version with a recoil lock inset into the right toggle-grip face. A prominent knob protruding to the left undoubtedly makes the gun easier to cock.

The box magazine was subsequently revised in accordance with German Patent 91998 of 10 October 1896. The original pattern had been inspired by Borchardt's experiences with the Lee rifle, but relied on the upper surface of the fabricated zigzag leaf spring to propel the cartridges upward. Experience showed that this was not robust enough to feed efficiently, and that the shock of recoil adversely affected the presentation of cartridges to the breech. The new magazine had an improved cartridge follower propelled by two coil springs, and the magazine base was noticeably wedge-shaped.

By the end of 1894, encouraging reports had been made about the pistol. For example, the US Army representative had reported that the Borchardt was 'a very accurate, close-shooting [accurate] weapon. The grip being about the centre of gravity makes the balance when held in the hand much better than with the ordinary revolver. It seems to possess great endurance.' On 22 November 1894, the *Boston Herald* reported a test undertaken by the US Navy. After claiming that it had been invented by 'an American Hugo Borchardt, now in Berlin', the newspaper reported that a hundred shots had been fired without a hitch. The exhibitor had been Georg Luger, the manufacturer's representative. A suggestion has been made that this pistol was No. 127, which displays an inlaid '1893' above 'H B', over the chamber, but the case is not proven.

By 1900, with the emergence of the Borchardt-Luger, the original Borchardt had lost much of the acclaim that had greeted it in the mid-1890s. H. B. C. Pollard, writing just two decades later in his book *Automatic Pistols*, dismissed the pistol as cumbersome and unreliable. But not everyone shared his opinion. In April 1920, in a review of Pollard's book, a correspondent of the British periodical *Arms & Explosives* wrote that 'nobody but those who were engaged in the arms trade at that time could appreciate first the incredulity and then the amazement which accompanied the exhibition by Mr H. F. L. Orcutt at his Cannon Street offices of the *hand-made* [my italics] model of the pistol, which was passed round during the time when the tools were being readied for quantity production.'

Henry Orcutt of 145 Cannon Street, London E.C., was Loewe's British agent. Unfortunately, it seems that this exhibition may not have occurred before the early spring of 1895 and it seems unlikely that commercial production of the Borchardt began as early as 1893. The tooling may well have been begun, but assembly clearly did not start for some time. Consequently, though there can be little doubt that the Borchardt was the first successful semi-automatic pistol to offer a locked breech, the 1894-pattern Bergmann may press it close as the first commercially successful semi-automatic.

The earliest promotional review to be published in a British professional journal seems to have appeared in *Engineering* in May 1895. The accompanying photographs show a gun with the old-pattern leaf-spring magazine, plain grips, and a large lanyard-ring eye on the back of the return spring housing. There is a chance that this is a very early piece, perhaps even a toolroom-made sample to guide series production. As most of the features of the refined version are already present, however, it is also very tempting to suggest that the gun is No. 19 (said to have been presented to Eley Brothers in the mid-1890s) and that the true production run began in the region of serial No. 30. Borchardt pistol No. 27, still 'in the white', known to have been demonstrated to Fabrique Nationale, has the stock lug on the operating-spring housing and Loewe marks above the chamber.

For the first production run, however, a transverse lug was substituted for the lanyard-ring eye; the latter had already been supplemented with a fixed loop on the left side of the frame. One of the most interesting of the surviving Loewe-made guns is No. 266, which was presented to President Porfirio Diaz of Mexico – possibly in 1896, marking the twentieth anniversary of his assumption of power. The gift supposedly came from Kaiser Wilhelm II, though there are no marks on the gun to prove an imperial connection. Perhaps the pistol was simply a gift from the representatives of Loewe, marking the adoption of the Mauser rifle by the Mexican Army.

On 4 November 1896, the ammunition-making business of Deutsche Metallpatronenfabrik of Karlsruhe (which Loewe already owned) was renamed 'Deutsche Waffen- und Munitionsfabriken' ('DWM'). On 10 December, the directors of Ludwig Loewe & Company agreed to transfer the Hollmanstrasse and Martinikenfelde factories to DWM, together with 'all rights to guns being made'. The transfer took effect on the first day of 1897. Shares held by Loewe in Mauser, Fabrique Nationale and Fegyver és Gépgyár Részventársáság were also transferred to DWM. Interest in the Borchardt also changed hands.

At least one fully-automatic C/93 had been made – tests showed that it could fire eight rounds in three-tenths of a second – and at least a thousand sets of C/93 components had been assembled by the end of 1896, all bearing the Loewe name above the chamber and an acknowledgement of Borchardt's original patent on the right side of the receiver. Whether *all* the parts-sets had been assembled is not known; demand had not proved to be great, and the first 'DWM' guns may have been assembled from parts that were already in store.

Before work continued, however, a few small changes were made. The most obvious is a simplification of the machining on the left side of the frame, where a narrow rib had formerly continued around the back of the trigger aperture. This was milled flat on DWM-marked guns, and a transverse pin was eliminated below the spring-plate let into the left side of the receiver. Guns of this type have SYSTEM BORCHARDT. PATENT. over DEUTSCHE WAFFEN- UND MUNITIONSFABRIKEN. above BERLIN. on the right side of the receiver.

Series production continued for a short period, but had probably terminated by the end of 1897 even though the 'Automatische Repetirpistole System Borchardt' was still being promoted in 1899. Engravings in DWM manuals, presumably perpetuated from earlier days, seem to show a Loewe-made gun with a DWM 'patent mark' toggle. The highest serial number of the DWM-made Borchardts reliably reported is 3013, suggesting that production was substantial.

Was the Borchardt as bad a design as modern writers customarily claim? Literature published by Loewe's (and later DWM's) agent, Hermann Boker & Co. of Duane Street, New York City, quotes the *New York Times* for 12 September 1897 as saying:

> 'A feature of yesterday's practice [at Creedmoor] was the testing of a new magazine pistol, an invention of Borchardt. Col. Butt and Major N. B. Thurston, the latter supervising the day's practice, conducted the tests. Tests at 25, 100 and 200 yards were made, and proved highly satisfactory. At 100 yards Major Thurston fired eight shots in fifteen seconds, and the score showed seven bull's eyes and one centre, a feat hitherto unaccomplished by a guardsman firing an ordinary revolver... '

There were many similar reactions. In January 1898, for example, the US *Commercial Advertiser* was claiming that the pistol, 'nothing more or less than a miniature Gatling Gun', was a novelty of the contemporaneous Sportsmen's Show.

The Borchardt had appeared at a time when smokeless propellant was in its infancy: in 1892, only five years had elapsed since the French Army had adopted the first smokeless rifle cartridge. The earliest batches of ammunition were dogged by variations in pressure, which were particularly important in the context of automatic operation. Some years elapsed before even the Maxim machine-gun could guarantee virtually jam-free operation. Yet Hugo Borchardt had attempted to solve all the problems in a weapon that weighed a fraction of the hefty Maxim.

The most reliable testimony to the efficacy of a properly-adjusted C/93 Borchardt appears in the *Reports of the Chief of Ordnance* for 1898, noting a trial of the Borchardt Automatic Pistol-Carbine. On 23 December 1897, a board of officers of the US Army[8] submitted its report to the Chief of the Ordnance Department, Colonel Alfred Mordecai.

The trials had been attended by Hans Tauscher, 'the inventor's representative', who had partially dismantled the gun and fired a single shot while holding the barrel and receiver in his hands to demonstrate the safety of the basic construction. Tauscher also demonstrated the fully-automatic gun, which had been demonstrated in the Loewe factory a year previously. The 'left end of the toggle joint was arranged to operate the sear so that when the Cartridge was inserted in the chamber and the trigger pulled, shots were fired automatically in about .2 second'.

Tauscher was unable to attend the remainder of the tests, fourteen of which were undertaken by the officers of the board. The first test was simply an examination of the gun, which, the board noted, contained 70 components, 'including 7 screws, 18 pins, studs and rivets, 7 flat and 5 coil springs excluding the stock and magazine'.

---

8. Comprising Captain James Rockwell Jr, Captain Charles Whipple and Lieutenant Tracy Dickson.

The first shots were fired to test the action, and the velocity was found to be 1,296.6ft/sec at 53ft. Field-stripping took 40 seconds; reassembly, 2 minutes 20. The rapidity-with-accuracy test was undertaken with an approximately man-size target, 6ft high and 2ft wide, at a range of 100 feet. With the stock fitted, 40 shots were fired in 68 seconds during the first trial (39 hits), and in 45 seconds (35 hits) in the second. Without the stock, the firers had more trouble: 12 hits out of 32 shots fired in 38 seconds. To see how many shots could be fired as quickly as possible, the gun was fired as a carbine (32 shots in 22 seconds) and 'as a revolver' (37 shots in 28, and then 26 seconds). The first jam occurred during the second series, owing to the accumulation of propellant fouling in the chamber that prevented the cartridge locating.

The accuracy trial showed just how well the Borchardt could shoot with the stock fitted. At 25 yards, the radius of the circle of shots was less than half-an-inch; at 75 yards, 1.39in; at 300 yards, 9.69in; and even at 500 yards – an arduous trial for a pistol – a radius of 15.86in was returned. Penetration through inch-thick pine boards placed an inch apart, 10 inches at 25 yards, had dropped to 3.5in at the longest distance. The commission reported that a variable wind blowing across the range had spoiled the results.

Yet the pistol-carbine was still capable of hitting a man-size target with reasonable regularity at ranges as great as 500 yards. The defective-cartridge trial broke the extractor, but the trial board was satisfied with the strength of construction. The excessive-charge trial was negotiated without a hitch; so, too, was a test in which the powder charge – usually 7 grains – was reduced to 5.5. The gun was then cleaned, having fired 402 rounds with only one jam.

The first endurance trial expended 997 rounds in 2 hours 37 minutes. The three jams were all due to defective cartridges in which the bullet had been seated too deeply. A second series of 1,000 rounds passed without incident, though one of the magazines cracked. In all 1,997 rounds had been fired, with only three cartridge-related jams… and this from a gun now characterised as unreliable. There was no measurable wear in the chamber, though the velocity at 53 feet had risen to 1,313.9ft/sec as a result of wearing of the lands and a consequent reduction in friction.

After preparation for the dust test, the mechanism failed to close properly after the first shot. After rusting, the pistol was fired again. The breech failed to close after the first two shots, but functioned satisfactorily thereafter. The gun was dismantled and thoroughly cleaned, and found to be in excellent condition except for some wear on the standing breech caused by the toggle roller. So 2,445 rounds had been fired, with four jams (one due to propellant fouling and three to defective cartridges), and the breech had failed to close three times during the dust and rust tests.

The board concluded:

'The great accuracy with which this pistol was made contributes largely… to its certainty of action. One of the features that mark the great superiority of this pistol over the

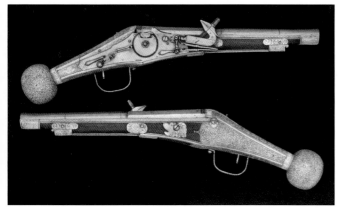

Left: *Typical wheel-locks, from Greener's* The Gun and Its Development *(1910 edition).*

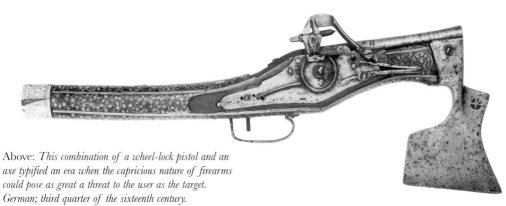

Above: *This combination of a wheel-lock pistol and an axe typified an era when the capricious nature of firearms could pose as great a threat to the user as the target. German; third quarter of the sixteenth century.*

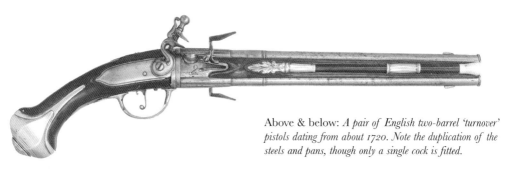

Above & below: *A pair of English two-barrel 'turnover' pistols dating from about 1720. Note the duplication of the steels and pans, though only a single cock is fitted.*

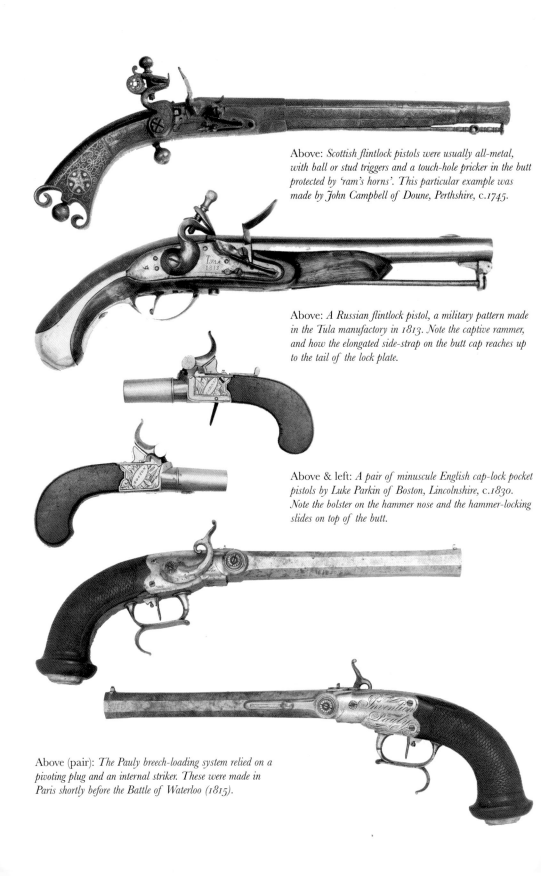

Above: *Scottish flintlock pistols were usually all-metal, with ball or stud triggers and a touch-hole pricker in the butt protected by 'ram's horns'. This particular example was made by John Campbell of Doune, Perthshire, c.1745.*

Above: *A Russian flintlock pistol, a military pattern made in the Tula manufactory in 1813. Note the captive rammer, and how the elongated side-strap on the butt cap reaches up to the tail of the lock plate.*

Above & left: *A pair of minuscule English cap-lock pocket pistols by Luke Parkin of Boston, Lincolnshire, c.1830. Note the bolster on the hammer nose and the hammer-locking slides on top of the butt.*

Above (pair): *The Pauly breech-loading system relied on a pivoting plug and an internal striker. These were made in Paris shortly before the Battle of Waterloo (1815).*

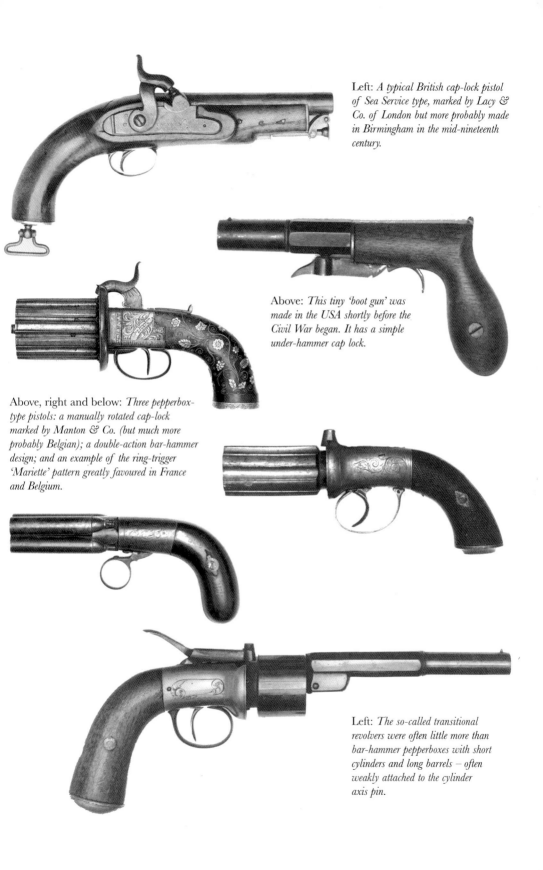

Left: *A typical British cap-lock pistol of Sea Service type, marked by Lacy & Co. of London but more probably made in Birmingham in the mid-nineteenth century.*

Above: *This tiny 'boot gun' was made in the USA shortly before the Civil War began. It has a simple under-hammer cap lock.*

Above, right and below: *Three pepperbox-type pistols: a manually rotated cap-lock marked by Manton & Co. (but much more probably Belgian); a double-action bar-hammer design; and an example of the ring-trigger 'Mariette' pattern greatly favoured in France and Belgium.*

Left: *The so-called transitional revolvers were often little more than bar-hammer pepperboxes with short cylinders and long barrels – often weakly attached to the cylinder axis pin.*

Above: *The Wesson & Leavitt revolver, manually operated and with an external hammer, resembled transitional designs in many respects. However, the barrel is attached to a strap running back over the cylinder and pivoted in the frame.*

Left: *A cased 1862-type Colt 'Police' revolver, with accessories including a powder flask and a bullet mould. Sets of this type were customarily made for the British market.*

Left: *An engraved Beaumont-Adams revolver, with accessories including a capper, a powder flask and a bullet mould in a fitted mahogany case.*

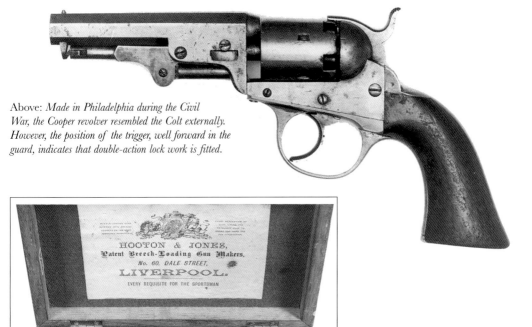

Above: *Made in Philadelphia during the Civil War, the Cooper revolver resembled the Colt externally. However, the position of the trigger, well forward in the guard, indicates that double-action lock work is fitted.*

Left: *A .38-calibre break-open or 'Top Break' Smith & Wesson third-model revolver, cased for the British market and retailed by Hooton & Jones of Liverpool.*

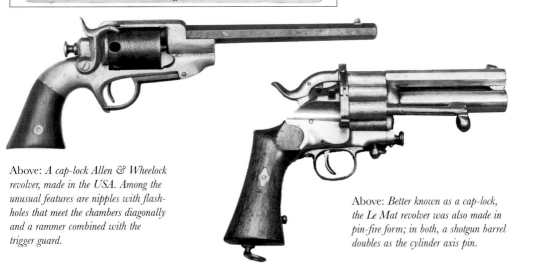

Above: *A cap-lock Allen & Wheelock revolver, made in the USA. Among the unusual features are nipples with flash-holes that meet the chambers diagonally and a rammer combined with the trigger guard.*

Above: *Better known as a cap-lock, the Le Mat revolver was also made in pin-fire form; in both, a shotgun barrel doubles as the cylinder axis pin.*

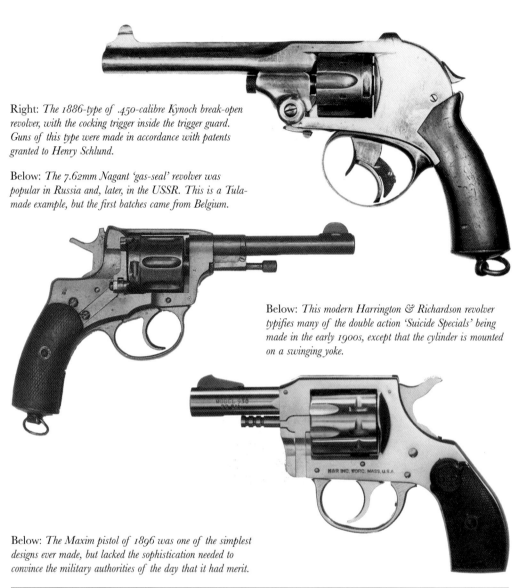

Right: *The 1886-type of .450-calibre Kynoch break-open revolver, with the cocking trigger inside the trigger guard. Guns of this type were made in accordance with patents granted to Henry Schlund.*

Below: *The 7.62mm Nagant 'gas-seal' revolver was popular in Russia and, later, in the USSR. This is a Tula-made example, but the first batches came from Belgium.*

Below: *This modern Harrington & Richardson revolver typifies many of the double action 'Suicide Specials' being made in the early 1900s, except that the cylinder is mounted on a swinging yoke.*

Below: *The Maxim pistol of 1896 was one of the simplest designs ever made, but lacked the sophistication needed to convince the military authorities of the day that it had merit.*

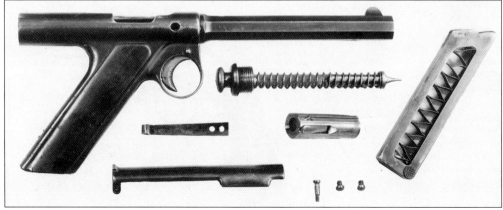

Right: *The reputation of the elegant Schönberger pistol, made to the patents of Josef Laumann, has undoubtedly been inflated in recent years – but there can be no argument that it was beautifully made.*

Right: *Despite its unusual appearance, with the grip set much farther forward than normal, the Borchardt handled and shot surprisingly well… though it made a better pistol-carbine.*

Right: *The Mauser C/96 rapidly eclipsed the Borchardt commercially, even though serious teething troubles took time to overcome. This is a short-barrelled 7.63mm 'Bolo' (so-called owing to perceived popularity with the Bolsheviks) with a ten-round magazine. Note the impressive tangent-leaf back sight and the deeply decorated grips.*

Right: *Bearing an external resemblance to the Mauser, the 5mm Spanish Charola y Anitua has the distinction of being the smallest-calibre pistol to offer a locked breech. This gun has Belgian proof marks, and was probably made in Liége.*

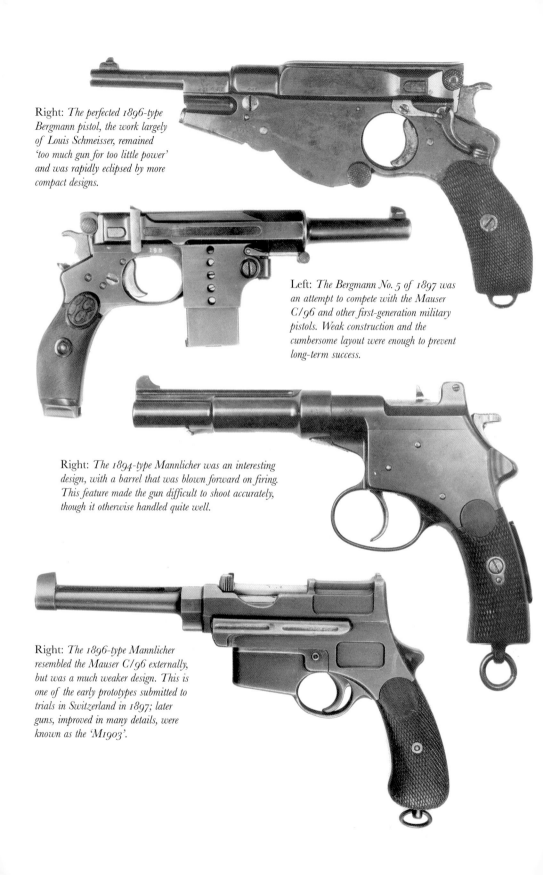

Right: *The perfected 1896-type Bergmann pistol, the work largely of Louis Schmeisser, remained 'too much gun for too little power' and was rapidly eclipsed by more compact designs.*

Left: *The Bergmann No. 5 of 1897 was an attempt to compete with the Mauser C/96 and other first-generation military pistols. Weak construction and the cumbersome layout were enough to prevent long-term success.*

Right: *The 1894-type Mannlicher was an interesting design, with a barrel that was blown forward on firing. This feature made the gun difficult to shoot accurately, though it otherwise handled quite well.*

Right: *The 1896-type Mannlicher resembled the Mauser C/96 externally, but was a much weaker design. This is one of the early prototypes submitted to trials in Switzerland in 1897; later guns, improved in many details, were known as the 'M1903'.*

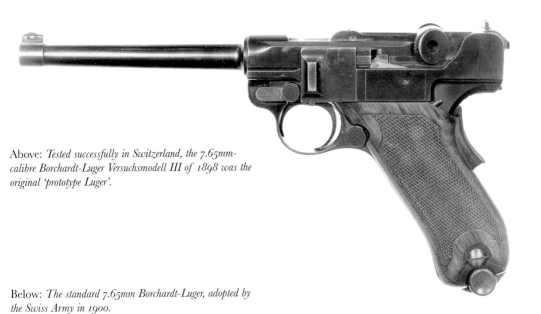

Above: *Tested successfully in Switzerland, the 7.65mm-calibre Borchardt-Luger Versuchsmodell III of 1898 was the original 'prototype Luger'.*

Below: *The standard 7.65mm Borchardt-Luger, adopted by the Swiss Army in 1900.*

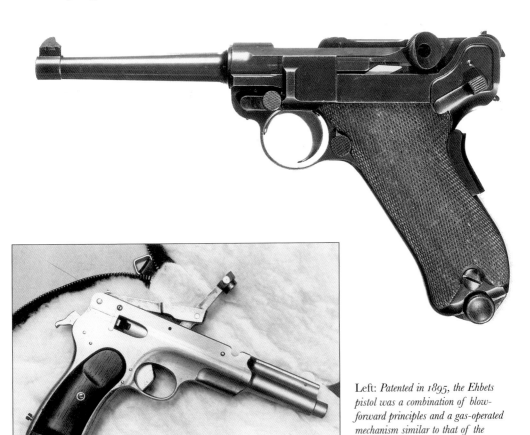

Left: *Patented in 1895, the Ehbets pistol was a combination of blow-forward principles and a gas-operated mechanism similar to that of the Browning-designed Colt 'Potato Digger' machine-gun. Only a few prototypes were made.*

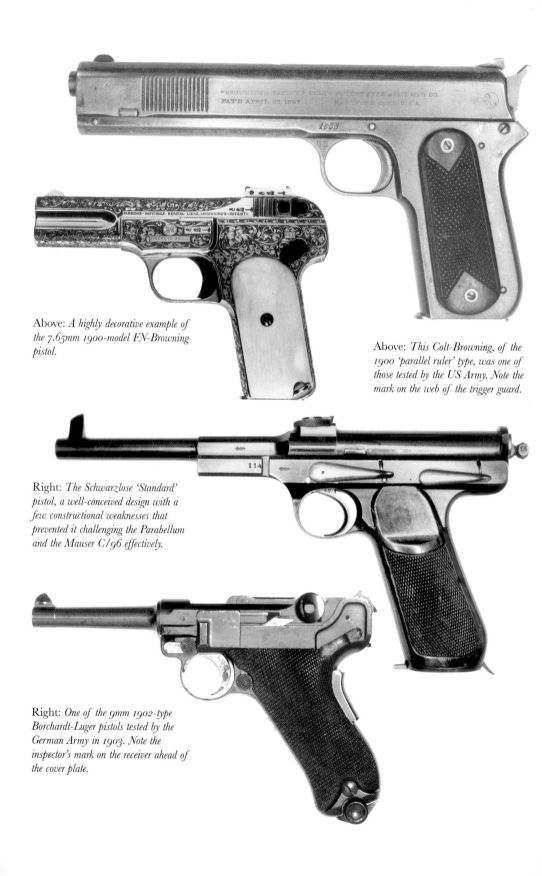

Above: *A highly decorative example of the 7.65mm 1900-model FN-Browning pistol.*

Above: *This Colt-Browning, of the 1900 'parallel ruler' type, was one of those tested by the US Army. Note the mark on the web of the trigger guard.*

Right: *The Schwarzlose 'Standard' pistol, a well-conceived design with a few constructional weaknesses that prevented it challenging the Parabellum and the Mauser C/96 effectively.*

Right: *One of the 9mm 1902-type Borchardt-Luger pistols tested by the German Army in 1903. Note the inspector's mark on the receiver ahead of the cover plate.*

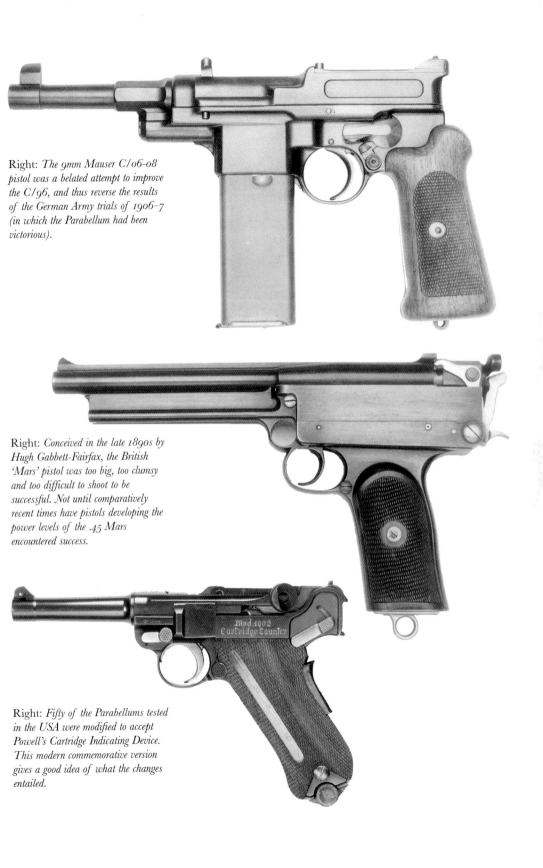

Right: *The 9mm Mauser C/06-08 pistol was a belated attempt to improve the C/96, and thus reverse the results of the German Army trials of 1906–7 (in which the Parabellum had been victorious).*

Right: *Conceived in the late 1890s by Hugh Gabbett-Fairfax, the British 'Mars' pistol was too big, too clumsy and too difficult to shoot to be successful. Not until comparatively recent times have pistols developing the power levels of the .45 Mars encountered success.*

Right: *Fifty of the Parabellums tested in the USA were modified to accept Powell's Cartridge Indicating Device. This modern commemorative version gives a good idea of what the changes entailed.*

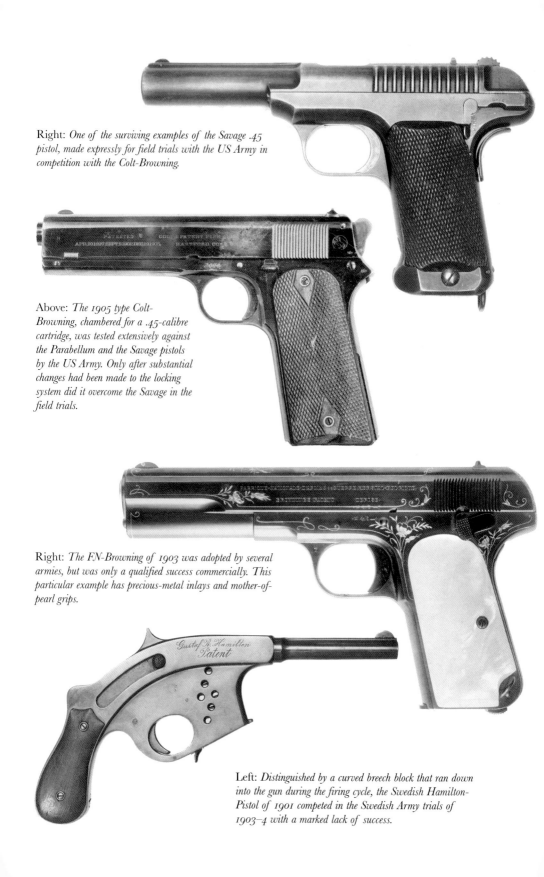

Right: *One of the surviving examples of the Savage .45 pistol, made expressly for field trials with the US Army in competition with the Colt-Browning.*

Above: *The 1905 type Colt-Browning, chambered for a .45-calibre cartridge, was tested extensively against the Parabellum and the Savage pistols by the US Army. Only after substantial changes had been made to the locking system did it overcome the Savage in the field trials.*

Right: *The FN-Browning of 1903 was adopted by several armies, but was only a qualified success commercially. This particular example has precious-metal inlays and mother-of-pearl grips.*

Left: *Distinguished by a curved breech block that ran down into the gun during the firing cycle, the Swedish Hamilton-Pistol of 1901 competed in the Swedish Army trials of 1903–4 with a marked lack of success.*

Right: *The 1910-type FN-Browning was an attempt to replace the 1900 pattern with something that looked more modern.*

Above: *The 'pocket size' 6.35mm-calibre FN-Browning was an outstanding success.*

Right: *This undated Pistole 1908 was made in 1909 by DWM, with the inspectors' marks on the left side of the receiver. It also lacks the stock lug that was added to the heel of the butt in August 1913.*

Left: *The Spanish Joha, possibly made for sale in Finland, was just one of the myriad copies of the 6.35mm FN-Browning of 1906.*

Right & below: *An example of the Navy Parabellum, the M1904, with its holster and stock. This is an example of the long frame 1908-type guns delivered during the First World War.*

Right: *Several hundred 9mm Mauser M12/14 pistols served during the First World War with the British, who had seized guns supplied from Germany to equip Brazilian warships building in British shipyards. The owner's name was probably added some time after 1918.*

Left: *The Repetierpistole M7 or 'Roth Steyr' was developed for the Austro-Hungarian cavalry prior to the First World War.*

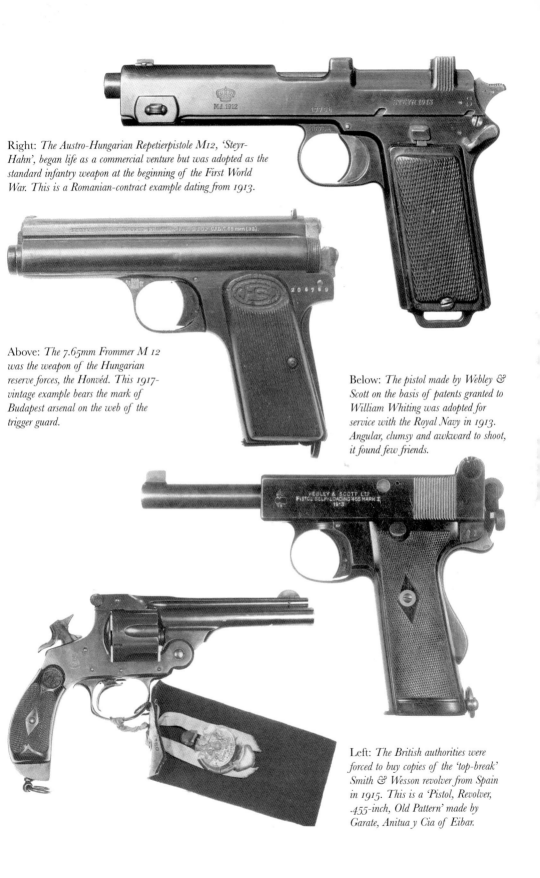

Right: *The Austro-Hungarian Repetierpistole M12, 'Steyr-Hahn', began life as a commercial venture but was adopted as the standard infantry weapon at the beginning of the First World War. This is a Romanian-contract example dating from 1913.*

Above: *The 7.65mm Frommer M 12 was the weapon of the Hungarian reserve forces, the Honvéd. This 1917-vintage example bears the mark of Budapest arsenal on the web of the trigger guard.*

Below: *The pistol made by Webley & Scott on the basis of patents granted to William Whiting was adopted for service with the Royal Navy in 1913. Angular, clumsy and awkward to shoot, it found few friends.*

Left: *The British authorities were forced to buy copies of the 'top-break' Smith & Wesson revolver from Spain in 1915. This is a 'Pistol, Revolver, .455-inch, Old Pattern' made by Garate, Anitua y Cia of Eibar.*

Right: *When the US Army entered the First World War in April 1917, supplies of .45 Colt-Browning M1911 pistols were meagre. Attempts were made to create alternative sources, but only Remington–UMC had delivered any guns by the Armistice.*

Below: *The .45-calibre pistol designed and patented by Grant Hammond was offered to the US Army in 1917, but failed to convince the testers that it had anything special to offer. Consequently, only a few guns were made.*

Above: *The 7.65mm Beretta blowback pistol was developed in 1915 to compete with the hordes of inferior Browning copies that had been purchased in Spain.*

Above: *The 1933-type Hämmerli-Martini target pistol was one of the outstanding performers in the inter-war period.*

Right: *The Hämmerli-Martini Model 106 was a modernised version of the M1933.*

service revolvers is the insertion of the cartridges into a chamber in the barrel and the retention therein of its case, until the bullet and gases have left the bore: this stops the disagreeable escape of gas and flame between the cylinder and barrel, reduces the weight of powder required to give the same velocity, diminishes the recoil and increases the accuracy. This is really the first marked advance made in the design of revolvers [sic] to which the attention of the Board has been called since the introduction of the metallic case cartridge. The butt stock can readily be attached to the grip and the weapon then becomes a short range carbine. The ammunition was excellent, except that occasionally a cartridge was found with the bullet forced back within the case against the powder... '

As the Borchardt had 'stood all the tests, to which it has been subjected by the board, in a highly satisfactory manner', Mordecai approved the findings of the report, but lack of funds prevented Borchardt Pistol-Carbines being purchased for extended trials.

On 22–23 June 1897, the Swiss Army ordnance department, the Kriegsmaterial-verwaltung or KMV, began trials in which guns tested by a commission two years earlier – the Bergmann and the Mannlicher – were pitted against new submissions from Borchardt and Mauser. The new committee[9] intended to test all four self-loading pistols against the control gun, an Ordonnanzrevolver 82. However, as the Bergmann and the Mannlicher had both been extensively tested two years previously and no improvements had been made since the trials, they were omitted to allow a more thorough test of the Borchardt and the Mauser to be undertaken.

The Loewe-made C/93, No. 95, was demonstrated by Georg Luger. After firing, handling and examination, the board reported that the Borchardt was not a fit substitute for the revolver owing to its excessive size and adverse balance. The pistol had also been tried by NCOs and men of the cavalry, as a light self-loading carbine, but complexity and poor balance had weighed against it.

The ballistic performance of the 7.65mm Borchardt cartridge was appreciably more impressive than the Ordonnanzpatrone 86 (fired in the control revolver) and attracted favourable comment. The 5.5gm jacketed lead-core bullet was propelled by a 0.45gm charge of Walsrode Jagdpulver, attaining a velocity of 410m/sec and a muzzle energy of 47.3mkg. By comparison, the Ordonnanzpatrone fired a 6.8gm bullet at only 221m/sec, its muzzle energy being only a little over a third that of the German design.

Advantageous though the small-calibre high-velocity Borchardt bullet seemed to be, the board realised that the good points were far outweighed by the pistol's size. The report gave the pistol length as 350mm and its weight as 1,310gm. Similar complaints were made about the Mauser C/96 and both pistols were rejected.

There is no doubt that these military trials were undertaken with pistols that had been carefully adjusted to work with specific batches of ammunition, and that this contributed

---

9. Chaired by Oberst von Orelli, head of the Technische Abteilung der KMV, its members were Oberst von Mechel; Oberst Rubin, direct of the Eidgenössische Munitionsfabrik; Major von Stürler, director of the Eidgenössische Waffenfabrik; Hauptmann Korrodi of the Technische Abteilung der KMV; Professor Amsler; and Herr Schenker, head of the Eidgenössische Munitionskontrolle.

to their success. However, the performance of the Borchardt in the US Army trials should be contrasted with those of the supposedly improved 7.65mm-calibre Borchardt-Luger in the trials of 1901 (33 assorted jams and misfires in 1,734 rounds during the endurance trial alone) and then with the .45 version in 1907 (31 in a grand total of 1,022).

The C/93 shot acceptably, but the lengthy overhang of the spring-housing at the rear of the frame made it difficult to holster. This could be solved only by moving the operating spring, substantially altering the basic design. Though the stages by which the Borchardt was transformed into the Borchardt-Luger are still disputed (*see below*), a solitary 'Improved Borchardt' (Übergangsmodell), serial number '1', replaced the C/93 in the Swiss trials of 1897.

Georg Luger had previously indicated that a 'smaller and lighter version' was already under development when the Swiss commission drew attention to the ungainly shape of the original Borchardt. Unfortunately, the Improved Borchardt was replaced by the earliest true Borchardt-Luger before the shooting trials began. The gun was returned to DWM and has since been lost.

It is popularly believed that a decision of Loewe's to let Mauser chamber a new pistol for the 7.65mm cartridge so antagonised Borchardt that he was unwilling to continue development. The key to this particular problem lies in the genesis of the cartridge. The Borchardt patent drawings show that the cartridge had been finalised by the spring of 1893, as the application was made in early summer. The earliest known examples are all the work of Deutsche Metallpatronenfabrik of Karlsruhe, subsequently incorporated in DWM. But did Hugo Borchardt actually design the cartridge himself? The only pertinent information comes from the review in *Arms & Explosives* cited previously, where it was noted that 'remarks Borchardt made proved the existence of a certain amount of soreness against Mauser, who, taking the cartridge worked out by Borchardt, found the construction of an improved pistol to fire it an easy matter, for he also had the faults of others to guide his design'.

The relationship between Ludwig Loewe & Co., Hugo Borchardt and Georg Luger has yet to be explained satisfactorily. Whatever rights the inventor of the cartridge once held were clearly assigned to Loewe as a condition of the now-lost contract controlling the exploitation of the Borchardt pistol. As Loewe held a substantial shareholding in Mauser, valued in 1896 at 2 million goldmarks, granting use of the cartridge made sound economic sense; Deutsche Metallpatronenfabrik (also owned by Loewe) was the only source of ammunition. Retaining a proven cartridge would obviously reduce development time and it may even be that the Feederle brothers – who designed the 'Mauser' auto-loader some time in 1894 – were already using Borchardt-type cartridges in their experiments.

Excepting the *Arms & Explosives* review mentioned previously, there is no real evidence that Borchardt regarded the use of 'his' cartridge as a grave breach of faith. But it takes no great stretch of the imagination to understand his feelings when the Mauser pistol left a greater mark on firearms history than Borchardt's own design.

Georg Luger was undoubtedly responsible for demonstrating the Borchardt on many occasions in the 1890s, and has been credited with refining the C/93 into the Borchardt-Luger. Writing in the 1930s, Adolf Fischer suggested that Hugo Borchardt (who, unlike Luger, had no military background) had been content merely to create a mechanism that worked, and could not understand the desire of military authorities to make it more combat-worthy. Though this is now widely accepted, it is worth considering an alternative; when DWM was formed at the end of 1896, it seems as though Borchardt, his skill as a designer well-proven, remained with the engineering side whereas Luger transferred to the new gunmaking organisation. When the necessity arose to refine the Borchardt pistol, therefore, it was inevitable that the work would fall on the shoulders of an employee of DWM instead of Loewe. So it is conceivable that Borchardt lost control of his basic pistol design largely by chance.

Though the C/93 had several severe disadvantages, it could operate very well when properly adjusted. However, the helical main spring was capricious and the guns worked only when adjusted to specific batches of ammunition. Smokeless propellant technology was in its infancy in the mid-1890s, allowing pressures to vary considerably from shot to shot, and as the tension in the Borchardt main spring was difficult to regulate without gunsmiths' tools, the commercial pistols rarely shot as well as the specially selected trial guns. The excessive rear overhang of the receiver and the main spring housing contributed greatly to poor balance, though the Borchardt made a passable light semi-automatic carbine when fitted with its sturdy shoulder stock. However, it was conceived as a pistol and was generally found wanting.[10]

The remainder of the life of a highly skilled engineer passed almost without notice. All that is known for certainty is that Borchardt was living at Königgratzer Strasse 66, Berlin, when his first patents were granted, and at Kantstrasse 31 in Berlin-Charlottenburg when he died of pneumonia on 8 May 1924. His inventions included shirt-neck shapers, machines to make ball-bearings, wire-straightening equipment, gas burners and electrical apparatus, but no authenticated portrait of him is known.

## The Borchardt Legacy

Hugo Borchardt deserves a much more prominent place than he currently occupies in the history of modern firearms. Subsequent events relegated his design to obscurity and stole its claim not only to be the first commercially successful semi-automatic pistol, but also the first to convince sceptical military agencies that such guns had a future. Much more successful was the Mauser pistol, designed by the three Feederle

---

10. Hugo Borchardt patented an improved pistol in 1909. Though this shared the general construction of the C/93, the changes were largely concerned with the construction of the trigger and its interaction with the sear: the specifications, British and German alike, do not explain precisely how the gun works. The width of the magazine and the vertical grip suggest that the operating spring cannot duplicate the layout of the perfected Borchardt-Luger, and thus that a leaf pattern lay under the rear of the frame. However, no surviving gun of this type is known. Borchardt and Luger also experimented with toggle-operated rifles, though no surviving examples of the former have been conclusively identified.

brothers in 1894, but developed (and eventually patented) under the aegis of Waffenfabrik Mauser.[11] Marketed from 1896 onward, officially as the 'Mauser-Selbstladepistole C/96' or colloquially as the 'broomhandle', the Mauser provided the Borchardt and then the Borchardt-Luger with strong competition. It had been submitted to the German Army very early in its development, and the Kaiser had fired one as early as 20 August 1896.[12]

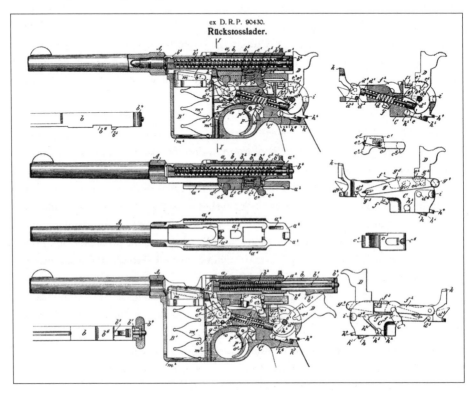

*Drawings of the Mauser C/96 pistol, from German Patent 90430.*

The C/96 operates on short-recoil principles and is locked by a sturdy block pivoting beneath the rear of the bolt. It was also beautifully made, the parts interlocking without so much as a screw. As a piece of nineteenth-century engineering, therefore, the Mauser was undoubtedly a triumph; but, considered as a practical proposition, it was too complicated to be produced cheaply.

---

11. See German No. 90430 of 1895. The patents were sought only in Mauser's name – typical of days when patents were sought in the name of a powerful, well-established figurehead. The identity of the actual designers often passed unnoticed, and many guns are now credited to 'inventors' who were simply the proprietors of the firms that developed them.

12. On 20 August 1896, the Kaiser had fired 20 rounds at 300 metres at the Katharinenholz practice range in Potsdam. The pistol was engraved accordingly, and was kept in the Oberndorf factory for many years.

The key to success lay in the powerful '7.63mm Mauser' cartridge, which was nothing more than a slight adaptation of the original Borchardt pattern achieved with the connivance of Ludwig Loewe & Company; Loewe had a large shareholding in Waffenfabrik Mauser, but Borchardt is said to have been convinced that Mauser 'pirated' the cartridge and acrimony continued until the adoption of the Borchardt-Luger by the German Army.

The earliest Mausers guns proved to be very susceptible to jamming, and many present-day champions of the design gloss over a serious flaw that probably cost the pistol its chances of adoption for the German Army. Impressive factory-staged endurance trials camouflaged the gloomy reports of contemporaneous military trials. In Britain in 1900, for example, there had been 55 jams in 180 shots before the experiments had been abandoned. A report made in August 1901 by the German rifle-testing commission, the Gewehr-Prüfüngs-Kommission or GPK, listed the major problems associated with the Mauser: jamming the spent cartridge case or new round in the breech, between the rear of the barrel and the front of the chamber; unintentional firing of two or more rounds at a time; failure of the hammer to remain cocked after the breech mechanism had returned, requiring the hammer to be re-cocked manually; failure of the action to stay open after the last round in the magazine had been fired and ejected; and failure of the action to open at all after firing.

The action of the C/96 was surprisingly violent, and could push bullets back into the case mouth unless they had been strongly crimped into the neck. A problem was also discovered with the angle of the earliest design of feed-way, which was pitched too sharply to feed cartridges smoothly into the chamber.

Mauser's elevated position in German society allowed him the chance to improve his weapons in circumstances where the products of lesser inventors would simply have been rejected. However, the 1901 GPK report, after detailing the problems listed above, also noted that one of the 'improved Mausers' had even fired two series of 500 rounds without misfiring.

Sales of the C/96 were boosted by the war between the British and the Boers in South Africa (1899–1902), by the Russo-Japanese War (1904–5) and by the unrest in Russia that culminated in the revolution of 1905. Breathed & Schroeder recorded in *System Mauser* that 46,509 Mausers had been sold between 1896 and 1905; the 100,000th dated from *c.*1910. Yet military acceptance still eluded Mauser. A few guns had been acquired in 1899 by the Italian Navy – the first European military agency to adopt a semi-automatic pistol – but most testers remained unconvinced. Guns rarely performed as efficiently before trial boards as in their promoters' factories, and delicate construction was inevitably exposed by rusting or in dust and sand.

Bearing a vague external affinity with the Mauser C/96, the Spanish Charola y Anitua pistol is rarely granted the attention it deserves. Said to have been designed in 1895, though patented by Eibar gunmaker Ignacío Charola only in 1897, the pistol was undoubtedly among the first successful small-calibre automatics.

Marketed with the assistance of businessman Gregorío Anitua, the Charola y Anitua had a box magazine ahead of the trigger. It chambered a tiny 5mm-calibre cartridge which was scarcely powerful enough to justify the wedge-type breech lock. The earliest examples were about 235mm long, had 104mm barrels and weighed about 850gm. Distinctive features included revolver-like lines, and the extended safety lever on the rear left side of the frame. Markings included the designation and the maker's name on top of the barrel, and a winged-bullet trademark on the left side of the frame above the trigger. The bullet was accompanied by a scroll displaying either MARCA REGIST<sup>DA</sup> or TRADE MARK.

The first guns were made in Spain by, or possibly for Charola y Anitua. They were not particularly successful, owing to the primitive state of metallurgy in the gunmaking district around Eibar, and components may subsequently have been purchased from Belgium. The identity of the manufacturer is not known, but, if serial numbers can be trusted, about 5,000 guns had been made when production ceased about 1904. The 5mm guns were more common than the 7mm type (chambering a cartridge introduced by DWM in 1900), but the greatest legacy was the smaller of the two cartridges – popularised in Belgium and central Europe in later years as the '5mm Clément'.

The Bergmann-Schmeisser pistol was another of the early designs to achieve success, but not until considerable development had taken place. The first of the guns, protected by German patent No. 76571 of 9 May 1893, was essentially the prototype of the so-called M1894, although it used a delayed-blowback system relying on the breech bolt being unseated from abutment against the receiver before it could run back and compress the return spring. This was achieved by pressure generated in the chamber acting on the bolt through the base of the cartridge case, relying on the inertia of the bolt, the pressure of the return spring and the frictional resistance set up between the bolt and the receiver as the former began to move. The efficacy of a system of this type is questionable and the designer, Louis Schmeisser, reverted to blowback operation on later designs. The external appearance of the 1893 (I) Bergmann-Schmeisser pistol foreshadowed the prototype of the 1893 (II) pattern, the major differences being internal; indeed, it seems likely that the only 1893 (I) gun was rebuilt to become the 1893 (II) prototype.

The promoters of the Bergmann-Schmeisser, Eisenwerke Gaggenau, asked the Swiss authorities to test a pistol as early as November 1892, but did not supply a sample until 14 January 1893. The Bergmann was subsequently tested against the standard 1882-pattern Ordonnanzrevolver, proving to be less reliable, but more accurate and faster-firing. Calibre was recorded as 7.75mm and the magazine was loaded with a clip of five special German-made cartridges.

The trials were completed on 18 March 1893, but although the Swiss were reasonably satisfied with the pistol's short-term performance, shortage of ammunition had restricted experimentation. Theodor Bergmann, who had attended the trials personally, was asked if the gun could be modified to fire the standard 7.5mm Swiss service-revolver cartridge – a rimmed straight-case design loaded with a round-nosed lead bullet and a charge of black powder. In collusion with Oberst Gressly of the Swiss Army, Bergmann soon supervised the production of suitably modified revolver cartridges in the federal ammunition factory in Thun. The first batch, loaded with a 0.18gm charge of semi-smokeless powder was ready by 16 May; a second consignment, with 0.20gm charges, was completed on 9 October. The design of the pistol had been simplified while the ammunition was being readied, and a new gun arrived in Switzerland at the beginning of 1894.

The gun submitted in January 1893 has sometimes been identified as the only Bergmann-Brauswetter, but there is no confirmatory evidence in the trial reports. The pistol submitted to the 1894 trials was recorded simply as an 'improved' (simplified?) version of the 1893 submission; there is nothing to suggest that the basic action had changed. The differences between the long-recoil Bergmann-Brauswetter and the delayed-blowback Bergmann-Schmeisser pistols would have been sufficiently important to attract the attention of the commissioners. The changes between the 1893 (I) and 1893 (II) Bergmann-Schmeissers, conversely, were much less obvious.[13]

The second important patent filed by Bergmann in 1893 – DRP 78500 of 10 June[14] – protected a simplified version of the first Schmeisser design, with a simple blowback mechanism substituted for the hesitation lock. The bolt reciprocated in the frame/receiver against the resistance of an under-barrel spring compressed by an extension rod running forward from the breech on the right side of the frame. The external spur hammer was cocked as the bolt ran back, the trigger mechanism resembled that of a single-action revolver, and a disconnector prevented fully automatic fire. A transverse bar in the bolt – the 'crosshead' in the patent specifications – abutted the receiver bridge at the limit of the recoil stroke. The return spring then returned the bolt, stripping a round from the magazine into the chamber.

A side plate over the clip-loaded magazine could be swung forward, taking the follower arm with it; a five-round clip was then placed in the magazine well and the side plate was shut. The follower arm, driven by a small coil spring beneath the barrel, pressed up on the cartridge column to ensure efficient feed. When the last cartridge had been chambered, the spent clip fell downward and out of the gun.

The first Bergmann-Schmeissers lacked an ejector, as the sharply tapered cartridge cases, made without extractor grooves, were to be blown from the chamber by the residual gas pressure in the breech. Extraction proved to be surprisingly efficient, but ejection – expelling the cases from the gun – was much more erratic, as it depended on

---

13. The pistol tested in January 1893 was apparently returned to Bergmann and has been lost. It is assumed to have been the delayed-blowback pattern. Two more guns were delivered from Gaggenau in January 1894; these, it is believed, are the two that survive in the Eidgenössische Waffenfabrik collection. One is not numbered and is clearly a prototype, as many of the individual parts are made of phosphor bronze.

14. See also German Patent 78881 of 13 February 1894, British Patent 11509/93 of 12 June 1893 and US Patent 547454 of 8 October 1895.

the case striking the blade-type ejector in the right way. The slightest deviation as the case flew out of the breech caused a poor strike on the ejector, and deflected the cases diagonally instead of vertically. The strike needed to be precise if the case was to miss the receiver walls. Occasionally, therefore, cases failed to clear the feed-way and the returning bolt jammed.

Trials of the Schmeisser-designed blowback began in Thun on 9 February 1894 against an Ordonnanzrevolver, using the special 7.5mm smokeless-propellant cartridges prepared the previous year. The pistol recorded a muzzle velocity of 220–233m/sec, compared with a mere 151–160m/sec for the revolver. (The latter had a shorter barrel, but its ammunition was loaded with black powder.)

The trials were judged to be inconclusive, and changes were presumably requested in the pistol. By the time work recommenced on 29 November 1894, Eisenwerke Gaggenau had submitted several new guns – two in 8mm calibre, two in 7.5mm, one standard and an experimental in 6.5mm, and one in 5mm.[15] Apart from the 7.5mm cartridges, which were loaded by the Eidgenössische Munitionsfabrik, ammunition was supplied exclusively by Deutsche Metallpatronenfabrik of Karlsruhe.

Ten single aimed rounds were fired through each of the pistols with the exception of the experimental piece (which was not fired), and rapid-fire trials were undertaken with the 8mm and 7.5mm guns. Six rounds – one in the chamber and five in the magazine – could be fired in as little as two seconds, while 30 aimed or up to 50 unaimed rounds could be fired in a minute. At a range of 6 metres, the pistol bullet pierced 57 wood boards, each 4mm thick, or 23 thin tin-plate sheets measuring 0.3mm apiece. The revolver pierced 24 boards and 12 tin sheets. Accuracy trials consisted of 30 rounds fired, freehand, at a 30-metre target.

There are no records of the pistols failing to operate satisfactorily, though there was presumably an occasional failure to extract or eject properly. The Swiss wanted to examine the rival designs before committing to any one particular gun, and Oberst Gressly had already written to the war department recommending against substituting the Bergmann-Schmeisser for the Ordonnazrevolver on the grounds that the high cost of changing handguns would not be repaid by the meagre benefits. The Bergmann-Schmeisser thus had very little chance of seeing military service.

Post-1894 Swiss specifications called for an 8mm-calibre pistol, shorter than 255mm and less than 900gm empty. None of the Bergmann-Schmeissers qualified, though the Swiss continued to experiment with the 7.5mm 1893 (II) blowback Bergmann-Schmeisser, with an under-barrel return spring, that had been acquired in January 1894.

On 27 May 1895, Oberst von Orelli informed the war department that Waffenfabrik Neuhausen (later SIG) wished to submit a Mannlicher pistol for trial. Two 1894-type 'blow forward' guns arrived on 29 May – one chambered for an 8mm cartridge and the

---

15. The Swiss records are exceptionally valuable, as they describe each of the pistols as prototypes or, in the case of the experimental 6.5mm specimen, as the 'first of its kind'. The experimental weapon, with a 're-positioned lock spring' protected by DRP 78881, was clearly a forerunner of the M1896.

other for the standard 7.6mm type – to be tested against the Bergmann and an Ordonnazrevolver 82. The 8mm Mannlicher gave the best penetration figures, but the Bergmann-Schmeisser, owing largely to its fixed barrel, proved to be the most accurate. Rapid-fire trials showed that the Manlicher, with a charger-loaded magazine, was quicker to use: 20 rounds were fired in 37 seconds, including reloading time, compared with 55 seconds for the clip-loaded Bergmann.

Twenty examples of each pistol were then ordered for extended trials, the Mannlichers from SIG and the Bergmanns from Eisenwerke Gaggenau. The German consignment duly appeared early in 1897, comprising improved M1896 guns instead of the obsolescent 1893 (II) pattern.

Blowback Bergmann-Schmeisser pistols were made in several sizes. The largest, the Bergmann-Militärisches-Pistole or M1894, originally chambered an 8mm round (excepting two made in early 1894 for the rimmed Swiss 7.5mm revolver cartridge). An 1894-vintage Bergmann catalogue states that the design could be adapted to most types of semi-automatic pistol and revolver ammunition if smokeless propellant was used.

Bergmann-Schmeissers of the '1896' pattern were first marketed in the autumn of 1895. They were very similar to the preceding semi-experimental guns, incorporating the revisions protected by DRP 78881 that included a return spring inside the reciprocating bolt. The design of the magazine side-plate provided the principal means of identifying transitional and production guns: the former had a raised thumb rib, the latter had two diagonal slots. The design and positioning of the safety lever on the left side of the frame above the trigger aperture was changed to facilitate operation. Production pistols also have an external safety-lever spring.

The magazine was substantially the same as that patented in 1893, loaded with a five-round single-sided pressed steel clip. The side plate was swung forward, the clip was placed in the feed-way, and the plate was replaced. Cartridges were fed into the chamber by a spring-loaded follower arm rotating around the same pivot as the magazine side-plate. The clip could be pulled out immediately (using the loop that protruded from the bottom of the magazine) to leave cartridges loose in the feed-way; but too much space was left between them and the receiver walls. However, the loop was apparently intended solely as a handling aid and less trouble ensued if the clip was left in place. It fell downward out of the magazine after the last round had been stripped into the chamber.

The first production 1896-type chambered the idiosyncratic *Randlöse Patronen ohne Auszieherrille* – rimless cartridges without extractor grooves – relying on residual gas pressure in the chamber to extract spent cases. Probably no more than 1,500 guns of this type were made in 5mm and 6.5mm calibres. A few of the 6.5mm-type guns, perhaps only about 200, were chambered for a straight-sided 8mm rimless No. 4 cartridge. These had a conventional extractor, but differed externally from the 6.5mm No. 3 only in the design of the barrel and the magazine bottom.

Bergmann-Schmeissers of the 'New Model' (1896 type) appeared on the commercial market in the autumn of 1895. They were very similar to the preceding semi-experimental military trials guns and had a return spring within the breech bolt. The magazine side-plate had two diagonal slots instead of a raised thumb rib, and the safety-lever spring was mounted externally.

Literature published by Eisenwerke Gaggenau about 1896 confirms that only three types of Bergmann pistol were being sold commercially at that time. The Pistole No. 3, chambered initially for the 6.5mm rimless/grooveless cartridge and then for its more conventional grooved successor, was about 250mm long and weighed 850gm empty. It was also the most widely distributed of the trio, as production has been estimated at about 3,250. This is sufficient to place the No. 3 among the most successful first-generation automatics.

The guns chambering the diminutive 5mm round were the first true semi-automatic pocket pistols. The earliest 5mm No. 1, according to Bergmann catalogues, was only 140mm long, 80mm high and 18mm thick. Empty weight was only 300gm. The magazine held five rimless/grooveless rounds, and the barrel and frame were forged in a single piece. Production is assumed to have been very small; few guns of this type survive. The 5mm No. 2 was distributed much more widely. The older pattern, probably dating from 1895–6, fired the rimless/grooveless ammunition and had a folding trigger. The barrel lug engaged a recess in the left frame rail, where it was held by a transverse screw. The guns were 175mm long, 110mm high and 22mm thick, and weighed 470gm. Serial numbers apparently ran upward from 1 to about 500. German proof marks – crown/crown 'U' – lay on the left side of barrel and frame, with '611' (the calibre, 611-bore), and PATENT/ BRÉVETÉ/S.G.D.G. on the frame ahead of the barrel locking-screw head.

The folding-trigger pocket pistol was unpopular, possibly owing to accidents caused by snagging the unprotected trigger, and a revised No. 2 appeared in the summer of 1896 – perhaps at about the time a conventional extractor was added to the 6.5mm No. 3. The perfected No. 2 had the trigger in an aperture in the frame behind the magazine well. It was slightly longer than its predecessor, though height and thickness were comparable. Overall length was about 195mm, empty weight being 550gm. The barrel lug was held by a transverse screw on the left side of the frame above the magazine follower/side-plate pivot. A fixed lanyard loop lay beneath the butt, a large 'B' was moulded into the grips, and the front sight was carried on a raised saddle.

The markings duplicated those of the folding-trigger No. 2, with an oval cartouche containing a lamp-carrying miner ('Bergmann' in German) on the left side of the magazine housing. The marks BERGMANN and V.C.S./SUHL also appeared, identifying the manufacturer as V. C. Schilling of Suhl. Serial numbers continued where those of the folding-trigger pattern had stopped, doubtless with a limited overlap as old components were expended. The highest reported number is 2,177, which suggests that about 1,700 new-type No. 2 pistols had been made.

A small hole drilled through the right side of the frame into the chamber of the perfected No. 2 has often attracted comment, though the Bergmann manual simply states that it '… enables [the firer] to ascertain whether there is a cartridge in the barrel'.

The bright brass case was easily caught by the eye. The port could double as a gas escape, but there is no evidence that Schmeisser ever had this in mind.

The performance of the Bergmann pistols is difficult to ascertain from the meagre evidence. The absence of an extractor from the earliest guns undoubtedly led to extraction/ejection failures, but these were corrected by adding a conventional extractor. On 24 July 1897, the British hunting and shooting-sports periodical *The Field* reviewed the Bergmann:

'Rumours of the excellent results obtainable with automatic pistols have for a long time past been in the air, but reliable information was not forthcoming. Quite recently, however, the Bergmann Patent Automatic Pistol Syndicate (of 24, Jewin Crescent, London, E.C.) submitted one of their weapons to us for examination and trial...

'The principle on which the mechanism works is at first sight rather startling, inasmuch as there is nothing rigid to close the breech – the inertia of the mass of metal forming the breech block alone being depended upon to back up the cartridge. This statement will, we believe, be read with astonishment by many shooters, especially those who pin their faith to a multiplicity of grips for securing the breech of guns. But although this system, looked at from the theoretical side, seems wanting, in practice it works perfectly. When the hammer falls the charge is exploded, and before the bullet leaves the muzzle the cartridge case commences to recoil, pushing before it the breech block, thus cocking the mechanism ready for the next shot. No extractor is necessary (although in the latest type an extractor is fitted to remove the cartridge in the event of a miss-fire), because the instant the recoiling cartridge case is clear of the chamber a spring is released which ejects it clear of the weapon. The breech block moves forward under the influence of a spring, and is held in the firing position until the next cartridge is fired.

'The accompanying illustration shows the weapon with the magazine open. It will be seen that the magazine holds five cartridges, and there may also be one in the chamber. The cartridges are carried in a spring clip, and the magazine may be replenished with great rapidity.

'The bullets, weighing 75grs., are of lead, with nickel steel mantles, and are propelled by 3grs. of smokeless powder. The actual velocity of the bullet at 10 yards from the muzzle is, on an average, about 800ft. per sec., and, in consequence of their unyielding nature, their penetrative powers are very high.

'With regard to rapidity of firing, six shots may be got off in two seconds, and thirty aimed shots in one minute.

'The pistol before us weighs 1lb. 15oz.; its calibre is 6.5 m.m. = .256 inch. We consider this bore rather small, but are given to understand that weapons of 9 m.m. = .354 inch calibre will shortly be placed upon the market.

'The mechanism of this pistol seems to be well thought out, and, as far as we are able to judge by our short acquaintance with it, works perfectly. There is one point to which we venture to call attention, and that is the awkward form of the stock; but, of course, this can easily be remedied.

'In our opinion, automatic pistols will eventually supplant the revolver, but whether the pistol under notice is sufficiently advanced to accomplish so great a revolution the future alone can decide... '

Two weeks later, on 7 August 1897, *The Field* illustrated a target shot at Pirbright by the celebrated marksman Walter Winans. Eighteen rounds were fired in 30 seconds (not including reloading time), 9 hitting the bull's eye of a standard 20-yard revolver target and 6 striking the innermost ring. There had been no stoppages of any kind.

Realising that the blowback system was unpopular militarily, Bergmann and Schmeisser developed the No. 5 pistol or Militärisches Modell. Protected by DRP 98318, this re-introduced a locked breech, achieved by displacing the tail of the bolt laterally into the receiver wall, and had a detachable box magazine with sight holes through the magazine and the frame to give a guide to the number of shots remaining. However, the clumsy layout and fragile look of the earlier guns was retained. Consequently, despite chambering a 7.8mm cartridge offering more power than the previous Bergmann rounds, the No. 5 never attracted much enthusiasm.[16] Production ceased after only a few hundred had been made, and attention focussed on a modification of the Schmeisser-designed Bergmann machine-gun lock. This was incorporated in the Bergmann 'Mars' pistol, adopted in Spain and Denmark in the early 1900s.

A modified version of the basic blowback pistols was made in the early 1900s as the 8mm Bergmann-Simplex, which had a detachable box magazine. A few thousand may have been made in Germany, though not by Schilling. It is often claimed that the guns were made in Liége, but they invariably bear German proof marks and one of the lesser Thuringian gunmakers was probably responsible. Manufacturing quality is not particularly good. The frame is comparatively soft, the one-piece rubber grip was fragile, and the extractor and ejector were both prone to fracture.

The Bergmanns worked well enough, but were primitive designs and certainly could not match the balance of a good revolver. They served the market for a self-loading 'pocket pistol' (even though the 5.5mm No. 2 was comparatively large) only until better designs, such as the FN-Browning, appeared early in the twentieth century. The loss of the production facilities and also of the principal designer – Schilling was acquired by Sempert & Krieghoff and Louis Schmeisser left for Rheinische Metallwaaren- & Maschinenfabrik – tolled the final knell.

The original Bergmann had many rivals. Among them were the pistols developed by Ferdinand von Mannlicher. The first of these, patented in Britain in September 1894 (No. 18281/94) and in the USA in April 1897 (No. 581296), was an unusual design in which the barrel was projected forward from the fixed breech to compress the return spring between the barrel and the front of the receiver. Releasing the trigger allowed the firing mechanism to be reconnected, whereupon the gun could be fired again either by thumb-cocking the hammer or simply pulling through on the trigger.

The 1894 model was comparatively simple, but the slam-loading feature was undesirable and the original rimmed cartridge was unsuitable for automatic action. The

---

16. In the Swiss trials of 1898, the No. 5 had been placed fourth of five, behind the Borchardt-Luger, Krnka-Roth and Mannlicher pistols. Only the presence of a box magazine allowed the Bergmann to beat the Mauser C/96, which the Swiss disliked intensely.

magazine was loaded from a charger. Most of these Mannlichers were chambered for a 7.6mm rimmed straight-case cartridge, but a few 6.5mm examples are known. One of the latter was tested in Switzerland against the Borchardt, predictably without success. About 200 blow-forward Mannlicher pistols seem to have been made.

In 1896, Mannlicher sought to protect two new pistols. The earlier, unexploited pattern protected an unusual blowback with a peculiar hammer immediately behind the magazine well and a long cocking lever whose spur protruded at the back of the frame. The first examples of the second 1896-type gun appeared in 1897, well before its inclusion in the Swiss trials. Very few were made before the end of the century, but the design was subsequently revived as the 'M1903'. Though it superficially resembles the Mauser C/96, the Mannlicher has a locking strut between the bolt and the rear of the receiver instead of a propped-up block under the bolt. The strength of the strut was barely adequate for even the low-powered variant of the 7.65mm Borchardt cartridge; firing the dimensionally identical 7.63mm Mauser round in an 'M1903' Mannlicher is potentially dangerous. Fragile construction was a notable characteristic of all the Mannlichers.

In 1898, Mannlicher sought patents for the guns that were later to be marketed as the models of 1900, 1901 and 1905 (*see Chapter 5*).

By 1890, the German military authorities had realised that the advances in small-arms design had overhauled the existing Commission revolvers of 1879 and 1883. Though the so-called 'mechanical repeaters' of inventors such as Gustav Bittner, Erwin Rieger, Franz Passler & Ferdinand Seidl, Josef Schulhof, Josef Laumann and others (*see Chapter 3*) were unsuitable for military service, they paved the way for the first true semi-automatic pistols. As early as 1891, tests were being undertaken by the Prussian GPK and procurement of revolvers had been suspended while the merits of 'repeating pistols' were assessed. Within a few years, the Germans became acutely aware that a semi-automatic would be adopted: they simply needed to find an appropriate design.

Early trialists included the Borchardt, the Mieg, the Mauser and the 'Spandauer Selbstladepistole M 1896', identified by Erlmeier & Brandt as a Schlegelmilch but possibly mistaken with a 'Mehrladepistole' by the same inventor. A few lightened double-action revolvers emanated from the Erfurt small-arms factory in 1896–7, but to no lasting effect.

The principal contender initially appeared to be the C/96. Mauser's newest rifle design had just been adopted as the Gewehr 88/97 and, as his guns had been serving the armies of the Deutsches Reich since 1872, Peter-Paul Mauser had naturally attained great prestige. His confidants included many high-ranking officials, his credentials were impeccable; and, indeed, one early C/96 had been test-fired by no less a person than Kaiser Wilhelm II.

Trials with the GPK had been encouraging enough for 145 guns to be ordered for extended trials. Delivered in June 1898, they were issued to the Infanterie-Schiess-Schule, detachments of the Garde-Jäger zu Pferde and the Leib-Garde-Husaren-

Regiment. The reports allowed the GPK to tell the War Ministry that the semi-automatic pistol was much more powerful and accurate than the Commission revolvers of 1879 and 1883, had a higher velocity and a flatter trajectory, and promised greater power. But there had been too many malfunctions and feed jams to permit immediate adoption, and the design of a stock and a holster required more thought. In January 1899, therefore, 124 additional Mausers were distributed to Infanterie-Regiment Nr. 48 and Nr. 72, Ulanen-Regiment Nr. 5 and Nr. 13, and Feldartillerie-Regiment Nr. 3. The three other German state armies reacted differently; Württemberg acquired 48 pistols of its own; Saxony merely sent observers to the Prussian tests; Bavaria decided to await developments.

While Mauser C/96 pistols were being tested in the German Army, a Mannlicher pistol arrived for trial, but the most influential of the powerful semi-automatic pistols being offered in 1900 was the Borchardt-Luger. When DWM succeeded to the business of Ludwig Loewe & Company, the C/93 or Borchardt was rapidly being overhauled by better designs. Though few of these proved to be as reliable as a properly regulated Borchardt, they were generally far less complicated. During 1897, therefore, Georg Luger began to redesign the pistol. He had been employed by Loewe for some years as a consulting engineer, and must have known Hugo Borchardt well.

The history of the Borchardt-Luger began in Switzerland, where the unsuccessful submission of a C/93 Borchardt in 1897 was rapidly followed by the offer of an 'Improved Borchardt'. This gun was recorded as having a 're-positioned recoil spring' (in the grip) and was appreciably smaller than the original trials Borchardt. Comparing the original C/93 with the drawings of the Swiss patent (17977 of 3 October 1898) – as well as the surviving Versuchsmodell 1898 in the Eidgenössische Waffenfabrik collection – allows some of the characteristics of the Improved Borchardt can be predicted. The mainspring had been moved from the spring-box housing, beneath the rear of the receiver, to a new position behind the removable magazine inside the grip. This allowed the grip to be raked backward, improving balance and letting a grip safety to replace the sliding Borchardt type.

However, as the roller that unlocked the toggle was retained, the true Improved Borchardt would be much longer than a Borchardt-Luger of comparable barrel length, but appreciably shorter than the C/93. Eugen Heer gives the overall length of the trials gun as 272mm and the barrel as 157mm; if both of these are correct, the action length of the gun is virtually the same as the perfected Borchardt-Luger. Had the barrel measured 127mm rather than '157' (a misprint?), the 'action length' of 145mm would fit the predictions more appropriately: the C/93 action is about 165mm long and that of the Borchardt-Luger is about 115mm. The full-length drawings accompanying DRP 109481 suggest that the barrel of the transitional pistol was considerably shorter than the Borchardt type.

The Borchardt-Luger Versuchsmodell of 1898 has a safety, sear and trigger system adopted from (but similar to) this Improved Borchardt, but the 1897 submission is unlikely to have featured any of the improvements to the safety system protected by DRP 109481 or the later Swiss Patent 18623 of January 1899.

But who was responsible for the transition from the clumsy Borchardt to the elegant Borchardt-Luger? DWM's fiftieth anniversary history, *50 Jahre Deutsche Waffen- und Munitionsfabriken*, states that:

> 'The Borchardt pistol's grip had been almost vertical, resulting in an unpleasant hold while shooting. What is more, at the end of the receiver had been a housing, comparatively large, containing the mainspring… all this adding to the pistol's length… Firearms designer Luger, who developed the Parabellum pistol, altered the grip-position in such a way that it corresponded to the natural hold while shooting. He repositioned the mainspring… in the grip, thus reducing the pistol's length and making it handier.'

This submission is supported by Adolf Fischer, who remarked in his memoirs that, while Borchardt was amiable and an excellent engineer, he lacked the military experience of ex-soldier Luger and could not appreciate the deficiencies of the C/93 judged from a military viewpoint.

By the summer of 1898, Luger had discarded the internal roller in favour of a method of breaking the toggle with inclined cam-ramps machined as part of the standing frame. When the gun was fired, recoil of the barrel and the receiver caused the toggle-grips to strike the cam-ramps – breaking the toggle upward so that the axis of the cross-pin, rotating about the fixed pivot, was raised above the bore thrust-axis. The toggle then continued to break upward until movement was stopped when a lug on the rear toggle-link struck the frame at the end of the recoil stroke. A spring in the back of the grip, acting through a spring lever, returned the breech block to the breech face and locked the action as the centreline of the transverse cross-pin dropped below the axis of the bore. The result was stronger, simpler and neater than its predecessor, though not as smooth or certain as the Borchardt roller.

Interestingly, Borchardt and Borchardt-Luger pistols originally included a special lock in the right toggle-grip. Similar retainers were often used in machine-guns whose breech blocks, returning with considerable momentum from the recoil stroke, could bounce back from the breech face. To ensure that their pistols locked properly, Bochardt initiated (and Luger perpetuated) a mechanism which locked into the frame when the breech block completed its return stroke and hit the breech face. Toggle-locks subsequently proved to be a system in which rebound suppressors are superfluous – rebound cannot take place once the cross-pin axis drops below the centreline of the bore – and the 'anti-bounce lock' was accordingly omitted from Parabellums made after 1905–6.

By 5 October 1898, the Swiss had six pistols to test: a Bergmann No. 3, a Bergmann No. 5, another Mannlicher, an improved Mauser C/96, a Krnka-Roth, and an Improved Borchardt (possibly fitted with Luger's trigger and safety). Before firing trials began, however, DWM asked to submit a new gun. The Improved Borchardt was replaced by the first two true Borchardt-Lugers – one described as a short-barrel type with a holster stock, the other simply with a 'longer barrel'.

The firing trials ended on 28 November, having included two series of 50 rounds rapid-fire, three targets fired at 50 metres for accuracy, and a 400-round endurance test without cleaning the guns. The Borchardt-Luger performed with hardly a misfire or jam, proved to be the most accurate, and was regarded as the best of the submissions by far. The Bergmann No. 5 and the Mauser C/96 had failed; the charger-loaded magazine and poor safety arrangements of the Krnka-Roth were disliked; and the Mannlicher (which had been placed third on the numerical scoring system) was preferred to all but the Borchardt-Luger. The worst feature of the Mannlicher was the magazine, ahead of the trigger, which had to be loaded from a charger through the top of the action.

The DWM pistols tested in Switzerland in November 1898 were the true prototypes of the Parabellum. The Swiss called these guns Versuchsmodelle III to distinguish them from the Modell I (the standard C/93 Borchardt) and the Model II (the Improved Borchardt of 1897). Luger's first pistol patents date from the end of September 1898, approximately contemporaneous with the appearance of the Versuchsmodell III in Switzerland, but months may elapse between application for a patent and the grant. Design improvements are continual and evidence based on patents can be unsatisfactory; in addition, Luger habitually applied for patents only after military adoption, extending protection to the furthest possible date.

The surviving Versuchsmodell III has a standard Borchardt-Luger cam-ramp action, but still retains characteristics of the Improved Borchardt of 1897. The trigger is still driven by a leaf spring, and pivots ahead of the trigger-plate; the same removable side-plate permits access to the safety mechanism. Yet, despite transitional features, all the basic operating principles of the Borchardt-Luger are present. The changes made in the Versuchsmodell IV of 1899 were largely superficial.[17]

The experimental Borchardt-Luger convinced the Swiss that it had great potential, but the trial board demanded a lockable grip-safety system to prevent accidental discharge. Luger's Swiss Patent 18623 of 2 January 1899 illustrates improved safeties, as well as flat toggle grips with a suggestion of a single raised rib.

After reviewing the previous year's trials, the Swiss authorities decided on a third series, to be held on 1–4 May with a prize of 5,000 Swiss francs. Two Borchardt-Lugers were delivered shortly before trials commenced on 1 May 1899. They embodied the

---

17. In 1975, a colour picture of a prototype Borchardt-Luger was added to the fourth printing of Harry Jones's book, *Luger Variations* (Volume 1), captioned as the '*Erste Original-pistole (Baujahr 1899) "System Borchardt-Luger" – Modell, das zum Seriennachbau diente. Vorrichtung und Lehrenbau: Deutsche Waffen- und Mutionsfabriken*' ['Original Borchardt-Luger system pistol, made in 1899. Pattern to guide series production. Designed and developed by DWM.'] The provenance of this gun is uncertain, and it is clearly not the 'first Luger', an honour belonging to the experimental pistol of 1898; the existence of 'System Borchardt-Luger' blueprints from January–February 1899 also seems to refute the 'Erste Originalpistole' claims.

improvements requested by the Swiss authorities a year previously, the principal change being the addition of a manually-operated safety lever in a distinctive recessed panel milled out of the left side of the frame.

The committee had also considered the Krnka-Roth and the Mauser C/96, but neither had progressed further than the previous submissions and so were refused further trials. A Browning-system gun had appeared from Fabrique Nationale, and details of a gun by the German inventor Albert Hauff also arrived. The principal contest was between the Borchardt-Luger and the Mannlicher Modell III. The previous Mannlicher, the Modell II or 1896-patent 'M1903', had performed with such distinction in 1898 that the Board was anxious to extend its successor the same courtesy.

Luger's two pistols, differing only in barrel length, were submitted to firing trials on 2 May and negotiated them without difficulty. They were recorded as 'improvements over the Modell 1898 III Borchardt-Luger', as the safety catches had been modified and the weight reduced. Georg Luger, who was present, stated that the 7.65mm pistols could be altered for any calibre between 7.3mm and 8mm simply by changing the barrel and the extractor; if the 7.65mm case-rim design could be used, even the extractor could be retained.

The retarded blowback Mannlicher-Pistole III provided no real competition to the Borchardt-Luger and the trials were soon complete. DWM was asked to supply at least twenty guns and a suitable quantity of ammunition, for field trials in the autumn of 1899, and if the gun could be lightened to 850gm or less. The twenty pre-production pistols arrived in Switzerland in October or November 1899. They were subsequently issued to a number of units – including the Walenstadt marksmanship school – with a request that reports should be submitted by March 1900.

A survivor of this period, submitted to the British Small Arms Committee in November 1900, No. 26, displays a hand-engraved Federal Cross above the chamber. British records note that two other guns of the six supplied for trial were 23 and 25, suggesting that the six were numbered either 21–6 or 23–8. One near-identical Swiss gun, No. 19, currently in the Eidgenössische Munitionsfabrik collection, may survive from the twenty field-trials guns of 1899. It is similar to No. 26 excepting a squared toggle-hinge interface instead of the improved radiussed pattern.

On 30 April 1900, the Swiss parliament, the Bundesrat, was advised to accept the Borchardt-Luger; and, on 4 May 1900 the 'Pistole, Ordonnanz 1900, System Borchardt-Luger' was adopted for the Swiss Army. On 24 December, Oberst von Orelli informed the KMV that the first 2,000 guns were expected to arrive in Switzerland at the beginning of 1901 at a cost, once the customs duties had been added, of 62 Swiss francs apiece.

The rapid success of the Borchardt-Luger was unusual, as many inventors struggled throughout the 1890s to provide a worthwhile automatic pistol. Among them was German-born Andreas Wilhelm Schwarzlose (1867–1936), whose greatest success came with the adoption of his machine-gun by the Austro-Hungarian Army. The earliest

Schwarzlose pistol, protected by British Patent 23881/92 of 27 December 1892, was virtually an automated form of the Remington rolling block, taking cartridges stored nose-down in a magazine chamber beneath the barrel. This aberration was succeeded by a ring-trigger pistol with a rotating bolt (British Patent 9490 of May 1895), and then by the so-called 'Standard' (British Patent 1934/98 of January 1898). The recoil-operated Standard was a good design, exploited commercially at the beginning of the twentieth century, and is included in Chapter 5 with the other Schwarzlose pistols.

## The Genius of John Browning

While Schwarzlose, Bergmann and Schmeisser were struggling to produce efficient designs, the American John Moses Browning (1855–1926) filed four differing pistol designs with the US Patent Office in 1897.[18] Early in 1897, the commercial manager of Fabrique Nationale d'Armes de Guerre, Hart O. Berg, was sent to the USA to seek improvements being made in bicycle manufacture. Berg met the Browning brothers on his North American travels, apparently accidentally, and a dialogue began.

John Browning had attained a considerable reputation as an inventor of firearms, as a range of his rifles and shotguns was being marketed by the Winchester Repeating Arms Company and a gas-operated machine-gun had been developed for Colt's Patent Fire Arms Manufacturing Company. Colt was also weighing the merits of several pistols designed and patented by Browning in 1895–7, the outcome of an agreement between the two parties signed on 24 July 1896.

Browning had initially licensed an early blowback pistol design (US Patent 580923), but Colt had decided that no suitable domestic market existed and the patent had reverted to the inventor. Browning casually mentioned to Berg that he sought a licensee for this patent, protecting the blowback pistol *'dont le verrouillage était opéré par la masse'* ('in which the lock was operated by the weight'), and Berg duly approached the FN Conseil d'Administration shortly after his return to Europe. An agreement was signed with Browning on 17 July 1897 by the President of Fabrique Nationale, Baron Charles de Marmol. The company's jubilee history, *Fabrique Nationale d'Armes de Guerre, 1889–1964*, pictures a receipt signed by John M. and Matthew S. Browning on 26 July: 'Received of the Fabrique Nationale d'Armes de Guerre, Two thousand dollars ($2,000⁰⁰). In payment on Automatic Pistol as per contract.'

The blowback pistol had been designed in 1894–5, as application for protection was made in the USA on 14 September 1895 (though the issue of a patent was delayed until 20 April 1897). Even before the printed specification had been published, Browning had refined the original design by replacing its distinctive internal bolt and 'hinge-crank' recoil unit with a simple bolt carried inside a full-length one piece slide. This slide had

---

18. On 10 July 1897, the agent of Colt's Patent Fire Arms Manufacturing Company in Britain, Phillip Justice, was granted British Patent 9871/1897 to protect the design of five different pistols. Four were Browning's work, the subjects of separate US Patents 580923–6, while the fifth – an aberrant blow-forward type also protected by US Patent 580935 – was due to Carl J. Ehbets.

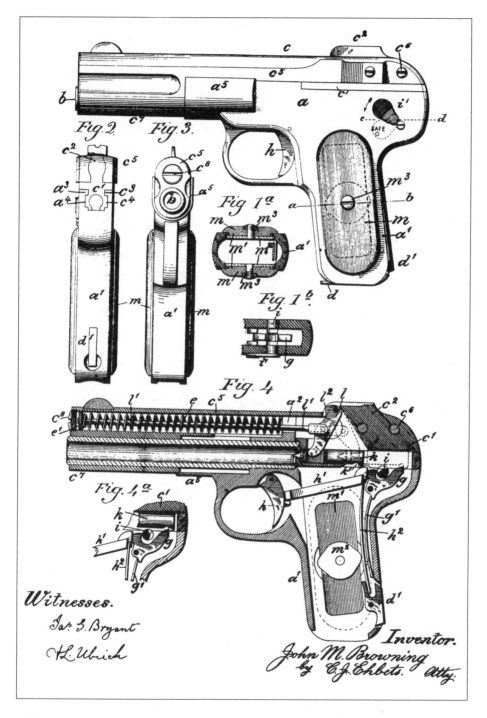

*US Patent 621747 of 21 March 1899 was granted to John M. Browning. It depicts the experimental forerunner of the FN-Browning M1900.*

been shown on US Patent 580926, application for which had been filed on 31 October 1896. Browning and FN sought further improvement in the 1896 design, and in 1898 requested more protection in several European countries. The application for the relevant British patent, 22455/98, was submitted on 25 October by a patent agent named Sidney Pitt, though its acceptance was delayed until 1 July 1899. However, a comparable German patent – DRP 101077 – dates from 6 February 1898.

The patent-specification drawings show a simple blowback pistol similar to the later 1900-type FN-Browning, which was little more than a refinement of the final experimental models of 1898–9 intended for series production. The recoil spring lay in a chamber above the barrel, while the mechanism contained very few parts and was easy to make.

The superiority of the perfected Browning blowback pistol was soon clear. As early as 1898, seeking a replacement for the Nagant-type officers' service revolver, the Belgians convened a committee at the Manufacture d'Armes de l'État (the state arms factory in Liége) to test handguns including the Nagant and Pieper revolvers, 'large and small' Brownings, a Bergmann, a Borchardt, a Mannlicher and a Krnka-Roth. Before the trials commenced, the Borchardt was replaced by the Borchardt-Luger, though not before the committee had expressed dislike of the older design.

Preliminary trials led to the rejection of all but the two Brownings, the Borchardt-Luger and the Mannlicher. The Departement de Guerre (War Department) then convened a second trials board in the Manufacture d'Armes de l'État late in 1899.[19] The small Browning won on account of its simplicity, light recoil and low cost, though the fact that it was already being made in Belgium was an undoubted advantage. The Borchardt-Luger had proved acceptably accurate, but breech-closure proved troublesome and the 7.65mm cartridge was considered too powerful for a service handgun. In this respect, the Belgian opinions presaged decisions taken in the Netherlands in 1903 and in Sweden in 1904. The Browning was finally adopted for officers of the Belgian Army on 3 July 1900.

Manufacture was naturally entrusted to Fabrique Nationale, although the guns were inspected and accepted by personnel of the Manufacture d'Armes de l'État. The first issues – initial contracts are believed to have amounted to 20,000 – were made to the Army officers, though their distribution was periodically revised as more guns were delivered: to the gendarmerie and some mounted artillerymen with effect from October 1901, to the non-commissioned officers of the élite cavalry from 6 May 1905, and to all men still carrying the obsolescent 1876 and 1883-type Nagant revolvers in October 1910. Even the officers and senior NCOs of the Garde Civique, the civil guard, had received semi-automatic pistols by the beginning of the First World War.

---

19. Its members were Général Donny; Colonel Pinte, 2e Régiment de Guides; Colonel Théunis, 9e Régiment de Ligne; Colonel Pioche, Carabiniers; Colonel Heynderick, État-Major; Major Vermeulen, État-Major, deputy inspector of ordnance; and Captaine le Marinel, commandant of the Télégraphistes.

Against such an impressive backcloth of official Belgian orders, the commercial versions of the M1900 FN-Browning sold very widely; an article published in 1904 in the *Revue de l'Armée Belge* stated that '*Ce succes est dû à l'adoption de cette arme, par beaucoup de pays; pour des services publics, gendarmerie, police ou autres, et en outre par des milliers d'officiers de toutes nationalities...* ' ('The success of the FN-Browning is due to its adoption by many countries; for the public services, gendarmerie, police and others, and, furthermore, by many officers of all nationalities... ')

Many countries tested the FN-Browning at the turn of the century. The *Proceedings* of the British Small Arms Committee meeting held at the Enfield firearms factory on 29 October 1900 noted that the British military attaché in Brussels had reported the adoption of the Browning pistol in Belgium, and the Small Arms Committee had subsequently asked if the calibre could be increased to 10.2mm (0.40in) to meet the contemporaneous British specification. The attaché reported on 24 October that FN's technicians doubted that the calibre of the gun could safely exceed 9mm. He also informed the Director General of Ordnance that the Belgian Army experts had also been initially suspicious of a bullet diameter as small as 7.65mm, but had overcome their objections and, according to a SAC Minute dated 12 November 1900, had acquired 4,500 pistols.

An example each of the Mle 1899 and the Mle 1900 ultimately arrived in Britain for trials. The pistols and 500 of their 7.65mm cartridges were given to the Chief Inspector of Small Arms (CISA) and a short trial of the 1899-type Browning was undertaken at Woolwich in December 1900. Only 80 rounds were expended, but the pistol was criticised for its poor penetration (only 6 or 7 half-inch boards at 25yd), the light weight of its bullet – only 74 grains – and its complicated field-stripping procedure. The CISA also opined that the calibre was much too small for military use, and that blowback principles were unsuited to more powerful loads. No further action was taken.

The 1900-type pistol was subsequently tested in 1901 by the captain of the Naval School of Gunnery, HMS *Excellent*, in comparison with the Mauser C/96, the service-pattern Webley revolver and a 'Borchardt' pistol – which was actually the 7.65mm 1900-model Borchardt-Luger. The report from *Excellent*, which was discussed in committee on 7 October 1901, noted that the FN-Browning was 'light and compact. Mechanism simple', but that it had a 'poor grip owing to the handle being too close to trigger', that its sighting arrangements required improvement, that the pull-off was rather heavy and that the cartridge contained a 'very small charge'. The Small Arms Committee noted *Excellent*'s report, but decided that it did not 'consider the "Browning"... suitable for the Service, and recommends that no further action be taken'.

The character of the Swedish trials was fundamentally different. Held in 1903–4 at the Infanteriskjutskolan – the infantry musketry school in Rosersberg – they became a straightforward contest in which two FN-Brownings were pitted against an assortment of other pistols, including Mannlichers, the Parabellum, a Frommer, a Swedish Hamilton and a Colt-Browning. The results are summarised in 'Försök med automatiska pistoler', in the 1904 *Artilleri-Tidskrift*. The Mle 1900 FN-Browning stood virtually no chance of adoption, because Fabrique Nationale had also submitted a much-improved 'försoksmödell 03' (fm/03). The trials ended when the Swedes adopted the fm/03 in 1907, and are summarised in the next chapter.

Records retained by Fabrique Nationale indicate that approximately 3,900 pistols were made in 1899, the majority of which, disregarding a handful of experimental antecedents, represented the 'Modèle 1899'. This gun is noticeably larger and heavier than the essentially similar Mle 1900: 183mm long, with a barrel measuring 122mm and an empty weight of 765gm, compared to 162mm, 102mm and 625gm. The Mle 1899 also has a plain frame instead of the panelled design that characterised its successor, and lacks the lanyard ring inevitably found on the bottom left side of the Mle 1900 butt. The Mle 1899 grips are also much smaller than the Mle 1900 type.

The earliest Mle 1900 specimens display FABRIQUE NATIONALE HERSTAL LIEGE in a single line on the left side of the slide, immediately above a small cartouche containing a pistol and a cursive FN monogram. The latter, together with BREVETE S.G.D.G. ('*Sans Garantie de Gouvernement*', 'without government guarantee') is struck into a raised panel milled on the left side of the frame. Serial numbers comprise one to three digits, appearing on the right side of the slide above the ejection port, on the right side of the back-sight base and on the right side of the frame directly in front of the ejection port. Liége proof marks are struck into the left side of the frame, slide and back sight; with FEU (fire) and SÛR (safe) alongside the safety lever.

The external appearance of the Mle 1900 FN-Browning was soon revised. A notable enlargement of the milled panels on the frame sides occurred, strengthening the frame at a point where a weakness had been found, and the grips were enlarged. Five broad slide-retraction grooves replaced the six narrow ones; and the small safety lever gained a chequered head instead of concentric circles. A lanyard ring appeared on the lower left side of the butt.

The markings were also revised: FABRIQUE NATIONALE D'ARMES de GUERRE HERSTAL BELGIQUE lies on the left side of the slide above the cartouche containing the FN monogram and pistol, which is stamped into the raised panel on the left side of the frame above BROWNING'S-PATENT/BREVETE S.G.D.G. The safety, proof and serial-number marks were unchanged.

Fabrique Nationale made the 100,000th 1900-type pistol in August 1904, according to Browning and Gentry's book *John M. Browning, American Gunmaker*; half a million had been made by 1909 and production was finally discontinued in 1910/11 at gun number 724,450. On 2 February 1914, the Liége newspaper *La Meuse* reported that the millionth Browning had been made on 10 June 1910, the majority of them being Mle 1900. The staggering total aptly illustrates the amazing impact of the simple and reliable Browning blowbacks, and their importance in the pre-1914 weapons-making industry. The FN-Brownings, more than any other single design, were responsible for the virtual disappearance of the European-made pocket revolver.

A catalogue distributed by Manufacture Française d'Armes et Cycles of Saint-Étienne in 1905–6 offered the standard Mle 1900 for 45 francs, with light overall engraving for 60 francs, with pearl grips for 70, and engraved and inlaid – the 'Modèle de Luxe' – for 100 francs. A box of twenty-five 7.65mm cartridges made by Société Française des Munitions (SFM), cost 2 francs 75 centimes, spare magazines were 2 francs 50, and two types of case were available: '*toile grenat, satin*' and '*beau cuir, velours*' (red cloth-covered with a satin lining, or plush-lined with a fine leather covering). Each gun was supplied with a screwdriver, a cleaning rod and three dummy cartridges. By way of comparison, Manufrance was selling the 1900-model Parabellum for 110 francs.

# 5
# *The Perfected Automatic Pistol, 1900–14*

When the twentieth century began, only a handful of automatic pistols had achieved success. A few – the Mauser, the Colt-Browning and the Borchardt-Luger – were destined for greater things, but most of the others soon fell by the wayside.

However, inventors usually believed theirs to be the perfect system, and the prizes to be gained through official adoption by a leading military power inevitably attracted large manufacturing businesses such as Fabrique Nationale, Österreichische Waffenfabrik and Waffenfabrik Mauser. Corporate backing could ensure that the guns would always be given a trial, and that changes demanded by testing commissions, which ruined the chances of many a private submission, could be implemented.

Chauvinism also played its part in military trials undertaken prior to the First World War, before standardisation on the weapons that had proved to be the most desirable – e.g., the Colt-Browning pistol – subjugated national pride. Prior to 1914, inventors would submit guns to trial whether or not their ideas had been sought. Many guns were turned away unfired; others were submitted to the most cursory tests, and then discarded. A handful proved good enough to be offered additional trials, but it was rare for 'one-off' independently-designed pistols to challenge the products of the arms barons. Those that did were often purchased by a manufacturer, either to facilitate development or to prevent them being exploited at all!

Some countries proved to be more chauvinistically inclined than others. Though this bias sometimes had the most unexpected side-effects, it more usually resulted in the adoption of an inferior weapon. The British wasted far too much time on the gargantuan Gabbett-Fairfax 'Mars', a true hand-cannon, and then adopted the cumbersome, unreliable Webley & Scott automatic at the expense not only of the Parabellum but also the Colt-Browning. The Austrian trials included guns submitted by Salvator & Dormus and Kromar as well as an assortment of Krnka-Roths; the Germans had tried the Schlegelmilch or 'Spandau-Selbstladepistole', the Hellfritzsch, the Mieg, the Fischer, the Vitali and some Frommers.

With the singular exception of Britain, with a history of open-minded adoptions, the countries with robust arms industries were least likely to adopt a foreign weapon. The

French were exceptionally introspective, particularly in regard to German weaponry. The long-standing political rivalry between the two nations, perennial haggling over Alsace-Lorraine and the bitter memories of the comparatively recent Franco-Prussian War (1870–1) all made the progress of a German design unlikely. Efficiency was never the major part of the demands.[1]

Though the Italian Regia Marina took a quantity of Mauser-Pistolen C/96 pistols in 1899, the first official adoption of a semi-automatic, there was little chance that the Army would follow suit if the Italian arms-making industry could find a suitable alternative. The US Army reacted similarly. The Borchardt-Luger was given a chance in 1901 and again in 1906/7, but the latter trials had been stacked against non-Browning designs by the selection of a Colt cartridge used by Browning during the development phase.

The gun with the best chance of adoption in national trials was inevitably the one that had been developed around a specific cartridge or, in the unusual case of a genuinely open competition, the design at the most advanced stage of development.

None of the handguns that had been designed for Theodor Bergmann by Louis Schmeisser proved to be militarily acceptable until the advent of the Bergmann 'Mars' (not to be confused with the British Gabbett-Fairfax gun of the same name) early in the twentieth century. As so much of Bergmann's fame rests on his role as an exploiter of others' ideas, it is ironic that, just as the Mars had been adopted by the Spanish Army, the production arrangement between Bergmann and V. C. Schilling & Company was terminated.

Bergmann's pocket pistols disappeared and the Mars, licensed to Anciens Établissements Pieper of Herstal-lèz-Liége in 1908, became the Bergmann-Bayard.[2] The Bergmann-Bayard was adopted by Denmark, and probably also by Greece prior to 1914, and several thousand were supplied to Spain to replace the worn-out Bergmann 'Mars' Mo. 1903. Elsewhere, however, the Mars was comparatively unsuccessful. It was clumsy and prone to jamming, but was unlucky in the US Army trials of 1906–7 – the German-made .45 ammunition was confiscated by the US Customs, preventing the Mars receiving a fair trial. And even the Danes may have adopted the Borchardt-Luger had DWM granted them a production licence.

After some curious-looking experiments, Andreas Schwarzlose developed an effectual 'Standard' pistol in 1898–1900. Unfortunately, in spite of good balance and comparatively simple construction, the pistol was not quite good enough to challenge the Mauser C/96 and the Borchardt-Luger. The biggest weakness was the ease with which the action could be clogged by mud and dirt. Production was substantial enough for large numbers of unwanted guns to remain in store until, in 1904–5, they were sold

---

1. The French had an unenviable record. Though the Lebel and Berthier infantry rifles were adequate, and much work had been expended on automatic rifles prior to 1914, the Army had a particularly poor collection of machine-guns. The Puteaux and Saint-Étienne designs, versions of the Hotchkiss 'improved' by government technicians, were both seriously flawed.

2. 'Bayard', accompanied by a knight on horseback, was Pieper's principal trademark.

to Russian revolutionaries at a bargain price. Production probably did not greatly exceed 1,500, which was minuscule compared with the output of FN-Brownings (100,000 by 4 August 1904), the Mauser C/96 (more than 46,000 by the end of 1905) and the Borchardt-Luger (about 30,000 by the end of 1905).

The Standard was a good design for its time, lacking only a reliable ejector, and failed more through its manufacturer's weakness than inherent design flaws. Schwarzlose, inspired by the adoption of his machine-gun by Austria-Hungary, then produced an unsuccessful toggle-lock pistol before progressing to the 1908-pattern blow-forward design. This was the most successful of the handful of pistol types to embody this quirky operating system.

### The German Pistol Trials and the Borchardt-Luger

The reports commissioned by the GPK concerning the issue of C/96 pistols for troop trials did not have to be submitted until November 1900: the Spandau munitions factory had made 17,050 live, 8,070 blank and 2,480 dummy cartridges that were to be used up first. The existence of the Borchardt-Luger was noted in September 1900, and another Mannlicher had been brought to the attention of the GPK. Neither pistol had then arrived. The Borchardt-Luger was submitted in December, however, and the Mannlicher followed in May 1901.

The Mannlicher blowbacks, elegant if somewhat fragile, were made by Waffenfabrik von Dreyse in Sömmerda (1900) and Österreichische Waffenfabriks-Gesellschaft in Steyr (1901–5). They achieved limited success as the service pistol of the Argentine Army, but rarely challenged the Borchardt-Luger in trials where complexity and price were not primary considerations. Joseph Schroeder has estimated that not more than 10,000 Mannlicher pistols were sold in a ten-year period, though perhaps the death of the inventor in 1904 contributed to the lack of lasting success.

On 18 February 1901, the GPK reported that trials with the C/96 had been unsuccessful: so many malfunctions had occurred, the commission confided, that the troops would rapidly lose confidence in the guns were they to be issued in quantity. Consequently, trials with the Mannlicher and the Borchardt-Luger (the 1900 model) had begun in earnest.

DWM supplied the GPK with a small number of 12cm-barrelled Swiss type Borchardt-Lugers, chambering the standard 7.65mm cartridge, in the spring of 1901. Late in August, the GPK reported on the progress with the Mauser C/96 and the Borchardt-Luger, the Mannlicher being dismissed in June as 'not [to] be used for military purposes'. As the Mauser C/96 was still suffering feed problems, the GPK asked Mauser to supply two modified guns. One was to have a short barrel, though to be otherwise identical with the trials guns obtained in 1898–9; the other was a 'reduced-weight type for officers'. Improved reliability was essential.

The GPK was now more interested in the Borchardt-Luger (lighter, handier and more efficient than the Mauser) than during the early trials. However, the Commission was concerned about the delicacy and complexity of the Borchardt-Luger, seeking a reduction in the number of parts and more power. There had also been complaints that the state of cocking was difficult to determine. Eventually, the GPK was to report that:

'Luger has declared himself unable to reduce the number of parts (59 compared with 37 in the Mauser pistol). Only the grip safety has been eliminated, resulting in alterations to the positive safety. The Commission has, however, initiated several improvements in order to prevent vital parts breaking and to increase the reliability of the pistol... The fact that one cannot see whether the pistol is cocked or not, has turned out to be disadvantageous... '

Another Mannlicher was submitted in December 1901 and finally, on 12 April 1902, a third series of field trials was devised. These were to revolve around 125 guns: 55 improved Mauser-Pistolen C/96, some with six-shot magazines and others with ten; 55 Borchardt-Lugers, 40 of which were 'without grip safeties' ('*ohne automatische Sicherung*'); and 15 Mannlichers, to be tested expressly for private purchase by the officers.

The third series of trials continued desultorily until September 1903. The GPK reported to the War Ministry at the beginning of December: the Borchardt-Luger had won. However, the absence of a loaded-chamber indicator was criticised, and the toggles had occasionally failed to close properly. By February 1904, Luger had been asked to make some improvements to the pistol and it is as well to consider the design of the trial guns of 1902–3. There seems little doubt that they were still 7.65mm 1900-pattern guns, through the barrel may have been reduced to 10cm in accord with the short-barrel Mauser. There would still have been the old-style dished toggle, and the toggle-lock. Though 40 were delivered without grip safeties, DWM could simply have omitted this part from otherwise standard guns – and there would be no distinctive sub-variant.

Several pistols survive from *c*.1903, numbered around 22000, with inspectors' marks (usually a crowned Fraktur 'D') on the front left side of the receiver. These are believed to have survived the third field trials. Most now chamber the 9mm Parabellum. In 1904, the Germans decided in principle to adopt the Borchardt-Luger, pending a few minor alterations, but Mauser successfully stalled proceedings for four years by persistently asking for 'new' designs (for example the C/06 and C/06-08) to be tested. Mauser also monopolised the pre-1914 commercial market, denied to DWM owing to the large military sales of the Parabellum.

The first mention of the Borchardt-Luger pistol in Britain appears in the *Minutes of the Proceedings of the Small Arms Committee* for 24 April 1900. An unspecified time previously, probably early in March, Trevor Dawson of Vickers Sons & Maxim had 'brought Herr Alexis Riese, Director of Deutsche Waffen- und Munitionsfabriken of Berlin, accompanied by the improver of the "Borchardt" pistol'. The weapon was a 'new prototype', Riese stating that manufacture could not begin until the production machinery had been revised.

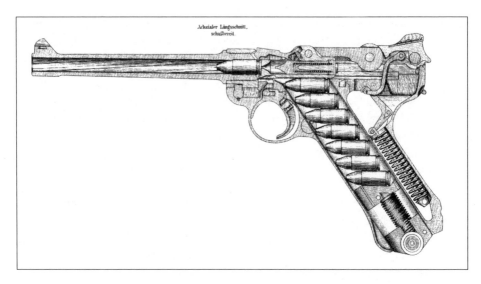

*A longitudinal section of the 1904 Navy Parabellum, from the original Kaiserliche Marine handbook.*

On 31 May 1900, the Secretary of the Committee asked Vickers Sons & Maxim to supply six guns and 3,000 cartridges for trials. The 'improver' of the design, Georg Luger, was to be asked if difficulty would be encountered in producing a version chambering .45in cartridges. On 13 October, Vickers replied that:

> '… we have now ready the six pistols, together with ammunition, which you asked for in your letter… In order to explain the action and several points of the pistol clearly to the Committee, we should be glad to have an appointment, so that we can bring the inventor, with a view of answering any special questions which they may wish to put, and to put the Committee in possession of all details connected with the general system. We would remark that the system made use of in this pistol is the same as that used in the Maxim gun, and in this respect we believe it would be an acceptable weapon for service, the principle having been tried under active service conditions.'

The Small Arms Committee agreed to see Luger and Vickers' representative, probably Trevor Dawson, on 22 October 1900, but Luger does not appear to have attended the meeting when the new pistols were exhibited. All six were issued to the Chief Inspector of Small Arms (CISA), and arrangements were to be made for trials at which Luger could represent the interests of DWM. The pistols were tested by CISA's department prior to 5 November, the report appearing four days later and forwarded to the Small Arms Committee by way of the Director-General of Ordnance.

> [The] 'Borchardt' [is] well made, is of good design, and handles comfortably. The breech bolt is strongly secured to the sideplates by means of a toggle joint and a stout axis pin; there is no liability of its being blown out into the firer's face. [CISA does not think that]

this pistol, or the Roth or Steyr automatic pistols, could be adapted to take the Webley cartridge, for, the magazine being in the handle, this large cartridge would make the handle unwieldy. An important advantage that this pistol possesses over the others mentioned above is the fact, when the eight rounds contained in the magazine have been fired, that the magazine can be replaced by a full one and fire resumed in four or five seconds. In the other pistols the magazine has to be reloaded from a clip [charger] which, even on a range, often does not work smoothly. The pistol may safely be carried ready loaded as there are two safety arrangements both of which act properly. One is automatic and is disconnected by gripping the stock, the other is operated as required by the thumb of the right hand. The pistol is easily stripped for cleaning or inspection without the aid of tools, it may be entirely dismantled with the aid of the small drift and screw-driver supplied. The latter is only required for the screw fastening the wood grips. There is no danger of a bullet remaining in the barrel on account of a light charge, and another cartridge being automatically loaded up and fired. Cartridges loaded with $1\frac{1}{2}$, 2 and $2\frac{1}{2}$ grains of powder used, fired the bullets out of the barrel but did not load up the next cartridge.

'The pistols have fired about 120 rounds, without a missfire or any failure. On one occasion the pistol was heavily dusted with sand before firing without interfering with the automatic action. The accuracy of the pistol was quite satisfactory, and the penetration was very good...[3]

'The bullet might be improved, for after passing through 15 2-inch planks it was not set up. The steel envelope in which the lead core is contained would probably wear the rifling unnecessarily much. The recoil in this pistol as in the other automatic pistols is but little felt.

'The pistol, on account of its having no cylinder, packs flatter in the holster than a revolver.

'In conclusion, this is a good serviceable weapon, and is much to be preferred to any of the other revolvers or automatic pistols we have had for trial. The only point I have not been able to ascertain is the wounding power of the bullet. Penetration tests into boards or clay blocks do not give a fair idea of this. I consider that this pistol is worthy of an extended trial.'

Vickers, Sons & Maxim reported the dimensions and basic performance of the Borchardt-Luger as: calibre, .299in [nominally 7.65mm, 0.302in]; groove depth, .004in; groove width, .177in; rifling, four grooves, right-hand twist; rifling pitch, one turn in 9.84in; barrel length, 4.8in; length of sight-base, 8.46in; overall length, 9.31in 'on the centre-line'; overall height, 5.3in; weight without magazine, 29.4oz; weight of empty magazine, 1.96oz; weight of each cartridge, .36oz or 162gr; weight of charge, .012oz, 5.25gr; weight of projectile, .21oz, 92.5gr; round length, 1.18in; muzzle velocity, 1,148ft/sec; maximum range at 27°30', 1,967yd.

---

3. Penetration in 2-inch thick pieces of deal, at 1-inch intervals, amounted to: Webley Mk 4 revolver, 9; 'Russian Revolver' (gas-seal Nagant), 11–12; Roth pistol, 5–7; Steyr pistol, 7; and Borchardt-Luger pistol, 14–15.

The Small Arms Committee recommended trials to determine the effectiveness of the comparatively small-diameter Luger bullet, compared with the Webley Mk 4 service revolver. Two pistols were sent to the School of Musketry at Hythe and the Royal Laboratory, Woolwich. One was retained by the Superintendent of the Royal Small Arms Factory at Enfield Lock, and the sixth was retained on behalf of the Director-General of Ordnance.

In January 1901, the Superintendent of the Royal Laboratory informed the Secretary of the Small Arms Committee that, as the best method of determining stopping power had not been resolved, nothing had been done with the Borchardt-Luger. The committee postponed action until 20 February, when the CISA submitted an explanation that no reliable method of gauging the 'hitting qualities' of pistol bullets existed. A series of comparative trials between the Borchardt-Luger and Webley pistols was to be used to develop a standard testing procedure.

The Commandant of the School of Musketry subsequently reported trials undertaken in December 1900 on 'two living sheep and one bullock which had just been pole-axed', which had been attended by Lt.-Col. James of the Royal Army Medical Corps. After examining the wounds in detail, James unsurprisingly concluded that the jacketed 7.65mm bullet was less lethal than the lead .455in Webley pattern, and was supported by the Professor of Military Surgery. The latter had written to the Director-General of the Army Medical Service that the:

> '... only wound of a non-vital part which may be depended on to immediately stop a man determined to come on at all risks, a Ghazi or other Eastern fanatic, for instance, is one which fractures the bones of the leg or thigh. Deformable bullets... sometimes cause enormous destruction of soft parts at short ranges, but, setting these aside, no bullets... can be expected to stop the rush of a determined man when they traverse unimportant soft tissues only. Great energy in a bullet by no means guarantees great stopping power; but size and weight of bullet combined with energy tend towards producing it. Since the days of the old round bullet, the energy put into small-arms projectiles has steadily been increased, while their diameter has been lessened; and with the latter condition their stopping power has steadily diminished.'

Simultaneously, the commandant of the School of Musketry reported that the Borchardt-Luger had undergone a very successful trial on the target range, the absence of recoil and rapid reloading contributing greatly to its superiority over the Webley service revolver.

The Small Arms Committee then planned trials in which the pistols under consideration were to be pitted against each other. On 7 October 1901, the final report arrived from the captain of the naval gunnery school, HMS *Excellent*. Each gun had fired 250 rounds. The Mauser C/96 was found to have no advantages at all, jammed continually, had a bad feed; and, if the gun was loaded and cocked, fired when the safety catch was moved from 'safe' to 'fire' without touching either the trigger or the hammer.

The blowback Browning was light and compact, with a simple mechanism; but its grip was awkward, the pull-off was regarded as too heavy, sighting arrangements were poor, and the cartridge was ineffectual. The Borchardt-Luger possessed the advantages of the Browning together with excellent sights, though recoil was considered to be 'rather heavy' (reversing the School of Musketry's opinion). The stopping power of the Webley was admired, but the revolver was heavy and less handy than the Browning and the Borchardt-Luger. Consequently, the Mauser C/96 and the Browning were rejected as 'unsuitable for military service', but the Borchardt-Luger was retained. However, 7.65mm was much too small a calibre to impress the British Army, which sought much greater 'man-stopping' power and judged everything by the .455 Webley revolver cartridge.

The enthusiasm with which Browning, Colt and others had embraced the automatic pistol initially failed to generate interest in the US Army, which remained convinced of the merits of the revolver. Trials undertaken in the late 1890s with a Borchardt pistol, which performed surprisingly well, were not enough to change conservative opinion. On 9 March 1901, however, the Board of Ordnance and Fortification met Hans Tauscher, the American representative of DWM, to order two Old Model 7.65mm Parabellums and 2,000 cartridges. The pistols arrived at Springfield Armory on 14 March. Four days later, a board of officers – Major John Greer, Captain John Thompson, Captain Frank Baker and Captain Odus Horney – assembled to meet Tauscher. The guns' calibre was recorded as 0.301in; empty weight was 1lb 13oz; the barrel was 4.625in long; the magazine held 8 rounds; and the propellant charge of 5.2 grains fired the 93.5 grain bullet at a velocity of 1,154ft/sec, measured at a distance of 53 feet from the muzzle.

Tauscher field-stripped a gun in only 3.75 seconds, replacing the pieces in 12.5. The entire weapon was dismantled in 79 seconds, and reassembled in 196 seconds. The best results in the rapid-fire trial, at a 'man-size' target, were obtained when Captain Horney hit the target 24 times in 30 shots in a little less than a minute.

No fewer than 1,734 rounds were fired in the endurance tests, with 33 assorted misfires and jams.[4] In the first series of 500 shots, trouble had arisen from insufficient striker protrusion, and cartridges had jumped out of the magazine as the breech block ran back. These had then jammed in the feed-way when the breech closed. In one instance, a misshapen cartridge case had even prevented the breech block seating properly.

Hans Tauscher, dissatisfied, wanted to modify the striker and the board agreed to repeat the 500-round endurance test. Six misfires were blamed on variable ammunition pressure failing to force the breech-block to the limit of its opening stroke; the front surface of the block caught in the cannelure of the top cartridge in the magazine as it returned, and jammed the action. The hold-open also proved to be too soft to function efficiently. Another 734 rounds were then fired, pausing after 200 to remove the hold-

4. The exterior of the pistol had been oiled after 300 rounds, the board recording that not only had the gun remained untouched since arriving in the USA but also that constant handling had removed most of its original lubrication.

open altogether. There were no cartridge mishaps in the last 534 rounds, the only failure being caused by the loss of the pin holding the toggle-lock.

The pistol passed a dust test without difficulty; but after a trial that involved 24 hours in the steam room, the mechanism was so thoroughly rusted that it failed to eject any of ten rounds fired. Tauscher asked the board to allow a light coating of oil to be applied externally, after which the gun fired 78 rounds with no problem. A final trial of the certainty of action was attempted with reduced-charge cartridges, but the gun handled them all satisfactorily.

The board, pleased with the results, sought a larger quantity of Old Model Parabellums for field trials. Lieutenant Colonel Frank Phipps, representing the committee, appeared before the Board of Ordnance in New York City on 4 April 1901 to press the claim. Subsequently, $15,000 was allotted to pay DWM for 1,000 guns and 200,000 7.65mm cartridges, to be delivered as soon as possible to New York Arsenal.

The consignment was shipped from Germany in August 1901. The guns were sent on arrival in the USA for inspection in Springfield Armory, and, on 31 December, one gun and its accessories were sent to Rock Island Arsenal with an urgent request for a thousand holsters. Several hundred guns had already gone to troops stationed in Cuba and the Philippine Islands. The holsters were duly completed on 23 January 1902. Five guns were issued to selected troops of the 1st, 4th, 5th, 7th, 8th, 10th, 11th, 12th, 13th, 14th and 15th Cavalry, and 61 assorted units in the Philippines. The balance – a hundred guns – was initially retained at Springfield Armory, though some were subsequently dispersed for trials.[5]

The reports were far from encouraging. Although the pistol was seen to be an improvement over other semi-automatics, most units expressed a preference for revolvers. On 21 October 1902, Captain M. W. Rowell, commanding D Troop, 11th Cavalry, stationed at Gerona in the Philippine Islands, replied that, in his opinion:

'… this pistol should not be adopted for use in US Cavalry, nor should it be carried by officers except by permission of their company and squadron commanders… My reasons for this opinion are as follows:

'1. Very great danger of accidental discharge. This danger exists in all pistols, but with this type it is increased. The danger is always present, even with fairly well trained troops and it becomes greater with partially trained men or with horses not thoroughly broken, conditions which now exist and which will recur from time to time in the Cavalry, under existing conditions.

'2. The mechanism while comparatively simple for so complicated a machine will not stand the wear and tear of service. Exposure to rain, dust and mud on field service will render the pistol unserviceable.

'3. Caliber too small. It is thought that no caliber less than .45 will produce a sufficiently powerful "stopping effect" or "shock" at the short ranges…

---

5. Ten may have gone to the US Academy at West Point, 15 to the Presidio in San Francisco, 10 to Fort Hamilton in Brooklyn and 40 to Fort Riley in Kansas.

A pair of 25-bore flintlock duelling pistols by John Manton of London, dating from 1805. Note the octagonal damascus-twist barrels. By courtesy of Bonhams

John Manton
GUN MAKER
To their Royal Highnesses
The Prince of Wales and Duke of York
No. 6, DOVER STREET.

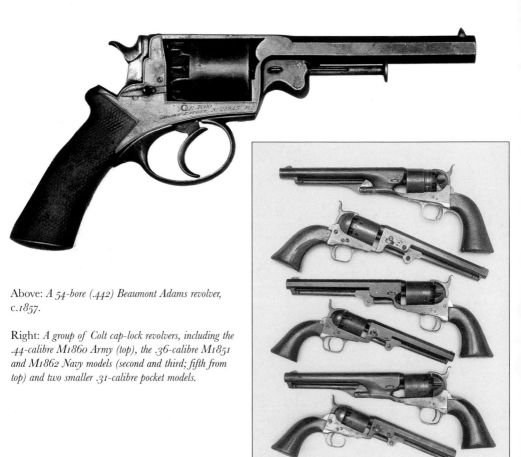

Above: *A 54-bore (.442) Beaumont Adams revolver,
c.1857.*

Right: *A group of Colt cap-lock revolvers, including the
.44-calibre M1860 Army (top), the .36-calibre M1851
and M1862 Navy models (second and third; fifth from
top) and two smaller .31-calibre pocket models.*

Below: *A 7.62mm-calibre M1895 Nagant gas-seal
revolver, made in the Tula arms factory in 1924.*

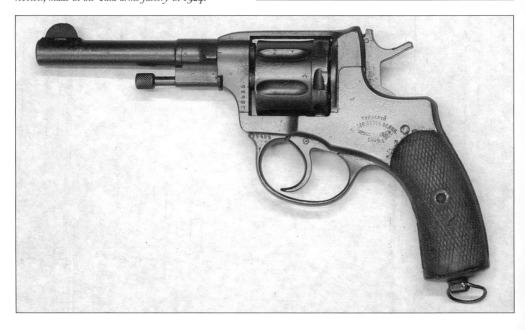

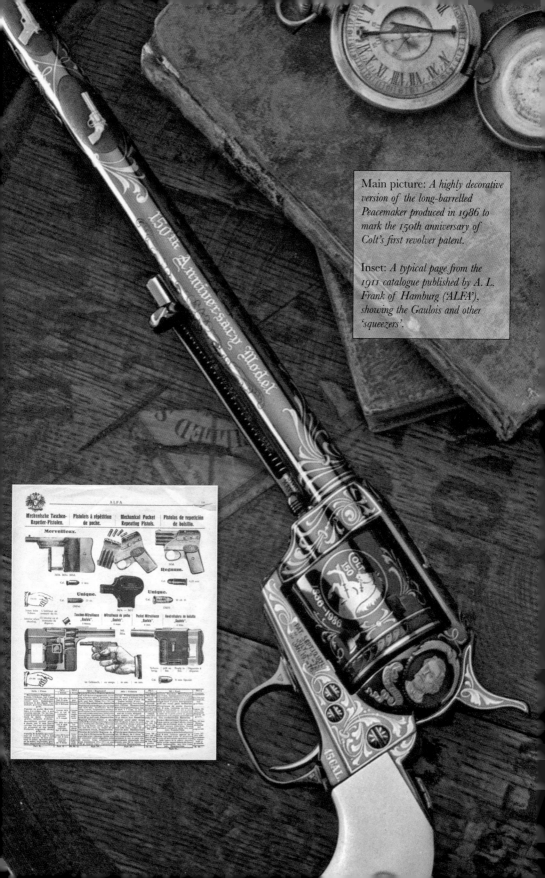

Main picture: *A highly decorative version of the long-barrelled Peacemaker produced in 1986 to mark the 150th anniversary of Colt's first revolver patent.*

Inset: *A typical page from the 1911 catalogue published by A. L. Frank of Hamburg ('ALFA'), showing the Gaulois and other 'squeezers'.*

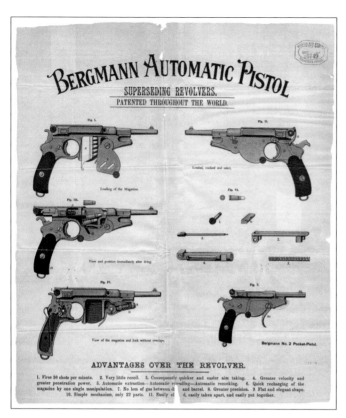

Above: *Made in Canada, the Para Ordnance pistol is just one of a legion of adaptations of the M1911 Colt-Browning, even though the materials used in construction represent the latest advances in steel-making.*

Below: *A sectional drawing of the Heckler & Koch P7.*

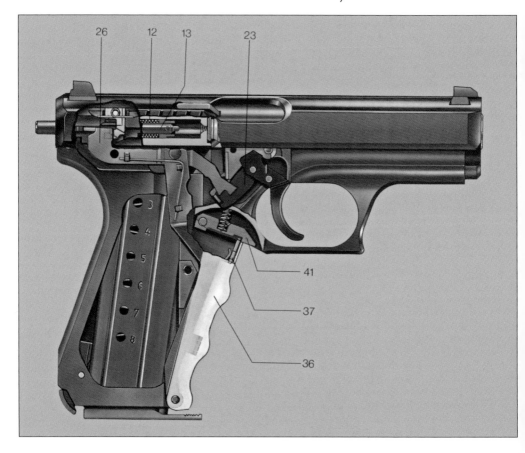

*The 9mm F.N-Browning Pistolet à Grande Puissance, better known as the 'GP', 'GP-35' or 'High Power', has had a long and distinguished career. Developed in the 1920s and introduced commercially in 1934, it has served the armed forces of more than sixty countries. The main illustration comes from an advertising leaflet published in 1985. The leaflets shown in the insets date from 1961, 1966 and 1972.*

Left: *The S&W M329 AirLite PD revolver.*

Above: *Made under licence, the S&W Model 99 pistol is based on the Walther of the same numerical designation with changes made to suit the North American military/police market.*

Left: *Typical advertising ephemera of the late twentieth century, in this case, published by Walther to promote the company's P5.*

'4. With reference to this pistol as a secondary arm it is not seen that either rapidity of aimed fire or a greater number of cartridges than six or seven or even the ability to reload the magazine are really essential… safety, sure action, and heavy caliber are in my opinion the three imperative features and it is believed that these objects are all best fulfilled by the best pattern single action cal. .45. The double action is objectionable in that its action is not sure while the trigger sets [sits] too far from the grip with the result that the grip and trigger do not fit the hand of the average soldier…

'5. This pistol, with respect to its magazine features, appears to infringe the use of the carbine… I can conceive of no circumstances worthy of mention in any class of warfare, where a reloaded revolver magazine will be necessary…

'I have had no opportunity to conduct exhaustive mechanical tests of this pistol and can make no recommendations for its improvement beyond recommending that it can be provided with such mechanism that in automatically cocking itself on discharge it also automatically locks itself at the same time thus removing the chief source of danger… '

Springfield recalled the surviving pistols to store in 1905 and, a year later, sold the remaining 770 to Francis Bannerman & Sons at public auction.[6] They had cost the US Treasury $15,630 ($14.75 for each gun and 88¢ for each extra magazine); the sale to Bannerman recouped merely $8,250.

The trials held in Britain and the USA highlighted the comparative lack of power in the 7.65mm cartridge. On 7 March 1902, the Director-General of Ordnance forwarded a letter from Vickers Sons & Maxim to the Small Arms Committee. 'We have the honour to inform you', it said, 'that, having communicated with our friends [DWM], we find that, although there are certain difficulties to be met with in producing an automatic pistol with a larger calibre than the one adopted for the Borchardt[-Luger] weapon, they are at the present time experimenting with a new weapon which they hope may give satisfactory results.'

The Small Arms Committee noted the contents of the letter, but took the matter no further. However, Vickers must have been sent a copy of the Small Arms Committee's final pistol requirements – for a gun firing a 200-grain bullet of not less than .40 calibre at a minimum of 1,200ft/sec. On 18 December 1902, Vickers informed the Director-General of Ordnance that it was:

'… practically impossible to submit a Borchardt[-Luger] pistol fulfilling the requirement specified… By actual experiment it is found that the maximum calibre which could be given to the Borchardt[-Luger] pistol is 9mm (i.e., .354-inch), firing a bullet weighing 8 grammes (123 grains). Such a pistol with its ammunition could be submitted for trials in the third week in January next [1903], and we would respectfully ask you to agree to try this pistol, as, in many respects, we feel confident that it would be found satisfactory, both

---

6. The 770 guns acquired by Bannerman & Sons were apparently numbered 6,167–96, 6,282, 6,361–7,108 and 7,147. This could suggest that the thousand acquired in 1901 were numbered 6,151–7,150, but only numbers 6,167, 6,361, 6,601 and 6,602 seem to have been mentioned in the field trial reports – all in a letter from Second Lieutenant Orlando Palmer of 7th Cavalry, stationed in Cuba.

as regards accuracy of fire, rapidity of fire and stopping power. Although the bullet is somewhat smaller than that which you have specified, we beg to state that the muzzle velocity is higher, and consequently the muzzle energy of the bullet will be as great as in the case of a weapon firing a heavier bullet with a larger calibre, and, on that account, possessing only a lower muzzle velocity… '

Yet despite the offer of the larger bullet, the British authorities were inclined to favour the 'Mars' pistol. This was the brainchild of Hugh Gabbett Fairfax who, according to the *Birmingham Daily Post* of 4 February 1899, had approached Webley in May 1898. Webley had been sufficiently impressed to make prototypes for the promoters, the Mars Automatic Pistol Syndicate, and these had been immediately brought to the attention of the War Office. Gabbett Fairfax had produced the most powerful semi-automatic of its generation, the characteristics of even the earliest examples anticipating the Small Arms Committee preference for a gun capable of firing a 200-grain bullet at 1,200ft/sec or more.

Design work is said to have been started in 1895, but very little progress had been made prior to the approach to Webley in the spring of 1898. The 'Mars' pistol was made in a variety of chamberings, including 8.5mm, .360 (or 9mm), and at least two .45 patterns. It operated on long-recoil principles, but was stupefyingly complicated.

The action of the breech was particularly odd. When the gun was fired, the barrel, receiver and breech-block assembly retreated to the end of a very long stroke. The breech block was then rotated out of engagement with the remainder of the mechanism, which returned to its original position and allowed the extractor, mounted on the breech block, to pull the spent case out of the chamber as the barrel ran forward to battery. When the barrel reached the limit of its travel, the ejector kicked the spent case clear of the breech. The breech block was then released to run forward, running a fresh cartridge forward from the cartridge-lifter into the breech and then re-locking the mechanism for the next shot.

'Mars' pistols were far too heavy for normal use. In addition, the unusually heavy reciprocating parts travelled so far backward that even experienced marksmen were unprepared for the shift in balance and were unable to keep the pistol on target. The muzzle customarily ended up pointing skywards; after one disillusioning trial, the captain of HMS *Excellent* made his feelings clear: 'No one who had fired [the Mars] wished to do so again.'

The greatest surprise was the length of time the British authorities actively tested the Mars pistols and the large number of trials undertaken with them. The promise of enough power to meet the ludicrously optimistic specifications was probably enough to convince the Small Arms Committee to grant an engineering catastrophe such indulgence. Even Webley became exasperated with Gabbett Fairfax's design, preferring instead to develop the ideas of its own chief designer, William Whiting.

Though the Small Arms Committee still received reports such as those of the military attaché in Washington, DC, describing the US Army trials, there was little chance that the disqualification of the Borchardt-Luger would be rescinded. But the British records are particularly valuable as they date the first '9mm Luger' pistols to January 1903.

## Pistols and the US Army, 1904–11

On 16 April 1903, in New York, the Board of Ordnance and Fortification met under the chairmanship of Lieutenant General Nelson A. Miles. Hans Tauscher had offered to submit several experimental 9mm Parabellums, and the Board suggested exchanging 50 of the original 7.65mm (1901) consignment for new large-calibre guns. A maximum of $35,000 was allotted to purchase 25,000 9mm cartridges, but it was expected that no other charge would be made owing to the terms of exchange.

Georg Luger arrived in New York City early in May 1903, bringing several prototype pistols[7] and a small quantity of ammunition. At the end of June 1903, the Board of Ordnance and Fortification asked Springfield Armory for a report on trials undertaken 'to enable it to select the most suitable length of barrel to be used with the fifty 9mm. Luger Automatic Pistols to be exchanged'. On 2 July, the officer commanding the Armory, Colonel Frank Phipps, replied that work had not been completed, but that three 9mm pistols had been submitted in differing barrel lengths. These were listed as $3^7/8$, $4^{11}/16$ and $5^{13}/16$ inches – 10, 12 and 15cm.

The final Springfield report was considered by the Board of Ordnance on 30 July 1903. The recommendations included the exchange of fifty 7.65mm for fifty 9mm pistols, and the addition to the latter of a cartridge-indicating device, credited to George H. Powell and approved by the Cavalry School at Fort Riley on 18 June.

Finally, on 13 August 1903, Colonel Phipps was requested to expedite the exchange of pistols and to send Luger the prototype (7.65mm?) gun fitted with the cartridge indicator. Tauscher was informed of matters four days later, but no deliveries had been made by October and ammunition experiments were still continuing. In December, Phipps, having contacted Tauscher, informed the Chief of Ordnance that: '… he [Tauscher] states under date of 4th inst. that the 50 9m/m Luger pistols cannot be expected until some time in February, the delay being caused by the work of attaching the Powell cartridge-indicating device.'

This proves that the indicators were fitted in Germany, though the prototype was probably converted at Springfield Armory or, conceivably, in the workshops at Fort Riley. Fifty 10cm-barrel 9mm guns numbered 22,401–22,450 arrived in the spring of 1904, being received at New York Arsenal on 20 April and dispatched to Fort Riley two days later. Half the total quantity was intended for the Light Artillery Board, and the remainder for the Cavalry Board. On 10 April 1907, 24 surviving 9mm Parabellums were returned to Springfield Armory. A letter written on 10 June 1908 by

---

7. The pistols delivered by Luger were prototypes with 'B'-suffix serial numbers. Two were apparently 10030B (12cm barrel), sold from Springfield to Dr Earl D. Fuller of Utica, New York State, on 7 November 1913, and 10060B (15cm barrel). Details of the third, 10cm-barrelled prototype remain unknown.

Captain W. A. Phillips, to the commanding officer of Springfield, describes the Powell
Device as:

> '... an indicating pointer attached to the follower in the magazine and sliding in a slot on
> the left side of the magazine. In the left grip is set a transparent celluloid strip about 3¼"
> long covering corresponding stops in the grip and magazine. There is a scale of black
> numbers numbered from the top 1 to 7, painted on the inside of the rear half of the
> celluloid strip, and then covered with metallic paint so that the numbers show black on
> a silver field. The end of the indicator on the magazine follower shows through the
> celluloid strip opposite a number showing the cartridges remaining in the magazine... it
> is believed that the left grip would be injured by the rough usage of service.'

The greatest obstacle to the success of the Borchardt-Luger in the USA was provided
by the designs of John M. Browning. Only the locked-breech Browning pistols can be
considered as direct competitors to the Borchardt-Luger, though in Sweden and the
Netherlands, blowback patterns were accepted instead. The guns were based on patents
granted to John M. Browning in 1897, and subsequent protection dating from 1902–13.
They were all made by Colt's Patent Fire Arms Manufacturing Co. of Hartford,
Connecticut, though the blowbacks were licensed to Fabrique Nationale in Europe.

Several prototypes were produced, one embodying what has become known as the
Browning dropping link. This used barrel recoil to disengage lugs on the barrel from
recesses in the underside of the slide, dropping the barrel on a pivoting linkage to
produce non-axial movement. Early guns used two 'parallel motion' links, one at the
muzzle and one at the breech. These were not especially successful, but were reliable
enough to beat the Parabellum and the Savage in the US trials of 1906–7. Browning
persisted, and in 1909 introduced a modification in which only a rear link was used.

Wear in the barrel bushing and the tolerances necessary to swing the barrel in its
housing made even the perfected Colt-Brownings less accurate than some of their rivals.
In the US Army trials, for example, the Borchardt-Luger and the Savage (both with
linear barrel movement) returned appreciably better shooting results than the
Brownings. The great merit of the Browning breech system undoubtedly lay in its
simplicity, reliability and unusual strength; one gun fired 6,000 consecutive rounds
without misfires or parts breakages. Though the Borchardt-Luger sometimes performed
similarly, firing 3,000 rounds non-stop during stringent German trials in 1901, the Colt
operated more reliably during the US Army trials.

In 1906, the US Army Board of Ordnance and Fortification decided to find the best
contemporary handgun. Since many designs had been rejected because of their
ineffectual or unacceptable cartridges, only guns chambering the M1906 round would be
considered for the trials scheduled for October. The specification demanded a magazine
capacity of six or more rounds, a muzzle velocity of not less than 800ft/sec with bullets
weighing at least 230gr, a locked breech with a 'solid bolt-head', vertical rather than
lateral ejection and a loading mechanism that would handle non-jacketed bullets.

The trials were soon postponed, allowing more time for submissions, and then Hans Tauscher admitted that the .45 Parabellum could not be delivered until early 1907. On 28 December 1906, Colonel Phillip Reade of the infantry, cavalrymen Major Joseph Dickman and Captain Guy Preston, Captain Ernest Scott of the artillery and Ordnance Captain John Rice reconvened at Springfield Armory and agreed to defer trials until 15 January 1907. As a further postponement proved necessary, the officers rejoined their units on 26 January. The board returned to Springfield on 20 March – Captain William Cruikshank replacing Captain Scott – to find pistols, revolvers and an 'automatic revolver' awaiting trial.

The Colt and Smith & Wesson revolvers were immediately rejected: the Board favoured a pistol; the products of both companies had been service issue for many years; their mechanical characteristics were well known; and neither incorporated improvements. Unsuitable calibre caused the rejection of the Glisenti, the Schouboe and the Krnka-Roth, leaving an interesting variety of private and corporate submissions. The Parabellum, the Colt-Browning and the Webley-Fosbery 'automatic revolver' were the products of experienced manufacturers; the Savage was submitted by a well-established firearms maker with no previous experience of automatic pistols; the Bergmann, though comparatively well known, had previously encountered little success; and there were even two designs – the White-Merrill and the Knoble – produced by hopeful inventors without appreciable backing.

The first decade of the twentieth century saw a sudden rise in interest in the USA in the semi-automatic pistol, which was largely due to the success of the Colt-Brownings. Consequently, many inventors produced working models and others prepared voluminous patent specifications in the hope of making their fortunes. They included famous names from an earlier era, and 'one-off' experimenters who rapidly slipped into obscurity. There were men such as Andrew Burgess, one of the most prolific (though not the most successful) of all American firearms inventors, who was granted several US patents[8] to protect blow-forward pistols – the later design relying on propellant gas bled from the bore to force the barrel and barrel shroud forward against the pressure of a large coil spring in a chamber beneath the barrel. Martin Bye of Worcester, Massachusetts, better know as a revolver designer (originally working in partnership with Iver Johnson), patented a pistol on 6 February 1906 (US No. 812015). Assigned by Bye to Harrington & Richardson, the patent illustrates a short-recoil design locked by a double-lug plate beneath the bolt.

Joseph Joachim Reifgraber of St Louis, Missouri, received protection for the first of his recoil-operated designs on 30 October 1906 (US No. 834753). A refined version of the Reifgraber pistol, patented in the USA on 27 July 1909 (No. 929491) was offered commercially by the Union Arms Company of Toledo, Ohio, prior to the First World War. The guns of Richard Flyberg of Halstad, Minnesota, (not to be confused with

8. Including No. 687448 of November 1901 and No. 762399 of April 1903.

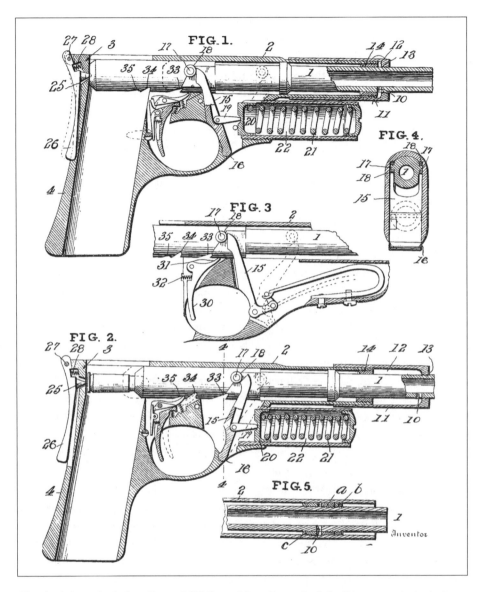

*The pistol shown in Andrew Burgess' US Patent No. 726399 of 28 April 1903 was an intriguing blow-forward design with the return spring in a chamber beneath the barrel.*

Andrew Fyrberg, designer of the Infallible pistol) were also short-recoil designs with, in the perfected version of US Patent 915087 of March 1909, a toggle-like linkage in the rear of the frame above and behind the grip to release the breech block to reciprocate within the closed frame.

Guns of these types may still exist, unrecognized for what they are, and there can be little doubt that a detailed study of these early American auto-loading pistols would be

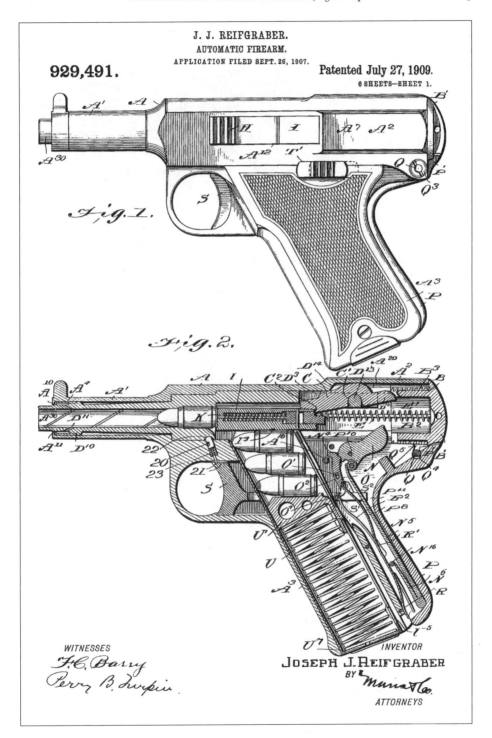

*Drawings from the Reifgraber patent, US No. 929491 of 27 July 1909.*

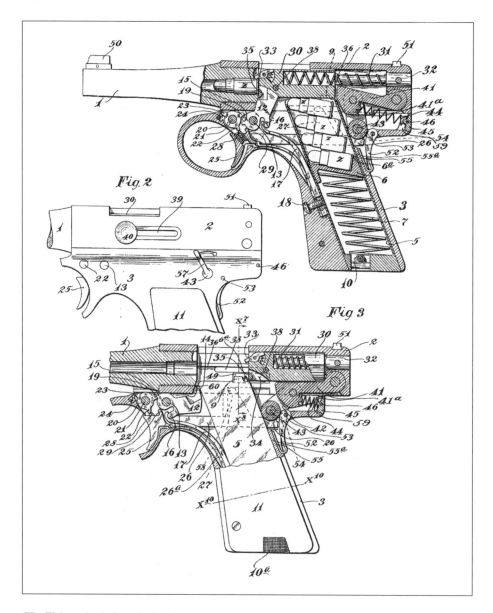

*The Flyberg pistol, from the drawings accompanying US Patent 915087 of 16 March 1909. Note the position of the hammer, directly behind the trigger at the front of the breech block.*

very interesting. For example, the exploits of Moritz Schrader of McKeesport, Pennsylvania, a Jewish Russian immigrant, were explored in an article by Joseph J. Schroeder in the third edition of *Gun Collector's Digest* (1981). Schrader received US Patents 965661 of 26 July 1910 and 968989 of 30 August 1910 to protect his unique .25-calibre and .32-calibre pistol designs.

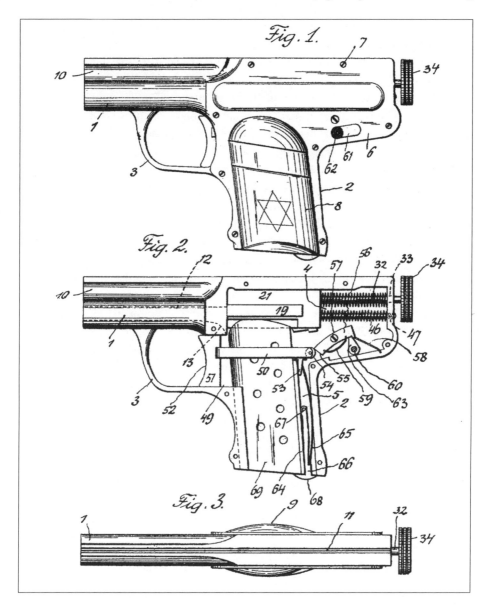

*Drawings from one of the US patents, 965661 of 26 July 1910, granted to Moritz Schrader to protect a blowback pistol design.*

A major problem faced by the individual experimenters was not so much the absence of skill or enthusiasm, but more the lack of funding or machine tools. They could rarely hope to challenge a large well-established gunmaker such as Colt, which not only had virtually every tool, gauge and machine desirable, but also well-staffed developmental facilities. The product of an internationally renowned gunmaking business had a far better chance of success than an unknown rival, even though the latter could be technically superior.

The fate that befell the two independent submissions in 1906 was, therefore, entirely predictable. The two Knobles (one single and one double-action) were rejected after the preliminary examination, to the chagrin of the inventor, William C. Knoble of Tacoma, Washington. The report stated that: 'A careful examination and several efforts to fire these weapons showed that they were so crudely manufactured as to render any test without value, smooth working being impossible.'

The White-Merrill was the subject of US Patent 888560, granted on 26 May 1908 to Joseph C. White of Chelsea, Massachusetts, and assigned to the White-Merrill Corporation of Boston. The application had been submitted in November 1905. The trials gun fired 211 rounds before being rejected because: '... its functioning was so unsatisfactory that the test was discontinued. The conception of a loading lever which permits loading by the pistol hand is commended, but its practical application was not entirely satisfactory' (owing to the powerful mainspring and the consequent effort required to cock the mechanism).

The special German-made ammunition for the .45 Bergmann 'Mars' had been impounded by the US Post and Customs Authority. As the hammer-fall was insufficient to fire the less sensitive primers of the Frankford Arsenal-loaded American cartridges, and 13 misfires occurred in 20 rounds, the Bergmann was promptly disqualified.

The board was fascinated by the Webley-Fosbery, which passed its tests only to be rejected. The introduction of an automatic feature in a revolver, said the board, was:

'not desirable for the military service. The only gain of importance being the more gradual take-up of recoil. The difficulty in reloading the arm on horseback after six shots have been fired, is the same as in any other revolver. The introduction of the automatic feature adds to the complication and weight of the weapon, and double-action is not present. It is therefore necessary either to carry this arm with the hammer cocked, and locked by the safety (which is not automatic), to cock using the thumb on the hammer, or to cock by forcing the body and barrel to the rear by pressure in the case of the first shot, or – if the recoiling parts do not move fully to the rear in firing or in the ease of misfire – the rotation of the cylinder and the cocking must be done by hand. The weight of the revolver is 2 pounds 10 ounces. In view of the above, the Board decided to discontinue the test... '

Only the Parabellum, the Colt-Browning and the Savage remained in contention, none of them entirely satisfactory. The handling characteristics of the Parabellum were greatly liked, as the rake of the grip made instinctive shooting very easy; the automatic and manual safeties, the loaded-chamber indicator, the accessibility of parts and vertical ejection were also praised, though the none-too-positive breech closure and problems encountered cocking against the powerful mainspring weighed against Luger's design.

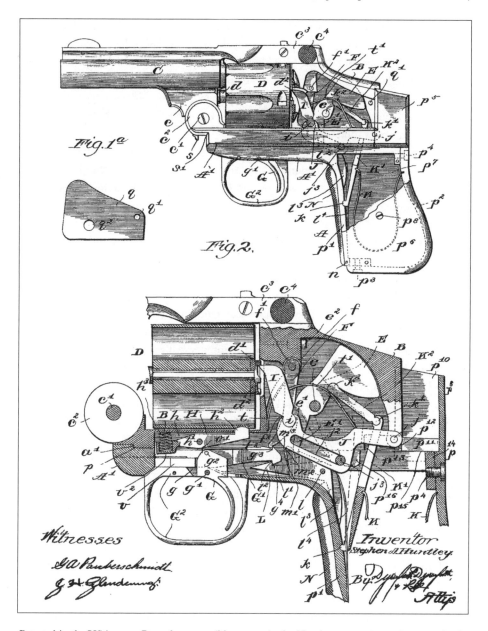

*Patented in the USA on 15 December 1903 (No. 747073), the Huntley automatic revolver was clearly inspired in concept – if not in detail – by the British Webley Fosbery.*

The Colt-Browning was compact, with a long barrel, but had no automatic safety, some poorly designed and inaccessible parts, lateral ejection, and required two hands to withdraw an empty magazine. The mechanism had twin dropping links that controlled the barrel/slide lock.

The Savage was, in some respects, the most interesting of the trialists. The eight-round magazine was approved, together with the 'way the pistol lies in the hand, the expulsion of the magazine by the pistol hand, and the ease with which the mechanism can be retracted'. Based on patents granted to Elbert H. Searle in 1904, the gun had been developed by a manufacturer with no previous pistol-making experience. The Savage Arms Company was trying to compete with two of the world's leading pistol-makers in a stringent military trial!

The Savage was the simplest, with just 34 parts compared with 43 for the Colt-Browning and 58 in the Parabellum. In addition, the springs used in the Savage were robust coils, whereas the mechanism of the Colt and the Parabellum included leaf springs. Shooting trials showed that the Parabellum, though encountering some problems, was by far the most accurate gun in the trials. Mean muzzle velocity had been determined as 819ft/sec for the Savage, 809ft/sec for the Parabellum and 775ft/sec for the Colt-Browning.

The dust test consisted of placing each pistol and magazines, empty and loaded, in a sealed box and then blasting them with fine sand for a minute. The barrel had been corked, and the firers were allowed to blow loose sand off external surfaces, but no other remedial work was allowed. The Savage managed the best performance, firing a magazine-load in a best time of 51.6 seconds, compared with 1 minute 53 seconds for the Colt-Browning and 2 minutes 32 seconds for the Parabellum. And if the dust test favoured the two American designs, the rusting trial gave an even clearer indication of their supremacy. The barrels were corked and the guns were immersed in a concentrated solution of salammoniac for five minutes, then hung to dry in a warm room for 22 hours. When the time came to fire them, all three guns had a good coat of rust. The Colt-Browning performed best, firing two magazines under its own power in 1 minute 8 seconds; the Savage took nearly 2 minutes, and the Parabellum, which required the toggle to be closed manually for each shot, took 3 minutes and 20 seconds to fire 14 shots.

At the end of the trials, the Colt had fired 959 rounds with 27 stoppages. By comparison, the Parabellum had had 31 failures in 1,022 rounds and the Savage had had 51 stoppages in 913. Most mishaps had been due to the inconsistent quality of the Frankford Arsenal cartridges. Luger had previously complained bitterly about the quality of the American ammunition sent to him, which developed an erratic average of 809ft/sec compared with a more constant 763ft/sec for the DWM pattern. The Parabellum had performed best in the endurance trial, with 8 stoppages compared with 24 for the Colt, but the Colt-Browning and the Savage had been superior in 'dust and rust'. The committee concluded that:

'From a careful consideration of the characteristics of each weapon and of the tests made by the Board, it is of the opinion that the Savage and Colt automatic pistols possess sufficient merit to warrant their being given a further test under service conditions... The Luger automatic pistol, although it possesses manifest advantages in many particulars, is

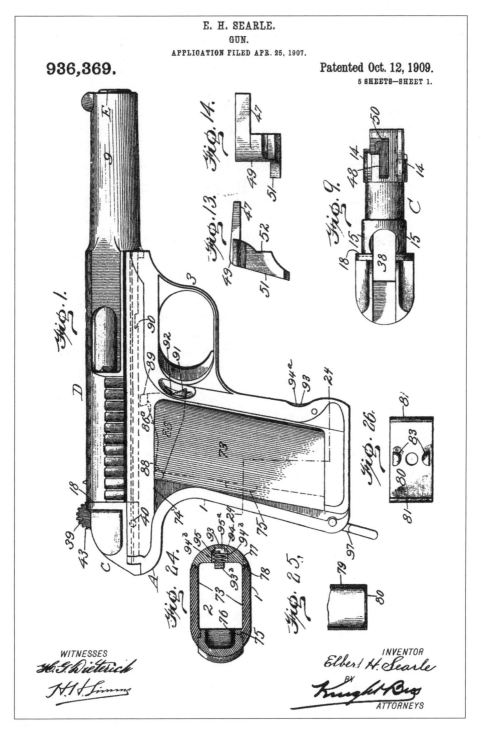

*Drawings of the Savage pistol, from Elbert Searle's US Patent 936369 of 12 October 1909.*

not recommended for a service test because its certainty of action, even with Luger ammunition, is not considered satisfactory because the final seating of the cartridge is not by positive spring action, and because the powder stated by Mr. Luger to be necessary for its satisfactory use is not now obtainable in this country.'

Colt and Savage were then each given orders for 200 of their pistols, and, on 18 May 1907, the Chief of Ordnance, Brigadier General Crozier, informed the US Army Adjutant-General that Colt had promised delivery for early 1908. Savage, however, at first declined the order owing to lack of production capacity. In the absence of the Savages, it was proposed to substitute 200 Parabellums. On 10 June, Hans Tauscher was asked to quote for the supply of 200 'Luger Automatic Pistols, caliber .45' and 100,000 cartridges. His reply of 12 August 1907 asked $48.75 for each Parabellum, two magazines and some spare parts, and $20 for each thousand cartridges. General Crozier placed the official order with DWM on 28 October 1907. On 16 April 1908, Tauscher told Crozier:

'Referring to your valued favour of the 13th ultimo [an enquiry into progress?]... I cannot accept the order for 200 Luger Automatic Pistols and 100,000 cartridges, etc. Thanking you for this order and the kind consideration shown me in this matter, I regret all the more the withdrawal of the Luger pistol from the competition, as this pistol (cal. 9m/m and 7.65m/m) has hitherto been adopted by the German Army and Navy and six other governments.'

The story of the Parabellum in the US Army was at an end.

On 25 October 1907, Crozier had finally placed an order with the Savage Arms Company for 200 pistols, with spare magazines and spare parts, for $65 apiece. This calls into question the widely accepted view that Savage only re-entered the race once DWM had withdrawn. It seems unlikely that Savage had declined the 25 October order so rapidly that the order was placed with DWM only three days later. But there is evidence to show that Savage was so committed to the development of the .32-calibre M1907 pistol for the commercial market that work on the .45-calibre guns was shelved. The assembly of the first gun altered in accordance with the recommendations of the original trials board – moving the back sight back from the muzzle, replacement of the original metal grips with wood, a grip safety, lateral ejection – did not occur until August 1908.

The 200 Savage contract guns, less five that had been pilfered on the way, did not reach Springfield Armory until 1 December 1908. The Colts had been there since March, but still the trials could not begin. Inspectors condemned virtually all of the Savages, and they were returned to Utica for attention. Unfortunately, only 128 of the consignment got back to the manufacturer – 72 had by now simply disappeared. Savage brought the returned guns up to the required standards, supplied 72 replacements, and then shipped them back to Springfield. Received on 16 March 1909, they passed inspection with only minor problems and were deemed fit for trial.

While Savage was struggling to improve the .45 Searle-system pistol in accordance with the US Army demands, John Browning and Colt's Patent Fire Arms Mfg Co. were also busily updating the M1905 Colt-Browning. In 1909, Browning designed an improved breech-locking system with only a single pivot at the breech, the muzzle being supported in the slide-mouth. Accuracy suffered compared with the earlier parallel-ruler system, but the new gun promised to be much more durable than its predecessor.

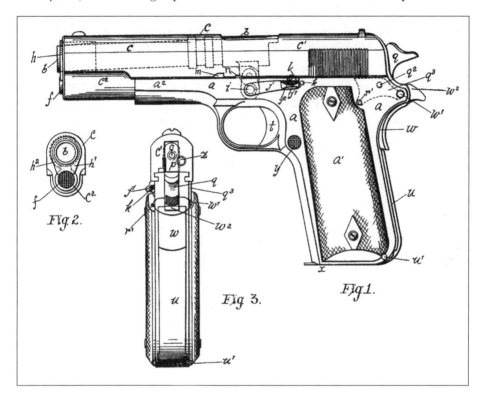

*Drawings of John Browning's single-link barrel depressor, from his US Patent 984519 of 14 February 1911.*

Unfortunately, the cavalry had been selected to test the pistols and the reports were unflattering: neither was judged to be superior to the revolvers that the cavalrymen had always preferred. The Board of Ordnance was still of the opinion that the Colt-Browning and the Savage were promising designs capable of improvement, and undertook another series of trials in mid-November 1910. These included a 1910-type Colt-Browning with the single-lug depressor, essentially the M1909 with the grip raked to improve handling characteristics; and an improved Savage. The Savage was judged to be simple and easily dismantled, but was unpleasant to fire owing to excessive recoil; the Colt-Browning was easier to fire, more accurate, and less prone to stoppages.

A final trial in March 1911 included a 6,000-round test of endurance, which the Colt negotiated without a single stoppage attributable to the gun. The Savage did extremely well for 5,000 rounds, but, in the last thousand-round series, jammed 31 times and broke five parts. The violent recoil of the Searle locking system, and possibly also inappropriate metallurgy, brought the exploits of the Savage to an end.

On 29 March 1911, the perfected Colt-Browning pistol was finally adopted by the US Army. An order for 31,344 guns went to Colt on 5 May 1911, and a licence was negotiated to allow production to begin in Springfield Armory once 50,000 pistols had been ordered. The US Army subsequently sold the Savage trials guns, and at least a few others were made in Utica for commercial sale. But total production scarcely exceeded (if it actually approached) 500 and the pistols are now very rarely encountered.

The 'Government Model' Browning gave Colt an important technical lead over the other US manufacturers of automatic pistols. By the time the US Army entered World War I in 1917, more than 75,000 M1911 pistols had been delivered by Colt and Springfield Armory; many others had gone to Russia and Britain for war service (*see Chapter 6*).

It has been alleged that the trials were deliberately manipulated in Colt's favour, but the facts refute this charge. The board appears to have carried out its work impartially, giving the foreign weapons every chance, even if the unstated preference was for an indigenous design. The relations between Colt and DWM were not good, the former filing a lawsuit alleging that the Parabellum infringed Browning's patents. This had not been resolved at the time of the trials, though Colt was to lose the final appeal in 1909. But there is no evidence that Colt had any influence on the conduct of the trials. However, the .45 M1906 cartridge was a government adaptation of a Colt automatic pistol cartridge of 1905, giving Browning a better opportunity to develop his pistol – about eighteen months, compared with the five or so accorded to the Parabellum and the Savage. The Savage faced the greatest problems, being entirely untried, but was almost a great triumph; after all, even though the 0.45in Parabellum was new, its toggle-link system had been in production for more than seven years.

The .32-calibre Savages were much more popular – ironically, even in military service, as they were purchased in quantity by the Portuguese Army during the First World War. They shared the locking system with the military trials pistols, and also had parts which interlocked without screws. The first gun was assembled in the company's Utica factory on 22 March 1908, chambering the .32 ASP (Automatic Savage Pistol) cartridge – a minor variant of the popular .32 ACP or 7.65mm Auto. The slides acknowledged the manufacturer and the patent date, PAT – NOV. 21. 1905, ahead of the calibre mark. The guns were 6½in long, had 4-inch barrels, and weighed about 19oz without their 10-round magazines. The grips were moulded plastic, and a round hammer protruded from the top of the slide until a spur-type hammer was substituted after 1919.

The retraction grooves were originally very broad, but a narrow pattern was soon substituted. The original ridged safety was exchanged at the beginning of 1909 for a chequered-head design, but this was superseded in 1912 by a special pattern amalgamated with a Lang Patent trigger-lock bar. The magazine-release catch in the front of the butt was altered in the middle of 1912, and a loaded-chamber indicator, patented on behalf of Charles Nelson in December 1913, was added shortly afterward.

The modified 1915-type .32 Savage appeared when serial numbers had reached the 130,000s. It had a concealed hammer and a grip safety system patented by William Swartz. The standard slide legend was changed in this period to SAVAGE ARMS CO. UTICA. N.Y. USA CAL. .32 above PATENTED NOVEMBER 21. 1905 – 7.65. M-M. Marks of this type were retained until 1920, when 'Savage Arms Corp.' replaced 'Savage Arms Co.' in the upper line.

The basic exposed-hammer pattern was not discontinued until April 1920, shortly after the refined M1917 had been introduced. Production amounted to about 208,800, making the .32-calibre Savages second only to Colt on the North American market. A large .380-calibre version of the Model 1907 was introduced in May 1913, numbers beginning at B2000, the prefix rapidly becoming a suffix. The .380 Savage was abandoned in 1920 after little more than 15,000 had been made.

High-speed photography undertaken in Germany in the 1920s is said to have shown that the Savage breech opened faster than that of the 1910-type FN-Browning and it can only be concluded that the Savage would not only have functioned just as well as a simple blowback but also have been easier and cheaper to make.

### Fabrique Nationale and the Browning Pistols

While Colt laboured with the locked-breech Browning, Fabrique Nationale was considering the future of the first blowback pistol. The Mle 1900 had been an outstanding success, but was clearly unsuitable for military service. However, some features could undoubtedly be improved, including the position of the recoil spring above the barrel and its use to actuate the striker.

Prototypes of a revised design had been made by June 1902, when the British military attaché in Brussels sent the Small Arms Committee a photograph of the new gun together with details of its cartridge – the so-called '9mm Browning Long', which propelled a bullet of 110 grains at 1,100ft/sec (7.1gm, 335m/sec). The development of the Mle 1903, as the gun came to be called, proceeded slowly: the specimen submitted to the Swedish Army in the winter of 1903, for example, was tested as the 'Experimental model 03' (Försöksmodell 03).

The *Revue de l'Armée Belge* published details of the new FN-Browning towards the end of 1903 in an article entitled 'Le Pistolet Automatique Browning, Calibre 9mm'. This opened by stating that:

'The question of the calibre of pistols, and also that of rifles, has long been the subject of controversy. The greatest difference of viewpoint is shown among the most distinguished and experienced officers and technicians. The question is unresolved… and each side has taken viewpoints that are completely different. The calibre [requirement] naturally varies according to the special circumstances in which an arm is used, and it is for this reason that the English, for example, who are often required to fight uncivilised peoples, prefer to sacrifice – in certain measure – the advantages of small-calibre weapons in sole favour of 'stopping power' [*pouvoir d'arrêt*] . It is in response to these special conditions that the Fabrique Nationale d'Armes de Guerre, at Herstal-lèz-Liége, has decided to devise a large-model automatic pistol ('*pistolet automatique grand modèle*') in 9mm calibre… '

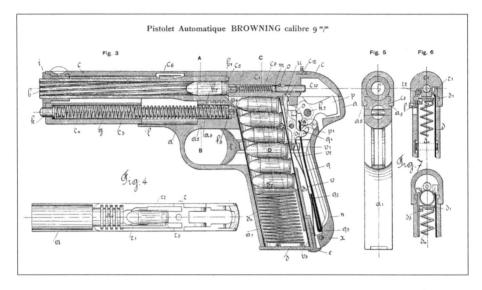

*Drawings of the 1903-type FN-Browning, from* Revue de l'Armée Belge *(1903).*

The gun described by the *Revue* differed greatly from its predecessors, the Mle 1899 and Mle 1900. Apart from the radical external alterations – the Mle 03 was neater and far more modern – the recoil spring lay beneath the barrel, to be compressed against the standing frame by a spring-housing attached to the lower part of the slide. The recoil spring was guided by a half-length rod, seated in a short tunnel cut into the standing frame below the chamber, and the barrel was anchored in the frame by five radial lugs. The trigger mechanism was radically altered to operate an internal hammer rather than a striker, though (owing to the width of the magazine well) the hammer struck a spring-loaded firing pin protruding from the breech block – which was forged integrally with the slide.

The Mle 03, although still a simple blowback, was a more powerful weapon than its FN-Browning predecessors. The *Revue de l'Armée Belge* records its muzzle velocity as 340m/sec, which gave a muzzle energy of slightly under 44mkg (1,115ft/sec and 320ft-lb). The performance of the pistol included accuracy assessed as rectangles, height × width, presumably shot freehand though the article does not make this clear. At 25 metres, the group measured 10.9cm × 8.0cm; at 50 metres, 14.5cm × 14.0cm;

at 100 metres, 40.0cm × 27.0cm; at 150 metres, 55.0cm × 63.0cm; and at 200 metres, 80.0cm × 84.5cm. The gun was sighted for 50 metres, which probably explains why the result at this distance was superior. Penetration in dry pinewood was 13.2–16.0cm at 25 metres (average 14.6cm); 12.8–15.0cm at 50 metres (13.9cm); 8.5–10.0cm at 100 metres (9.3cm); 7.5–8.5cm at 150 metres (8.0cm); and 7.0–7.5 at 200 metres (7.3cm).

The mere fact that the Mle 1903 lacked a breech-lock hastened its rejection by several armies: the British refused even to entertain its submission until the calibre had been increased to at least 0.4in and the bullet weight had been all but doubled. Many European countries, however, saw the semi-automatic pistol purely as a close-range defensive weapon, favouring simplicity at the expense of power. Sweden, Belgium, the Netherlands and others were included in this group.

The Swedish authorities tested the Mle 1903 and the obsolescent Mle 1900 in the Infanteriskjutskolan, Rosersberg, in 1903–4. Competitors included the Parabellum, the Colt-Browning, a Mannlicher and Mannlicher 'Karbin-Pistol', the Swedish Hamilton and the Frommer. The FN-Brownings were known as the No. 1 and No. 2, or m/00 and fm/03 (Försöksmodell 03, 'Experimental model 03'); together with the Hamilton, they represented the blowbacks.

The extensive trials programme contained accuracy, penetration, rust, sand and endurance tests, from which the FN-Browning No. 2, or fm/03, emerged with credit. According to the *Artilleri-Tidskrift* (1904), shooting at disappearing half-figure targets resulted in 10 per cent hits for the m/87 Nagant service revolver; 11 per cent for the FN-Browning No. 1, m/00; 18 per cent for the Mannlicher Karbin-Pistol; 23 per cent for the M1900 Parabellum; 24 per cent for the 'm/01' Mannlicher; 32 per cent for the Colt-Browning m/00 and the Frommer; and 40 per cent for the FN-Browning No. 2, fm/03. The Hamilton pistol had been withdrawn.

One Browning No. 2 fired 1,340 rounds during the endurance trial – including 450 without cleaning – with minimal trouble. The extractor had broken at 790, but the only other problems had been a handful of misfeeds. Its accuracy was, however, inferior to that of the Parabellum. Results of 50 per cent dispersion measurements of targets shot from a rest gave a 3.8cm circle for the FN-Browning and 2.9cm for the Parabellum at a distance of 10 metres; 14.4cm and 7.8cm at 30 metres; 22.3cm and 13.8cm at 50 metres; 60.7cm and 26.2cm at 100 metres; and 128.0cm and 62.2cm at 200 metres.

The Parabellum showed itself to be the more accurate on account of its longer barrel, more powerful cartridge and the aerodynamically superior bullet shape; this was most evident in the long-range results. Consequently, the Parabellum and the Mannlicher were retained for further trials, but the FN-Browning blowback, simpler and easier to maintain than either of them, was ultimately adopted as the 9mm Pistol m/07. The first guns were purchased from Fabrique Nationale, the sole supplier until Husqvarna Våpenfabriks AB commenced tooling when Belgian supplies were stopped by the First World War.

The Mle 03 was also purchased in quantity by Belgium, by Russia, Turkey and the Royal Netherlands Army. Small numbers are also said to have been acquired by the

Royal Danish Army prior to the adoption of the Pistol m/1910, the Bergmann-Bayard. However, Arne Orloff's article 'Pistolforsiøg ved Skydeskolen for Håndvåben 1899–1911', in *Vaabenhistoriske Aarbøger* XVII, makes no mention of any large-scale army purchase – other than a few acquired for trials – and it is concluded that bulk deliveries (if any) were destined for the police, border guards or customs service.

Many private sales were made to military personnel, particularly officers, prior to the beginning of the First World War. According to the ALFA catalogue of 1911, the Mle 03 could be purchased in Germany for 98 marks 80 pfennigs. The price included a spare magazine, a screwdriver, a cleaning rod, three dummy cartridges and a cardboard box. Each spare magazine sold for 4 marks 80, while 114 marks bought the pistol complete with its detachable wooden holster-stock. The 1906-pattern Parabellum, by comparison, was then selling for 122 marks.

The Mle 1903 was originally sold under a number of different names, including 'Pistolet Automatique Browning, Grande Modèle', 'Pistolet Automatique Browning, Modèle de Guerre' and 'Pistolet Automatique Browning, Calibre 9mm'. The Mle 03 designation originated in the Belgian Army but subsequently became commonly used on the commercial market after the introduction of the Mle 1910.

The standard Belgian FN-Browning Mle 1903 pistols display FABRIQUE NATIONALE D'ARMES de GUERRE HERSTAL BELGIQUE over BROWNING'S-PATENT DEPOSE on the left side of the slide, together with Liége proof marks on the mid-point of the slide and the frame. The proofs are repeated on the right side of the barrel, visible through the ejection port, and the master serial number lies on the right side of the frame above the trigger guard. It is repeated inside both grips, on the underside of the barrel beneath the breech, inside the hammer recess in the top rear of the slide and on the left side of the barrel bushing. Small factory inspectors' marks – a 'Y' in a square, '6' on the trigger guard – appear on individual components.

The first Swedish m/07 pistols were purchased from Fabrique Nationale, but will often be found with Swedish government inspectors' marks (tiny crowns) on many of their parts and unit markings on the left side of the frame above the grip. Examples of the latter read '15 № 779', the 779th gun issued to the 15th Infantry Regiment (Alvsborgs Regemente). Later guns were made by Husqvarna, where about 94,731 were made between 1917 and c.1941: 88,586 for the army and 6,145 for export and private sale. Husqvarna pistols were made in every year except 1925, 1927–32 and 1934–7, the greatest yearly totals occurring in 1918 and 1940 – the first to re-equip the Army as rapidly as possible, the latter in the panic during the early stages of the Second World War. Small-scale assembly continued until 1944.

All m/07 pistols chambered the 9mm Browning Long cartridge, apart from the guns numbered 80,931–80,945, which were unsuccessfully adapted for the 9mm Parabellum. The first guns were marked HUSQVARNA VAPENFABRIKS AKTIEBOLAG on the left side of the slide, though SYSTEM BROWNING was later added below the company name. Location of the serial numbers follows Belgian practice, while unit markings are invariably present on the frame or slide. The grips of Husqvarna-made Brownings have a 'crown h' moulding rather than an FN monogram, but Swedish and Belgian products are otherwise very similar. The m/07, whether made by Fabrique Nationale or Husqvarna, was issued with a lanyard ring on the heel of the butt, a lanyard (*pistolsnodd*), a cleaning rod (*läskstång*), three spare magazines, a leather holster (*pistolfodral*) and a double-chambered oil bottle (*oljedosa*).

A thousand guns were sold to Turkey in *c.*1906; standard Fabrique Nationale company markings and Liége proof marks are clearly evident, but most also display an Arabic inscription on the right side of the slide which, it is believed, translates as a police property mark. Five thousand pistols were sold to Russia in 1904, with a mark of crossed Mosin-Nagant rifles on top of the slide, but their destination is unclear. They may have been used by Army officers, or perhaps by a specialised force such as the Okhrana (secret police). Small quantities of Mle 03 were also acquired by the Paraguayan Army about 1908, marked with an enwreathed enrayed five-point star and the legend REPUBLICA DEL PARAGUAY on top of the slide.

A special wooden holster-stock may sometimes be found with the Mle 1903. Its body has a hinged lid which opens to reveal compartments for a spare magazine and the cleaning rod; and which is securely closed by a chequered-head spring steel bar that locks over an additional bar inlet in the stock body. The steel stock tip slides onto rails machined along the bottom edge of the butt, where it is locked by a spring catch.

To capitalise on the better accuracy obtainable from stock-fitted pistols, Fabrique Nationale optimistically made some tangent-leaf back sights to be mounted on top of the Mle 03 slide. These were graduated from 200 to 1,000 metres in fifty-metre or hundred-metre increments, but were of little real value on a low-powered blowback pistol.

About 153,173 Mle 1903 pistols seem to have been made, 94,731 by Husqvarna and 58,442 by Fabrique Nationale. Production is believed to have ceased in Belgium in 1909 though Browning & Gentry, in *John M. Browning, American Gunmaker*, record the date as 1939 (a misprint?). Husqvarna, however, continued to make m/07 Swedish Army Brownings into the 1940s.

### The Browning Copies

A good example of the fluctuating fortunes of the small handgun was provided by the introduction of the 6.35mm Browning pocket pistol, which, greeted with great acclaim, inspired a frantic rush to find a suitable competitor. These trends were most obvious in Europe; for though the Browning was made under licence in the USA by Colt, North American purchasers were, by and large, firmly wedded to the revolver and regarded the low-powered semi-automatic with suspicion.

Browning's patents prevented direct copies of his pistol being made in most European countries, where any infringements could often be pursued with vigour through the courts, and ensured that many of the earliest rival designs were ineffectual: the need to find 'something different' hamstrung many inventors, who were forced to make guns that were often much more complicated to manufacture than the FN-Browning and often structurally weaker. Most of the earliest guns appeared in Belgium, made by gunmakers such as Clément and Pieper in and around Liége. Comparatively few of them survived the German occupation of Belgium during the First World War to reappear after the fighting had ceased.

The most productive copyists – judged in terms of quantity, if not quality – resided in the Basque region straddling the Franco-Spanish border. The small provincial town of Eibar was the traditional centre of the Spanish gunmaking industry, renowned for the diversity of its wares. There had never been a shortage of men eager to follow the gunmakers' calling, and there had been occasional flashes of inventiveness: Orbea had made a working gas-operated revolver in 1863 and the best products offered good standards of material and workmanship. However, at the other end of the scale, the products could be truly awful. Though a proof house existed in Eibar, no mandatory proof existed in Spain until 1925; tests were left to the individual conscience. When the first FN-Browning pocket pistols appeared, enterprising Spanish gunmakers saw their chance.

The first boom period of the Spanish pocket automatic lay in the years immediately prior to the First World War, when a variety of near-facsimiles of the Belgian prototype were promoted. Not all of them were poor; from this period, well-known gunmaking companies such as Esperanza y Unceta (later 'Astra') and Gabilondo y Cia laid the foundations of long-term success, but for each well-organised business there were ten cottage workshops. David Penn, writing in the British periodical *Handgunner*, once summarised the situation in an article entitled 'The Golden Age of Spanish Trash' – harsh, but fair.

The basic pre-1914 guns duplicate the Browning, though shortcuts were taken to minimise the need for complicated machining operations (few Eibar gunsmiths of the day had sophisticated machine tools), simplify construction, and save money. Consequently, the way in which the barrel was attached to the frame was greatly simplified, the magazine catch became a simple spring-latch on the butt heel, and the grip safety catch was customarily abandoned. Changes were also made to the manual safety catch.

Identifying the individual guns is often very difficult. Though it is probable that few of them were made in large numbers (excepting the Victoria and others made by larger gunmaking establishments), their markings try to tell another story. Trademarks and brand names ranging from 'AAA' to 'Zwylacka' help to hide the source, aided by the appearance of distributors' marks (in Spain, France and elsewhere) and a variety of insignia, illustrations and mottoes moulded into the grips.

An individual brand name may help to date a particular gun. The 'Titanic', for example, was named to mark the commissioning of RMS *Titanic* of the White Star Line, the largest passenger liner of its day, and not the tragic sinking only a few months later, so these guns most probably date from 1912. The derivation of others was less obvious and the names have often attracted considerable scorn. The 'Stosel' or 'Stossel' is one, but the derivation would have been obvious when it was introduced in 1910: General Anatoly Mikhailovich Stössel was seen as the heroic Russian defender of Port Arthur during the war with Japan (1904–5), which had generated great public interest at the time.[9] The 'Terrible' was named after the British first-class protected cruiser that had attained notoriety during the South African War (1899–1902); and 'Destructor', 'Furor' and 'Terror' all commemorated ships of the Spanish Navy. *Furor* had been sunk during the brief war between Spain and the USA in 1898.

Another curiosity is 'Peral', which has sometimes been identified as a misspelling of 'Pearl'. Isaac Peral y Caballero was a naval engineer, responsible for building Spain's first successful submarine in 1888 – a landmark in national achievements. The tiny vessel was withdrawn in 1909, to be preserved on public display, and it is likely that the gun dates from immediately after this date.

On the other side of the world, the existence of the Mauser C/96 appears to have inspired the Japanese designer Kijiro Nambu, whose autobiography claims that experimentation dated back to the '30th Year Automatic Pistol Plan' of 1897; by 1902, he had perfected the 8mm 'Nambu-type self-acting pistol' (*Nambu-shiki jido ken-ju*) by combining the pivoting locking block of the C/96 with the box magazine and general lines of the Borchardt-Luger. Uniquely, the coil-pattern main spring lay in a separate chamber on the left side of the bolt. Distinguished by their extraordinarily small trigger guards, these guns were made by the Tokyo Artillery Arsenal between *c.*1903 and 1906. A modified pattern was then made by the Tokyo Gas & Electric Company, some of these being purchased by the Imperial Navy during the First World War. A 7mm-calibre derivative was also produced in small numbers.

---

9. Baron von Stössel (1848–1915), though publicly lauded as a hero during the war, was court-martialled in 1907 for unnecessarily surrendering Port Arthur after a siege lasting 148 days. He was sentenced to death, but this was commuted to ten years' imprisonment. Stössel was then pardoned by Tsar Nicolas II in 1909.

# 6

# *The First World War*

The origins of the First World War were rooted in disparate causes, the rise of militant nationalism and the demands of ethnic minorities for self-government being only two of them. But the flashpoint is well known: Sarajevo, capital of Bosnia-Herzogovina. At this time, Bosnia-Herzogovina was a province of the Austro-Hungarian empire, a weak alliance of minorities held together largely by the popularity of the ageing emperor Franz Josef.[1]

On 28 June 1914, Gavrilo Princip, Nedjelko Cabrinovič and four other supporters of the so-called Black Hand society (in Serbo-Croat, *Ujedinjenje ili Smrt*, 'Union or Death'), committed to the union of the South Slavs, seized the opportunity to attack Erzherzog Franz Ferdinand von Österreich-Este – nephew of Kaiser Franz Josef and heir to the Austro-Hungarian throne – during a visit to Sarajevo. An initial attempt to bomb the archduke's car failed when the missile bounced under the next vehicle in the cavalcade, though the resulting explosion injured several of the passengers, and, ironically, was to seal Franz Ferdinand's fate. An unexpected change in route, apparently to allow the royal visitor to visit the injured in a nearby hospital, soon presented Princip with another opportunity. Approaching the car, pointing an FN-Browning pistol, he fatally wounded both the archduke and his wife before being overpowered.[2]

Few people could foresee the extent to which the struggle would involve the armies of the world, nor that the conflict would be protracted. When the fighting began, most people were buoyant; the war, they said, would be over by Christmas and all the participants sensed victory. But 1914 dragged into 1915; and then into 1916; and then into another New Year with no end in sight.

---

1. Franz Josef was 83 in July 1914, and had reigned for 66 years. His life had been marred by the suicide of his only son Rudolf in the Mayerling tragedy (1887), and by the assassination of his consort Elizabeth von Bayern by anarchists (1898). He lived until 1916.

2. Gavrilo Princip was born in July 1894, a quirk of fate that was to save him from death: imperial law decreed that no one under the age of twenty at the time of a crime could be executed or sentenced to more than twenty years in prison. Suffering from tuberculosis even at the time of the assassination, he died in hospital in 1918. Princip always claimed that he had aimed at the military governor of Bosnia and had hit Herzogin Sophie accidentally.

The Germans made rapid progress initially, moving through Belgium in accordance with the latest version of the Schlieffen Plan and outflanking the French defences. Just when victory seemed certain, however, the Russians unexpectedly invaded East Prussia and troops were withdrawn from the German right wing in Flanders. Thus weakened, the Germans faltered against stubborn resistance from the French and the British Expeditionary Force, whose extraordinary performance at Mons entered the annals of British military mythology. Turned away from Paris, though victorious at Tannenberg in the east, the Germans had been denied their major goal. Much of the remainder of the war on the Western Front degenerated into entrenched stalemate.

As the conflict escalated, however, even countries that had resisted conscription (such as Britain) were forced to order men to the colours in ever-increasing numbers. To arm them, ever-increasing numbers of guns were needed.

### Handguns: The Central Powers

In August 1914, the regular armies of Austria-Hungary, Britain, France, Germany, Italy and Russia were properly equipped, though the Balkan War of 1912–13 had taken a toll of the weapons of Greece, Bulgaria, Serbia, Romania and Turkey.

Front-line German units were armed with pistols, although substantial quantities of M1879 and M1883 Reichsrevolvers were still in second-line service or held in reserve. The 7.65mm Dreyse blowback, designed by Louis Schmeisser, was popular with German state police, particularly in Saxony, and the 7.65mm Roth-Sauer – a woefully underpowered locked-breech design – was used in some numbers, according to the *Deutsches Kolonial-Lexicon* (1920), by the rural gendarmerie or Landes-Polizei in German South West Africa.[3]

The Austro-Hungarian cavalrymen, and most other mounted units, had the Roth-Steyr; the infantry and the second-line units had the 1898-type Rast & Gasser revolver. The majority of the Allied armies had revolvers – the British Webley, the French Mle. 92 ('Modèle d'Ordonnance' or 'Lebel') and the Russian gas-seal Nagant of 1895. The exception was provided by Italy, where the Mo. 910 'Glisenti' pistol had been introduced to supersede the 1889-type Bodeo revolver. Most of these guns were durable enough for military service and acceptably efficient. The Parabellum was probably the most combat-worthy of the semi-automatics, and the auto-ejecting Webley, with its man-stopping .455-calibre bullet, was unquestionably the best of the revolvers.

Vast new conscript armies were clamouring for arms by 1915, but the established gunmakers were incapable of supplying their demands. An obvious stratagem was to accelerate production of regulation-pattern guns, recruiting extra contractors if necessary, and virtually every country tried this method first. It soon became obvious that, even with production running at full capacity, shortages would still be evident. Fresh solutions were needed.

---

3. Though no original documentation has yet been found, a few Roth-Sauer pistols have been found in southern Africa with special 'C'-prefix serial numbers and 'L.P.' markings.

In Germany, when the original 50,000-gun contract for the Pistole 1908 (Parabellum 'Luger') had been negotiated with DWM in 1909, the authorities had been astute enough to acquire production rights. The primary intention was to secure employment in the government arsenals – Spandau, Erfurt and Danzig – and avoid the problems that could arise when supply depended on a single source. Consequently, a duplicate set of machinery had been installed in the Erfurt arms factory in 1909–10 and the government paid a royalty to Luger and DWM on each gun made at the arsenal. The finish of Erfurt-made Pistolen 1908 rarely compares favourably to DWM examples – particularly when material and machine-time ran increasingly short towards the end of the war. All of the guns bore chamber dates, beginning in 1911, and had the standard crowned Fraktur inspectors' letters on the right side of the receiver alongside the displayed eagle military proof marks. In common with contemporary DWM products, the proof mark was repeated on the barrel and the breech block, and the last two digits of the serial number (together with a profusion of inspectors' marks) appeared on most parts.

The standard Parabellum, the Pistole 1908, was being issued in 1914 to officers,[4] artillerymen, and cavalrymen whose principal weapon would otherwise have been a sword. In the *Ehrenbuch des Deutschen Heeres*, Major F. W. Deiss states that they were also carried by some infantry non-commissioned officers, hospital personnel and stretcher bearers. Most of the gunners, drivers and non-commissioned officers of the field artillery still carried old 1879- and 1883-type revolvers when the fighting began, but these were subsequently replaced by lange Pistolen 08 or 9mm Mauser Pistolen C/96.

By August 1914, DWM and Erfurt had delivered about a quarter-million Parabellums, though the precise total is difficult to assess. DWM apparently made about 208,000 guns by the outbreak of the war, with Erfurt contributing another 50,000. No sooner did hostilities commence in earnest than a notable shortage of Navy Parabellums, Pistolen 1904, became evident; things had become so bad that early in October 1914, only six pistols of this type remained in store. This reflected a state of affairs that was common, in some degree, with all weapons in all armies. The immediate solution to the shortage of Navy Parabellums was to secure delivery of the contract placed earlier in 1914.[5]

The Army and the Landwehr[6] were also experiencing shortages of the Pistole 1908,

---

4. Officers were expected to buy their own personal weapons, acquiring not only Parabellums from DWM's commercial output, but also Mausers and an array of other handguns. However, officers who were commissioned from the ranks of the senior non-commissioned officers were allowed to retain their pistols if a suitable payment was made.

5. Once most of these guns had been delivered, the Reichs-Marine-Amt placed another order with DWM: W.III.19614 of 29 August 1916 called for a further 8,000 guns. DWM was asked to strive for a monthly delivery of at least 800 guns, starting, if at all possible, in October.

6. In the German Army, the Landwehr provided a means of preparing recruits for service from the age of 17 to 20. They were then posted to the Army or the Supplementary Reserve, or rejected as unfit for service. Regular soldiers served for two or three years in peacetime, then a period in the reserve until, at 28, they were sent back to the Landwehr *I. Aufgebot* ('first draft'); those who had originally been drafted into the reserve were released at the age of 32 into the Landwehr *II. Aufgebot* (trained men) or the Landsturm *I. Aufgebot* (untrained men). Finally, in the year of their 39th birthday, everyone was transferred into the Landsturm *II. Aufgebot*. Service obligations lasted until the age of 45.

even though the major revisions that had proved to be necessary – reintroduction of a hold-open, addition of a stock-lug – had already been made. Production in the DWM and Erfurt factories was accelerated as fast and as far as possible, but the Parabellum was notoriously difficult and time-consuming to make. Consequently, comparatively little use could be made of sub-contractors.[7]

The Germans mobilised more than 13 million men during the First World War, and losses of weapons by attrition were commensurately large. Shortages of serviceable small-arms were soon apparent, in common with all the combatant armies, and the Germans quickly ran short not only of Parabellums but also of the old Reichsrevolvers that had been serving the second-line formations.

Continued shortages brought Mauser a contract for 150,000 9mm C/96 pistols, and the Bavarians even ordered Austro-Hungarian Repetierpistolen M12 (Steyr-Hahn) after 1916, but the Oberste Heeres-Leitung (OHL, Army High Command) was eventually forced to sanction the issue of many non-regulation weapons. Some, like the curious Langenhan FL-Selbstlader were specially designed for the Army; other *Behelfspistolen* (or 'temporary pistols') were simply acquired from commercial sources in occupied Belgium as well as in Germany. These guns were usually issued to medical personnel, train and lines-of-communication troops, none of whom had much need of combat-worthy handguns, to release better pistols for combat.

Information passed to the Kriegsministerium by the Waffen- und Munitions-Beschaffungs-Amt in August 1917, *Preise für Pistolen und Revolver*, lists a variety of acceptable handguns in addition to the three regulation Parabellums and the two Commission revolvers. Those acquired in Germany included 7.63mm and 9mm Mauser C/96 pistols, with or without the holster-stock; the short-lived Walther 9mm-calibre 'Modell 6'; and a large number of guns chambered for the 7.65mm Auto (.32 ACP) round – Beholla, Dreyse, Jäger, Langenhan, Mauser, Meffert (Dreyse and Walther types), Menta, Sauer and Walther. There was even official sanction for the Hungarian 7.65mm Frommer-Stop. Among the Belgian products were the 9mm Pieper; the 9mm Bayard, 'large' (Bergmann-Bayard) and 'small'; 9mm FN-Brownings, 'large' and 'small'; the 9mm Browning, 'large, with stock'; the 7.65mm Pieper; the 7.65mm Bayard; and a selection of 6.35mm 'Lütticher Pistolen' ('Liége pistols').

The Mauser C/96 was undoubtedly the best *Behelfspistole* – the most powerful, eagerly sought and reckoned on a par with the long-barrel Parabellum; 150,000 of the 9mm Parabellum version were ordered in 1916, at least 140,000 being delivered before the end of the war. Among the smaller guns, the Walther Modell 4 was particularly efficient; but the first FL-Selbstlader made by Langenhan of Zella St. Blasii was so poorly designed that the breech block could fly out of the gun if its retaining screw loosened. A quirky 'locking system' could disengage when the 9mm Dreyse became worn, and the

---

7. The Bavarian factory at Amberg played no part in the production process (contrary to some claims), participation by the Spandau factory was restricted to the very end of the war, and plans for Bosch of Stuttgart to make Pistolen 08 for the Württemberg Army had not been finalised by the Armistice.

continual battering of 9mm Parabellum ammunition proved too much for the blowback Walther Modell 6.

The Parabellum performed acceptably on active service provided the mechanism was kept reasonably clean. Fortunately, its holster, the Pistolentasche 1908, gave considerable protection from the elements and minimised the effects of the mud of the Western Front. There were very few complaints about the alleged jamming proclivities. The biggest problem was the exposed sear bar, though the Parabellum was relatively easy to field-strip for cleaning. In the trenches, particularly when the armies in the West were stalemated, there were sufficient lulls between attacks, bombardments and counter-attacks to permit weapons to be cleaned. Many survivors have testified that this was regular practice, having the priceless advantages of passing the time and maintaining something on which lives depended. The Germans also often had an advantage over their British and French opponents; their original positions, at least, were usually well-entrenched and often above the water-table. Thus, the Germans were sometimes spared the worst of the clogging mud.

A light coat of oil usually cleared a Parabellum immobilised by anything other than a feed jam. However, as triggers, sears and trigger-plates required hand-fitting during manufacture, the consequences of mismatching parts could be fatal:

'Years ago I purchased a Luger from an elderly man who had been a captain in the British Army in the First World War. He was in the trenches in France and during an attack a German officer came within a yard of him. The German pointed a four-inch barrel Luger at him and pulled the trigger. The gun didn't fire and he had time to hit back with a shovel. He brought the gun home and for the next 48 years it stood… in his living room. When I got it home, I discovered why it didn't fire. All the numbered parts matched except the side plate. Someone had assembled that pistol and put back the wrong side plate. This mistake saved that British officer's life… '[8]

As a result of the experiences of the First World War, partly because so many pistols were retrieved as souvenirs, the Parabellum gained a remarkable reputation. Its recoil is surprisingly light, with none of the twisting or bucking that affects the big Colt-Brownings, though the rise of the toggle through the line of sight is initially quite disconcerting. The Borchardt-Luger action is smoother and more progressive than many heavy-slide linear-breech systems in which massive parts recoil through considerable distances, and the change in its centre of gravity as the parts run back is less in the Parabellum than in many comparably powerful handguns. Although noticeably muzzle-light, the Parabellums are much more pleasant to fire than many other 9mm pistols. This was appreciated by the Germans, and by many of their opponents who used captured Pistolen 1908 illicitly.

---

8. From a review of Charles Kenyon's book *Lugers at Random*, in the British periodical *Guns Review*, Vol. 10, No. 8 (August 1970).

The Parabellum soon came to be regarded as a symbol of technology and militarism. It is on this that its success as a collectors' piece is based, but this reputation is disproportionate to its effect on handgun design in the decade that followed the First World War. Writing in 1919–20, Pollard, in *Automatic Pistols*, stated that:

'The weapon [the "Luger-Borchardt", as he calls it] is the lineal descendant of the original Borchardt, but has been very much improved. The barrel and breech block recoil together until lugs on the frame force up the toggle joint and allow bolt and barrel to separate. The sear is somewhat unusually placed being at the side of the action and is somewhat free to clog, but taken as a whole the pistol is well made and well designed. It has an excellent grip, an easy safety catch, and is easily dismounted for cleaning though difficult to reassemble. The trigger-pull is rather long and creeping, but it shoots extremely well, lies low in the hand, and has an excellent service foresight... The parts are interchangeable and well made, and the extractor on top of the bolt serves as an indicator to tell whether the chamber is loaded or not. The first portion of the bolt travel serves to cock the striker, so the weapon may he carried loaded but not cocked, and cocked by a short pull up on the toggle without clearing the chamber.

'As a piece of design it is curiously efficient, but its small calibre, high velocity and rather delicate lock work are points against it as a purely military arm. It is really very German in its psychology – it is wonderfully designed – theoretically capable of great things, but when taken practically it tends to break down through over-organization, and its very virtues become defects.'

This view was at least partly refuted by the men in the trenches, who felt that the automatic pistol gave them an advantage over the revolver-equipped British and French alike. However, when the war in northern France became bogged down, literally as well as metaphorically, it became obvious that, though an infantry rifle and a long bayonet were useful to repel raiders or reach down into the trench, they were a great disadvantage at close quarters on a muddy, slimy trench-floor. The *Frontschweine* – experienced men who had survived their first weeks of combat – soon proved to be adroit improvisers: in hand-to-hand combat, a dagger or a sharpened trench spade was often the equal of a handgun.

Like many armies, the Germans had once been keen on the pistol-carbine. Cavalry and artillerymen were issued with bolt-action magazine carbines, but even these were deemed to be unnecessarily clumsy. The first result had been the adoption of the naval Parabellum, the Pistole 1904, accompanied by a board-like shoulder stock to which the holster was attached. The longer barrel – 5.9in/150mm – and the adjustable two-position back sight were claimed to give experienced marksmen a reasonable chance of hitting a man-size target at distances as great as 200 metres.

The success of the Pistole 1904 had encouraged the German Army to adopt the 'lange Pistole 1908' (LP. 1908), the so-called 'artillery Luger', shortly before the First World War had begun – 3 June 1913 in Prussia, Saxony and Württemberg, 12 September 1913 in Bavaria. With a 20cm-barrel and a tangent-leaf back sight graduated to 1,000 metres, the L.P. 1908 had been issued to field and garrison artillerymen, airmen and other specialised units by July 1914. With unjustifiable optimism, the training manual claimed that 'head size' targets could be engaged at ranges as great as 800 metres, but the combination of increased accurate range and a high rate of fire made the L.P. 1908 popular with the troops. Its principal weakness was the eight-round magazine, which was inappropriate for close-range trench fighting where firepower was pre-requisite.

Like others – among them the Austro-Hungarians and, later, the US Army – the Germans realised that fully-automatic pistols could have a place on the battlefield. In 1916, a Swiss inventor, Heinrich Senn, patented a conversion which ultimately inspired the development of the Fürrer submachine-gun, and Georg Luger himself demonstrated a fully automatic carbine-type conversion of the Parabellum to Prussian airmen in 1917. However, the guns emptied their magazines in a flash and rapidly over-heated to a point where the chamber temperature was sufficient to 'cook off' a round without the assistance of the firing-pin. The light weight of the conversions also made them uncontrollable, and the experiments were abandoned in favour of work on submachine-guns such as the Villar Perosa and the Bergmann.

Trials with the Mondragon automatic rifle had been undertaken in Germany throughout 1915, and small numbers of these Mexican-designed, Swiss-made rifles had been issued for service. The limited capacity of the original box magazines had been overcome by providing spring-driven drum magazines that could seat in the original feed-way. Though complicated and delicate, these took up much less space beneath a gun than a conventional box magazine of similar capacity. The Gewehr-Prufungs-Kommission quickly concluded that if magazines of this type could be used with the Mondragon, the concept could be suited to the lange Pistolen 08.

The design of the 'snail' magazine has been attributed to two Austro-Hungarians, Tatarek and von Benkö, on the basis of a British patent filed in 1911. However, the Parabellum magazine was patented by Friedrich Blum, whose domicile (Budapest) suggests that he, too, was Hungarian.[9]

The Blum magazine was a success. According to papers found in the Hauptstaatsarchiv Stuttgart, three contractors were to be involved in production: Gebrüder Bing Metallwarenfahrik AG of Nürnberg, the Ackerstrasse factory of Allgemeine Elektrizitäts-Gesellschaft in Berlin, and Vereinigte Automaten-Fabriken Pelzer & Co. of Köln-Ehrenfeld. Bing seems to have produced most of the *Trommelmagazine*; no Köln-made examples have yet been found. The first pattern was too weak: subsequent batches had reinforcing ribs, improved magazine bracing and, ultimately, a perfected folding winding lever.

---

9. In January 1913, Blum had been associated with Tatarek, Franz Kretz and Bela von Döry in a patent protecting a gas-operated rifle (DRP 275,651). It has been suggested that Blum, a financier or agent, provided the backing not only for this rifle but also an adaptation of the Tatarek–von Benkö magazine specifically intended for the Parabellum. The most obvious improvements are the telescoping winding lever and angled magazine-feed.

Heavy, unwieldy and delicate they may have been, but the Blum magazines held 32 rounds. The first issues appear to have been made in 1917, the year in which the relevant manual, *Anleitung zur langen Pistole 08 mit ansteckbarem Trommelmagazin (T.M.)*, states that the '*Kasten für TM. 08*' (the magazine box) contained five drum magazines, one loading tool and some ammunition.[10] Thin sheet-steel or pressed-tin feed covers were subsequently issued to protect the mouths of the *Trommelmagazine* when they were separated from the guns.

The *Trommelmagazin* manual shows that the pistol, holster and shoulder-stock were suspended on a strap carried over the left shoulder, while two drum magazines dangled from the belt in canvas holdalls. But the semi-automatic Parabellum would have been superseded by submachine-guns had the war not ended in 1918, even though the Bergmann Maschinenpistole, the first true submachine-gun to be made in quantity, was apparently never adopted officially. *Trommelmagazine* were also issued with the Bergmann, with the detachable collar adaptor.

In 1914, the Austro-Hungarians had the Repetierpistole M7, based on patents granted in 1898–1905 to Karel Krnka and Georg Roth, intended expressly for the cavalry, and made in both Austria and Hungary. The standard M 98 revolver is now better known as the 'Rast & Gasser' after its original manufacturer, and the Hungarian reserve, the Honvéd, had the recoil-operated Frommer Pisztoly 12M. All three guns were solid and workmanlike, but the pistols were difficult to make and there were far too few of them to equip all the troops mobilised in 1914. Like Germany, Austria-Hungary promptly reissued obsolescent Gasser and Gasser-Kropatschek revolvers from store.

The Roth-Steyr was complicated and difficult to make, and the principal manufacturer, Österreichische Waffenfabriks-Gesellschaft (OEWG), Austria's premier privately-owned small-arms manufacturer, determined to produce a better weapon that would achieve commercial sale. The work has been credited to Karl Murgthaler, but claims made in the patent specifications seem to credit most of the finer detail to Helmut Bachner and Adolf Jungmayr. Design of the new pistol had been completed by 1912, when it was not only offered commercially (as the 'M1911') but also sold in some quantity to Chile (Navy) and Romania (Army). Gun number '01', suitably cased, was presented on 18 August 1913 to Kaiser Franz Joseph, but there is no evidence to prove that it was newly made: it may have been the first of a series tested by the Austro-Hungarian Army, but trials were still under way when the First World War began.

---

10. Several unloading tools have been discovered, and while there is no evidence that they were official issue during the First World War, it is equally clear that some are genuine. During the late 1920s, C. G. Haenel of Suhl developed a straight 32-round magazine for the MP. 28, II. The police were glad to rid themselves of the TM. 08 issued with the MP. 18, I, serious accidents having occurred during unloading, and complied immediately. *Trommelagazine* were returned to the stores in the early/mid-1930s, their accessories including a few '*Entleerer zum Trommelmagazin*' (unloading tools) converted from pre-1918 loading tools in the police armouries. Not only do genuine tools exist, therefore, but a reasonable explanation is possible for their comparative crudity. Semi-official status also explains diversity of design.

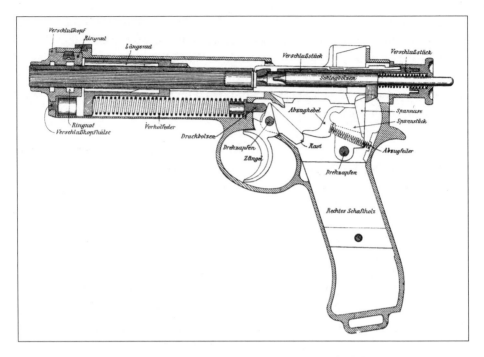

*A longitudinal section of the Austro-Hungarian Repetierpistole M7 or 'Roth-Steyr', a long-recoil design of considerable complexity. The drawing is taken from the Army manual.*

However, as the M 1911 Steyr pistol was clearly better than the older Roth-Steyr, it was pressed into service as the 'Repetierpistole M12' and Österreichische Waffenfabriks-Gesellschaft made about 275,000 during the period of hostilities. The gun provided the basis for the only machine-pistol to be issued in quantity during the First World War, the Repetierpistole M12/16. Developed in 1915 by OEWG for the Austro-Hungarian troops fighting on the Southern Front, to counter Italian firepower provided by the two-barrelled Villar Perosa, the first fifty M12/16 pistols were issued for trials in February 1916.[11] Cyclic rate proved to be 800rds/min, which exposed the limitations of the eight-round magazine and a special sixteen-round detachable box was substituted. A selector lay on the right side of the frame above the grip. Five thousand machine pistols were ordered in September 1916, with the highest priority, and an inventory taken on 1 November 1918 revealed that there were still 9,873 M12/16 pistols in service in the Tyrol and on the Isonzo Front.

Curiously, though its own armies were desperately short of handguns, the Austrian government accepted two orders from the Bavarians – one in 1916 and the other in 1918 – which explains why M12 pistols and their holsters are occasionally found with the

11. Austrian Patent No. 79594 was granted to Österreichische Waffenfabriks-Gesellschaft on 15 May 1919 to protect the auto-firing system of the M12/16, but the initial application had been made on 19 December 1916.

Right: *The Japanese 14th Year Type pistol was the first attempt to provide the Army with a standard infantry handgun since the Meiji 26th Year Type revolver of 1893. The Nambu pistol, on which the 14th Year Type was loosely based, had been purchased for trials but had never enjoyed universal recognition.*

Above: *The Czechoslovak vz. 22 pistol was derived from the Nickl-Pistole, made by Mauser during the First World War. This is 9mm-calibre gun No. 26. Note the large 'N' on the frame.*

Below: *The FN-Browning M10/22 was little more than an enlarged version of the pre-war M10. Note how the standard slide was extended with a light sheet-steel shroud.*

Above: *This 7.65mm Walther PP was made towards the end of the Second World War. Note the use of the manufacturer's code 'ac', though the Walther banner still appears on the grip.*

Above right: *The Mauser Schnellfeuerpistole, shown here with its wood-body holster stock, was an attempt to compete with Mauser-type machine pistols being made in Spain. This is the Model 712, based on a patent granted to Karl Westinger in 1936. Note the selector on the frame behind the trigger.*

Left: *The Polish 9mm Radom or 'Vis 35', was an adaptation of the Colt-Browning. Sturdy and reliable, it was made throughout the war under German supervision – with ever-declining quality.*

Right: *The Le Français 'Type Militaire' pistol chambered the 9mm Browning Long cartridge. Among its unusual features were a barrel that could be tipped to load a single round and a trigger blade supported by a small wheel. This example has a plain heavy barrel; earlier versions were usually finned.*

Right: *The French Army adopted the SACM Mle 35-A pistol, but production had only just begun in 1940. The pistol was pleasant to handle, but fired the woefully underpowered 7.65mm Longue cartridge and had a crude safety catch.*

Above: *The Finnish m/35 L (Lahti) pistol resembles the Parabellum in shape and size, though it is entirely different internally. This gun, No. 2333, comes from the first production run.*

Right: *The Italian Beretta Mo. 34, in 7.65mm and 9mm Short, was simple and effective. This is a commercial version.*

Above: *The Japanese 8mm Type 94 pistol was a quirky design, with an exposed sear bar in a channel on the left side of the frame and a grip that was suited to gloves.*

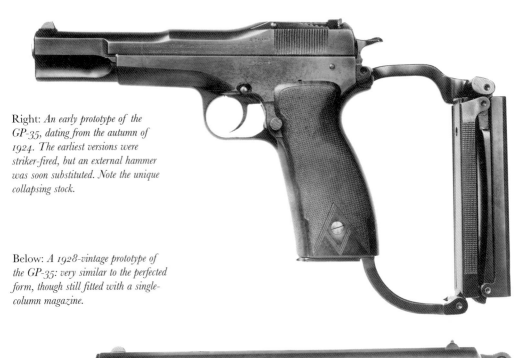

Right: *An early prototype of the GP-35, dating from the autumn of 1924. The earliest versions were striker-fired, but an external hammer was soon substituted. Note the unique collapsing stock.*

Below: *A 1928-vintage prototype of the GP-35: very similar to the perfected form, though still fitted with a single-column magazine.*

Above: *Made in Eibar by Bonifacio Echeverria, the 9mm-calibre Star Super B was just one of many Colt-Browning pistols made in Spain between the wars.*

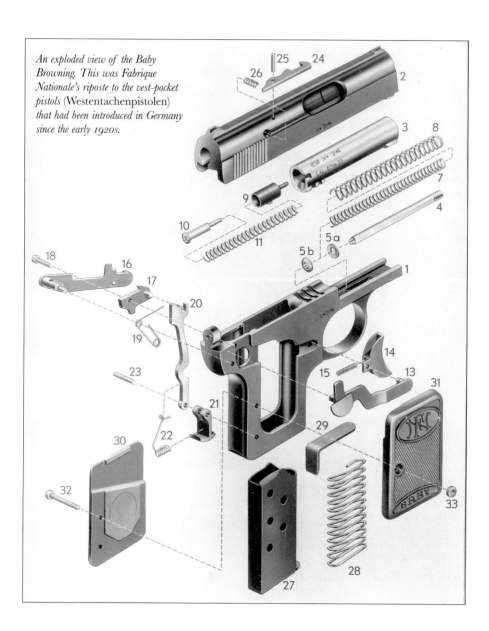

An exploded view of the Baby Browning. This was Fabrique Nationale's riposte to the vest-pocket pistols (Westentachenpistolen) that had been introduced in Germany since the early 1920s.

Left: *The Spanish Astra 200 was one of many pistols inspired by the FN-Brownings.*

Right: *The diminutive Baby Browning of 1932.*

A '50th year' commemorative version of the S&W .357 Magnum revolver, made in 1985 to honour the original introduction – 8 April 1935.

Below: *The double-action Walther P. 38 was introduced in April 1940. It was to replace the P. 08 (Parabellum), but never entirely superseded the earlier design. This is a standard Walther-made ('ac') example dating from 1941.*

Above: *Designed by Myška, the ČZ vz. 38 was adopted by the Czechoslovak Army just as the Germans sequestered Bohemia and Moravia. Many guns were subsequently impressed into Wehrmacht service, but they were unpopular: the grip was uncomfortable and double-action trigger pull was far too heavy.*

Left: *This* Volkspistole *of 1944, believed to have been the Mauser V.7082, embodies a gas-delayed blowback system. This was never developed satisfactorily during the Second World War, but has since been influential.*

Right: *As Germany's defeat approached, attempts were made to provide weapons suitable for the last line of defence. This 9mm enlargement of the PP, made largely of stampings, probably dates from the end of 1944.*

Above: *Mindful that production may fall short of demand, the US authorities developed a stamped-steel version of the M1911A1 service pistol. However, supplies of handguns did not run as short as predicted, and the fighting ended before more could be done.*

Above: *The Hi Standard Model G 380, chambered for the .380 Auto (9mm Short) cartridge, was developed immediately after the Second World War from the guns that had served as military trainers.*

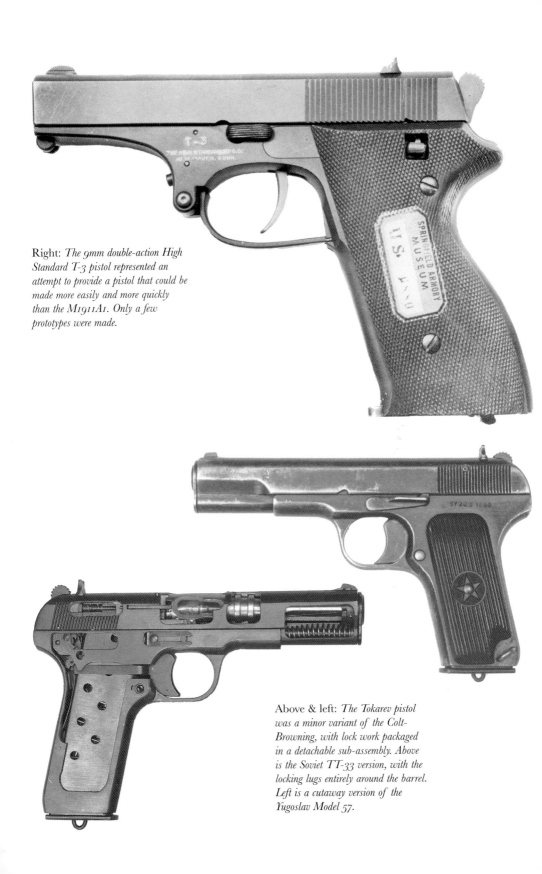

Right: *The 9mm double-action High Standard T-3 pistol represented an attempt to provide a pistol that could be made more easily and more quickly than the M1911A1. Only a few prototypes were made.*

Above & left: *The Tokarev pistol was a minor variant of the Colt-Browning, with lock work packaged in a detachable sub-assembly. Above is the Soviet TT-33 version, with the locking lugs entirely around the barrel. Left is a cutaway version of the Yugoslav Model 57.*

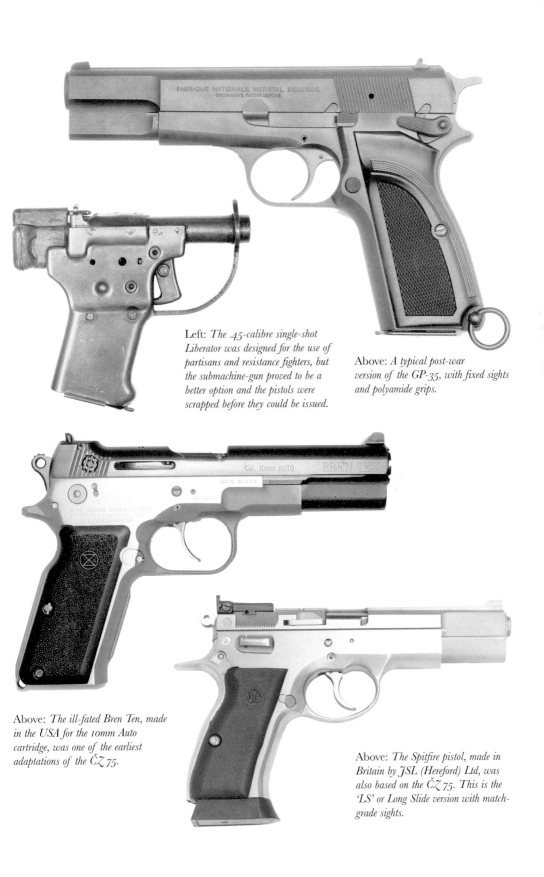

Left: *The .45-calibre single-shot Liberator was designed for the use of partisans and resistance fighters, but the submachine-gun proved to be a better option and the pistols were scrapped before they could be issued.*

Above: *A typical post-war version of the GP-35, with fixed sights and polyamide grips.*

Above: *The ill-fated Bren Ten, made in the USA for the 10mm Auto cartridge, was one of the earliest adaptations of the ČZ 75.*

Above: *The Spitfire pistol, made in Britain by JSL (Hereford) Ltd, was also based on the ČZ 75. This is the 'LS' or Long Slide version with match-grade sights.*

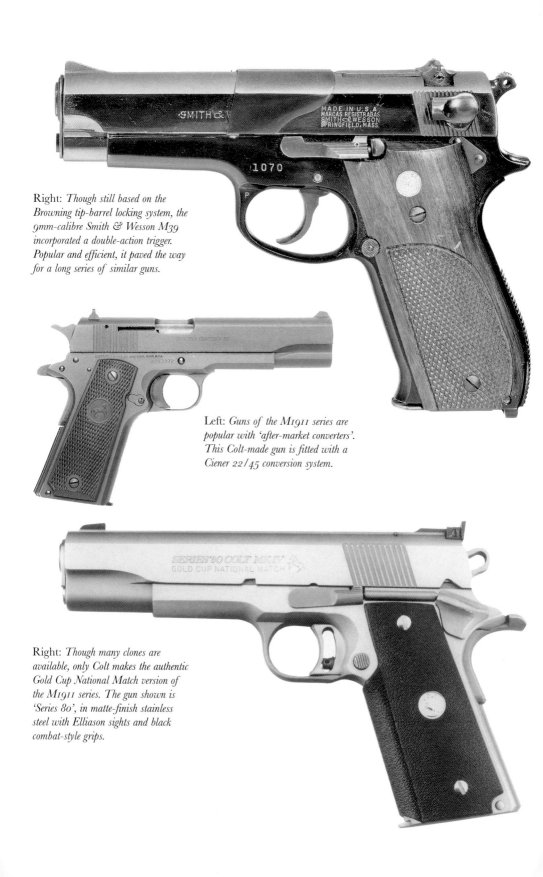

Right: *Though still based on the Browning tip-barrel locking system, the 9mm-calibre Smith & Wesson M39 incorporated a double-action trigger. Popular and efficient, it paved the way for a long series of similar guns.*

Left: *Guns of the M1911 series are popular with 'after-market converters'. This Colt-made gun is fitted with a Ciener 22/45 conversion system.*

Right: *Though many clones are available, only Colt makes the authentic Gold Cup National Match version of the M1911 series. The gun shown is 'Series 80', in matte-finish stainless steel with Elliason sights and black combat-style grips.*

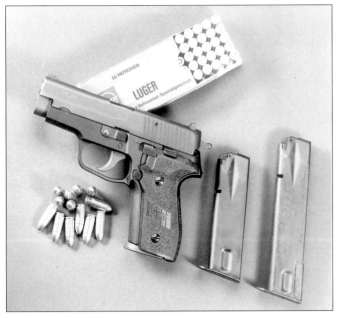

Left: *The SIG-Sauer P228 of the 1980s embodied not only a double-action trigger system and a variation of the tip-barrel lock, but also some up-to-date manufacturing techniques. The standard (short) magazine holds thirteen rounds.*

Right: *The 9mm Helwan pistol was a variant of the Beretta Mo. 951 made under licence in Egypt in the 1960s.*

Above: *The 9mm Beretta 92G is a minor modification of the '92 series', adopted by the French armed forces in 1990.*

Right: *A cutaway drawing of the Ruger Mk I .22-calibre pistol.*

Left: *The 9mm Ruger P85 is a modern double-action combat/police pistol, with a steel slide and a cast alloy frame. The controls are all ambidextrous.*

Right: *Incorporating a gas-delay system, the 9mm Steyr GB was submitted for trials with the Austrian, US and other armies in the early 1980s without encountering success.*

Above: *The unexpected winner of the Austrian trials was the Glock, which has since been an outstanding success throughout the world. This is the standard pattern, the 9mm Glock 17, with a standard-length slide and grip.*

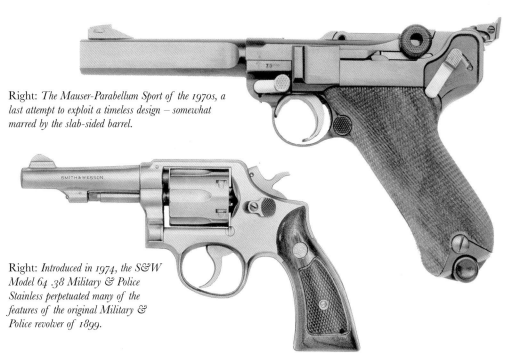

Right: *The Mauser-Parabellum Sport of the 1970s, a last attempt to exploit a timeless design – somewhat marred by the slab-sided barrel.*

Right: *Introduced in 1974, the S&W Model 64 .38 Military & Police Stainless perpetuated many of the features of the original Military & Police revolver of 1899.*

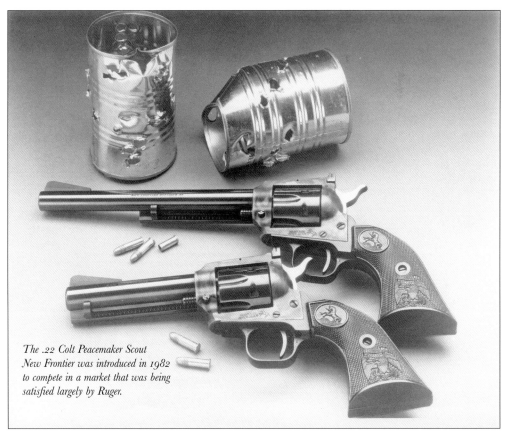

*The .22 Colt Peacemaker Scout New Frontier was introduced in 1982 to compete in a market that was being satisfied largely by Ruger.*

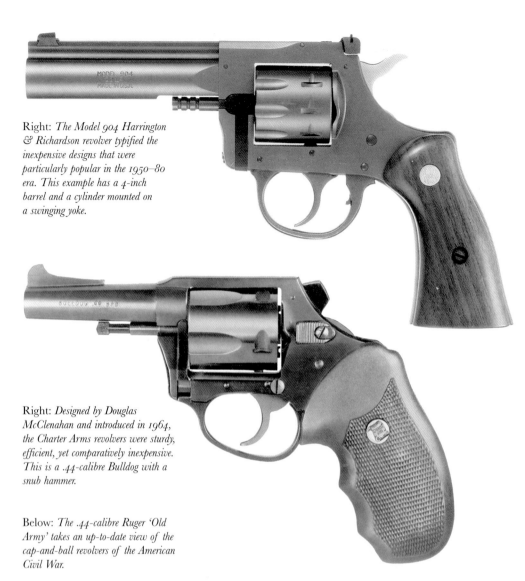

Right: *The Model 904 Harrington & Richardson revolver typified the inexpensive designs that were particularly popular in the 1950–80 era. This example has a 4-inch barrel and a cylinder mounted on a swinging yoke.*

Right: *Designed by Douglas McClenahan and introduced in 1964, the Charter Arms revolvers were sturdy, efficient, yet comparatively inexpensive. This is a .44-calibre Bulldog with a snub hammer.*

Below: *The .44-calibre Ruger 'Old Army' takes an up-to-date view of the cap-and-ball revolvers of the American Civil War.*

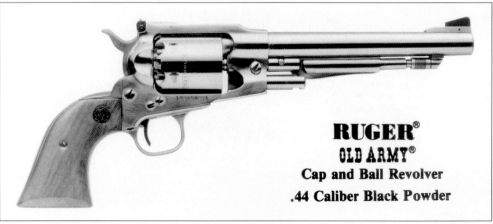

**RUGER®**
**OLD ARMY®**
Cap and Ball Revolver
.44 Caliber Black Powder

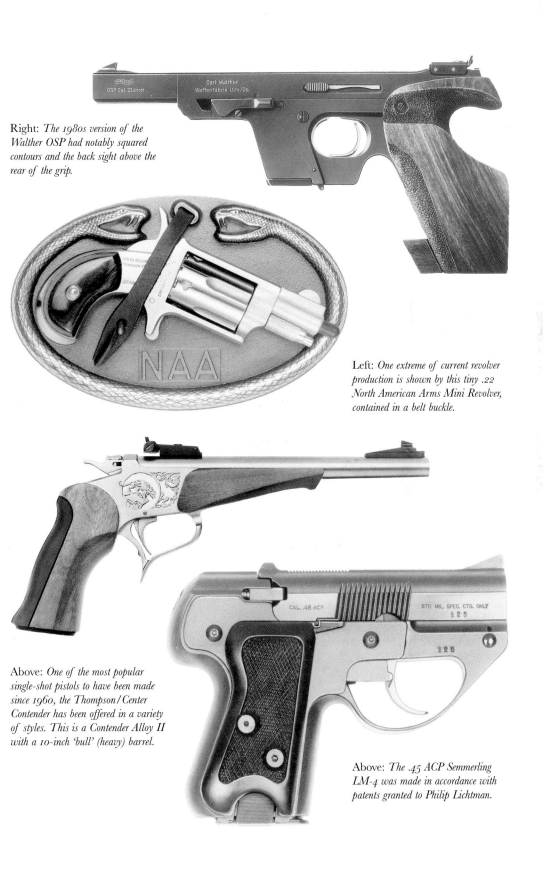

Right: *The 1980s version of the Walther OSP had notably squared contours and the back sight above the rear of the grip.*

Left: *One extreme of current revolver production is shown by this tiny .22 North American Arms Mini Revolver, contained in a belt buckle.*

Above: *One of the most popular single-shot pistols to have been made since 1960, the Thompson/Center Contender has been offered in a variety of styles. This is a Contender Alloy II with a 10-inch 'bull' (heavy) barrel.*

Above: *The .45 ACP Semmerling LM-4 was made in accordance with patents granted to Philip Lichtman.*

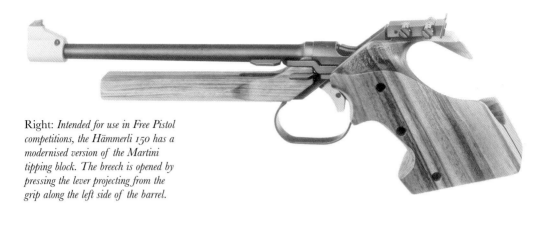

Right: *Intended for use in Free Pistol competitions, the Hämmerli 150 has a modernised version of the Martini tipping block. The breech is opened by pressing the lever projecting from the grip along the left side of the barrel.*

Left: *Developed in Britain in the 1970s, the Victory Arms MC-5 readily accepted changes in calibre, but never found widespread acceptance.*

Right: *The Walther M99 typifies the trend towards synthetic and alloy construction. Particular attention is now paid to 'human engineering' to improve handling qualities.*

marks of Bavarian Army corps or clothing depots. The only other pistol regularly used by the Austrian Army appears to have been the 1909-model 7.65mm pocket pistol made by Steyr under licence from the Belgian Pieper company.

The Bulgarians, allied with the Central Powers, had acquired 10,000 Parabellums shortly before the war began, differing from the Pistole 1908 only in markings and the provision of a lanyard ring on the butt-heel; Romania had small quantities of the 1911-model Austrian Steyr; and Turkey had 1903-model FN-Browning blowbacks. Each also had supplies of earlier weapons, usually Gasser- or Smith & Wesson-type revolvers and Mauser C/96 pistols.

## Handguns: The Allies

After protracted experimentation with a variety of handguns, including the 1905-type Colt-Browning, the British Royal Navy adopted the Webley 'Pistol, Self Loading, .455 Mark I' (or 'Mark I N') in 1913. The Mark I was the culmination of a series of large-calibre guns developed by William Whiting from 1903 onward.[12] Its action was locked by a barrel lug engaging a corresponding recess in the slide-top. When the gun fired, recoil forced diagonal ribs on the side of the barrel block downwards in grooves cut in the frame side, disengaging the locking lug and allowing the slide to reciprocate. Two locating holes in the magazine back uniquely allowed the entire magazine to be held in reserve while the action was operated as a single loader.

Though Whiting's locking system proved to be sturdy and efficient when clean, it was easily jammed by mud. As the gun was also quite heavy – 2lb 8oz empty – and the grip was much too square to the bore to assist snap-shooting, the Webley autoloader was soon relegated to subsidiary duties. A modification of the original Navy Mark I with a drum-pattern back sight, an auxiliary hammer lock and a shoulder stock was authorised for the Royal Flying Corps in 1915 ('Mark I No. 2'), but was retired as soon as aircraft machine-guns became commonplace.

The standard British Army handgun in August 1914 was a revolver, the six-chambered .455-calibre Webley 'Pistol' Mk IV that had been adopted in 1899. Though longer barrels are occasionally encountered on officers' guns, the regulation length was 4 inches; the bird's-head butt had been inherited from the preceding Mark III, but the revolver was otherwise a standard break-open pattern with an efficient auto-extracting system. Complaints were received from the trenches that the Webley was difficult to grasp with muddied hands. In May 1915, therefore, the Mark VI appeared with a 6-inch barrel and an angular grip with a pronounced hump behind the hammer. The lengthened barrel is believed to have been intended to increase the sight radius and hence improve the accuracy of shooting among subalterns fresh from the playing fields of England.

---

12. Beginning with British Patent 19032/1903, Whiting received several patents protecting locked-breech operating systems – including British 3820/1904, 17856/1904 and 25028/1904, and US 803948 (1905), 804694 (1905) and 939882 (1909).

The Webley was the best combat revolver issued during the First World War: it was strong, incorporated a latch preventing the hammer reaching the chambered round unless the breech was properly shut, and had particularly rapid extraction/ejection. The ease with which the Webley could be replenished occupied the thoughts of many inventors, the one tangible result being the introduction of Prideaux's Instantaneous Revolver Magazine in 1915. The Webley was also the only military revolver to be fitted with a bayonet, patented by Lieutenant Arthur Pritchard in 1915 and made by W. W. Greener from the blades of old French Gras sword bayonets.

The output of Webley Mark VI revolvers was prodigious, the initial government contract asking for 2,500 guns per week for the duration of the war. But even this was insufficient, and the War Office, in desperation, acquired as many .455-chambered Colt and Smith & Wesson revolvers as possible, together with some .455 Colt Government Model semi-automatic pistols (*see below*).

Among the most numerous, and most impressive of the purchases were the 'New Century' Smith & Wessons. Introduced in 1908, these were distinguished by a third locking point in the form of a latch in the cylinder lock to reinforce the usual breech-face and barrel-lug locking points. Often known as the 'Triple Lock', the guns also had a shrouded ejector rod beneath the barrel. They were big, strong, and beautifully made; but this combination came at a price, as the New Century required very precise assembly for everything to lock together smoothly. Consequently, only 15,375 were made for the commercial market in a variety of chamberings, and another 5,000 were supplied to Britain early in the First World War. These had 6.4-inch barrels chambering the .455 (Webley revolver) service cartridge, blue finish, and War Department 'Broad Arrow' property marks. The original Triple Lock version of the New Century was then superseded by a simpler form, lacking both the auxiliary locking latch and the ejector-rod shroud. This modification is believed to have been undertaken at British request, to accelerate deliveries, as most of the 69,800 revolvers made in 1915–17 went to Britain in .455-calibre. Production continued after the fighting had ceased, and revolvers of this pattern were still being offered commercially as late as 1937.

Large numbers of .455 Smith & Wesson-type top-break revolvers – 'Pistol, Old Pattern with 5-inch Barrel', No. 1 and No. 2 Mark I' – were ordered from Garate, Anitua y Cia and Trocaola, Aranzabal y Cia of Eibar, Spain, and issued with effect from 8 November 1915. The Garate y Anitua revolver (No. 1 Mark I) has 'GAC' monograms on the side of the frame beneath the hammer and on the bakelite grips, the grips are squared off above the protruding bird's-head pommel, and the back of the trigger guard tends to be squared; the Trocaola y Aranzabal guns (No. 2 Mark I), conversely, have 'TAC' monograms on the frame, their chequered bird's-head grips extend to the base of the butt, and the trigger-guard backs are almost always rounded.

Very few of the Spanish-made guns saw combat; indeed, there is some evidence to suggest that they were inappropriate for their purpose. Lt.-Col. Robert Wilson, in his book *Automatic Pistols* (1943), stated – after a diatribe against Spanish guns in general –

that: 'All Spanish arms were withdrawn from the British Service as unreliable and dangerous in 1917.' If true, they must have been withdrawn to store: both revolver patterns were not declared obsolete until October 1921, when it is assumed that survivors were either scrapped or sold at auction.

When the First World War began, the Spanish gunmaking industry encountered a crisis as the commercial markets on which it depended, particularly in Europe, collapsed. Sales of what would now be called 'back-up guns' were made to individual soldiers, particularly in France (where the issue of handguns was inadequate), but the quantities did not initially make up for the loss of commercial sales. But salvation was at hand. The First World War did not end at Christmas 1914, as had been widely predicted; instead, the slaughter of thousands of men and the loss of thousands of guns continued to gain momentum. Individual governments reacted to the loss of weapons by accelerating production in the state-owned ordnance factories, by enlarging production facilities or building new ones; by impressing captured equipment; and, particularly in the case of Britain, ordering small-arms from the USA, initially uncommitted to the war but with unrivalled production capacity. None of this would have had much effect on Spanish gunmaking, had it not been for France.

The French Army suffered terrible casualties during the First World War and the losses of equipment were similarly prodigious. But France had the weakest manufacturing base of the major participants, excepting Russia, and lacked the ability to make guns in huge quantities; the capacity of the ordnance factories was limited and the gunmaking centre of Saint-Étienne, relying largely on handwork, was not geared to mass production.

The desperate need for personal-defence weapons persuaded the French authorities to turn to the Spanish gunmakers. This was made easier by the strong links between the Basques in southern France and those in Spain, many of whom scarcely recognised the Franco-Spanish border that they believed to split their homeland. There were family ties between the gunmakers of Hendaye on one side and Eibar on the other, and it was natural that the groups would band together. There had been little real difference between the pocket pistols made in France and Spain prior to the war, except that the French examples (which were often imported from Spain 'in the white') had to undergo mandatory proof.

The French government commission initially selected 8mm Lebel copies of the solid-frame Smith & Wesson revolver, but these could not be made quickly enough to restore losses. A solution was then found in the form of the inexpensive blowbacks adapted from the early FN-Brownings. A large quantity of 'Star'-brand pistols was purchased from Bonifacio Echeverria y Cia of Eibar, and a contract for militarised versions of the 'Ruby' – initially calling for 10,000 pistols monthly – was given to Gabilondo y Urresti of Guernica. The 'Ruby' was a 7.65mm-calibre enlargement of the original FN-Browning pocket pistol with an eight-round box magazine in the butt. A lanyard ring was added to the right side of the butt heel, and the grips were wood instead of moulded rubber. Losses continued to exceed supplies, and so the Gabilondo y Urresti contract was tripled to 30,000 guns monthly. As this was far more than the Guernica facilities could handle, Gabilondo y Urresti recruited five additional gunmaking businesses as prime sub-contractors: SA Alkartasuna, Fábrica de Armas, of Guernica; Beistegui Hermanos of Eibar; Eceolaza y Vicinai of Eibar; Hijos de Angel Echeverria of Eibar; and Bruno Salaverria y Cia of Eibar. By the end of 1918, at least 200,000 pistols had been made and at least eleven more gunmaking businesses had been recruited to supply parts.

The 7.65mm Ruby pistols made by the best of the sub-contractors worked adequately, but the worst of them were truly terrible. After the end of World War I, the newly-formed armies of Finland and the Kingdom of Serbs, Croats and Slovenes (later 'Yugoslavia') inherited many of the survivors of French issue.

In 1914, the Russian Army had been content with the fascinating obr. 1895g revolver ('Nagant Gas-seal'). This had been supplemented prior to 1910 by small numbers of 1903-model FN-Brownings and even a few New Model Parabellums, though the pistols appear to have been reserved for officers, police and internal security units. Many Mauser C/96 pistols had also been acquired by officers. Apart from accelerating production of obr. 1895g revolvers in the Tula factory, and rehabilitating surviving Smith & Wesson-type guns (made by Smith & Wesson, Loewe and Tula), the Russians did very little: small numbers of .45 Colt semi-automatics were acquired in 1916–17, along with some Ruby blowbacks diverted from France, but there is no evidence of mass purchasing. The Russian soldiery simply went without handguns.

The Italians had adopted the Mo. 910 or 'Glisenti' pistol shortly before the war began, and had been steadily supplementing the existing Mo. 1889 ('Bodeo') revolvers. Issue appears to have been to officers and NCOs, leaving the revolvers to the rank and file. Promoted at different times by Società Siderugica Glisenti and Metallurgica Bresciana gia Temprini (which also made the 'Brixia' derivative for commercial sale), the Mo. 910 had a dangerous superficial affinity with the Parabellum.[13] However, its reciprocating bolt was locked by a comparatively weak strut and, as the frame was particularly weak on one side of the magazine well, the 9mm Mo. 910 cartridge was appreciably weaker than the 9mm Parabellum. Unfortunately, the two cartridges were dimensionally identical: the German cartridge could easily be fired in the Glisenti, soon straining it irreparably.

The Italians rapidly discovered that supplies of Glisenti pistols and Bodeo revolvers could neither equip the conscript armies nor cope with the tremendous losses. Large numbers of Ruby-type 7.65mm blowbacks were purchased in Spain in 1915–16. However, the Italians appear to have been more discerning than the French and encouraged the indigenous gunmaking industry to provide alternatives. This inspired

---

13. There is still some argument over the precise origins of the Glisenti. Some have seen the work of the Swiss designers Haussler & Roch in its construction. In addition, though the British patent was granted to the Glisenti company, the US patent (which is sometimes a more accurate reflection of invention) names Alessandro Provaglio of Carcino, 'assignor to Metallurgica Bresciana Gia Tempini'. The patent, No. 985632 of 28 February 1911, had been sought as early as April 1906.

Beretta, never previously regarded as a mass-producer of handguns, to develop an efficient little 7.65mm blowback pistol as the 'Mo. 915' (or 'Mo. 15'). Ordered into immediate mass production, this was to provide the basis of Beretta's subsequent dominance of the Italian pistol market.

Among the minor allies, Belgium had had a selection of sturdy solid-frame Nagant revolvers, alongside the FN-Browning blowback pistol models of 1900 and 1903. Most of these, however, were seized by the Germans after the invasion of Belgium in 1914; the remnants of the Belgian Army engaged on the Western Front carried British or French handguns.

When the United States of America was finally drawn into World War I in 1917, the standard handgun was the .45 Colt M1911 semi-automatic pistol – undoubtedly the best of its type to see service prior to 1918 and destined to emerge with its reputation unsullied at the Armistice. Colt's Patent Fire Arms Mfg Co. had always been keen to market guns in Europe, where the Browning-patent blowbacks made in Belgium by Fabrique Nationale were selling particularly well. A meeting between representatives of Colt and FN was convened in 1910, but does not seem to have had lasting results; the FN management was understandably keen to resist promoting the .45 M1911 Colt-Browning, as this would undoubtedly reduce sales of the cheaper but less powerful 9mm M1903 FN-Browning. Consequently, the European sales of the Colt-Brownings were handled by agencies such as Amerikanische Waffen- u. Munitionsfabrik of Hamburg (until 1912) and the London Armoury Co. Ltd (after Colt relinquished its London warehouse in 1913). LAC was the official distributor for the British Empire, but it seems that Colt undertook its own representation in continental Europe in years immediately prior to the First World War. These brought successes such as the sale of 10,000 Army Special revolvers to Greece – an order subsequently increased to 50,000 when the fighting brought an end to deliveries of Bergmann-Bayard pistols from Belgium – and the adoption of the M1911 in Norway.

On 15 January 1915, the British Government appointed J. P. Morgan & Company of New York as official purchasing agents, a relationship that lasted until the USA entered the war in April 1917. The acquisitions included a substantial number of M1911 Colt-Brownings.

Between August 1914 and April 1919, Colt managed to export more than 70,000 of these pistols, often taken from regular commercial production and numbered in the same ranges. Canada acquired 4,900 in late 1914; France took 5,000 in December 1915 and January 1916.[14] By far the largest purchases were made by Tsarist Russia, which took 47,100 from February 1916 to January 1917. These had 'C'-prefix serial numbers in the 23,000–80,000 range, and had the Cyrillic АНГЛ ЗАКАЗ. on the right side of the frame. The British government was the next most important purchaser. The earliest guns, a little more than 5,000 with 'C' prefix numbers, were taken at random from commercial

---

14. Five hundred additional M1911 pistols were sent to France in December 1917 from Springfield Armory production.

production and chambered the .45 ACP service cartridge. About 600 guns were then supplied by way of the London Armoury Company, with 'W'-prefix numbers but chambered for the 'Cartridge, Pistol, Self-Loading, Webley, .455-inch Mark I' that had been adopted by the Admiralty in 1912.[15] They were then followed by substantial quantities of similar guns acquired directly through J. P. Morgan. British Colt-Brownings had the standard maker's mark, patent claims and Rampant Colt logo on the left side of the slide, with COLT AUTOMATIC over CALIBRE 455 on the right side of the slide and GOVERNMENT MODEL on the right side of the frame above serial numbers such as W107755.

Colt ledgers show the dispatch of 200 guns to the London Armoury Company in July 1915, mostly numbered in the W19001–W19200 group, and another 400 in January 1916 (W29001–W29444 with gaps). Orders subsequently placed by the War Offfice (and, later, the Ministry of Munitions), included one for 500 guns in May 1916 and another for 1,900 guns and 4,000 spare magazines in June 1916. A total of about 1,700 pistols numbered between W40500 and W97000 had been supplied in accordance with the latter order by April 1917. At this point, administration of contracts passed from the War Office to the Ministry of Munitions. By September 1917, the British were complaining that Colt's Patent Fire Arms Mfg Co. was unduly favouring the US Army and had cut supplies to Europe; it took the intervention of General Crozier, the Chief of Ordnance, to ensure that supplies recommenced. An order placed in November 1917 for 5,000 guns and 15,000 spare magazines was completed in November 1918, and a second placed in May 1918, for 10,000 guns and 30,000 additional magazines was terminated in April 1919 after 5,000 pistols and 24,000 magazines had been shipped to Britain.

In addition to the marks on the slide and the frame, Colt-Brownings supplied in accordance with official military contracts bore the broad arrow, inspector's marks, and the 'crossed pennants' indicating that they had passed military proof. Many survived to serve in the Second World War – see Chapter 8.

The US Ordnance Department soon discovered that having sufficient handguns for the regular forces was not the same thing as being able to equip a rapidly mobilising reserve, or to account for losses during even a month's combat. In April 1917, fewer than 75,000 M1911 pistols – made by Colt and Springfield Armory – were on issue or in store, representing a tenth of the requirement.

Mindful of the huge demands being made on Colt, which was still only satisfying a quarter of the demand by the summer of 1917, the Secretary of the Army not only placed new contracts for 2.55 million M1911 pistols with Remington, Savage and Winchester, but also recruited several precision-engineering companies with no gunmaking experience: among them, the National Cash Register Company of Dayton, Ohio, made cash registers and comptometers, whereas the Lanston Monotype Company of Philadelphia, Pennsylvania, made type-casting machinery.

---

15. It was renamed 'Cartridge, Pistol, Self-Loading, .455-inch Mark I' in 1916. The Mark Iz was similar, but had a load of nitrocellulose propellant instead of cordite.

By the Armistice, only Remington had delivered guns (13,152 of them), though the formerly Ross-owned Dominion Rifle factory in Quebec, renamed the North American Arms Company, may have assembled about a hundred early in 1919. The total number of Colt-Brownings on hand on 11 November 1918 amounted to 643,755 against a predicted requirement for about 2.8 million by 1 January 1919!

The US Government also contracted with Colt and Smith & Wesson for revolvers chambering the standard rimless .45 pistol cartridge, which would drop through Colt chambers and stop in some Smith & Wessons only against a shallow ring on which the case mouth could seal. Neither type of extractor could work with rimless cases, which not only prevented existing revolvers being taken into service but also required the production line to be halted (at a critical time) while changes were made. Before remedial work could begin, however, Joseph Wesson designed the so-called 'Half-moon Clip': a spring-steel clip or plate, retaining three rounds by slipping into the ejector groove, which not only held the cartridges in the chambers but also allowed the extractors to grip satisfactorily. The Colt New Service and the Smith & Wesson .44 Hand Ejector ('New Century') revolvers were adapted simply by shortening the back of the cylinder to accommodate the width of the clips; 151,700 highly efficient Colts and 153,311 Smith & Wessons were officially purchased between 6 April 1917 and the end of 1918, being known collectively as the 'Model of 1917'.

When the USA entered the First World War, the Navy worried, with justification, not only that the Army would have first call on deliveries of the M1911 Colt-Browning but also that sufficient handguns would be difficult to obtain. Consequently, trials were undertaken with several other .45-calibre pistols. These included the recoil-operated Hammond, tested in the summer of 1917, and the elegant Pedersen-designed hesitation blowback that was to be made by Remington–UMC.

Designed by Grant Hammond of New Haven, Connecticut, and apparently made by either Harrington & Richardson or what was to become the High Standard Mfg Co., the .45 Hammond was a large gun with a slender 6.75-inch barrel protruding from the frame, an enclosed bolt, an exposed hammer, and a noticeably raked grip.[16] Though there was a vague external affinity with the Parabellum, the mechanism was locked by a single cam-shape lug on the frame engaging a vertical spring-loaded plunger in the bolt. This was a comparatively weak design, but the pistol proved to handle very well and shot accurately owing partly to the length of the barrel and partly to the linear recoil. The most unorthodox feature was the automatic ejection of an empty magazine, but the Hammond was deemed to be inferior to the M1911 and the project foundered.

The gun submitted by John Pedersen of Jackson, Wyoming, was altogether different. Pedersen was an experienced rifle designer – particularly for Remington – and is now

---

16. Surviving guns are generally marked by the 'Grant Hammond Mfg. Corp., New Haven, Conn., U.S.A.' and refer to a patent granted on 4 May 1915 ('other patents pending'). The finalised Grant Hammond pistol patent, US No. 1363040, was not granted until 21 December 1921; however, the application had been filed on 1 November 1917. The '4 May 1915' date refers to an earlier patent, 1138379, sought on 3 February 1914 to protect a simplified pistol.

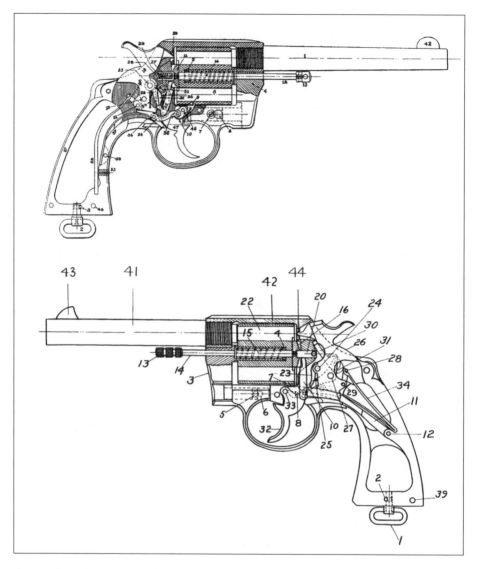

*A comparison of the Colt New Model Army Revolver (M1894, top) and the Colt New Service Revolver (M1909, bottom). The drawings are taken from the US Army military handbooks.*

generally renowned as the most brilliant production engineer among the best-known gun designers. Protected by US Patent 1348733,[17] the pistol embodied a 'momentum block system', delayed-blowback, relying on the interaction of carefully shaped surfaces

---

17. Pedersen proved himself capable of designing many of the fixtures, gauges and tools required to make his guns, and his patents often reflect this meticulous approach. The master patent for the pistol contains an almost unbelievable 122 pages – including nineteen pages of detailed drawings. Granted on 3 August 1920, it had originally been sought on 30 July 1915 and then again on 17 July 1917.

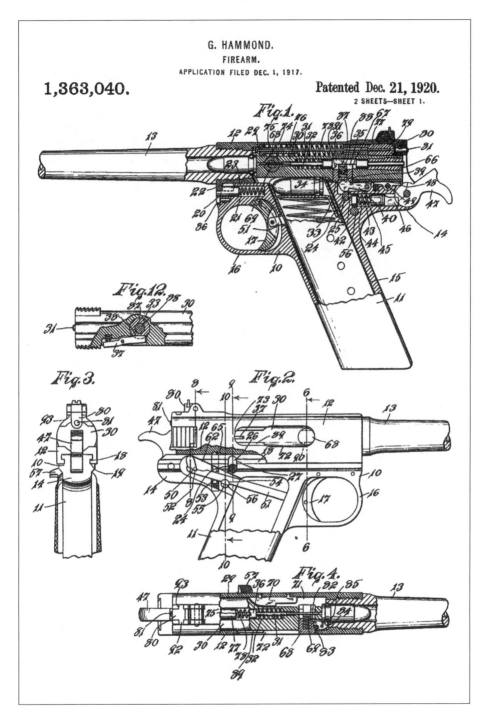

*A sheet of drawings from US Patent 1363040 of 21 December 1920, granted to protect the pistol designed by Grant Hammond.*

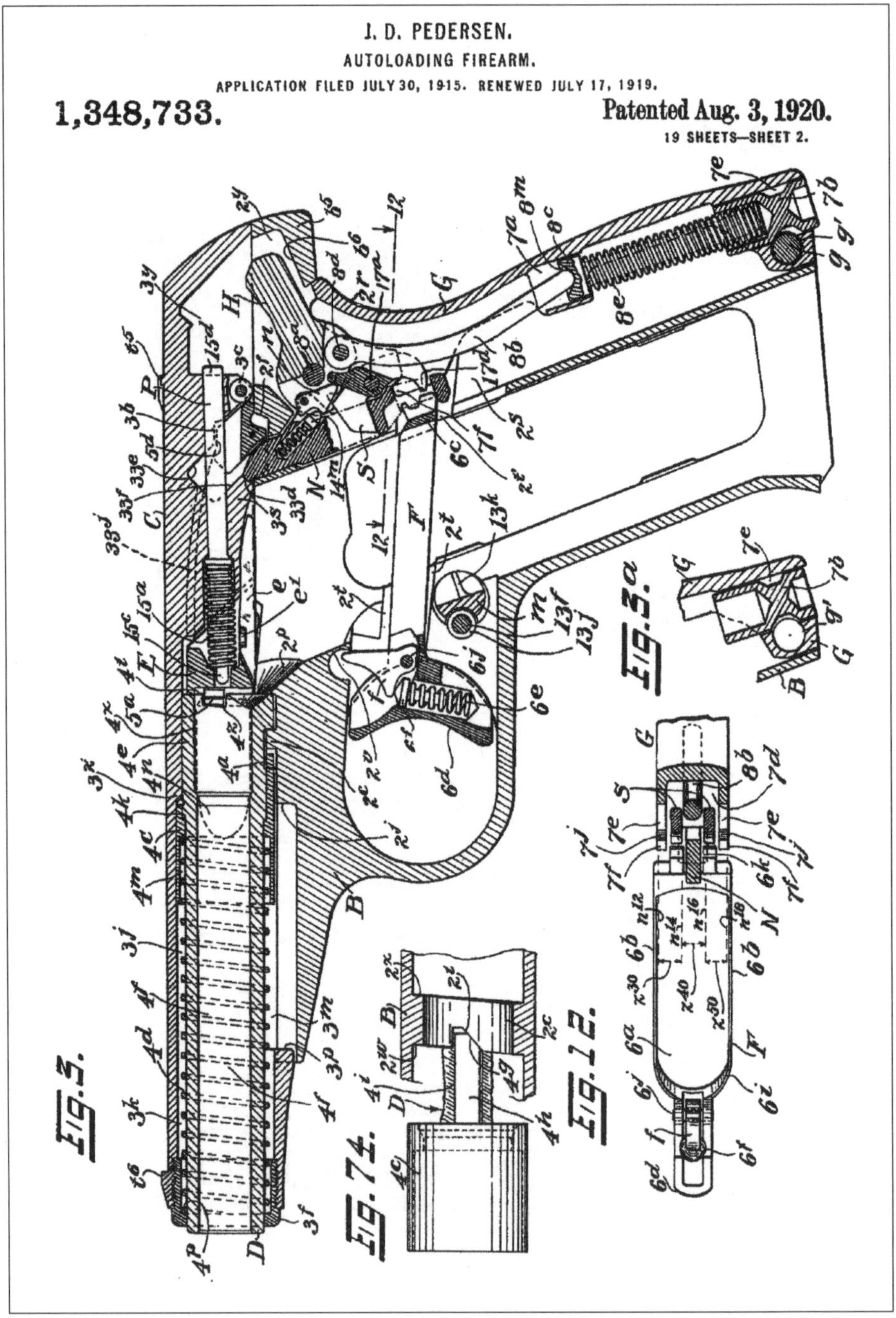
J. D. PEDERSEN.
AUTOLOADING FIREARM.
APPLICATION FILED JULY 30, 1915. RENEWED JULY 17, 1919.
1,348,733.
Patented Aug. 3, 1920.
19 SHEETS—SHEET 2.

*John Pedersen was one of the most gifted firearms designers of the twentieth century. This drawing is taken from US Patent 1348733, granted on 3 August 1920 to protect what became the Remington Model 51.*

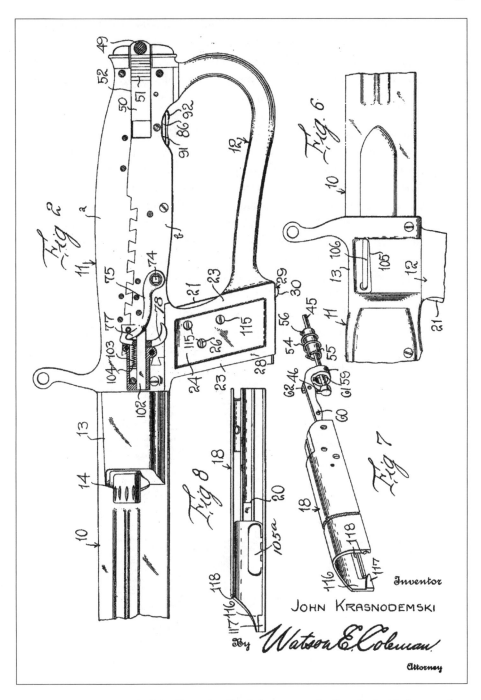

*The sword-pistol patented by John Krasnodemski relied on an auto-loading pistol with the magazine incorporated in the knuckle bow. Just one of many aberrant ideas originating in the First World War, it was never made in quantity.*

in the multi-part bolt to delay the opening of the breech until the chamber pressure had dropped to a safe level. The slide and the lightweight breech block move back about 0.08-inch (2mm) when the gun fires, until the block is stopped by a shoulder or transom in the frame and the slide continues to move to the rear. Shortly afterward, a ramp inside the slide lifted the breech block from engagement with the transom and the parts ran back together.

The system proved to operate with surprising ease and, though the war ended before the US Navy could standardise the Remington-Pedersen as the preferred substitute for the M1911 Colt-Browning, the basic design went on to become the Remington Model 51 pocket/personal-defence pistol – and encouraged Pedersen to produce the toggle-lock rifles that came close to persuading the Army to adopt them.

The ferocity of trench-fighting encouraged the development of many unorthodox weapons, from reintroductions of the Welsh Knife – a short sword of medieval origins – to a bayonet for the Webley revolver. It was only to be expected that the idea of combining different types of weapons would reappear, as it had done during virtually every major conflict fought since the Middle Ages. Typical of the designs produced by well-meaning, often well-educated inventors whose experience of combat conditions was non-existent was the pistol-sword patented by John Krasnodemski of Wausau, Wisconsin, in August 1917 (US No. 1238527), which had the action of a striker-fired automatic pistol within the sword hilt and a magazine forming part of the knuckle bow.

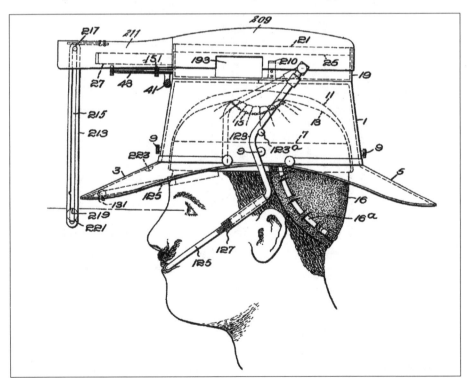

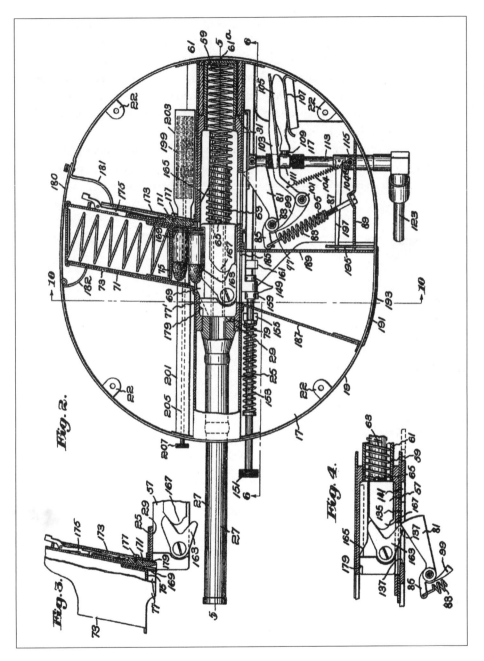

*Patented on 2 December 1919 by Albert Pratt, the 'Hat Gun' (left) would have been an eccentric addition to a soldier's arsenal. The gun in the helmet was fired by a pressure tube in the firer's mouth. From US Patent 1323609. The cross-section of the Pratt Hat Gun (above) shows that the gun was an auto-loading repeater. It would have been heavy enough to have had an unbalancing effect on the head – even ignoring the effects of recoil.*

Even more bizarre was the 'hat gun' of Albert Pratt of Lyndon, Vermont, protected by US Patents 1183492 and 1323609.[18] The perfected design had a large-calibre automatic pistol in a high-crown broad-brimmed hat, feeding laterally from a magazine in the right side, ejecting to the left, and fired by a 'mouth trigger' – a blow-tube leading up above the firer's left ear. The sight dangled down from the gun-muzzle shroud when needed. The idea was obviously totally impractical, yet the Pratt hat gun could probably have been used, without the auxiliary sight, simply by 'aiming' the head at a target. It is interesting to speculate if such an idea could be translated into reality with modern technology; it is even possible to see in it the genesis of the type of head-up display that can incorporate a gun sight operating on the look-and-shoot principle…

---

18. US Patent 1183492 was sought in and granted on 16 May 1916; US Patent 1323609 was sought in May 1916 and granted in December 1919.

# 7
## *Between the Wars*

When the First World War ended at 11.00 a.m. on 11 November 1918, a fantastic quantity of weapons became superfluous. Attempts were made to cancel contracts that had been let 'for the duration' and decline delivery of the thousands of guns that were arriving daily at the inspection points. Another major problem was provided by the collection and disposal of equipment taken from the German and Austro-Hungarian Armies after the collapse of their imperial regimes.

Many people hailed the end of the 'war to end all wars', welcoming the League of Nations as a first step to universal disarmament and lasting global peace. How wrong they were to be proved! The fragmentation of the empires allowed ethnic groups to seize control of their own affairs, and self-governance led to the creation of new states from the old. However, the widespread desire for autonomy was inevitably accompanied by new tensions. The situation soon became effectively a new powder-keg.

Germany had lost Alsace and Lorraine (Elsass-Löthringen) to France in the west, and, in the east, Silesia (Schlesien) and parts of Prussia had become part of newly-emergent Poland – which had mostly been a Russian province. A socialist revolution briefly threatened to pull Bavaria away from the Reich, but was ruthlessly crushed by right-wing forces and the establishment of the Weimar Republic gave a veneer of unity.

The population of Austria-Hungary had never been as homogeneous as that of Germany: Austria and Hungary immediately declared independence, the Czechs and the Slovaks united to form a new state, but the most radical changes occurred in the Balkans. Some Austrian territory was ceded to Italy, and the 'Kingdom of Croats, Serbs and Slovenes' (known after 1929 as Yugoslavia) was formed from the south-eastern extremities of old Habsburg dominions and the independent state of Serbia. The Russians had lost control of Finland and Poland; and three new states, Estonia, Latvia and Lithuania, carved themselves out of the part of European Russia that had fringed the Baltic.

No self-respecting authority could exist without police and armed forces, and all of the new states immediately set about arming themselves. Initially, this was often achieved simply by seizing weapons that were in store: the Finns, for example, gained large numbers of ex-Russian Mosin-Nagant rifles, Maxim machine-guns and Nagant revolvers from the old tsarist arsenal in Helsinki.

Poland used a collection of ex-Russian and ex-German stores, reflecting the country's geographical position; the Serbs, Croats and Slovenes relied on ex-Serbian Mauser rifles and ex-Austro-Hungarian Mannlichers. Many of the emergent nations, however, were determined to make guns of their own. This was partly due to national pride, but also to the desire to avoid dependence on external supplies that could be cut in time of war.

Poland inherited the Mauser rifle-making machinery that had been in the former state-owned German manufactory in Danzig (Gdansk), and then built a new factory in Radom. Czechoslovakia included Bohemia, a fertile source of gunmaking expertise since the sixteenth century, and had soon installed machinery in Brno to make Mauser rifles. The Kingdom of Serbs, Croats and Slovenes bought an entire Mauser rifle-making production line from Fabrique Nationale, installing it in Kragujevač.

## Fabrique Nationale and the Brownings

Handguns were generally accorded low priority, but the Czechoslovaks and, later, the Poles developed designs of their own. The Serbs, Croats and Slovenes preferred to rely on Fabrique Nationale for their pistols, which included the FN-Browning Mle 10/22. This was a minor variant of the Mle 1910, with a longer barrel and an extended grip, designed in response to an order for 60,000 9mm Short pistols (and 6 million suitable cartridges) placed with FN by the government 'du royaume des Serbes, Croates et Slovenes' on 23 February 1923.

The size of the 1923 order was insufficient to justify developing an entirely new design, forcing Fabrique Nationale's Bureau d'Études (Design Office) to meet the contract criteria in an ingenious way. The barrel of the Mle 1910 personal-defence pistol was lengthened and its slide was extended by a light sheet-steel shroud, attached to the muzzle with a bayonet joint and locked by a sliding spring-loaded catch on the lower left side of the slide/extension joint. The butt was lengthened to accommodate a longer magazine, a blade-type front sight was attached to the slide extension, a standing 'V'-notch open back sight was added to the rear of the slide, and there was a lanyard ring on the bottom left side of the butt.

The contract for the Serbs, Croats and Slovenes was fulfilled by 1925, and orders were subsequently obtained from the Royal Netherlands Army in about 1926–8 and what had by then become Yugoslavia in the early 1930s. The FN-Brownings were issued in the Netherlands as 'M25 No. 2' pistols. The FN company history notes that the second Yugoslav and the Dutch orders totalled 40,000 guns. The Mle 10/22 pistol was also marketed commercially in 7.65mm Auto and 9mm Short chamberings; several hundred thousand were made, and production continued under German control after the invasion of Belgium in 1940 – until the Allies reoccupied the Herstal factory in September 1944. Belgian production recommenced in the 1950s, but finally ceased in about 1959.

The earliest Mle 10/22 pistols had slides with the old-style serifed inscription FABRIQUE NATIONALE D'ARMES de GUERRE HERSTAL BELGIQUE over BROWNING'S PATENT DEPOSE on the left side. The old Liége proof marks were to be found on the mid-point of the left side of the slide and frame, and sometimes on the side of barrel above the serial number and calibre designation CAL 7$^{M}$/$_{M}$65 OR CAL 9$^{M}$/$_{M}$. However, the smaller-calibre mark seems to have been used very rarely; unmarked 7.65mm guns seem to have been the rule rather than the exception. Factory inspectors' marks, such as an encircled 'FN' over M, were to be found on parts such as the trigger-guard bow. The master serial number initially appeared on the right side of the frame above the trigger and was repeated in full on the right side of the barrel shroud, inside the upper rear of the slide, and often on the right side of the barrel above the calibre mark. Consequently, the serial number and the calibre designation were usually visible through the ejection port. Pistols made after the early 1930s bore a revised sans-serif inscription FABRIQUE NATIONALE D'ARMES DE GUERRE-HERSTAL-BELGIQUE over the usual patent mark; though it occupied much the same width as its serifed predecessor, the space between the words PATENT and DEPOSE was eliminated. The pistols made for Yugoslavia bore the standard FN marks and Belgian proofs, but the majority of those examined bore Cyrillic markings on the right side of the receiver. These, which included a repetition of the master serial number, usually translate as 'Officers' or 'State Troops', but one has also been seen with the marks of the Split police department.

It has been suggested that the first 60,000 pistols sent to the Yugoslavs – apparently numbered from 1 – were made with special grips, though those examined, their numbers ranging from 5,118 to 49,356, all had the standard FN monogram pattern. However, pistol 62,420, pictured by Smith & Smith in *Small Arms of the World*, does have grips displaying three encircled pictograms: from top to bottom, a double-headed eagle from the Serbian coat-of-arms, a crown and a 'wild man' carrying a club. Unfortunately, no other examples of this grip have yet been reported; it seems plausible that a few thousand guns could have been so altered for élite units, though the slide markings on the 'Smith' gun are standard. But it seems from the photograph that the frame number does not match the slide number, which in turn differs from those on the barrel and muzzle extension. Consequently, the grips may not have been made by FN, but instead have been added in Yugoslavia.

The second Yugoslav contract consisted of standard FN guns in the low 200,000s (for example 227,033 and 231,260), all of which had standard FN monogram grips. Pistol number 227,048 was a standard commercial gun, suggesting that they were supplied at random from commercial production. The marks 'FN' encircled and 'S' appeared on the trigger guards, in addition to other inspectors' marks.

The pistols acquired by the Koninklijke Nederlanse Leger during the 1920s and 1930s bore standard FN marks and Belgian proofs. Most also acquired a large crowned 'W' cypher of the queen of the Netherlands, Wilhelmina, on the slide or frame.

Browning & Gentry, in *John Browning: American Gunmaker*, state that 396,865 Mle 10/22 pistols had been made by 1961, but this clearly excludes the several hundreds of thousands made under German supervision during the Second World War (*see Chapter 8*).

## The Pistol in Japan

The Japanese armed forces had played little part in the First World War, though the inactivity after the capture of Tsingtao (Qingdao) early in the fighting allowed large numbers of rifles to be sold to the Allies – in particular, Britain and Russia. This largesse did not extend to pistols, as supplies were comparatively low. The Japanese relied on the Meiji 26th Year revolver, a break-open design dating from 1893, and officers were still keener on the sword than the gun. However, attempts had been made to introduce the *Ko-gata* Nambu self-loading pistol prior to 1914. The original Nambu was regarded as too complicated to be mass-produced sufficiently cheaply and development of a new design had already begun when the great earthquake of 1923 destroyed a large part of Tokyo and disrupted production.

A new pistol was developed in Tokyo arsenal by a military commission headed by Kijiro Nambu, by then ranking as a general. The result was the introduction to the Army in 1925 of the Taisho 14th year Type Pistol (*Tai-sho ju-yon nenshiki kenju*): 1925 was the fourteenth year of the Taisho *nengō*, or reign-period. The Imperial Navy delayed adoption of the new pistol until 1927.

The committee simplified the mechanism of the original Nambu, but as the Japanese lacked experience of handgun design, the 14th Year Type pistol was unnecessarily complicated and only moderately efficient, though the design of the 14th Year Type parts permitted quicker and easier production, since fine manufacturing tolerances were no longer necessary. The Nambu frame was simplified so that it bridges the receiver only at the rear, where it supports the V-notch back sight; and the asymmetrical bolt-return-spring chamber was eliminated. The sides of the 14th Year Type receiver are flat. The barrel and receiver, forged and machined in a single piece as those of the old Nambu had been, reflected the continuing influence of the Mauser C/96 pistols acquired prior to the Russo-Japanese War of 1904–5.

The 14th Year Type barrel and receiver run back within the frame until their travel is stopped by a vertical blade on the trigger sub-group, whereupon the bolt separates from the propped-up locking block and continues backwards within the receiver. Coil springs lie on each side of the bolt in specially machined channels, to control recoil and the bolt-return stroke by bearing against lugs on the frame. The springs work efficiently despite the lack of guides or pins, as they are supported by the bolt-body and the walls of the receiver. The shape and machining of the locking piece have been greatly revised, though it remains a separate propped-up block beneath the rear of the receiver (where it engages a recess in the bolt). However, the circular transverse tip of the locking-piece shaft passes between the sides of the bifurcated receiver block, unlike the original Nambu in which a hollow locking unit engages a solid receiver block.

The tail of the striker protrudes below the bolt instead of from the left side, and the sear and disconnector system was altered. A lug on the trigger – replacing the spring-loaded disconnector plunger on the tip of the Nambu sear bar – acts in conjunction with the receiver stop-lug to prevent the trigger meshing with the sear until the breech has been reloaded and the trigger has been released. The spring-loaded sear consists of a simple bar with its tip bent through 90 degrees to pass under the bolt and engage the striker, and is raised by a step on the tail of the trigger. It gives a light pull, lighter than even the original Nambu, although some inherent 'creep' occurs because the sear nose has to move vertically to release the striker.

Unfortunately, no mechanical safety mechanism was built into the trigger unit, and the disconnector only ensures that the trigger and sear bar do not mesh during the reloading cycle. As a result, the striker can be jarred out of engagement with the sear bar by the shock of the bolt hitting the breech face and a loaded gun will fire. This normally happens in guns where the sear-to-striker contact is insufficient.

The grip safety of the *Ko-gata* Nambu that had blocked the trigger until it was squeezed (not always infallibly) was replaced by a multi-purpose lever-operated device on the left side of the frame above the trigger aperture. The pistol can be fired when the lever is pushed upwards and forwards through 180 degrees; rotating the lever backwards locks the barrel/receiver group and prevents the sear moving vertically. Finally, once the left grip has been removed, the lever can be rotated downwards until it can be taken out of the frame completely. The trigger sub-group, locked by the safety lever spindle, is slid downwards and the retraction grip unscrewed from the bolt. The receiver can then be run forward and off the frame.

The safety is efficient and effective, but can only be operated by the fingers of the non-firing hand. Better designs – such as the German Parabellum – can be reached by the thumb of the firing hand without removing the finger from the trigger or unduly disturbing aim. The 14th Year Type also has a magazine safety taking the form of a horizontally pivoted block in the top front of the magazine well. The nose of the block tilts into the well when the magazine is removed, and its tail intercepts the trigger so that the gun cannot fire. The block rotates to disengage the block-tail from the trigger when the magazine is inserted in the feed-way and pushed fully home. The feature is, however, of dubious utility and has attracted many critical reviews.

The 14th Year Type magazine is retained by a spring-loaded transverse catch that lies behind the trigger on the left side of the frame. Guns made after 1940, some months after the introduction of the large or winter trigger-guard, will be found with an auxiliary magazine-retaining spring on the front of the grip. This secures the magazine in addition to the standard cross-bolt. The auxiliary retainer was a good idea in view of the magazine safety and the problems arising from a lost magazine.

Magazines dating later than mid-1940 have a special aperture in the front of the body to retain the cartridge follower in its lowest position; when the magazine needs replenishing, the depressor button is simply pushed down and slightly forward to lock under the notch, disconnecting the follower spring so that cartridges can simply be dropped into the magazine. Should the firer forget to disengage the follower from its retaining notch, however, the gun will not load because the magazine spring is not lifting the cartridge column. The auxiliary magazine-retaining spring pushes through the aperture in the front of the magazine body, reconnecting the feed system if the firer has omitted to do so.

One inexplicably bad feature of the 14th Year Type pistol was the absence of a separate mechanical hold-open. The magazine follower keeps the bolt back after the last round has been chambered, fired and ejected. Others had previously experimented with this system but it was universally agreed to be inefficient. There are two principal disadvantages: pressure from a powerful mainspring often makes it difficult to withdraw the magazine, and the breech closes when the magazine is reloaded so that the slide must be retracted to load the first new cartridge. The former problem is especially notable in the 14th Year Type, whose double mainsprings are often reinforced by an auxiliary magazine spring on the lower front of the grip.

The earliest pistols will be found with bolt-retraction grips consisting of three separate circular milled flanges, small trigger guards, and no auxiliary magazine-retaining springs. Firing instruction appears on the safety lever surround, and the designation *ju-yon nenshiki* (14th Year Type) in kanji characters lies on the left rear of the frame. The serial number may be found on the right rear of the frame, where it is invariably prefixed by the arsenal's trademark, and the frame panel behind the grip bears the date of manufacture – for example '12.7', the seventh month of the twelfth year of the Showa *nengō*, equated to July 1937. The character for the Showa reign-period often appears in conjunction with the date figures. Inspectors' marks may be found on some of the larger parts, notably the frame and the receiver.

The earliest pistols were made of passably good material and were generally well finished; their blueing was often equal to many of the best contemporary Western products. The poor parts-fit, however, generally meant that even major components would rarely interchange and it is evident that appreciable hand finishing, in the early years as well as the last days of the war, was necessary on each gun. Production, judged by Western standards, proceeded at a snail's pace.

The output of 14th Year Type pistols between 1926 and 1937 is difficult to assess, as six sets of marks are found prefixing the serial numbers. The marks of the government-owned arsenals in Tokyo (Koishikawa) and Nagoya (Atsuta) arsenals, and of the initially privately operated Nambu-Seisakusho/Chuo Kogyo factory, are readily identifiable, but the others are not. The key lies in the interpretation of the characters that were widely used to distinguish minor design variations among bombs, fuses, cannon and other military stores.

The Japanese had simply adopted a cyclical serial-numbering system in which blocks of 99,999 units were given a distinguishing prefix in much the same way as the Germans had done with their small-arms. The kana phonetic alphabet provided the basis for the prefix marks, as the simple characters made legible punches. The sequence followed that of the *Iroha* poem, which contains nearly fifty symbols (from 'i' to 'su') without repetition. Only the first two kana characters, 'i' and 'ro' appeared on the pistols, as none of the contractors reached the third and fourth blocks 'ha' and 'ni'.[1] Japanese rifle production was far higher and many more of the kana prefix characters were used as a result.

Initial production was entrusted to the Army arsenals in the Atsuta district of Nagoya and the Koishikawa district of Tokyo, the former completing tooling in 1926 and the latter a year later. The first 14th Year Type pistols were completed in Nagoya-Atsuta in November 1926, and in the Tokyo (Koishikawa) factory, rebuilt after the 1923 earthquake, in May 1928: Frederick E. Leithe's *Japanese Hand Guns* pictures Nagoya-made gun No. 835, dated July 1927, and Tokyo gun No. 886 of August 1928. Production in Tokyo arsenal ceased in 1931, when about 27,000 had been assembled – the destruction caused by the earthquake had been so great that the military authorities had decided to move the arsenal to a new site in Kokura in the summer of 1933. Parts were still being made in Tokyo for the 14th Year pistol as late as 1935, but they were sent to Kokura for assembly.

The history of the Nagoya Army arsenal, which also inspected and accepted the guns made by Nambu-Seisakusho/Chuo Kogyo, is less clear. Manufacture of 14th Year pistols apparently stopped late in 1932 when the production machinery was sold to the Nambu-Seisakusho company[2] and installed in a factory in the Kitatama district of Tokyo. The earliest Nambu-made 14th Year Type pistol examined, No. 8303, dates from January 1934. Production began again in Nagoya arsenal during the Second World War.

### The Czechoslovak Story

In Czechoslovakia, the establishment of a robust arms industry was achieved surprisingly quickly after independence had been gained from the Austro-Hungarian Empire. This was helped by the inclusion of the renowned Škoda works in the new country, and by the rapid creation of a Mauser-rifle production line in Prague and then Brno. Once resources had been allocated to the major priorities, attention turned to pistols.

Two Bohemian designers had already achieved limited success: Josef Nickl had patented a rotating-barrel pistol that had been tested by Waffenfabrik Mauser during the First World War, and Alois Tomiška (1876–1946) had been an early pioneer of double-action firing systems. His patents, originally filed shortly before the First World

---

1. The serial numbers of Japanese pistols, rifles and machine-guns, therefore, should be written as *i*-18734 or *ro*-7757, as it is possible to find three Nagoya-made 14th Year pistols with identical numbers, though one is 2345, one *i*-2345 and the third *ro*-2345.

2. Nambu-Selsakusho factory was renamed Chuo Kogyo Kabushiki Kaisha in 1936, when Nambu merged with Taisei Kogyo KK, and seems to have been the only contractor active between 1933 and 1941.

War, encouraged the production of 'Little Tom' pistols (the anglicised form of Tomiška's name) by Wiener Waffenfabrik. Dating these pistols is still speculative: though they follow the pre-1914 patents in many respects, the proof marks of surviving examples are almost exclusively dated in the 1921–30 period.

The Little Tom was a fixed-barrel blowback with the return spring around the barrel, a safety catch above the trigger, and a double-action lock with an external hammer. The slide design ensured that only the serrated tip of the hammer protruded. Access to the lock-work could be gained simply by sliding open a plate on the right side of the frame, once the slide had been removed. The first guns were marked WIENER WAFFENFABRIK above PATENT on the left side of the slide, with 'Little Tom' on a ribbon moulded into the grips. Guns made after the end of the First World War displayed WIENER WAFFENFABRIK. PATENT. LITTLE TOM. CAL. 7 $^{65M}$/$_M$ (or '6 35$^M$/$_M$') in a single line on the left side of the slide. Exports to North America or the British Empire also often had an additional (.25) or (.32) mark. A 'WWF' monogram lies on a small brass medallion set into the grip.

Tomiška continued to develop handguns, including the 'Fox' for Jihočeská Zbrojovka, and worked as a consultant for Česká Zbrojovka. He also traded independently as a gunsmith for some time; many small blowbacks will be found with his marks. Some Little Tom pistols were made – or perhaps sold – by Tomiška in Czechoslovakia, with slides marked ALOIS TOMISKA – PLZEN – PATENT LITTLE TOM 6.35MM (.25) and an 'AT' monogram on the grip medallion.

The first to be adopted officially by the Czechoslovakian authorities was the Praga, an undistinguished 7.65mm-calibre blowback. Zbrojovka Praga had been formed shortly before the end of the First World War by gunmaker Antonin Novotný, to make a simplified form of the 1910-type FN-Browning for the Austro-Hungarian Army. Hostilities finished before much could be achieved, and Novotný sought to find a market in newly-created Czechoslovakia. The Praga, known to the Army as the 'vz. 21', had vertically ribbed wooden grips and a safety catch on the rear left side of the frame. Unlike the FN-Browning, the prototype had a separate breech-block pinned into the slide, and used the front inner surface of the slide to constrain the main spring instead of a separate bush. A few guns were purchased for evaluation, but their quality was so poor that they were soon discarded by the army; a few were also sold to the police – one has been seen with the marks of the Prague municipal police force – but these, too, were rapidly superseded by sturdier guns. Zbrojovka Praga also offered pistols commercially, with plastic grips bearing PRAGA in a circular cartouche, but sales were so poor that liquidation was concluded in 1926.[3]

The Státní zbrojovka a strojírna v Brně ('State armament and engineering works in Brno') was founded by the Czechoslovak government in November 1918 in a former

---

3. There was also a 6.35mm (.25-calibre) Praga, a minuscule gun with a finger-grip in the front upper surface of the pressed-steel slide. However, this was not a one-hand cocking system: retracting the slide with the finger merely allowed the folding trigger to spring down beneath the frame.

Austro-Hungarian artillery arsenal in Brno-Zábrdovice. At the beginning of February 1919, the trading name was changed to 'Československé Statní Závody na Výrobu Zbraní'[4] and development of a pistol began. The Pistol 'N' was the work of Josef Nickl, an ex-Mauser engineer who had helped to organise production of Mauser rifles in the Brno factory. During the First World War, the management of Waffenfabrik Mauser had granted Nickl the facilities to develop guns which had included a version of the 7.65mm 1910-type Mauser locked by rotating the barrel. Nickl produced an improved design in 1921, with an external hammer instead of a striker, and the Pistol 'N' was officially adopted on 19 July 1922 after successfully overcoming Tomiška and Zbrojovka Praga rivals. About 18,000 guns were subsequently made in Brno.

A lug on each side of the barrel engaged slots in the slide walls, and an additional helical lug under the barrel engaged in a groove in the frame. When the gun fired, the barrel and slide moved backward until the helical lug acted in a groove to rotate the barrel through about 20 degrees. This released the slide lugs and the barrel was brought to a halt, allowing the slide to complete the extraction/reloading cycle. The barrel was driven forward as the slide closed, turning back into engagement with the slide. The Pistol 'N' (vz. 22) was beautifully made, and could easily be identified by the lack of an overhang above the rear of the grip. The bulbous slide had diagonal retracting ribs, and the lock-cover plate on the left side of the frame above the grip was marked '9.mm.N'. above 'Čs. st. zbrojovka, Brno'.

The Czechoslovak government had soon decided to centralise manufacture of military handguns, and work on the vz. 22 was passed to Česká Zbrojovka of Strakonice.[5] It is assumed that a few guns were made (or at least assembled) in the Strakonice factory, but the inability of deliveries to meet governmental demands posed a problem. The vz. 22 was too complicated to mass-produce – its 9mm Short chambering was really too weak to justify the complexity of the locked breech – and so František Myška simplified the mechanism to produce the vz. 24. Most of the alterations were minor, such as the substitution of hard rubber grips for wood, though a magazine safety system was fitted. The marks included ČESKÁ ZBROJOVKA A.S. v PRAZE impressed in the top rib of the slide ahead of the serial number that also appeared on the front right side of the frame. A concentric 'encircled CZ' trademark and marks in the form 'J' and '37' (the inspector's mark and the last two digits of the date) separated by the lion of Bohemia were also used. Factory records reveal that a 9mm Parabellum version, fitted for a shoulder stock, was made for trials with the Turkish Army, but no gun of this type has yet been found.

Myška , who could see no good reason for a locked breech, soon proposed substituting a simple 7.65mm-caliber blowback. This was similar externally to the vz. 24, though the

---

4. The state-owned business was ultimately reorganized as the privately-owned Československá Zbrojovka AS in June 1924.
5. Jihočeská Zbrojovka was founded in 1919 in Pilsen to make the 6.35mm blowback pistol marketed as the 'Fox'. A move to Strakonice occurred in 1921, and in 1923 Česká Zbrojovka (as the company had become) obtained the contract to produce pistols for the Czechoslovak Army.

slide-retraction grooves were milled vertically. Known as the vz. 27 in military and police service, the pistol was still being made in quantity when the Germans annexed Bohemia and Moravia in 1939. A decision had been taken to replace the Army's vz. 24 with the double-action vz. 39, but no bulk deliveries had been made. Consequently, the new pistol is described in Chapter 8.

### Double-Action: The Walther Polizei-Pistole

The introduction of the Polizei-Pistole, generally known by the abbreviation 'PP', revolutionized the part of the firearms industry that was making pocket and personal-defence pistols. Up to that time, the Browning blowbacks made by Fabrique Nationale and Colt (not to mention the legion of Spanish copies) had held a virtual monopoly.

The Walther pistol was known to the factory as the 'Selbstlade-Pistole Modell 1930', after the year of its first commercial appearance, but was based on a series of patents granted to Fritz Walther in 1928–9. Initial advertising listed the dimensions as 170mm overall, with a 98mm barrel, and a weight of about 600 grams. The gun was 22mm thick and about 109mm high, and carried a detachable eight-round box magazine in the butt. It chambered the popular 7.65mm Auto (.32 ACP) and 9mm Short (.380 ACP) cartridges.

The earliest catalogue illustrations show 'The New Walther Police Model' with a slide marked *Waffenfabrik Walther. Zella-Mehlis (Thür.)* over *Walther's Patent. Cal. 7.65m/m* ahead of the banner trademark, which lies in front of the safety-lever thumb piece. No gun has yet been found matching this artist's impression, however. The Walther banner is shown moulded into the base of the injection-moulded plastic grips, a signal pin is present above the hammer, and a magazine extension is stated as available. It is notable that there is no 'Mod. PP' mark on the gun; Walther apparently intended to call the gun 'Modell 10', continuing the previous numerical sequence, before having a last-minute change of mind.

The PP was undoubtedly the first commercially successful pistol embodying a double-action trigger system that could fire by thumb-cocking the hammer or by simply pulling through on the trigger. Most previous pistols had used a single-action system in which the hammer had to be thumb-cocked or the slide retracted to cock-and-load. However, though Walther is due the credit for the first successful application, he is certainly not due the credit as the father of double-action. Such triggers had been successfully applied to pepperboxes and revolvers in the nineteenth century – Cooper, Remington and other designs had seen service in the American Civil War – and many major manufacturers had successfully marketed them prior to 1914.

Though the problems with automatics were more difficult to solve, largely because of the comparative violence of the action, the Russian Korovin and the Bohemian Tomiška had both developed workable systems prior to the First World War. Though exploitation of Korovin's pattern was delayed by the Russian Revolution and the subsequent civil war until the late 1920s (making the TK a near-contemporary of the

Polizei-Pistole), Tomiška's ideas were briefly exploited in the 'Little Tom', first made by Wiener Waffenfabrik and then, after the disintegration of the Austro-Hungarian empire in 1918, in Tomiška's own workshops in emergent Czechoslovakia.

Production of the Little Tom was small, perhaps no more than 20,000; but this allowed the gun to attain sufficient reputation to attract Walther's attention. It is here that the researcher is presented with a choice that either brands Fritz Walther as a sympathetic negotiator or a ruthless exploiter, depending on viewpoint. In 1922, Walther approached Tomiška, supposedly intending to market guns incorporating the latter's patents. After purchasing the rights, however, Walther either deliberately stalled until 1929 – when the patents expired through non-renewal – or laboured unsuccessfully for several years to adapt the Little Tom to mass-production methods. During this time, Walther amalgamated the best of Tomiška's ideas with some of his own, and approached the Deutsches Patentamt with his perfected designs.

Whatever the truth, the Polizei-Pistole was an infinitely better weapon than the Little Tom: it was strong, durable in spite of its complexity, elegantly designed and cleverly packaged. In 1930, it had no peer. The first guns chambered the popular-but-ineffectual 7.65mm Auto and 9mm Short cartridges, numbered from 750001 and continuing, interspersed with PPK, up to 999999. The sequence recommenced at 100,001P in 1939. Slides displayed the banner trademark ahead of **Waffenfabrik Walther. Zella-Mehlis (Thür.)** over **Walther's Patent Cal. 9m/m.** The designation mark, **Mod. PP**, lay behind the maker's mark ahead of the safety-catch thumb piece. The pistols were officially known as the 'Selbstlade-Pistole Walther, Polizei Modell, Kaliber 9mm kurz', but this was widely abbreviated to 'P W PP Kal. 9' or 'P W PP Kal. 7,65'. The 7.65mm slides are marked identically with the 9mm version, excepting that **Cal. 7.65m/m** is substituted.

The Polizei-Pistole was offered to the commercial market in the middle of 1930, encountering instant success. The gun was intended as a small holster pistol but the state police of Prussia apparently indicated that a smaller pistol would be necessary for concealment in a shoulder holster. The result was what is now generally known as the 'Polizei-Pistole, Kriminal' or 'PPK'; the origin of the designation, however, is still questionable. Explanations offered for the 'K' suffix include *Kriminal*[-*polizei*], *kurz* and *klein* – from the Prussian plain-clothes policemen, its reduced overall length and generally smaller construction respectively. In all cases, the abbreviation should have been written 'KPP' rather than PPK, but the latter has persisted.[6] The first PPK seems

---

6. Even Walther ultimately added it into the slide-marking dies. But this proves nothing: neither the 1943 edition of Karl Fischer's *Waffen- und Schiesstechnischer Leitfaden für die Ordnungspolizei* nor the inserted Walther broadsheet that originally accompanied it mention the Kriminalpolizei in connexion with the pistol. The broadsheet actually states: 'In den Abbildungen... ist das Modell PPK gezeigt, welches sich von dem Modell PP *durch kleinere* [my emphasis] Abmessungen unterscheidet, im übrigen jedoch die gleichen Funktionsteile besitzt.' ("In the drawings the Model PPK is shown, which differs from the Model PP in *smaller dimensions*, [but] in other respects, however, has the same functional parts.') There is a suspicion that the gun was originally called the Kleine Polizei-Pistolen ('small police pistol') until Walther discovered the advertising merits of the term Kriminalpolizei.

to have reached the commercial market in 1931. Gun 754958 is a PPK marked as a Polizei-Pistole, but has a frame lacking the rear strap.[7]

The outstanding feature of the Polizei-Pistole was its trigger/safety mechanism. Pressure on the trigger draws the trigger bar forward, rotating the hammer by the action of the sear bar on the hammer-lifting arm. At the same time, the sear also lifts the hammer lock by pressing upward on it; only when the hammer lock is fully elevated can the hammer strike the firing pin. At all other times, the passage of hammer to pin is prevented by the interposition of the hammer lock on the hammer-body projection. When the hammer-lifting arm has rotated the hammer to its rearward limit, the sear disengages and the hammer flies forward to a position where (now that the hammer lock has been lifted) it can strike the head of the firing pin.

The gun then fires, whereupon the slide reciprocates, rides back over the hammer and forces it back until it can engage the sear. The trigger bar has been disconnected from the sear during the recoil stroke, forcing the firer to release the trigger before the trigger bar can be pulled back to re-engage the sear. The contact between the trigger bar and the sear is surrounded by the metal of the sear itself, resulting in a captive system that is all but incapable of malfunctioning. The trigger mechanism can be operated by thumb-cocking the hammer, when, owing to the deletion of the motion on which most energy was required – rotating the hammer to full-cock by pressing the trigger – better accuracy resulted from the appreciably lighter pressure needed to release the hammer from the sear.

The safety system is activated by rotating the transverse stem of the catch, by means of a thumb-lever protruding from the left side of the slide above the grip. This action rotates the solid portion of the catch-spindle through a hole cut in the firing-pin body and securely prevents the pin from moving forward or back.

At the same time the hammer, which in normal operation can strike the firing pin (as long as the hammer lock has been lifted clear by the sear bar) by means of the cut-away rear portion of the catch spindle, is prevented from going right forward by the solid spindle surface. Further rotation of the thumb lever trips the hammer-disconnecting lever, allowing the hammer to fly forward towards the firing pin. But it actually strikes the hammer lock, and additional safety is provided by the catch spindle and the positive firing-pin lock; there is no way in which the hammer can reach and strike the firing pin. Equally, there is no way that the normally inertia-type firing pin, now mechanically locked by the catch spindle cut-outs, can move forward to strike the primer of a chambered cartridge.

The PP and PPK also have an interesting dismantling system derived from the Modell 9, in which the slide can be removed simply by cocking the action (having checked that the gun is clear), pulling down on the trigger-guard bow, and pulling the slide to the rear. It then disengages the frame and can be slid gently forward.

---

7. The prototype PPK is believed to have had a reduced but conventionally forged grip, with front and back straps, and separate grips; the perfected version had an abbreviated grip with only a front strap, plus an enveloping one-piece grip.

The earliest guns had a complicated firing-pin assembly comprising the catch lever, the small firing-pin piece, its spring and a retaining piece, the firing-pin block (pinned in the slide), the long firing-pin piece and its spring. Unnecessarily complicated, the assembly was soon simplified and the riband spring powering the firing-pin lock was substituted by a small coil pattern. Both of these changes had been made by the time of the introduction of the PPK, but were not quite contemporaneous. The first stage was to simplify the firing-pin assembly, which thereafter consisted of the 90-degree safety-catch stem and firing-pin block (in the slide), together with a one-piece firing pin powered by a small coil spring. The replacement of the riband-pattern firing-pin lock spring occurred next, together with revisions to the frame and sear. When the PPK appeared, it featured an abbreviated grip with only a front strap, enveloping one-piece grips and a shortened frame.

However, as the sear rotates through an aperture cut in the frame-side, the latter is particularly weak in the area of the back-strap joint even in the Polizei-Pistole. The alloy frames were soon found to crack, and an alteration to the machining was subsequently made to allow a bridge of metal to act as a strengthener. This necessitated a change in the sear design, and the trigger-bar actuating spring was discarded after the trigger spring was bent far enough to fulfil the spring's function.

A further modification to the safety catch was made in the mid-1930s, when the support block for the firing pin, previously pinned into the slide, became an integral part of the slide machining. The barrel was rebated for part of its length to increase the clearance for the recoil spring, the signal pin was revised (its spring moved from behind the shoulder to in front) and the hammer was grooved to clear it.

The oldest frames can be recognised by the large recess in the right side for the riband spring. A few original guns were modified for the new firing-pin/spring assembly, probably when they returned to the factory for repair after supplies of the original components had been exhausted. Many of these have their serial numbers engraved on the right side of the slide ahead of the retraction grooves.

Many of the original Polizei-Pistolen also lacked the signal pin (or loaded-chamber indicator) that protruded from the rear of the slide above the hammer when there was a cartridge in the chamber. This feature was originally optional, but proved so popular that it was virtually standard after 1933. As late as 1935, however, Polizei-Pistolen were being offered for RM 46.50 with the signal pin or RM 45 without it. The prices for the smaller PPK were RM 43.50 and RM 42 respectively. As indicated above, the earliest PP hammers were not grooved to accommodate the signal-pin, which was driven forward to nick the rim of the chambered cartridge each time the hammer fell. This oversight was soon corrected, and is rarely if ever encountered on the PPK. The late-wartime pistols omitted the pin to simplify production.

Walther was more than satisfied with the PP; interest was considerable, and initial sales were most gratifying. Consequently, 6.35mm (.25 ACP) and 5.6mm lfb (.22 Long Rifle rim-fire) versions appeared in 1933 to special order.

The 6.35mm Polizei-Pistole was far from successful and it is believed that a little fewer than 500 of them were produced before this particular pattern was abandoned in 1935. It has been reported that there were 180 PP and about 300 PPK in this feeble chambering. Numbered between 775000 and 780000, their slides bore the standard company banner trademark ahead of *Waffenfabrik Walther. Zella-Mehlis (Thür.)* over *Walther's Patent Cal. 6.35m/m*. The gun-pattern, *Mod. PP* (or *PPK*) lies behind the main portion immediately ahead of the safety-catch thumb-piece. Close examination reveals that the *Cal. 6.35m/m* slide marking was hand-stamped, the remainder of the mark being rolled-in. It is much less even than its more conventional alternatives.

The failure of the 6.35mm Walther was due to the ineffectual cartridge. The guns were made to Walther's usual standards (at Walther's usual price), but few people used guns of this calibre as anything other than last-ditch personal protection. It was pointless acquiring such a large, well-made gun when there were legions of compact 'suicide specials' to be had at a quarter of the cost.

The 5.56mm (.22) rim-fire derivative of the basic Polizei-Pistole design, also introduced in 1933, proved to be a better commercial proposition than the ill-fated 6.35mm gun; more than 5,000 were made in 1933–5. The ignition system was altered and the signal pin was omitted: otherwise, it would have rested on the primer-containing cartridge rim. Some rim-fire PPs were purchased by the German Heereswaffenamt and the Reichszeugmeisterei for training purposes, but not in the quantities of the full-bore guns. The slide marking was conventional, except for 'Cal. .22 LR'; this was hand-stamped on the earliest guns, but, once Walther realised that the rim-fire variant would be successful, the calibre became part of the slide-inscription die and is indistinguishable from the remainder. The guns cost RM 49.50 in the mid-1930s, but the special extra-long walnut grips were RM 10.50 extra.

No decision to discontinue production was ever taken, but the wartime concentration on 7.65mm and 9mm guns meant that few rim-fires were made after about 1940 – though, ironically, many of the last guns made in 1945 (in the 430,000 group) chambered 5.6mm lfb.

All PP and PPK were rifled with six grooves, but the clockwise twist made one complete turn in 190mm (6.35mm), 210mm (.22 and 9mm) or 240mm (7.65mm). They were widely favoured by the police, paramilitary and military authorities. Some of the political formations of the Third Reich period began to buy guns as early as 1935–6, when all pistols, PP and PPK alike, were numbered in a single cumulative block. In about 1939, numbers reached a million and each gun-type was split into separate sequences. Numbering of Polizei-Pistolen recommenced at 100001P, their smaller cousins beginning at 100001K (though a few were made with seven-digit numbers between 1000001 and 1007000).

In about 1938, the 90-degree safety catch was replaced by a short-throw 60-degree pattern and a change was made in the slide design to accommodate it. The original heavyweight hammer, with a small transverse hole, was replaced by a lightened pattern with a markedly larger hole. Apart from changes of marking-die, however, no serious alterations were made until the Second World War.

Unlike the alloy slides of the experimental Armee- and Heeres-Pistolen of the late 1930s, which proved incapable of withstanding the battering of 9mm Parabellum ammunition, the duraluminium PP slide was successful enough to find wide use. The lower power of the 7.65mm Auto and 9mm Short cartridges prevented fretting (wear caused by excessive friction or abrasion between steel and alloy parts). These guns were made in the regular serial-number ranges, being developed experimentally in the mid-1930s and offered commercially from 1937. Pre-war examples had the metal anodised an attractive shade of blue, but most wartime examples exhibit a baked-on black paint finish. Some pistols were specially finished; some wore nickel plating, others were chromed, and a few were even etched or engraved for special presentation. Gold plating and inlaying, gilding and silver-finishing were also occasionally used, although the vast majority of pistols were quite standard.

Accessories for the Polizei-Pistolen included a luminous radium night sight, or *Leuchtkorn*, that clipped around standard front sights in which a distinctive notch had been cut; extension magazines, some containing two additional rounds and others with luminous bases, were also available.

Polizei-Pistolen originally bore the commercial crown-over-'N' ('crown/N') nitro-proof mark, until this was replaced under the 1939 law – with effect from 1 April 1940 – by an eagle/N mark. Observing serial numbers suggests that virtually all guns below 143500P and 242165K display crown/N; that the official changeover occurred somewhere in the region of 162000P and 255000K; and that almost all guns above 184300P and 261000K have the eagle/N mark. Guns between 143500P and 184300P, or 242165K and 25500K may be found with either.

Police pistols usually bear a large eagle/swastika mark, the swastika being stylised into a circle. The mark is accompanied by a letter ('C' or 'F' on Walthers) signifying the principal inspector's mark.[8] The mark of the supervisor of the Zella-Mehlis bureau, whose personal number was 359, will be found beneath tiny stylised eagle marks on Polizei-Pistolen accepted into the Army. Other common marks include the encircled 'RZM' of the Reichszeugmeisterei, which accepted guns for the Schutzstaffel or SS; 'D.R.P.', usually on the grip straps, which indicates service with the postal authorities, or Deutsches Reichspost; 'NSKK' or 'N.S.K.K.', rarely encountered, was the distinctive logo of the Nationalsozialistische Kraftfahrkorps, or state transport service; 'S.A.' or, more rarely, 'S.A. der N.S.D.A.P.' for the Sturm-Abteilung; 'R.F.V.' for the forestry service, or Reichsförstverwaltung; 'R.J.' for the Reichs-Justizministerium; and a series of Bavarian police marks, taking the form of 'P.D.M.' or 'P.D.N.' for Polizei-Direktion München and Polizei-Direktion Nürnberg respectively. Guns which are marked

---

8. Inspector 'C' accepted PPs numbered below about 350000P and PPKs below 410000; inspector 'F' then replaced 'C', continuing to approve guns numbered as high as 375000P and 430000K.

'Rplt.', for Rigspoliti ('state police'), were used in Denmark after the end of the Second World War.

The NSKK Polizei-Pistolen are particularly rare. One particular block between 994001 and 994999 featured a special slide-inscription die in which the standard Walther legend is narrowed to make room for the NSKK eagle Hoheitsabzeichen. It is probable that these guns were actually intended for presentation, but no evidence of this has yet been found. Sturm-Abteilung guns usually display an inventory mark on the front grip strap, or the name of the SA-Gruppe in full – for example *SA der NSDAP* over *Gruppe Thüringen*.

## Poland and the Radom

Like the Czechoslovaks, the Poles were also in dire need of handguns in the immediate post-independence period, as only a few ex-Russian revolvers had been retrieved. The first step was to construct a new arms factory, Fabryka Bronie w Radomiu, where work began in 1920. Radom became the principal source of Polish small-arms – including a copy of the 1895-type Nagant 'gas-seal' revolver and the Vis or 'Radom' automatic.

To ensure that no time was wasted, the Polish authorities decided to adopt the Czechoslovakian vz. 24 pistol. However, this did not meet the approval of Pyotr Wilniewczyc, an engineer employed by the National Armament Factory (*Państwowej Wytwórni Uzbrojenia*, PWU), who had seen a letter from the Department of Armaments indicating the impending acquisition of a licence. Wilniewczyc objected strongly to the adoption of the vz. 24, partly on technical grounds but also because it seemed pointless to pay licensing fees if an indigenous alternative existed. So vocal were his protests that the Polish authorities allowed Wilniewczyc to develop his own idea which, at the time, was little more than a sketch. The management of the PWU granted two months to prepare a design and two months to prepare a prototype – but only if the designer could convince the Ministry of Armaments that there was enough merit in his scheme to delay the contract.

Two days later, Wilniewczyc had prepared a specification and some drawings for what was labelled the 'PWU Military Pistol M1928'. Though it did not exist as anything other than an idea, the covering letter submitted by the PWU suggested that work had been under way for some time. Wilniewczyc then met the director of the machine-gun factory in Warsaw, Jan Skyrzpinski, and a partnership was struck. When the Department of Armaments indicated that the contract for the vz. 24 could be delayed for ninety days, the designers were ready to proceed. Though other projects sometimes took priority, Wilniewczyc and Skrzpinski had completed the drawings by the autumn of 1930 and the first 'WiS' prototype[9] was readied in the machine-gun factory in February 1931. Concurrently, protection had been sought from the Polish patent office, though patent No. 15567 was not granted until 8 February 1932.

---

9. The designers intended the gun to be known by their initials, but the Department of Armaments changed 'WiS' to *Vis* – the Latin word for 'force'.

Extensive testing on the Zielonka range, near Warsaw, was encouraging. The gun fired inadvertently during the drop tests, a fault that could easily be rectified by altering the sear, and it was mistakenly immersed in cement instead of sand during the dust test. Miraculously, the mechanism was put back into working order before the cement could set.

Wilniewczyc and Skrzpinski sold rights in the patent to the Polish government in March 1933, and a small quantity of pistols was made for field trials. These led to changes in the contours of the frame behind the grip, smoothing several uncomfortable edges, and a hammer-release lever was added to the left rear of the slide; the first deliveries to the Polish Army of the Pistolet 'Vis' wojskowy wz. 35 (commonly known as the 'Radom') occurred in 1935. By 7 September 1939, 18,000 had been made. Work continued after the Germans invaded Poland in 1940 – *see Chapter 8.*

The Vis was a bulky and rather heavy weapon for its calibre but, because of its weight, very comfortable to shoot. It was a modified Browning design, using a shaped cam beneath the breech to disengage lugs on the barrel from the inside of the slide as the latter recoiled. The action was similar to that of the Browning High-Power. A recoil-spring guide rod was added to prevent the spring buckling, and a safety lever was let into the rear of the grip. The manual safety catch was replaced with a hammer release, on the left rear of the slide, which drew the firing pin back into the breech when pressed downward – and then, disconcertingly, allowed the hammer to fall. The goal was that the pistol could then be carried safely with a round in the chamber, to be readied for firing simply by thumbing back the hammer. At the rear of the frame was a stripping catch, resembling the safety lever found on a Colt M1911, but it did nothing except lock the slide back when dismantling the pistol.

Radom pistols bore the Polish eagle on the left side of the frame, separating the place and date of manufacture (e.g., RADOM over '1937r') from the designation and an acknowledgement of the patent (VIS–wz. 35 over PAT. NR. 15567). The first 3,000 had frames and slides of a light steel alloy, but the components proved to be too weak and standard carbon steel was substituted. An 'FB' motif within an inverted triangle (*Fabryka Broni*, 'arms factory') appeared on the left-hand chequered plastic grip, with 'VIS' on the right.

### France: Le Français and Petter

Though the French Army authorities had not been keen on pistols, preferring the 1892-type revolver, events of the First World War conspired against them. The thousands of Ruby pistols that had been bought in Spain – in desperation – had proved to be poorly made and comparatively ineffective, but had also shown that the semi-automatic pistol was easily (and therefore comparatively cheaply) made in quantity.

Development work began soon after the First World War, but with no great enthusiasm or urgency. In fact, the first French pistol to be successful was a private development. Étienne Mimard (1862–1944), associated with Manufacture Française des

Armes et Cycles of Saint-Étienne, had sought protection for his design as early as
August 1913. The patent was successfully obtained in 1914 and a few 'Le Français' pistols
had been made prior to August 1914. The First World War put paid to series-production
plans, but they were successfully resurrected after hostilities ceased.

Initially made only as a 6.35mm-calibre pocket pistol, the Le Français was a blowback
with a 'drop-down' barrel hinged at the front of the frame and a self-cocking striker.
Pressing the barrel-release lever, the principal novelty, allows the breech to rise clear of
the slide in much the same manner as the Belgian Pieper design. The barrel catch is
linked to the magazine to ensure that the barrel flies open as the magazine is withdrawn,
preventing inadvertent firing of a round left in the chamber.

The slide is conventional in appearance, but an 'L'-shaped lever, beneath the left grip
plate, is pivoted close to the lower edge of the grip; its vertical limb engages the slide,
while the short toe presses up against the coil-type recoil spring placed vertically in the
front edge of the grip. The striker, striker spring and striker-retracting spring are all
carried within the slide. When the trigger is pressed, the trigger bar forces the striker
back against the mainspring and is then cammed free, allowing the striker to fly forward
to fire the cartridge. There is no extractor, the empty case being blown from the
chamber by residual gas pressure as the slide opens.

The magazine is often found with a spring clip on its bottom plate, allowing the
carriage of an extra cartridge. After the magazine is inserted this spare round is taken
and loaded into the chamber and the barrel closed. The guns made prior to 1945 lacked
retraction grips, as there was no need to retract the slide to cock or chamber a round.
The magazine of the 9mm Army model can be partly withdrawn and locked clear of
the slide, allowing single rounds to be fired by inserting them directly into the chamber
while a full magazine is kept in reserve.

The design of the Le Français was ingenious, and the 6.35mm guns were very
successful commercially. Introduced in 1914, the Modèle de Poche ('Pocket Model') was
made until 1966. The grips, usually with an enwreathed 'MF' monogram trademark,
were held by two screws until 1928 and one thereafter. The design of the sear spring was
changed at about the same time, and the original butt catch, which was formed
integrally with the base of the magazine, was replaced in 1935 by a conventional cross-
bolt. Catalogues published in the 1920s listed the guns as No. 1 to No. 4, depending on
the degree of decoration, but by 1939 they were being numbered in the 800 series.

The Type 'Policeman' of 1922, originally identified as No. 5 to No. 8 depending on
decoration, was a 6.35mm pocket pistol with a 3.3-inch barrel protruding from the slide.
There was also a short-lived 6.35mm/.22 LR rim-fire convertible target pistol, Type
'Champion', with a 5.9-inch barrel and a special magazine extension (*rallonge*) with
sprung straps that could be slipped over the grip. The gun was sold as the 'No. 10', or
as the 'No. 15' as part of a cased set. Production was confined to 1926–33.

The military version of the Le Français, Type 'Armée', was never as popular as its
promoters had hoped. Its cause was not helped by the chambering, for the 9mm

Browning Long round that was widely judged to be too weak to be effective in combat. Guns had been tested by the French Army in 1928–33, but were rejected owing to the reliance on residual gas pressure to extract a spent case, by concerns over the durability of the double-action trigger system, and by the absence of an exposed hammer. The military Le Français pistol was 8 inches long, with a 5-inch barrel, and weighed about 37oz empty. Catalogues dating from the late 1920s allocate the model numbers 12 (plain), 14 (lightly engraved) and 16 (deluxe engraving) to the army pistols, the designations changing to 850, 856 and 862 respectively by 1938.

The plain barrel/slide design lasted until, in 1931, circumferential grooves were added to the breech and longitudinal flutes were milled in the barrel beneath the chamber to reduce weight to about 32oz. Concurrently, wooden grips with a plain brass disc replaced the original composition type displaying an enwreathed 'MF' monogram. A loop on the base of the post-1931 magazines accepted a single cartridge, which was used to load the chamber once the barrel had been tipped open. Many Le Français pistols served during the Second World War, when the slide was reinforced and a gas-escape hole was cut through the face of the breech-block into the striker channel.

Though the Le Français was a failure militarily, the French Army had become convinced that a semi-automatic pistol should be adopted. Consequently, designers attached to the small-arms factories – particularly that in Saint-Étienne – began work at a leisurely pace by seeking the opinions of commercial manufacturers before proceeding with a series of experimental pistols. The odd-looking 'SE-MAS Type A No. 4' of 1932 was the last of this group, a blowback chambering the idiosyncratic French 7.65mm Longue cartridge. The return spring was concentric with the barrel, and the firing mechanism in the rear of the slide included a suspended hammer.

Trials with the SE-MAS, the Le Français, a 7.65mm Longue version of the pre-production FN-Browning Pistolet à Grande Puissance (GP-35), and the SACM (Petter) pistols resulted in a victory for the last-named. It had been developed on the basis of patents granted in 1934 to Swiss-born Charles Petter, though, truthfully, there was little novelty in yet another variation of the Browning swinging-link system excepting the detachable self-contained firing mechanism.

The Mle 1935A SACM-Petter proved to be well made, comfortable to hold, and extremely reliable. However, the safety catch through the rear tip of the slide was no more than a crude half-round shaft to block the fall of the hammer onto the firing pin. But the worst feature was unquestionably the feeble 7.65mm Longue cartridge, which fired an 87-grain bullet at only 1,100ft/sec. Production of the Petter-type pistols began in the SACM factory in Cholet in 1938, and the first batches of a 10,500-gun order had been delivered to the Army by the end of the year. Yet when the Franco-German 'Armistice' was declared in the summer of 1940, the order was still incomplete. Production continued under German supervision (*see Chapter 8*).

The Mle 1935A, a conventional design, was not particularly easy to make. In 1938, therefore, with the threat of war growing daily, designers in the Saint-Étienne factory

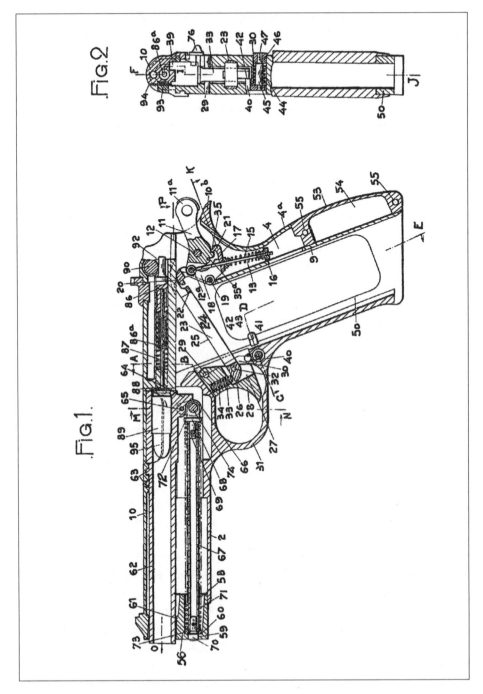

*The French Mle 1935A pistol was designed by Charles Petter, to whom US Patent No. 2139203 was granted on 6 December 1938. The principal improvement on the Colt-Browning concerned the firing mechanism, which was packaged in a readily removable sub-assembly.*

were ordered to simplify the pistol. The intention was to re-equip the Army as soon as possible. The new gun, the Mle 1935S, was much more angular. In addition, the locking lugs of the 'A' were replaced on the 'S' with a rising block, and the safety bolt was replaced by a hammer-blocking safety catch. The simplified Mle 1935S was to be made by the three principal French small-arms factories – Châtellerault, Saint-Étienne and Tulle – and by two private contractors, SACM and SAGEM, but only a few thousand had been made by June 1940. Work then stopped, as the Germans had more important uses for the arms factories than making handguns.

Markings on the original '35A' included the designation and the serial number (e.g., ℬ1178A) above S.A.C.M. on the left side of the frame. The pistols were 194mm long, with a 110mm barrel, and weighed only 670 grams empty. The later Mle 1935S was 188mm long, had a 119mm barrel, and had an empty weight of 780 grams. Its markings included the arsenal mark on the left side of the slide ('MAC' for Châtellerault, 'MAS' for Saint-Étienne or 'MAT' for Tulle), with the designation MODELE 1935 S on the right, above CAL. 7,65 L and a serial number (e.g., MAC–C 1023)

## Finland: The Lahti

Immediately after Finland gained independence from Russia in 1917, small-arms seized from the ex-tsarist arsenal at Helsinki formed the bulk of the Army's weapons: Mosin-Nagant rifles, for example, were retained by the Finns until the early 1960s. The Russian storehouse did not contain many handguns, and so the Finnish Army initially had FN-Browning pocket automatics and Mauser-Pistolen C/96 brought back from the First World War. Nine thousand Ruby blowbacks were then acquired from France shortly after the Armistice.

The Rubies, issued as Pistooli m/19, were little more than a stop-gap. The Parabellum was considered to be the best readily available design in the early 1920s and was standardised in Finland as the Pistooli m/23 Pb. The initial choice of the Parabellum was influenced by the number of Finnish volunteers who had served with the German Army during the First World War and formed the nucleus of the embryonic Finnish Army, along with others who had served the Russians. It is believed that about 8,000 7.65mm New Model pistols, with 98mm barrels but no grip safeties, were acquired from DWM in 1923–30.

Finnish Army m/23 Parabellums often bore marking discs, and unit markings were stamped into the board-type shoulder stocks. For example, one stock is marked 11.S.J.R.2.K.K.K. – the 11th gun issued to the second machine-gun company (*konekivääri-kompania*) of the Savo Rifle Regiment, or Savon Jääkärirykmentti. It also bears the four-digit number '7539', the serial number of the gun with which the stock was issued. The pistols and rifles issued to the Finnish Army bore these marking discs prior to 1940, when the system was abandoned.

Some of the Finnish m/23 pistols were refurbished during the 1930s, when 9.8cm and 12cm replacement barrels, some in 7.65mm, others in 9mm, were made by Oy

Tikkakoski Ab. Though some m/23 Parabellums had been passed to the 'Protective Corps' (the Suojeluskunta-Organisation, or Sk.Org.), the police and the prison service prior to the Winter War, survivors saw active service in 1939–40 and again in the 'Continuation War' of 1941–4.[10]

By the end of the 1920s, however, worried by the comparatively poor performance of the Parabellum in sub-zero conditions, the Finns had decided to develop a handgun of their own. The talented firearms designer Aimo Johannes Lahti, best remembered for the 'Suomi' submachine-gun, began his pistol designs against this backcloth, which explains why his perfected m/35 L copied some features of the m/23 Pb.

However, the vertically-opening toggle-lock of the Parabellum was very susceptible to variations in ammunition pressure, and the way in which the breech block travelled back within the receiver exposed the interior of the action to the entry of snow and dirt. Despite its undeniably superb balance and safety features, the Parabellum was temperamental in sub-zero conditions: snow jammed the mechanism, cold froze the action solid. The toggle-lock was quite clearly an undesirable feature.

Lahti seems to have fused the best features of the Parabellum with the suitably modified locking system of the Danish Bergmann-Bayard. This claim has been and will doubtless continue to be disputed – but it seems probable that the then-current Danish service pistol, the m/1910–21, was tested in Finland before the Parabellum was adopted in the mid-1920s, and Lahti was familiar with its design. The vertically moving Bergmann-Bayard locking block, designed by Louis Schmeisser for the Bergmann machine-gun, had been patented in 1901 and was known to be strong, simple and reliable. However, the Bergmann 'Mars' and Bergmann-Bayard pistols were long and badly balanced: placing the magazine in front of the trigger had lost the advantages of a compact locking unit.

Lahti obviously saw potential in the Bergmann action and set to work in 1928. Development proceeded slowly, as he was involved in other projects, but the prototype pistols had been perfected by 1932 and the designs were immediately submitted to the Finnish patent office in Helsinki. Patent 15716 was granted on 16 February 1934.

The Lahti pistol operates on a short-recoil system, in which the rearward movement of the locked parts is less than the length of the cartridge case, and is locked by a vertically moving yoke (or inverted 'U'-block) in the receiver above the rear of the grip. There are three major groups of components – the frame, the barrel and receiver, and the breechblock and locking unit. The mechanism also includes a two-armed accelerator lever pivoted in the front left side of the receiver. As the receiver and bolt recoil, locked together, the lower arm of the accelerator bears on the frame and rotates the lever around its central pivot. Just as the inverted-U block rises into the roof of the

10. With Lahtis in short supply and only a few Parabellums available, the Finns also acquired the FN-Browning GP-35 for the Air Force and the Beretta Mo. 34 for the Protective Corps. Many of these pistols were discarded after the Finns signed a peace treaty with the Soviet Union to end the Continuation War, but the 7.65mm m/23 Parabellums were not declared obsolete until the early 1980s.

receiver, the longer arm of the accelerator comes into contact with the left side of the freed bolt. The design of the lever ensures that the upper arm acts at a mechanical advantage and, moving faster than the recoil velocity, gives the bolt an additional thrust.

Accelerators are often found in machine-guns such as the Browning, to increase the cyclic rate or improve the efficiency of poor feed systems. But they are very rarely found in handgun designs. There has been much speculation about the function of the Lahti accelerator, particularly in relation to the unusually long 'short recoil' stroke required to unlock the bolt – at 7mm, almost twice as long as most other short-recoil designs. Some writers have suggested that Aimo Lahti deliberately adopted a slow-acting mechanism of the most positive type, accepting that a relatively long 'locked recoil' had little significance in a semi-automatic weapon.

The accelerator was not essential in the design of the m/35 L, and, in 1940, a batch of pistols was made without it. However, operation proved to be unsatisfactory in extreme cold and the accelerator was rapidly reinstated not only on all subsequent pistols but also on replacement slides made in the 1950s and 1960s. Guns fitted with accelerators were always regarded by the Finns as more efficient than those without them.

The basic design of the Lahti is generally considered to be excellent, excepting the safety lever mechanism. The exceedingly simple magazine safety (a spring-loaded bar forced to retain the bolt by the magazine follower button) works perfectly; but the lever safety unit is curious. A radial lever placed nearly vertically behind the left grip can be rotated backwards to its safe position, marked 'V' for *Varma*, Finnish for 'safe'. The transverse lever pivot carries a lug that locks the sear solidly into the intermediate and full-cock notches on the hammer. Locking the hammer at full cock is understandable; in the intermediate position, much less so. The latter prevents the bolt being retracted over the hammer and supposedly allows the hammer to be dropped safely onto a loaded chamber when the safety catch has been pushed forward and the trigger pulled. The unsatisfactory nature of this arrangement cannot be emphasised too strongly: Finnish service ammunition may have insensitive primers, but other cartridges may very well not.

This criticism apart, the Lahti is a first-class service pistol with an efficient action which is isolated, as far as possible, from the effects of mud and dust. Though easily field stripped, the gun is relatively heavy and can only be completely stripped in a workshop. However, these drawbacks are considerably outweighed by its advantages.

In March 1934, the inventor sold the production rights to the Finnish defence ministry and tooling in the Valtions Kivääritehdas (VKT), the state rifle factory in Jyväskylä, began a year later. The first examples of the Pistooli m/35 L appeared early in 1936 and small numbers had been issued before the Russo-Finnish 'Winter War' (*Talvisota*) began in 1939, though rearmament had only begun in earnest at the beginning of the year. Had production capacity not been allotted to the m/26 Lahti-Saloranta light machine-gun and the m/31 Suomi (Lahti) submachine-gun, the pistol could have been introduced several years earlier than it was.

The original pistol type was officially known as the m/35 L Perusmalli ('basic model') and bore a considerable resemblance to the Parabellum, largely because of its unsupported barrel, the angle and position of its grip and incorporation of a Parabellum-type radial dismantling lever on the front left side of the frame. A closer inspection, however, reveals that not only is there no toggle mechanism, but also that only one aperture lies in the angular receiver; the ejection port on the right side is cut through to the bolt.

Early Lahti pistols can be recognised by the distinctive machining of the receiver, which displays several milled-out panels including one running the entire length of the right side and another running half the length of the left. The base of the latter contains the spring-steel ejector. A housing for the blade-type loaded chamber indicator may be found on top of the receiver, while a prominent protrusion at the rear – running forward from the locking block reinforce chamber – contains a spring to lock the inverted U-block into the bolt. The top of the locking piece recess contains an oil-impregnated pad to lubricate the wide friction-generating surfaces.

The injection-moulded plastic grips always display the 'VKT' monogram. The serial numbers are stamped into the left side of the frame and the receiver, and sometimes on the underside of the barrel and on the top rear of the bolt. The 'VKT' mark, the designation 'L-35' and the Finnish Army property mark ('SA' within a square) are usually struck into the top of the receiver. About 200 experimental wooden shoulder/holster stocks were issued in 1937, but were never adopted officially though many guns (even those numbered in the 6,000s) had stock lugs.

### The Later Japanese Guns

The bizarre appearance of the Type 94 (1934: year 2594 on the *Jimmu nengō* calendar system), the oddest of the Japanese service pistols, has excited much controversy. There seems little doubt that it was conceived about 1929, either as a compact replacement for the 14th Year Type or to suit the crews of armoured vehicles and aircraft. However, though Kijiro Nambu has been linked with its design, suggestions have been made that his role was little more than as a consultant and that the details was undertaken by the staff of Nambu Seisakusho. So many changes were made that military trials were not negotiated satisfactorily until the mid-1930s.

Made exclusively by the former Nambu-Seisakusho Kabushiki Kaisha factory in Tokyo-Kitatama, and marketed commercially as 'Self-acting [automatic] Pistol, Type B', the Type 94 bears no resemblance whatever to the earlier Nambu and 14th Year Type pistols. Some features resemble a Browning, although the similarity is no more than superficial. Its odd, deep receiver, and the frame bridged for the passage of the slide and breechblock assembly, are most distinctive. It also has an oddly designed grip, which cannot be mistaken. Some writers consider the grip to be comfortable, provided the firer's hand is gloved, but others have been much less complimentary. The grip contains the six-round box magazine, widely considered to be too small for a service pistol. A capacity of between eight and ten rounds was considered to be ideal in the 1930s, but the FN GP-35 was already being offered with thirteen.

The recoil-operated Type 94 is locked by a separate block that floats independently between two lugs under the chamber end of the barrel. The locking unit is controlled by cam-ways cut into the frame, and locks into a transverse notch cut across the underside of the slide. The barrel/slide group recoils through about 2.5–3mm as the gun is fired, whereupon the locking block begins its downward movement. It is completely disengaged, and after 2.5–3mm further travel the barrel is halted as its lug strikes the frame in front of the trigger, and the slide is released to run back alone. The main spring is compressed between the slide and the barrel until it halts recoil, and then returns the parts to rest, transferring a new round from the magazine to the chamber and camming the locking block up and into its recesses in the slide.

Undoubtedly the worst feature of the unusual firing mechanism is its long sear bar, lying in a channel on the left side of the frame, which converts the vertical movement of the trigger into lateral movement of the sear by the action of a spring-loaded plunger on top of the trigger. This plunger projects at 90 degrees to the sear bar and is shaped into a cam, which engages an oblique cam-way in the sear nose. The sear bar moves towards the right side of the frame as the trigger is pulled, disengaging its tail from the hammer.

When the gun fires and recoils, the barrel stop lug strikes a cam on the front of the trigger plunger and forces the plunger head down against its spring, disconnecting the plunger (and thus the trigger) from the sear nose. The sear spring then forces the sear tail back into engagement with the hammer, but the plunger cannot re-engage the sear nose until the firer has released the trigger. The device consequently takes care of disconnection and the phenomenon of trigger 'clutch'.

The Type 94 incorporates a magazine safety and a manual safety. The latter, a lever pattern, lies on the left rear of the frame where it can be rotated across the sear bar to lock the sear tail securely into the hammer. Simple and very effective, it can be applied by the thumb of the firing hand without unduly disturbing aim – unlike the clumsy unit fitted to the earlier 14th Year Type pistol. The magazine safety is a very simple design, and its construction is merged with that of the magazine release cross-bolt. When the magazine is removed from the feed-way, the tip of the magazine safety springs into the gap and its tail is lifted into a notch cut in the back of the trigger. Although this is a reasonably effective safety device, the design of the sear bar – which can release the hammer when its external surface is struck – makes it possible to fire the gun even with the magazine removed, though this was hardly the primary function of the external sear. The usefulness of any magazine safety is, however, questionable; there can be no valid reason for its inclusion in a military weapon, regardless of its efficiency. The gun often cannot be fired if the magazine is lost, even though loose cartridges may be readily available.

A hold-open was omitted from the Type 94, just as it had been from the Nambu and the 14th Year Type, and the magazine follower held the slide open after the last round had been loaded, fired and ejected.

The weaker mainspring of the Type 94 made the task of withdrawing the magazine rather easier than it had been with the 14th Year Type pistols. As the magazine follower was removed from contact with the breech block, the slide ran forward onto an empty chamber. When a fresh magazine was inserted in the feed-way and pushed home, the slide had to be manually retracted and returned to cock and load. Many contemporary military pistols had devices to retain their open slides until the new magazine was inserted, after which the tripping of a button or lever caused the slide to run forward to load. This eliminated the separate retraction and return strokes, and saved time.

Despite their mistakes, the designers of the Type 94 eliminated some of the bad features of the earlier 14th Year Type. The latter's suspect striker mechanism was replaced by a powerful internal hammer, and the Type 94 rarely suffered the misfires that had often characterised its predecessor. The manual and trigger safeties were much better than those of the 14th Year Type, but a new drawback negated each improvement. The strange trigger had a 'creepy' pull of between 4,000 and 4,500 grams, and the exposed sear, lying in its channel on the outside of the frame, could be operated simply by striking the front of the bar without touching the trigger (regardless of whether the magazine safety was engaged). And the method of achieving disconnection was efficient only so far as trigger 'clutch' was concerned, as the movement of the sear could be impeded externally, by pushing or jamming it, to prevent the disconnection system working. In cases such as this, the slide rolled the hammer back on recoil, but the sear tail could not lock satisfactorily in the hammer body; and as the slide returned, the hammer simply rotated forward to rest against the firing pin. The chambered cartridge was not generally ignited, as the blow imparted to the inertia-type pin was insufficient. There is potentially far more danger in striking the exposed sear to release a fully-cocked hammer; the gun will then fire and reload quite normally.[11]

The locking system of the Type 94 is theoretically efficient, but the poor quality of guns made late in the war, and the exposure of the tops of the locking piece in open recesses in the slide-side, caused a number of accidents. Guns fired before they were fully locked, or when the lock had worn or jammed. The action was consequently transformed into a simple blowback and damage to parts ensued. It is clear that this type of malfunction was rare but that it did happen occasionally. Compared with the 14th Year Type pistol, the Type 94 had a better safety and a much better ignition system in which the hammer replaced a striker; but its trigger and sear unit was far worse, and the magazine capacity of a mere six rounds was insufficient for combat use.

The production history of the Type 94 is something of a mystery. The first guns were made by Nambu-Seisakusho KK (later to become part of Chuo Kogyo KK) in about

---

11. A theory, now discredited, has been advanced that the exposed bar permitted Japanese soldiers to commit suicide as they passed their loaded pistols, butt first, to their captors. However, the pressure required to release the cocked sear is considerable, and the bar must be struck rather than simply pushed.

1935, but production was slow and fewer than 3,000 guns had been made in the Tokyo-Kitatama factory before the commencement of the Sino-Japanese War in July 1937. Frederick Leithe illustrated gun number 3177, dating from September of the same year. The marks applied to the pistols followed standard Japanese practice, as the arsenal mark and the serial number appear on the rear right side of the frame; pistols numbered below about 7500 (mid-1939) have the mark of Nagoya arsenal separated from the Nambu/Chuo Kogyo mark, which prefixes the serial number group. These separated number groups, applied by separate punches, may indicate that the guns were made in Tokyo and subsequently inspected and accepted in Nagoya. Later guns have the arsenal and manufacturer's markings close together below the date (but not struck with one punch) and this may indicate that the guns were assembled, inspected and accepted under full government control. Whether this happened in Tokyo-Kitatama or in Nagoya-Toriimatsu is open to debate, but it is believed that the former plant was nationalised in 1939 and the pistol machinery may have been moved to the latter, where it was apparently found in 1945.

The date of manufacture (or, perhaps, acceptance) appears on the right rear of the frame, together with the Showa reign mark. The marks on the left side of the frame are confined to the designation *kuyon shiki* (94 Type), above the trigger aperture, and characters for 'fire' and 'safe' on the safety lever surround. Many magazines, triggers, breech blocks and some other major components bear the last three digits of the serial number. This indicates that the guns were largely hand-finished and that vital parts were not totally interchangeable.

## Spanish Handguns Between the Wars

The fortunes of the Spanish gunmakers took another tumble after the end of the First World War, largely because so many completed guns and millions of individual parts were being readied when the 'for the duration' contracts were cancelled. The emergence of new countries, often facing internal strife and with military and police forces to create, was a temporary outlet – even emergent states such as Yugoslavia soon followed the conventional purchasing channels by buying guns and production machinery from Fabrique Nationale. These included large numbers of the M10/22 FN-Browning pistol, which removed any need for cheap Spanish imitations.

Deprived of the lucrative military market, the Spanish gunmakers returned to their commercial markets and the hubbub that had characterised wartime Eibar rapidly subsided. Unsurprisingly, in view of the post-war glut of unwanted weaponry, comparatively few people wanted low-grade Spanish blowbacks when a Luger pistol or a Smith & Wesson revolver could be had for next to nothing. Even though reliance was still placed on handwork, and costs were comparatively low, one immediate consequence was the demise of many small gunmaking businesses in Eibar and Guernica. The rise of several larger businesses, such as Echeverria ('Star'), Esperanza y Unceta ('Astra') and Gabilondo y Cia ('Llama'), offered sufficient prospects of employment for the worst effects of the slump to be avoided. In addition, the introduction of mandatory proof in Spain in 1925 soon improved the quality of the guns.

There was also a trend towards better design, often based on the streamlined FN-Browning M1910 pocket/personal-defence pistol. A few gunmakers were even prepared to apply a little ingenuity to their products, ensuring that they were not just another straightforward copy of the blowback FN-Brownings. The Charola y Anitua of the 1890s, which remained the locked-breech pistol with the smallest calibre until comparatively recent times, is considered in greater detail in Chapter 4. Another oddity was the Jo-Lo-Ar, with a one-hand cocking lever on the right side of the slide. Designed by José de Lopez Arnaiz and protected by Spanish Patents 68027 and 70235, the gun was made in small numbers in the 1920s – in 9mm Short, 9mm Bergmann-Bayard (allegedly for the Peruvian Army) and even .45 ACP – by Hijos de Calixto Arrizabalaga of Eibar. The relevant British patent (206093) dates from April 1923.

The end for many of the individual gunmakers came at the close of the Spanish Civil War, when the victorious Nationalists exacted revenge on the largely pro-Republican Basques by bringing the production of pistols and sporting guns forcibly to an end. Only the major employers were spared, for reasons that are not entirely clear. Consequently, the 'Astra', 'Llama' and 'Star' brands that were being applied to surprisingly good-quality Colt-Browning pistols and Smith & Wesson-type revolvers when the war began have all lasted until the present day.

### The Pistolet à Grande Puissance

The most successful handgun to be introduced between the wars was the FN-Browning 'Pistolet à Grande Puissance' ('High Power Pistol'), though its strengths did not become truly evident until the 1950s. The origins of the design lay in the desire of John Browning to improve the 1911-type guns made, extremely successfully, by Colt. Among his goals were to refine the trigger mechanism, as the original Colt-Browning was thought to be too simple to give a good trigger pull; a desire to increase the capacity of the magazine forced a reduction in the size of the cartridge, acceptance of the 9mm Parabellum coincidentally increasing the chances of success in Europe. A series of prototypes, made from 1922 onward by Fabrique Nationale,[12] allowed a patent to be

---

12. Fabrique Nationale d'Armes de Guerre, widely known simply as 'FN', had been formed by a group of Belgian gunmakers and entrepreneurs in 1889, to manufacture whatever infantry rifle the Belgian government decided to adopt. This proved to be a Mauser, leading to litigation when FN attempted to fulfil an export order placed by Chile in December 1894. A cartel was formed of Waffenfabrik Mauser, Deutsche Waffen- u. Munitionsfabriken, Österreichische Waffenfabriks-Gesellschaft and FN in 1897, to carve up the Mauser rifle-market between them in pre-defined proportions, and German interests acquired a majority shareholding in FN. After the end of the First World War, however, non-Belgian holdings were declared untenable and the Union Financière et Industrielle Liégeoise retrieved the 5,700 shares held by DWM. Once again, Fabrique Nationale had been returned to Belgian ownership. A lucrative arms trade was rapidly re-established on the basis of the Mauser rifle, no longer fettered by patents or ownership disputes.

sought and granted in the USA. This protected a striker-fired pistol with a barrel that was depressed not by the well-established pivoting link but by a cam-track in a lug beneath the chamber. Trials undertaken by FN showed that the system worked efficiently, but the striker was unpopular; consequently, by 1928, a hammer had replaced the striker and the gun had taken a shape that was essentially similar to the perfected version. John Browning had died unexpectedly in Liége in the winter of 1926, and so the final changes were undertaken by the Bureau d'Études, the FN design office, under the direction of Dieudonné Saive.

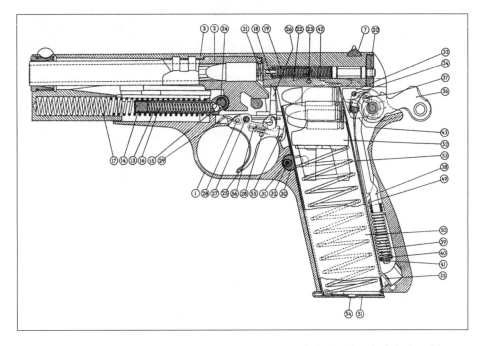

*A section of the FN-Browning GP-35, showing the way in which the breech end of the barrel is tipped downward to lower lugs on the barrel from their recesses inside the top of the slide.*

By 1929, the new pistol was virtually ready to enter series production. But then came the Wall Street Crash and the Great Depression, a period of great hardship in which the FN workforce declined from its pre-Crash establishment of 9,138 to only 2,580 by 1934. The worst of the crisis then passed, allowing the Belgian government to adopt the pistol officially and the first of a few small pre-1939 export orders to be fulfilled.[13] One of the greatest advantages of the GP-35 was the magazine, holding 13 rounds in a

---

13. The 75th anniversary history, *Fabrique Nationale 1889–1964*, records pre-1940 sales of 56,500 'Pistolets à grande puissance', notably to Belgium, Lithuania, Estonia and Peru. The book also records that China had acquired 164,500 Mauser rifles, 5,000 GP pistols, 6,470 Browning Automatic Rifles, 357 FN-Browning machine-guns and a huge quantity of cartridges in 1935–40, to help in the struggle against Japan, but it is assumed that the pistols had been counted into the 56,500 total.

staggered column, and the gun as a whole soon proved to be robust and efficient – though it is still debated whether its greater complexity reduced its advantages over the M1911 Colt-Browning in these particular respects.

## The Olympia Pistole

In the 1932 Los Angeles Olympic Games, the German Oberleutnant Heinz Hax unexpectedly won a silver medal in the rapid fire pistol-shooting competition, beating marksmen armed almost exclusively with the Colt Woodsman. In 1934, the Germans began to train a team for the 1936 Olympics, which were to be held in Berlin. A good performance was essential and, as it was recognized that Hax's earlier success owed more to his skill than the comparatively crude Walther pistol, the Deutscher Schützen-Verband asked Fritz Walther to prepare an improved design while Rheinisch-Westfälische Sprengstoff (RWS) worked hard to improve the standard of German rim-fire ammunition.

The Walther Olympia-Modell was given to the German team early in 1935. It was distinguished by an exposed hammer and long frame-spur that extended backward over the firer's wrist. A sight-block could be attached to the frame extension to increase the sight radius; unfortunately, if predictably, attaching one sight to the slide and the other to the frame magnified the effects of wear. Accuracy was not what had been expected and the guns were soon returned to the factory.

Throughout the spring of 1935, Walther worked to improve the Olympia Modell. Finally, an enclosed-hammer lock was developed and the gun reappeared as the Olympia-Pistole in the autumn of 1935. Its release coincided with RWS's greatly improved .22 LR cartridge and the team managers were well satisfied. Experiments with muzzle brakes and counter-weights led to the development of a .22 Short version for the rapid-fire contests. The Walther pistol had now gained an alloy slide, an improved magazine and a greatly modified extractor; its performance was now truly world-class, helped by the RWS .22 Short cartridge. Mass production began in the early part of 1936, the .22 Short guns being intended for target shooting and the steel-slide .22 LR examples for sporting purposes. With the standard barrel, the former weighed 815gm and the latter 890gm.

Pre-Olympic competitions in Hungary and Sweden convinced the Germans that they had a world-beater; by the time of the Olympic Games, however, other marksmen had bought new Walthers and the results were not quite what the Germans were seeking! The Walthers eclipsed their rivals comprehensively in the rapid-fire competition, taking the first five places. The Germans van Oyen and Hax took the gold and silver, followed by the Swede Ullmann (bronze), a Greek and then another Swede in fifth place. In addition, Händrick, the German winner of the modern pentathlon, had used a Walther in the pistol-shooting competition.

Before the Walther was introduced, few marksmen had been keen to use semi-automatic pistols in top-class competition owing to their comparative crudity. The triggers, especially when strikers rather than hammers were used, were rarely as precise or delicate as those of the finer single-action revolvers. The Olympia-Pistole removed most of these fears at a single stroke and, more than any other single gun, established the autoloader firmly on the target-shooting scene. It is fair to say that many target pistols have been judged by the standards of the Olympia-Pistole for the past fifty years… and have often been found wanting. In a class of shooting renowned for the rapidity of technological change, this is indeed a tribute to the excellence of the basic design.

The left side of Walther-made slides displayed the company's banner trademark ahead of *Waffenfabrik Walther. Zella-Mehlis (Thür.)* above *Walther's Patent.* The words *Olympia-Pistole* lay above the magazine-release catch. Serial numbers of up to four digits were struck into the rear left side of the slide, behind the retraction grooves, and into the left side of the frame immediately below the slide number. The frame number generally displays an additional 'O' suffix, no doubt representing 'Olympia', while all or parts of the number graced the barrel and the left side of the magazine extension. Standard German proof marks, crown/N, were applied to the barrel, the slide and the frame. No guns have yet been verified with the eagle/N marks applied, under the 1939 law, with effect from 1 April 1940.

Walther apparently undertook considerable research into rifling profiles and twist-pitches before settling on six-groove clockwise twist making one complete turn in 450mm. Several differing guns were marketed before the beginning of the Second World War halted production, but all shared the same basic enclosed-hammer mechanism. They were often advertised under the model-number 184, but it has yet to be determined whether this was Walther's or had simply been applied by one of the large wholesale houses. It is sometimes difficult to establish precisely which model is being described, as the supplementary weights sold with the *Funfkampfmodell*, for example, would also fit the *Schnellfeuermodell*.

The *Schnellfeuermodell* was the standard production variant, made with an alloy slide and chambering the .22 Short rim-fire cartridge for rapid-fire competitions. The barrel measured 190mm, but only a single 350-gram frame weight was sold with the guns – bringing the total 'all-up' weight to 1,130 grams. The guns had a six-round detachable box magazine and could be recognised by the heavy cylindrical barrel noticeably 'stepped' in front of the frame-tip.

Offered with a cylindrical barrel of 170 or 190mm, but with only two small frame weights, the *Sportmodell*, although otherwise similar to the rapid-fire gun, had a steel slide and chambered the .22 LR cartridge. Six- and ten-round magazines were obtainable.

Intended for the shooting discipline of the modern pentathlon competition, the *Funfkampfmodell* chambered the .22 LR rim-fire round (5.6mm lfb). Three supplementary weights could be fitted to guide rails under the slab-side barrel and the front of the frame. The frame weight curved back under the trigger guard to minimize the effects of a snatched trigger pull. The barrel weight had no effect on recoil, because the slide reciprocated independently. The front sight was an adjustable blade, the back sight an open U-notch; and the chequered walnut grip – in some shooters' opinion the best mass-produced pattern ever made – amply filled the hand, particularly after 1939 when the heel was flared. The thumb-piece was generally chequered, which was not permitted on rapid-fire guns. A wooden extension on the magazine base acted as an integral part of the grip, but did not protrude. *Funfkampfmodelle* had 245mm barrels, though shorter non-standard variations were made on special order. The overall length was about 332mm, sight radius being 295mm. The magazine held ten .22 LR rim-fire cartridges. The standard guns weighed nearly 900 grams without the three auxiliary weights, which added an extra 390–400 grams. These had rounded fronts, rather than the squared weights associated with the *Sportmodell*. A few presentation models were made with exchangeable alloy slides, an additional barrel and six-round magazines adapted for the .22 Short cartridge.

The *Standardmodell* was essentially similar to the *Funfkampfmodell*, but is generally found with a 190mm cylindrical barrel and squared auxiliary weights. The frame weight is much the same as the *Funfkampf*'s, but the three small barrel weights attach in the most peculiar manner. Unlike the 184F, which has a rail beneath the barrel to which the weights are attached directly, the standard pistol requires an odd upper weight with an extension collar around the muzzle; this weight attaches directly to the frame weight at the back, and in turn accepts the two smaller under-weights. When fully assembled, the pistol has a distinctly odd look about it.

Designed for hunting, the *Jagdmodell* was simply a 12cm-barrelled version of the basic design; 200mm overall and weighing 765gm with an empty magazine, it could not accept auxiliary weights. Though the standard chambering was .22 LR, an alloy-slide .22 Short rim-fire variant could also be obtained. Magazine capacities were generally ten and six rounds respectively.

How many Olympia-Pistolen were made prior to the Second World War is not known with certainty, though serial numbers suggest that the total was no greater than 12,500. The highest known number is 120750. It is worth recording that Hämmerli's first post-war broadsheets illustrated a genuine pre-1939 gun, serial number 85230, with its Walther marks touched-out and replaced by Hämmerli's.

## Revolvers and Combination Guns

Comparatively little change occurred in revolver design between the wars. The military status of these guns was being questioned everywhere expect in Britain, where the .38 Enfield replaced the .455 Webley as the standard service weapon, and the Depression of the 1930s persuaded most manufacturers (if they survived) to concentrate on existing designs. In the USA, this meant that Colt and Smith & Wesson continued to rely on their established solid-frame swing-cylinder designs, while Harrington & Richardson and Iver Johnson relied on anything from inexpensive solid-frame guns to surprisingly sophisticated break-open auto-ejectors.

Perhaps the most important introduction concerned a cartridge: the .357 Smith &

Wesson Magnum, developed by Philip Sharpe and Douglas Wesson by elongating the rimmed case of the .38 Special of 1902 to provide a much more powerful load – typically developing 535ft-lb with a 158-grain bullet compared with only 200ft-lb for its predecessor. The first production revolver, a minor variant of the 'N'-frame S&W 38/44 Model Hand Ejector of 1930, was completed on 8 April 1935; and, after a comparatively slow start, demand grew; the .357 was, after all, the most powerful revolver cartridge available until the introduction of the .44 Magnum twenty years later.

If the reputation of the revolver was eclipsed, at least militarily, the penchant for combination weapons not only survived the First World War but gained added impetus from the grim realities of trench warfare. Penknife guns were surprisingly popular. Designed to be readily concealed, the Defender and the Huntsman, 3in and 4in long respectively, were offered in the early 1920s by the American Novelty Company of Chicago. They were similar to the nineteenth-century Rogers patterns, but relied on a radial firing lever set into the upper strap of the grip instead of a pivoting trigger latch. An advert placed in 1923 in *Popular Science Monthly*, showing one of these guns being used to protect a child from a mad dog, claimed that they were a:

> '… practical pocket firearm! Easy to carry, absolutely safe, and has a thousand uses. Not a toy, but a sturdy well-made combination knife and pistol of finely tempered steel. Shoots regular .22 cal. Cartridges – hard and straight… American made and guaranteed.'

Straight-grip pen- and clasp-knife pistols were very easily disguised, but difficult to hold and aim. In these respects they were inferior to the pistol-grip patterns. Typical of the latter was the 'Little Pal', made by the L. G. Polhemus Manufacturing Company of Miami in Arizona. It was apparently offered in differing forms, as one gun is marked MOD. 23 – 22 SHORTS ONLY and another reportedly chambers .25 ACP. The Little Pal was basically a bolt-action pistol with additional knife blades beneath the muzzle. The guns generally had a simulated bone or staghorn fore-end and chequered plastic grips displaying an encircled 'S' mark.

# 8

## *The Second World War*

By 1939, ill-feeling had been simmering in Europe for several years and it had been obvious to many people – including military authorities – that war was inevitable. In Europe, many nations viewed the intentions of a Germany led by Adolf Hitler with suspicion; Austria and large parts of Czechoslovakia had already been assimilated into the Third Reich, and peace was being maintained increasingly uneasily. In the Far East, the Chinese and the Japanese had been locked in bitter conflict since 1937, while the border between the Soviet Union and Manchuria, by then a Japanese vassal state, was another source of dispute.

When Germany invaded Poland in September 1939, the die had been cast. Bound by the guarantees of treaties, Britain and then France declared war on Germany. But the campaigns were to be unexpectedly decisive. Once the 'Phoney War' had been concluded, the Germans surged through Belgium and, with unpredicted rapidity, forced the French to capitulate. Britain survived only by virtue of the English Channel, which provided a barrier that even German technology proved unable to conquer. Like the 'war to end wars' a quarter-century earlier, the Second World War was destined to last for years instead of months. A German invasion in the summer of 1941 forced the USSR into grudging co-operation with the Allies, and the Japanese attack on Pearl Harbor brought the USA into the war at the end of the year. Yet even the great industrial might of the USA was unable to subdue the Japanese without a long and bloody drive across the Pacific, or bring a rapid end to the war in post D-Day Europe. Once again, the ability of industry to supply the demands of the warring armies was put to the test.

In September 1939, the supply of handguns in most European armies was in a state of flux. Only the British had a settled issue – the .38-calibre Enfield revolver, adapted in controversial circumstances from the Webley. The Czechs, Finns and Poles had only recently approved the vz. 38, the wz. 35 Radom and the L-35 Lahti respectively, and series production of each of these three pistols had hardly got under way by 1939. The French had adopted the Mle 1935 SACM-Petter only four years earlier, and government technicians had been desperately trying to accelerate production by refining the design; the Italians were still re-equipping with the 1934-type blowback Beretta; the Belgians were issuing the first FN GP-35 pistols; and even the Germans, having accepted that the P. o8 (Parabellum) was too difficult to make, were still in the throes of developing a successor.

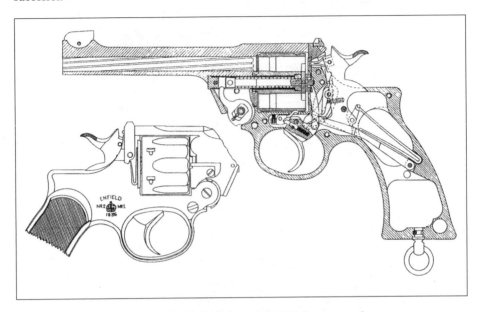

*The British No. 2 Mk I revolver, the 'Enfield', from the British Army manual.*

## Handguns and the German Envelopment of Europe

Though many words have been written about the service career and production history of the Walther P. 38, the steps from the blowback Militärische Pistole (an enlarged PP) of 1934, through the locked breech concealed-hammer Armee-Pistole of 1937 to the exposed-hammer Heeres-Pistole of 1938 have yet to be satisfactorily explained. What is certain, however, is that the Walther was not approved for issue until 1940 and not made in any real numbers until 1941. By 1945, despite being made not only by Walther but also by Mauser and Spreewerke, it had still failed to replace the Parabellum. This was partly due to its sophistication; simpler than the P. o8 in all respects excepting the safety and trigger mechanism, it remained complicated and comparatively difficult to make.

One of the great successes of the 1939–45 period was the FN-Browning GP-35 or 'High Power' pistol, which achieved the distinction of being mass-produced by the Allies and the Axis simultaneously – the former in the Inglis factory in Canada, and the latter in the sequestered Fabrique Nationale factory. Long before hostilities commenced, the Belgian government, well aware that the Liége district could not be satisfactorily defended against German incursions, had made plans to transfer as much equipment as possible from the FN factory in Herstal to Bruges, Anzeghem-près-Coutrai and even the Mécanouty suburb of Paris if war seemed inevitable. But the strength of *Blitzkrieg* caught the Belgians totally unprepared: the first Wehrmacht units crossed the border on

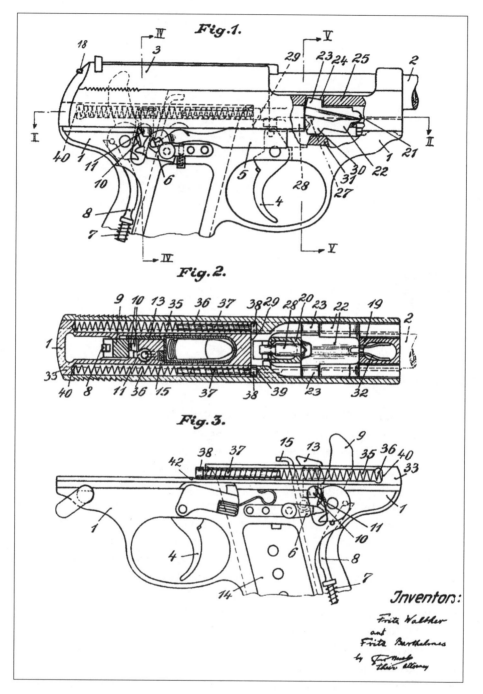

US Patent 2135992 (8 November 1938) protected the locking mechanism and trigger system of the internal-hammer Walther Armee-Pistole, which subsequently was adapted to become the external-hammer P. 38.

10 May 1940, entered Liége in triumph on 12 May, and the Belgian Army capitulated just sixteen days later. The FN factory in Herstal was captured, though much of the tooling and equipment of the ammunition factory in Bruges was evacuated to Toulon on four special trains.[1]

The German occupation forces wasted no time putting the Herstal factory to good use, unlike their predecessors in 1914. On 17 May two of the FN managers living in Liége were ordered to recommence production, but refused. Their stand was upheld by the president and vice-president of the FN Conseil d'Administration, but this was not enough to prevent the Germans seizing the factory and its inventory of complete and semi-complete weapons. On 20 May, the factory was confiscated for the duration of hostilities. Representatives arrived from the industrial-equipment section of the Oberkommando der Wehrmacht and Mauser-Werke, and work resumed. On 19 June, control of the Herstal factory was given to Deutsche Waffen- u. Munitionsfabriken – ironically, as DWM had been forced to sell shares held in FN in the aftermath of the First World War.

A Heereswaffenamt sub-bureau[2] was installed in September 1940 and production of weaponry commenced in earnest. FN-Browning GP-35 pistols were made alongside parts for the P. 38, the Karabiner 98k and the Maschinenkanone 108. Production of the Mle 10/22 also continued in Herstal-lèz-Liége under German control until August 1944, when the Germans withdrew, under pressure from the approaching Allies. The last German troops left the area early in September and the first Allied units entered Herstal on 8 September. During the occupation, 363,200 10/22 pistols were accepted by the Heereswaffenamt. Yearly production, according to Robert Whittington in his book *German Pistols and Holsters*, amounted to 200 in 1940, 45,000 in 1941, 69,000 in 1942, 166,000 in 1943 and 83,000 in 1944. The Mle 10/22 was given the Fremdengeräte designations *Pistole 626 (b)*, in 7.65mm Auto chambering, or *Pistole 641 (b)* in 9mm Short. A list of foreign military equipment had been drawn up by German military intelligence long before the Second World Wear and numbered to a master sequence.

The slides of the 10/22 pistols made under German supervision were marked FABRIQUE NATIONALE D'ARMES de GUERRE HERSTAL BELGIQUE over BROWNING'S PATENT DEPOSE on the left side, while the inspectors' marks of the Heereswaffenamt sub-bureaux 103, 140 or 613 were struck into various parts such as slide, frame and barrel. Whittington stated that:

'Serial numbers were a continuation of those numbers on the Belgian weapons, which had approached 70,000. Use of digits continued above 100,000 and even 200,000

---

1. The German invasion of France, which was similarly rapid and comparably successful, forced the French to surrender before the factory could be reconstructed. It finally fell into German hands when control of arms-making facilities in the 'Zone Libre' ('Vichy') was transferred in 1942.

2. This was controlled by Inspector No. 613 until November/December 1940, when he was replaced by No. 103. Inspector No. 140 relieved No. 103 in 1942. The identity of the men concerned has yet to be established beyond doubt.

without a letter. The majority of the numbers were reduced to a maximum of five digits with a small letter added  −  a with the second 100,000, b with the third 100,000, and c when production exceeded 300,000… '

Despite this claim, it will be seen that a disparity exists. The total number of guns that could have been made under the 'Whittington system', even assuming the serial numbers run as high as 99999c (though the highest reported during research has been 54851c), could scarcely have exceeded 330,000 − that is the remaining 30,000 in the 'Belgian serial number block' below 100,000, and three completed blocks of 100,000 each (a, b and c suffixes). This does not tally with the official HWaA procurement figures of 363,200; and Fabrique Nationale had made at least 200,000 Mle 10/22 pistols prior to the German invasion, since guns delivered to Yugoslavia in the early 1930s have been seen with numbers as high as 231,260. It is believed, therefore, that the Germans recommenced production at number 1 and ran onwards to about 63200c (that is 363,200). It is true that the serial suffix letters were not applied consistently and that some guns in the second block, for instance, were numbered in the form '165431' while others in the same group were '65431a'.

The HWaA procured many more 7.65mm than 9mm Mle 10/22 pistols, the latter being made only until the supplies of existing parts were exhausted. The quality of guns made in the early years of German control was generally quite good, but deteriorated rapidly after 1942. Many guns from this era exhibit rough machining marks and coarsely chequered wooden grips. When the FN factory was retaken by the Allies, nearly a quarter of the machine tools had already been taken back to Germany, and the Bruges (ammunition) and Zutendael (primers) factories had been destroyed. Subsequently some of the 6,000 V-1 flying bombs fired into Belgium damaged the structure of the FN Herstal factory far more than the retreating German Army had been able to achieve.[3]

In Czechoslovakia, from 1939 until 1945, the 7.65mm-calibre vz. 27 service pistols were made under German supervision as 'Pistolen 27 (t)'; their slides were marked BÖHMISCHE WAFFENFABRIK A.G. IN PRAG, a literal German translation of the original Czechoslovak marking. Most of the pistols made for the Wehrmacht and the police had vertical retraction grooves instead of the diagonal pattern associated with pre-1940 output; Pistole Modell 27 [space] Kal. 7,65 appeared on the left side of the slide. In 1941, however, the slide-top marking was abandoned in favor of the manufacturer's code 'fnh' ahead of the designation/calibre mark.

The vz. 38 pistol was the work of František Myška (1899–1972). Based on the lock-work of the 6.35mm ČZ 1936 pocket pistol, protected by Czechoslovak Patent no. 2814

3. The company's 75th anniversary history records that 1,976 (or 24 per cent) of the original 8,113 machine tools had been removed by September 1944. After the war had ended, the Office de Récuperation Economique de la Mission Militaire Belge managed to retrieve 1,228 machines − 331 from Germany and 897 from other parts of Belgium where they had been dumped during the German retreat. However, substantial numbers of tools had been installed in the DWM factory in Poznań (Poland) and they had been seized by the Russians.

(1927), it was intended for cavalry service. The 'vz. 37', chambered for the 9mm Short round, was made in small numbers to allow field trials to be undertaken. A few minor changes were then introduced, among them an alteration to the dismantling catch and the left side of the frame, and the perfected design was adopted by the Czechoslovak Army in April 1938 as the 'vz. 38'. The tip-slide construction was protected by patent No. 65558, granted to Česká Zbrojovka ackiová společnost of Strakonice on 6 November 1936.

Most commentators have considered the introduction of the vz. 38 to have been a mistake. Although firing the comparatively weak 9mm Short cartridge, the pistol was as large as those chambering 9mm Parabellum; and the stiffness of the self-cocking action made accurate shooting impossible without long and arduous practice. The only virtue was the ease of dismantling; a catch at the side released the slide/barrel unit to tip on a transverse pivot in the front of the frame. This allowed the slide to be slipped from the rear of the barrel, and a side-plate could be slid off to expose the lock-work.

An order for 41,000 guns was placed in June 1938, but no issues had been made when the Germans occupied the Strakonice factory. The pistols were immediately assimilated into German service as 'Pistolen 39(t)', all but 3,000 Luftwaffe-issue guns going to the Army.

The 1937-type guns displayed the manufacturer's name ČESKÁ ZBROJOVKA A.S. V PRAZE on the left side of the frame; vz. 38 were marked ČESKÁ ZBROJOVKA AKC. SPOL. V PRAZE on the slide beneath the ejection port. Most have inspectors' marks in the form 'F8' and '39' separated by the twin-tailed lion of Bohemia, the final digits giving the date ('39' = 1939). German displayed-eagle WaA 77 inspectors' marks may also be present.

In German-occupied Poland, managerial staff were imported from Steyr-Daimler-Puch and output of the VIS-35 or 'Radom' was diverted to the Wehrmacht. These pistols customarily bear German proof and inspectors' markings. Slides are marked F.B.RADOM VIS MODEL 35. PAT. NR. 15567 in a single line, usually above the German designation P.35 (P.). Designation marks will also be found on reissued ex-Polish weapons. Interestingly, the Radom factory was one of the very few munitions-makers never to be allocated a production code by the Germans; it operated under its own name throughout the war.

The construction and finish of wz. 35 pistols made prior to 1943 were eminently acceptable, but a progressive deterioration led to the supersession of good-quality blueing by a grey-green phosphate finish; the omission of the stock-slot on the heel of the butt; the deletion of the stripping catch on the left rear of the frame; and the substitution of radially-grooved wooden grips for finely chequered plastic. In addition, the pins driven through the frame to retain the hammer, the sear and the grip-safety lever were replaced with rolpins.

When the Germans evacuated Radom in the face of the Russian advance, in the autumn of 1944, large numbers of components were evacuated to the Steyr factory (or to one of its subsidiaries) and work continued into 1945. The quality of these, which bear the code 'bnz' was exceptionally poor. Total production of Radom pistolsunder German control has been estimated at 310,000 guns.

The German armed forces, paramilitary organisations such as the SA and the SS, and the police forces relied greatly on small-calibre blowbacks, including the Walther PP/PPK series, the Mauser HSc and the Sauer 38 (h). All three of these were efficient designs, with the Sauer perhaps the most advanced.

Changes were made as the war progressed to accelerate production. As far as the Walthers are concerned, the pronounced step behind the rear trigger-guard pivot of the Walther PP and PPK, below the magazine catch, was eliminated in 1943 to save machine time. The projection of the frame beneath the hammer was lengthened slightly in much the same period. This appears to have occurred in the region of gun number 250000P but, as with so many of these revisions, some degree of overlap is to be expected. As parts are often already on hand when changes are specified, hybrid guns always result until supplies are exhausted.

As the war progressed, so the standard of finish declined from a rich commercial blue to a blue wash over the major components. The fine polishing and attention to detail that had characterised Walther's peacetime wares was sacrificed in pursuit of speed, post-1942 examples often showing coarse milling marks, and previously squared-off edges that had become sloppily rounded. And, finally, shortages of oil forced the substitution of pressed-wood grips for the original injection-moulded plastic varieties. A few even had experimental grey phosphate finishes, comparable to Parkerization.

A few guns were made in 1945 with the code letters 'ac' replacing the banner trademark on the slide. These pistols are marked, typically, '384771P' above a large 'ac' on the right side of the slide (not the left) and were apparently confined to the 370000–394000P block. A further 2,000 guns were then made in the last few weeks of the war, bearing no marks at all other than an occasional proof.

Many 7.65mm guns will be found with lanyard loops set in a screwed-in eye on the base of the butt on the left side; most of these were added after the war by the French, to virtually any gun that was considered in good enough condition for issue to the French armed forces. The few original German loops were fixed on the base of the butt behind the magazine well.

Production continued until the end of the Second World War, when the PPK numbers had reached the low 430000 block and continued with an 'A' suffix. The highest known numbers are 431332K and 433521A for the PPK, compared with 396979P for a standard Polizei-Pistole.

## Handguns and Japan

The beginning of the Sino-Japanese War in 1937 intensified production of the Japanese 14th Year Type handguns: 11,000 were made by Chuo Kogyo between March 1936 and March 1937, but more than 25,000 left the factory between March 1937 and March 1938. No mechanical or constructional alterations were made until it was discovered during campaigns in Manchuria that a gloved finger could not enter the small trigger guard. In about November 1939, therefore, in the region of gun number 70,000, Chuo Kogyo introduced an enlarged trigger guard.

An auxiliary magazine-retaining spring was added to the front of the butt in mid-1940 and the length of the striker was reduced from 75mm to 65mm at about the same time. The latter gave a longer striker fall, counteracting the progressive deterioration of the striker spring and overcoming ignition problems caused by insensitive ammunition. However, the striker modification was little more than a token solution to a very serious problem, as the power and design of the striker spring should also have been reconsidered. The locking-piece lugs on the 'short striker' pistols are cut longitudinally to allow the striker to pass by.

Chuo-Kogyo reached gun 99999 in September or October of 1941; the highest known number, 98963, bears a September date. The numbers then recommenced at *i*-01. Pistol *i*-8948 was made in August 1942, which indicates that there was a steady slowing of production owing, perhaps, to a shift in priorities – Chuo Kogyo was also making machine-guns. Production of the 14th Year Type pistols continued until early in 1944, when it ceased in favour of the Type 94. Gun *i*-19799 is the highest known number and was made in April 1944. No pistols are known to have been made in 1945, though some may have been assembled from parts. The factory had been put on a war footing in 1939; yearly production quantities prior to 1938 were understandably much less than the figures quoted here for 1939–45, but are not known with as much precision.

The lowest number yet noted on a wartime Nagoya-Toriimatsu pistol is *i*-41003, dating from May 1942. Whether the no-prefix block, 1–99999, had been completed is not currently known and the kana symbol may only have been used to distinguish wartime from pre-war. If Nagoya's assembly was reasonably consistent, and assuming that the first pistol of the second run was *i*-01, it seems reasonable to conclude that the factory recommenced manufacturing 14th Year pistols in the 15th or 16th years of the Showa *nengō* (1940 or 1941). The former is more likely, as the maximum annual production capacity of the factory has been listed as '20,000 pistols'. The highest known *i*-prefix number was made in October 1943, and the lowest *ro*-number in January 1944. Consequently, *i*-99999 must have been reached late in 1943 and another series began. Most post-1944 Nagoya pistols have plain-knurled (or flangeless) retraction grips.

The factory continued to make the guns until the middle of 1945, when numbers reached the *ro*-72000 block. An illustration in the first volume of the *Gun Collector's Digest* indicates that *ro*-72027 and *ro*-72028 were found unfinished in the Toriimatsu factory after Japan had capitulated, which gives an accurate guide to the state of production. These two guns have three-flange retraction grips rather than the plain-knurled or plain-surface variety, but the factory may simply have been using old parts. The finish of many guns made in the last months of 1944 and the first half of 1945 was awful, but the need was more for quantity than quality.

Owing to a largely unsatisfactory assessment of the relationship between the first and second Nagoya-Toriimatsu production runs, the total may be as much as 90,000 greater than has been claimed. Slightly more than 400,000 14th Year Type pistols may, therefore, have been made.

There are many differing opinions of the pistol, most of which are uncomplimentary. The most damning is Robert Wilson's, but he had at least taken the opportunity to assess the value of the Japanese weapon under combat conditions. Even accepting his notoriously low opinion of anything that was Japanese, the assessment is quite accurate; the 14th Year magazine 'safety', the poor quality of the striker spring and the method of magazine removal are bad features, fully deserving criticism. But it is unfair to decry the Japanese pistols solely on the grounds that they were poorly made. German and Russian industry was also responsible for some notably badly made weapons, particularly when conditions had become chaotic through heavy bombing or wholesale relocation.

Yet faint praise cannot excuse the worst features of the 14th Year Type Pistol, particularly the weakness of the striker spring. Wilson, then stationed in Borneo, seized his opportunity to test the certainty of action in pistols surrendered after September 1945. He reported that:

'… these pistols [three 14th Year and two *Ko-gata* Nambus] were in poor condition; they were battered, rusty and had presumably seen much service. Ammunition… was obtained from an apparently untouched store, but it was later discovered that this… had been made in 1941 [and] it was impossible to say how long it had been in store in the tropics. In this distinctly unscientific series of experiments, a total of 148 rounds were [*sic*] fired from two examples of the Year 14 and one example of the Nambu.'

The results were illuminating – first, 14th Year Type Pistol No. 86356 fired 64 rounds with 46 misfires and one failure to feed. The same pistol was then fired again, with a new striker spring, and there were no misfires in ten shots fired. Next came 14th Year Type Pistol *i*-13846, which fired 33 rounds with 24 misfires, and lastly *Ko-gata* Nambu No. 9265 (made by TGE) which encountered 10 misfires in 40 rounds.

Colonel Wilson thought that the tests were largely inconclusive:

'… due chiefly to their rough nature and the fact that the ammunition employed could not be relied upon. However, it seems reasonable to suggest that Test 1 demonstrated a weak and rapidly tiring spring, possibly of poor quality in the first place, also that from the limited data obtained the Nambu behaved better than the Year 14… '

Even allowing for the deterioration of the cartridges – and the quality of Japanese propellants was sometimes very poor indeed – the trials clearly showed some of the problems confronting the soldiery.

The Japanese Type 94 pistol was also being made in quantity when the Second World War began in Europe. A change in the sear contours and the rear left side of the frame was made in the period 1939–40, and a flattened sear bar tail replaced the earlier stepped variety. Most of the pistols made before the middle of 1940 were of good materials and displayed acceptable surface finish, but the quality of finish and materials declined steadily until, by the beginning of 1943, the products had become noticeably bad. By 1944 the quality had declined even more, and the last few made in 1945 were among the worst service handguns ever manufactured. Their parts fitted extraordinarily badly and their surface finish consisted of little more than tool marks and blemishes.

Production was never spectacular and remained steady; only some 72,000 guns were made in the decade 1935–45. However, the Nambu/Chuo Kogyo/Nagoya-Toriimatsu conglomerate also made 14th Year Type pistols, to which priority was presumably initially accorded since they were infantry weapons; the Type 94 was issued to air crews, tank crews and some officers, and was required in relatively smaller numbers. It is also conceivable that the large amount of hand finishing required by the Type 94 acted as a brake, as the figures indicate that there was no marked increase in production towards the end of the war. The facilities were estimated to have been capable of making 20,000 Type 94 and 45,000 14th Year Type pistols per annum in 1944–5, though these targets were never reached. The Nagoya-Toriimatsu factory was badly damaged by American air raids and this may have restricted output.

### The Lahti in Wartime

In eastern Europe, about 4,000 Finnish L-35 Lahti pistols had been made by the beginning of the Winter War with the USSR in 1939. The field campaigns proved that the Lahti, designed by a Finn for service in Finland, was outstandingly reliable. Robert Wilson reported that:

> 'Early in 1942 the writer [Wilson] met a British officer of Swedish origin who had served with the Finnish Army in the Winter War of 1939–40. This officer thought very highly of the Lahti pistol... He recalled an incident during the Winter War when his sub-unit was attacking leaguered Russian tanks under cover of a heavy snow storm. He described how nearly all the weapons available, both Finnish and Russian, machine-guns, machine carbines and even rifles, were put out of action by the freezing snow. But the Lahti pistols of his unit were unaffected.'[4]

Unfortunately, pistols were in short supply and the Finns were forced to use any they could acquire. Nagant revolvers and Tokarev pistols, FN-Brownings, Mausers and Parabellums were all used wherever and whenever possible, but accurate records of captured Russian weapons were not kept – the Finns were so desperately short of handguns, valuable in hand-to-hand combat, that they rarely gave up captured examples to be refurbished, inventoried and reissued.

---

4. Lt.-Col. R. K. Wilson, 'Low Velocity Automatic Arms', unpublished manuscript.

Production of the m/35 L continued during the war, when a few were made in Jyväskylä without the accelerator. It is assumed that they date from early 1940, the elimination of the accelerator representing an attempt to simplify production. The m/35 L Type II was only made for a few months: probably fewer than 500 existed. Construction and markings remained the same as the Type I. However, the auxiliary spring controlling the locking unit was discarded as the weight of the inverted U-block proved sufficient to ensure engagement with the bolt. The machining of the receiver was simplified since the locking-piece spring housing was no longer necessary.

Series production – quantities were never large – continued in the state rifle factory after the end of the Winter War, but experience gained in the fighting had shown that a few design changes were desirable before production continued still further. In the region of gun 5,250, therefore, the design of the receiver was changed and the resulting m/35 L Type III differed in several respects from Types I and II. The back edge of the loaded-chamber indicator housing was squared instead of rounded, and the sides of the receiver were milled flush as far as the protruding reinforce containing the locking piece. The spring-steel ejector was still inset in the lower left side of the receiver but the oil-impregnated lubricating pad was omitted from the locking block housing. Experience with the Type II Lahti had shown that the accelerator was desirable, though not essential to the weapon's operation, and it was promptly reintroduced. The Type III was made in the state rifle factory until 1949–50, although production was slow as much time was expended on hand-finishing and assembly. It seems that fewer than 10,000 guns were made, though many other estimates have been offered.[5]

By the late 1950s, many of the guns in service were beginning to show signs of wear and an inherent design weakness had led to many being discarded – simply because their receivers and bolts had been declared obsolescent or unserviceable. A small quantity of replacement receivers and bolts was ordered from Valtions Metallitehdas ('Valmet') in 1958–61 and fitted to old frames. The new receivers are usually – but not always – marked VALMET and L-35 across the top surface, and are identical with those of the Types III and IV Lahti pistols apart from the omission of the loaded-chamber indicator and its prominent housing. The new bolts discarded the older full-length recoil spring and guide rod assembly, which was replaced with a spring guided by a short rod attached to the bolt; the spring floats at its rear end and bears against the standing breech. Additionally, the incline of the firing pin tunnel was reduced relative to the major longitudinal axis of the bolt. It has sometimes been suggested that Valmet made completely new guns, but the work was apparently confined exclusively to fitting new receivers and bolts in refurbished frames. These guns are known as m/35 L *Vammakoski* ('repaired').

---

5. In addition to regular production, several hundred pistols were assembled in the late 1940s from blemished and oversized parts that, though materially sound, had been rejected by the Army inspectors. These m/35 L Type IV pistols were sold privately to Army officers; identical with the Type III, they had squared loaded-chamber indicator housings, plain-milled receivers and serial numbers such as V 0239 and V 0292. The Sotamuseo states that about a thousand guns were made in the 'V 0' series and it is believed that numbers ran from V 01 to about V 0970.

The m/35 is regarded as a very accurate weapon, which its linear barrel movement and the long receiver/frame support ensured. The receiver, of course, acts as a fixed extension of the barrel. The service pistols were expected to put eight shots in a 15cm circle at 50m when new. Some Finnish sources claim that the Lahti is subject to jamming, which may be due to the elimination of the locking-block spring and the oil-impregnated lubricating pad as pistols from the first production run functioned flawlessly during the Winter War. However, owing to a peculiarity in the feed system, the mechanism will only function satisfactorily with cartridges loaded with ogival bullets; truncated (flatnose) bullets cannot be guaranteed to feed properly.

## Production and the Stress of War

Reaching production targets set by governments and military authorities was one of the biggest problems of the Second World War, when soldiers often lost more guns in combat than industry could make to replace them. The shortfall in the production of handguns presented most of the warring armies with problems. Handguns were traditionally made by only a handful of manufacturers, and even the recruitment of new ones often failed to answer demand. Another limiting factor was the decline in the reputation of the handgun as a combat weapon, as the rise of the submachine-gun during the inter-war period had called the utility of the pistol into question. Though submachine-guns were generally confined to pistol ammunition, they had much larger magazines and were capable of firing automatically without the problems of controllability that inevitably made lightweight handgun-size 'machine pistols' difficult to shoot accurately.

It is true to say that almost all of the pre-1940 submachine-guns were too complicated to make in quantity. The German MP. 38 and MP. 40 (the mis-called 'Schmeissers') were among the most efficient, but even they were made in accordance with pre-war ideas of what a gun of this type should be; even though some advanced fabrication methods had been employed in embryonic form, manufacture was still firmly based on traditional precision-engineering techniques. Consequently, production in 1940–5 was limited to about 950,000 guns.

By way of comparison, the production of P. 08 (Parabellum) pistols – mainly by Mauser-Werke AG, but with a few thousand from Krieghoff – is estimated to have amounted to 499,448 between March 1939 and October 1942. The total output of the Parabellum's supposed successor, the Walther P. 38, reached about 1,175,000 by 30 April 1945. The influence of increased production and the impressment of Walther, Mauser and Sauer blowbacks (not to mention the guns that were being made under German supervision in Czechoslovakia and Poland, or bought in Hungary) is implicit in the rise of the Wehrmacht pistol inventory from 552,962 in September 1940 to more than 1.6 million in August 1944. However, losses were also stupendous, more than 52,000 in July 1944 alone.

In an effort to provide ever more handguns, increasingly desperate (and ultimately unproductive) efforts were put into the development of *Volkspistolen* (People's Pistols') in the last six months of the war.[6] But the quantities would have been as nothing compared to the output of MP. 3008, a simplified derivative of the Sten gun, which was projected to reach 200,000 *monthly* by the summer of 1945. In the event, the simplified pistols had little effect on the German war effort. However, their legacy could be seen in post-war developments such as the Heckler & Koch PSP (P7) and the Steyr GB.

In Britain, the picture was a little different. Handgun acquisitions included nearly 26,000 .455-calibre No. 1 (Webley) revolvers, 192,500 .38-calibre No. 2 (Enfield) revolvers, 120,000 .38-calibre Webley Mk IV revolvers, and 400,000 assorted revolvers – including large numbers of .38 Colts and Smith & Wessons – ordered in the USA in 1940–2. Output of Sten Guns during the Second World War is said to have been 4,184,237, excluding pilot models made in 1941. (In addition, there were about 80,000 Lanchesters and at least 514,000 Thompsons of various patterns.)

The authorities in the United States were better placed to secure the supply of handguns, being able to channel into military service the commercial production of Colt, Smith & Wesson and some lesser revolver makers such as Harrington & Richardson and Iver Johnson. However, production of the M1911A1 Colt-Browning service pistol was confined at the outbreak of war to Colt, and the problems of answering sudden increases in demand were much as they had been during the earlier war. And they were answered in much the same way: by the recruitment of additional contractors with experience of precision engineering, backed by legions of sub-contractors to provide some of the lesser parts.

Unlike the WWI manufacturing programme, which failed to provide tangible results by the time of the November 1918 Armistice, the later efforts were successful: in addition to 520,316 supplied by Colt's Patent Fire Arms Mfg Co. (December 1940–September 1945), 1,032,000 guns were made in 1942–5 by Remington-Rand, Inc., of Syracuse, New York; 369,000 in 1943–5 by the Ithaca Gun Company of Ithaca, New York; and 55,000 by the Union Switch & Signal Company of Swissvale, Pennsylvania, in 1943.[7] These quantities proved to be sufficient to meet requirements, restricting Union Switch & Signal to a single contract, yet they were eclipsed by the output of the M1 carbines – which rose from less than 400 by June 1942, at the start of work, to 2,892,697 by the end of 1943. By the end of the war with Japan, 15th August 1945, more than 5 million carbines had been issued.[8]

---

6. For additional details, see John Walter, *Guns of the Third Reich* (2004), pp. 190–2.

7. When tenders for the M1911A1 were advertised, eight bids were received: from several well-known firearms makers such as Harrington & Richardson, Iver Johnson, Marlin, Savage and Winchester, the Burroughs Adding Machine Company, the Lanston Monotype Machine Company, and the Singer Mfg Co. 'Educational contracts' for 500 guns apiece were given to Harrington & Richardson and Singer; the former made no guns at all, whereas Singer delivered all of its order. However, the authorities then decided that Singer had more important priorities, and the gauges, tools, jigs and fixtures for the pistol were sent to the Ithaca Gun Company.

8. It has been estimated that about 6.2 million M1, M1A1, M2 and M3 Carbines had been made by the end of the war with Japan in August 1945. See John Walter, *The Rifle Story* (2006), pp. 231–7. By comparison, wartime acceptance of M1911A1 pistols was put at 1,878,742.

Attempts were made to simplify the basic M1911A1, leading to a design made largely of sheet-steel stampings that was claimed not only to make production much quicker but also save substantial quantities of valuable raw material. Only about a dozen pistols of this type were made, but they were substantially heavier than the standard M1911A1 and the output of conventional pistols proved to be more than sufficient to meet demand. The project was quietly dropped when the fighting ceased.

Production figures for the USSR are much more difficult to authenticate, but show a distinct tendency to concentrate on simple submachine-guns at the expense of the Tokarev pistol and the venerable Nagant 'gas-seal' revolver, which had re-entered production largely because the recoiling barrel of the Tokarev did not suit the pistol to the firing ports of armoured vehicles. Fragmentary acceptance figures show that about 280,000 pistols and 134,000 revolvers were made in 1941–2; the output of submachine-guns (PPSh and PPS) in 1942 alone amounted to 1.5 million.

Among the simplest of the handguns to be made in quantity during the war was the single-shot Liberator, developed on behalf of the US Joint Psychological Warfare Committee by a team led by George Hyde and made by the Inland Division of General Motors. Hyde is best known for his submachine-guns.

Known officially as the 'Flare Projector, Caliber .45' (FP-45) to disguise their true purpose, Liberators were to be dropped behind German lines to arm partisans and resistance personnel. A million were ordered in May 1942 and delivered within a calendar month by the Guide Lamp Division factory in Anderson, Indiana, at a total cost of $1,710,000. The design was basic in the extreme, relying on stampings and spot-welding, and several of the parts fulfilled more than one function. Liberators were easy to conceal – only 5½in long, they had a 4¼-inch smooth-bore barrel and weighed 21½oz – and were each packed in a waxed waterproof carton, accompanied by a pictorial instruction sheet and ten .45 ACP cartridges hidden inside the hollow butt.

Pulling the locking block back and turning it to the left through ninety degrees cocked the striker and allowed the breech-plate to be slid vertically to open the chamber. A spent case could be punched out with a separate ejector rod (a stout twig could often suffice) and a new round was pushed into the chamber. The breech-plate was closed, the locking block was turned back and pushed forward, and the Liberator could be fired.

About 500,000 guns were shipped to Britain, the remainder going to China and the Pacific. Few were ever used; the Far Eastern theatres were sceptical of the crudity of the single-shot Liberator and its very poor accuracy. The story in Europe was no better. Production of Sten Guns in Britain had accelerated to such a level that the authorities sensibly decided that a 9mm submachine-gun – particularly one which shared a standard German service cartridge – was much more useful than a crude pistol which would be useless once its ten .45 rounds had been expended. Consequently, most of the Liberators were dumped in the Irish Sea or simply melted down to allow their valuable steel content to be recycled.

# 9
# *The Modern Era*

The history of the handgun in the second half of the twentieth century – effectively, since the end of the Second World War – can be divided into several parts. Perpetuating production of the guns that had served in wartime was one obvious way of answering any handgun shortage, even though large numbers of war-surplus weapons made this unlikely. Another method was to invest in new ideas and new technology, but this was potentially expensive and sufficient of a risk to discourage all but the bravest (or most foolhardy) investors. The rise in competition shooting on a scale unknown prior to 1939 was a third factor; and the substantial growth of recreational and 're-enactment' shooting was a fourth.

The defeat of the principal Axis power, Germany, initially removed from the equation guns such as the Luger, the Walther P. 38, the Walther PP/PPK series, the Mauser HSc, and the Sauer 38 (H); the other major enemy state, Japan, had had little to offer in the way of handguns. Britain ended the war still using the Enfield revolver, a minor modification of the venerable Webley; the armed forces of the USA remained faithful to the 'A1' upgrade of the .45-calibre Colt-Browning of 1911; and the Russians, somewhat grudgingly, had committed to the Tokarev.

The end of the war wrought another large-scale change in the European map. The surge of the Soviet armies into Germany from the east allowed the USSR to re-establish its domination in areas where Russia had lost control in 1917 – Poland and the Baltic republics of Estonia, Latvia and Lithuania. In addition, the emergence of pro-Soviet regimes in the German Democratic Republic ('East Germany'), Czechoslovakia, Hungary, Bulgaria and Romania left only Finland and the leftist but non-aligned Yugoslavia as bastions against Soviet domination of eastern Europe.

One common result of Sovietisation was the abandonment of individual small-arms designs in favour of Soviet regulation patterns, which, as far as handguns were concerned, meant first the Tokarev ('TT') and then the Makarov ('PM'). Work on the Polish Radom or 'VIS-35' did not recommence after the war had ended,[1] which was at

---

1. However, from 1992 onwards, small numbers of pistols were made in Poland by Zaklady Metalowe Lucznik of Radom to satisfy the collector/re-enactment market. They were made *(continued opposite)*

least partly due to the dispersal by the Germans of a part of the production line. Czechoslovakia briefly recommenced work on the vz. 27, production of which had been continued under German supervision as the Pistole 27 (t), but had soon proceeded to the ČZ 50 blowback and the fascinating vz. 52, a roller-locked military handgun that soon encountered Soviet disfavour. None of the Baltic states had made handguns of their own during the their brief inter-war independence, and the Yugoslavs had bought almost all of theirs in Belgium from Fabrique Nationale. Eventually, the Yugoslav Zavodi Crvena Zastava (ZCZ, 'Red Banner Factory') made copies of the Tokarev pistol and a smaller, if externally similar blowback.

## The Commercial Scene

However, there were still fortunes to be made. The greatest success of the post-1945 handgun industry, at least until comparatively recent times, was the FN-Browning GP-35 or 'High Power'. Its pre-war origins, described in greater detail in *Chapter 7*, led to sales to a variety of countries by 1939 – and then to production under German auspices during the Second World War (*see Chapter 8*).

When hostilities ceased, the Herstal factory, which had been making articles as diverse as jerry cans and 'mud grips' (enabling tank tracks to get a better grip) for the US armed forces, began the refurbishment of small-arms. The quantities were enormous: more than 2.1 million were treated between 6 June 1945 and 23 June 1946. The Browning Arms Company once again began to buy FN-made shotguns and hunting rifles, and new markets for military small-arms were explored. By 1950, business had grown from the sales of limited quantities of handguns destined for police in Belgium, France, the Netherlands, Germany and Greece to much more substantial orders for war matériel placed by China, Egypt and Venezuela. The GP-35 was one of the major beneficiaries not only of the reconstruction of business but also of the gradual move towards the issue of standard guns in virtually all NATO-aligned armies other than France and the USA.[2]

In addition to the GP, prior to the advent of the Glock (*see below*), the only handguns to see widespread success were the Beretta 951/Beretta 92 series, based on a locking system adapted from that of the Walther P. 38; the SIG-Sauer series; and the traditionally-made ČZ 75/ČZ 85 series made by Česká Zbrojovka in Uhersky Brod (now in the Czech Republic). The SIG-Sauer and Czechoslovak pistols are all basically variations of the Colt-Browning tip-barrel locking system, but have double-action triggers and – in some versions at least – ambidextrous controls. Among the most obvious differences is that the Swiss guns used advanced metalworking techniques to

---

in accordance with a 1937-vintage set of blueprints and are difficult to distinguish at a glance from the pre-1940 examples.

2. An idea of the growth can be gained from statistics relevant to the FAL (light automatic rifle), which had been adopted only by a single country in 1953 but by no fewer than 49 by 1964. The GP-35 benefited from this success, about 250,000 being made in the same period for military and police forces throughout the world.

keep quality high and costs down in a notoriously expensive country, whereas the Czechs, with lower labour costs, could afford to perpetuate much more traditional gunmaking methods.[3] The ČZ 75 has been deemed good enough to copy in Italy (by Bernardelli and Tanfoglio), in Switzerland (by ITM), in Britain (by John Slough), in Israel (by Bul) and in Turkey (by Sarsilmaz).

Another class of handgun, particularly popular in North America, is often termed the 'after-market upgrade'. Typical of these are the hordes of customised pistols based on the 1911-type Colt-Browning, which has a unique place in handgun mythology and is still extremely popular among IPSC target shooters. Some of the changes are comparatively minor, confined to re-shaping grips, extending the safety levers, or duplicating the controls so that the gun becomes ambidextrous; others are more radical – changes in the bushing in which the barrel pivots, usually in an attempt to enhance accuracy, or the use of cam-finger depressors instead of the original pivoting link.[4] A few guns even incorporate the locking system pioneered by SIG, relying on a sturdy squared lug rising into the ejection opening in the top of the slide instead of the more conventional barrel ribs rising into recesses in the interior of the slide-top.

Among the many 'Colt converters' are Auto-Ordnance Corporation of Blauvelt, New York; Les Baer Custom, Inc., of Hillsdale, Illinois; Ed Brown Products, Inc., of Perry, Missouri; Entréprise Arms, Inc., of Irwindale, California; Kimber Mfg. Co., of Yonkers, New York; and Springfield Armory of Geneseo, Illinois. Dan Wesson Firearms of Norwich, New York, and Smith & Wesson also offer customised versions of the M1911/M1911A1 series, in addition to the many variations still made by the Colt Manufacturing Company. Outside the USA, Para-Ordnance, Inc., of Scarborough, Ontario, Canada, and Peters Stahl GmbH of Paderborn, Germany, have also contributed excellent 1911-type pistols.

The locked-breech Ruger and Smith & Wesson pistols, though operating similarly to the Colt-Brownings, are rarely used as the basis for conversions. One exception to this was the ASP, marketed by Armament Systems & Procedures of Appleton, Wisconsin, which was effectively a Smith & Wesson Model 639 adapted to serve as a 'concealed carry' personal-defence weapon. All external projections were suppressed or rounded-off, including the hammer spur, transparent grips were fitted to allow the contents of the magazine (which was appropriately slotted) to be assessed at a glance, and a Guttersnipe sight allowed the firer to shoot quicker and more accurately than the standard fixed sights would allow.

When the Second World War ended, the production of rim-fire handguns, which had been suspended for the duration of hostilities with the exception of guns such as the

---

3. By the 1990s, however, spiralling costs in the Czech Republic caused Česká Zbrojovka to introduce the CZ 100, with a polymer frame and a variety of synthetic fittings.

4. Smith & Wesson pistols, for example, feature barrel bushings bought from Briley Mfg., Inc., of Houston, Texas; hammers and safety levers from the Chip McCormick Corporation of Manchaca, Texas; sights from Novak's, Inc., of Parkersburg, West Virginia; and beavertails and magazines from Wilson Combat of Berryville, Arkansas.

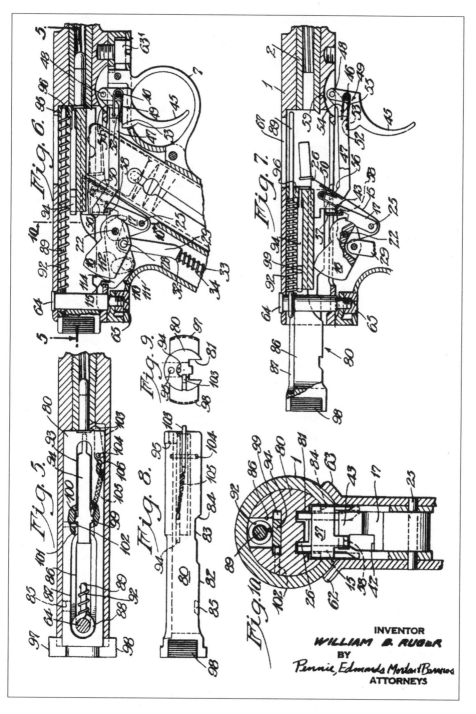

*One of the pages of drawings accompanying US Patent 2655839, granted on 20 October 1953 to William Ruger to protect the Mark I .22 rim-fire pistol.*

High Standards that had seen military use,[5] began again with the re-introduction of pre-1941 designs. The Colt Woodsman reappeared, as did the basic High Standard patterns, but a more innovative approach was taken by the late William Batterman 'Bill' Ruger (1916–2002). Ruger and his partner Alexander Sturm were keen to exploit a blowback pistol, gauging that a niche existed for a gun that looked like the German Parabellum, 'Luger' in US parlance, but chambered inexpensive .22 LR rim-fire ammunition. The similarity of the names 'Luger' and 'Ruger' was coincidental, but a great marketing asset nevertheless.

Sturm, Ruger & Co. was established in 1949 to make the 'Mark I Automatic Pistol', the first deliveries being made in 1951.[6] The success of the .22 pistol, which was soon adopted by the US armed forces as a training aid, encouraged Ruger to develop the Single Six, a rim-fire version of the Colt Model P ('Peacemaker') revolver introduced in 1953, before introducing the first of a long line of high-class centre-fire revolvers: the Blackhawk of 1955. The genesis of the Ruger firearms is readily accessible in the form of an article by John C. Dougan in the 2004 *Guns Digest*. The millionth .22 LR Ruger pistol was made in 1979 and the millionth double-action Ruger revolver – a line begun in 1971 by the Security Six – dated from 1983.[7]

### Military Trials: Beretta and Glock

By the early 1980s, it was obvious to many in the US Army that the M1911A1 Colt-Browning, a design which was then seventy years old, was due for replacement. An 'XM9' pistol competition was subsequently announced by the Joint Services Small Arms Program (JSSAP), 'Requests for Test Samples' being sent to manufacturers, importers, designers and other interested parties in November 1983. The progress of the trials, which ran from February to August 1984, has been widely reviewed and is comparatively well known. Not only were the tests characterised by the awful performance of some of the best-known European guns, something that reflected the trials of 1907 (*see Chapter 4*), but there was also an acrimonious spat between the US authorities and Smith & Wesson. The gunmaker felt that the Beretta M92, which was declared the victor (and subsequently adopted as the Pistol M9), had been unfairly favoured. Correspondence flew backwards and forwards for some years, but the authorities stood by their decision and Smith & Wesson had to be content with small orders placed on behalf of Special Forces, the FBI and a handful of police forces.

---

5. Many were used for basic training, but others – particularly the silenced High Standard Model B – were issued to the OSS and other specialist forces for use as assassins' weapons.

6. The US Patent protecting the .22 Ruger pistol, No. 2655839, was not granted until 20 October 1953, nearly *seven* years after the application had been filed on 5 November 1946.

7. The Mark I pistol, specially engraved and inlaid in gold, was sold by auction at the 1980 NRA meeting; the Security-Six revolver, similarly decorated, was auctioned at the 1985 SHOT Show. The proceeds of both sales went to shooting charities. In 1998, Bill Ruger himself gave a million dollars to fund the National Firearms Museum and another million dollars to allow the Buffalo Bill Historical Center to establish the Cody Firearms Museum.

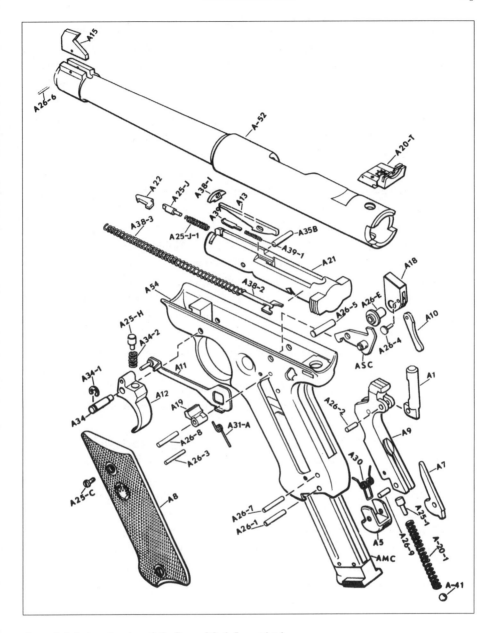

*An exploded-view drawing of the Ruger Mark I .22 pistol.*

Driven by the decision to replace the M1911A1 Colt-Browning, Ruger also began development of a 9mm-calibre automatic pistol. Introduced commercially in 1987, the P85 had had much to offer but was too late to take part in the XM9 trials; consequently, though many differing models have been prepared, it has never been able to challenge the Colt-Browning and the Smith & Wesson commercially.

In Europe, the worldwide sales of the FN-Browning GP-35 were sufficient to repel most of the challenges to its supremacy, even though the Walther P1 (the post-1957 version of the P. 38) and a near-relation, the Beretta M92, were adopted in Germany and Italy respectively. By 1980, however, even the GP was beginning to look dated. The trigger mechanism was restricted to single action, the safety controls were comparatively crude, and a reliance on traditional construction presaged expense. When the Austrian Army announced a competition to replace the GP in military service, a variety of handguns appeared. Many observers reckoned that the established reputation of the SIG-Sauer would be crucial, though others suspected that the Austrian origins of the Steyr GB would guarantee victory, even though whispers were heard that the pistol was not as efficient as it should be.

The GB was an interesting design. It had been developed in the early 1970s by a team of Steyr engineers led by Ulrich Zedrosser and Satish Malhotra, on the basis of some of the *Volkspistolen* developed in Germany at the end of the Second World War, and was the subject of a number of patents.[8] Before work began in Austria, however, small-scale production was begun in the USA by an importer, Les Rogak, who had formed LES, Inc., in Morton Grove, Illinois. The precise circumstances of this arrangement have never been revealed. However, the introduction of the Rogak Pi-18 was a disaster: quality was so poor that the gas bleed, the cornerstone of the delayed-blowback operating system, was exceptionally unreliable. Some of the last guns were made as blowbacks, relying on compressible fibre washers to absorb the recoil, and the project foundered in the late 1970s when Steyr filed a lawsuit. It has been estimated that only a little over 2,000 pistols had been made (1974–9).

The advent of the Austrian Army pistol trials encouraged Steyr-Daimler-Puch to re-engineer the Pi-18, which became the 'GB' (for *Gasbremse*, 'gas brake'). Many changes were made: the magazine was refined, a de-cocking system replaced the manual safety catch of the Pi-18, the magazine release catch was moved from the heel of the butt to the web behind the trigger, and the contours of the muzzle bushing were altered. The front of the trigger guard was squared to facilitate a two-hand grip.

Though the GB performed far better than the Pi-18 had ever done, the unexpected winner of the Austrian trials was a submission by Gaston Glock; 25,000 guns were ordered for the Austrian armed forces in 1983 and, a year later, Norway's became the first NATO army to buy them. The GB was entered in the XM9 trials in the USA, proving to be simpler than the better-known Heckler & Koch PSP, exceptionally accurate, and easy to handle. But it was less reliable than the control pistol (the M1911A1) and elimination came in May 1984. A few paramilitary sales were made to Pakistan and Lebanon in the mid-1980s, but the commercial appeal of the GB was too limited to ensure long-term success. Work stopped in 1986, after about 15,000–20,000 examples had been made, and the last batch of pistols was imported into the USA in November 1988.

---

8. For example German patents 4369593 and 4573280.

Protected by US Patent No. 4539889, granted to Gaston Glock of Vienna on 10 September 1985,[9] the basic design is a variation of the Colt-Browning, relying on a tipping barrel controlled by a shaped lug, but the pistols all embody the 'Safe Trigger System' protected by patents granted in many countries. The essence is a 'trigger within the trigger', a pivoting lever set into the leading edge of the actual trigger to lock the action until pressed inwards by the firer's finger. This is done unconsciously, and has proved to be very effective.

The Glock embodies so many synthetic parts that it subsequently came to be misleadingly described as the gun that could pass through X-ray equipment without being detected. In fact, the metal barrel, metal springs and an array of minor components were quite sufficient to alert any security system, and the slide has always been a mixture of polymers and metal alloy.

The guns can also be recognised by their squared contours and synthetic frames. The surface of the original frames was plain, with the grip areas roughened, but the so-called 'Pebble Frame' was substituted in January 1986; this was, in turn, replaced by an improved version with chequering on the grip straps (March 1989) and then with finger grooves on the straps and an extended under-barrel rail to accept laser projectors and similar accessories (June 1995). The version current in 2005 also had a key operated immobiliser in the rear of the grip behind the magazine well.

Like many modern military handguns, the Glocks are made in many differing versions. Among them are the Compact and Sub-Compact guns, with short and ultra-short grips. Though magazine capacities range from 9 to 33 rounds, depending on calibre and size, they must sometimes be matched to individual guns: consequently, the Sub-Compact magazine will only enter the butt of the Sub-Compact pistols, though the guns can accept any of the longer magazines. Similarly, the Compact magazine will fit the Compact and Sub-Compact versions, but not pistols with standard or full-length grips.

The standard Glock, the Model 17, has just 34 parts (including two small pins). The magazine is a 17-round double-column design, the controls are ambidextrous, and the double-action trigger system actuates a striker. Manual safety catches are deemed irrelevant, as the Glock is fitted with a trigger safety, a firing-pin lock, and an automatic trigger-bar safety that prevents firing unless the action is properly locked and the trigger is being pressed correctly. The Model 17 is about 7.3in long, with a polygonally rifled 4.5-inch barrel, and weighs about 22oz without a magazine. Details of the many different versions of the Glock will be found in the manufacturer's literature, on the company website, or summarised in books such as *Pistols of the World* (4th edition, 2004, pp. 143–5).

The magnitude of this unexpected success almost overwhelmed the small Glock factory in Deutsch-Wagram, which had been founded in 1963 to make grenades, entrenching tools and combat knives, and the initial orders were completed only with

9. The application had been made in the USA on 29 April 1982; the original Austrian patent application, however, had dated from 30 April 1981.

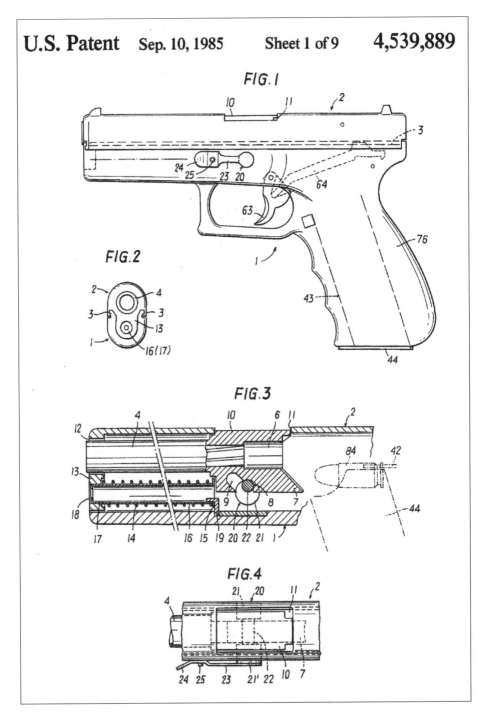

The first sheet of US Patent 4539889 (10 September 1985), granted to Gaston Glock to protect the basic design of the Glock pistol.

the assistance of subcontractors. As the success grew, however, Glock AG opened new factories in Smyrna, Georgia, USA (1985); in Hong Kong (1988); in Ferlach, the traditional Austrian gunmaking centre (1988); and in Montevideo, Uruguay (1990). The 2 millionth Glock pistol was exhibited in January 1999 at the SHOT Show. The guns have been adopted by police and military authorities throughout the world, and have been greatly favoured by Special Forces. They have an enviable reputation for durability and efficiency.

### The Revolver

Though the stock of the automatic pistol has quite clearly risen greatly since 1945, this has not necessarily been to the detriment of the revolver. Revolvers are easier to make and, in the opinion of some observers, easier and safer to use – particularly after the forcible introduction of transfer-bar systems by the US Gun Control Act of 1968. Though some of the old-time mass producers met their end in the post-war period (Iver Johnson and Harrington & Richardson among them), Colt, Ruger and Smith & Wesson all still offer sophisticated designs of revolver. Charter Arms was just one of many new manufacturers to appear in the USA in the 1960s, and, despite tribulations, continued to offer good quality but comparatively inexpensive swing-cylinder revolvers into the 1990s.

European manufacturing in recent years has been confined largely to insignificant personal-defence/recreational revolvers, high-grade target revolvers and 'Western' replicas. Occasional attempts have been made to re-introduce the revolver as a personal-defence weapon – by Fabrique Nationale, Luigi Franchi and others – but none has succeeded, and the automatic pistol remains supreme. Hermann Weihrauch oHG of Mellrichstadt (Germany) offers guns ranging from inexpensive 'plinkers' to good-quality target-shooting revolvers with anatomical grips and micro-adjustable sights, but is more the exception than the rule. Revolvers are still made in Spain by Astra-Unceta y Cia and Llama-Gabilondo y Cia, but the products of Rossi and Taurus in Brazil are, perhaps, not only better known but more widely distributed.

The antithesis of the single-shot derringer, the 'boot gun' and the assortment of rim-fire mini-revolvers, the large-bore ultra-power revolver has its origins in the .357 Magnum cartridge described in Chapter 7. Among the most important post-war developments was the introduction of the .44 [Remington] Magnum – popularised by the Clint Eastwood 'Dirty Harry' films, but introduced commercially in 1955. For many years, this remained the yardstick against which other handgun cartridges were judged. Another 'super power' attempt was made with the .454 Magnum Revolver cartridge developed by Dick Casull and Jack Fulmer in 1957–8, typically firing a 260-grain bullet with a muzzle velocity of 1,725ft/sec (1,720ft-lb); originally chambered in single-action Colt and Ruger revolvers, this subsequently became associated with the Freedom Arms Company guns now known as the 'Model 83'.

Where the .454 Casull cartridge led, others followed. The .475 and .500 Linebaugh rounds, adapted from .348 Winchester and .45-70 Government rifle cases, were developed in the late 1980s by John Linebaugh of Maryville, Montana, to fire bullets weighing more than 400 grains at muzzle velocities in excess of 1,250ft/sec (1,390ft-lb). The first guns were .45 single-action Colts with special five-round cylinders instead of the original six; now, however, the Ruger Bisley is the preferred basis for conversion. The Freedom Arms M83 has also been chambered for .475 Linebaugh cartridges.

Among other 'Big Bore' revolvers is the Magnum Research BFR, which has been offered in an assortment of rifle chamberings – .444 Marlin and .45-70 Government among them – alongside high-powered handgun rounds such as .480/475 BFR and .500 Smith & Wesson. This is an area in which experimentation will doubtless continue for many years.

### Target Shooting: Hämmerli and Walther

The needs of international target-shooting are still usually satisfied with highly specialised automatic pistols (for Standard and Rapid-fire competitions) and the sophisticated single-shot pistols (for Free Pistol competitions) that often derive from Aydt, Martini and similar dropping-block designs favoured prior to 1939.

Among the finest of the first generation of post-war automatic pistols was the Hämmerli-Walther, derived from the Olympia-Pistole that had taken several gold medals during the 1936 Berlin Olympic Games. Hämmerli had had a long and distinguished gunmaking tradition, including Martini-action single shot Free Pistols introduced in 1931, and the directors were keen to re-establish supremacy after 1945. Exactly when Walther and the Hämmerli management began discussions is not known, but meetings undoubtedly took place informally soon after the end of the Second World War. The first contract between the two parties was signed in March 1950, superseded in December 1954 by a modified version. Walther was to be allowed to resume production in Germany if the Allies allowed,[10] and, for some reason, South Africa was excepted from the worldwide sales rights.

The Hämmerli-Walther Model 200 was the first of the new guns, though differing little from the originals in most respects other than the markings on the slide. The slide had twenty grooves instead of the original Walther 22, still milled vertically, and the design of the sights and barrel weights remained unchanged. Three weights adding up to 700gm could be used in five differing combinations to suit the firer and the type of competition.

Comparing a 1952-vintage Hämmerli sectional drawing with a pre-war Walther equivalent emphasises how few changes had been made. However, there are slight but insignificant machining differences between the two types of gun, particularly to the

10. It has been claimed that a small quantity of Olympia-Pistolen, no more than fifty, was assembled in Ulm in the late 1950s from a mixture of old Walther and new Hämmerli parts. No details are known of the serial numbers, nor of any characteristics – other than markings – that would distinguish them from either pre-1939 Walther or post-1950 Hämmerli products.

lower rear part of the grip.[11] The slides of Swiss-made guns were marked *Lenzburg Hämmerli-Walther Switzerland* on the left side, ahead of *Olympia-Pistole*, and the combination of block, cursive and italic lettering looked decidedly odd. Serial numbers lay on the front right side of the slide and frame, and on the barrel; the proof marks were Swiss commercial, in the form of small crosses. Numbers began at O-100 for the .22 Short rapid-fire pistols, and O-5000 for the .22 LR standard pistols; the first in each group were delivered on 5 April and 27 August 1952 respectively.

Comparatively few changes were made to the basic design, though a three-slot compensator was added in 1954 (reduced to two slots in 1957) and the original fixed trigger was altered in 1956 to an adjustable pattern placed noticeably nearer the centre of the trigger guard. The design of the supplementary weights was altered in 1957 to conform to new UIT rules. The two frame weights were discarded; the size and shape of the standard barrel weight were altered; and a supplementary weight was introduced to clip beneath the barrel weight. At about the same time, the grooves milled in the slide became diagonal instead of vertical.

The Model 200 was 295mm long, with a 190mm barrel, and weighed 850gm (.22 Short version, alloy slide) or 940gm (.22 LR, steel slide) with an empty eight-round magazine. The auxiliary weights could add up to 290gm. Rifling remained the pre-war six-groove type, twisting to the right to make a turn in 450mm. The standard gun cost 425 Swiss francs in 1952, but ornamentation in the form of engraving and precious-metal inlay could easily add a hundred francs or more.

Derivatives of the basic gun included the Model 201 (1955–7), made with a 240mm barrel for target shooting under specific national target-shooting rules rather than those of the UIT. The Model 202 was similar, but had a wide French walnut palm-rest grip for Free Pistol competitions. Available in .22 Short or .22 LR, it was only marketed in 1955–7. The Model 203 was a minor variation of the 200, introduced in 1956 after a change was made to UIT rules in the wake of the Melbourne Olympic Games. This had been caused by the Soviet MTsZ-1, which was essentially a standard Margolin MTs with the action inverted so that the barrel lay below the firing hand. The intention was to reduce the tendency of the muzzle to rotate upward during rapid fire, but the gun was deemed to be too long and too radical to allow in competition.

Though the Hämmerli-Walther Model 203 shared the revised weights of the post-1957 Model 200, the palm-rest grip was narrowed to fall within the 150mm depth and 50mm width specified by the revised Free Pistol rules. The M203 was 315mm long, with a 190mm barrel, and, with all the supplementary weights in place, weighed 1,180gm (.22 Short) or 1,260gm (.22 LR). Magazines held six Short or eight LR cartridges.

The Model 204, known as the 'Amerikamodell', was a modification of the 200 introduced to conform to National Rifle Association (NRA) rules. The European

---

11. The original production machinery seems to have been taken by the Russians from the Walther factory in Zella-Mehlis, but may subsequently have been used to make the East German BUHAG target pistol of the 1950s – which was virtually an Olympia-Pistole with an exposed hammer.

marksmen of the 1950s were accustomed to moving the front sight vertically and the back sight laterally to achieve hits, but this was alien to U.S practice; consequently, the Amerikamodell had a fixed front sight and a multi-directional micro-adjustable back sight on the slide. The trigger pull and the sighting radius were also adjusted to NRA requirements, and a special hold-open mechanism was added to hold the slide back after the last round had been ejected until a new magazine was inserted in the feed-way; the slides of the European guns closed as soon as the empty magazine had been removed.

The 204 was offered with three supplementary weights, two that fitted beneath the frame and one – the largest – beneath the barrel. Made only in .22 LR rim-fire, the Model 204 was offered until 1963. It was 298mm long, weighed a maximum of 1,370gm (post-1958 two-weight system), and had non-adjustable French walnut thumb-rest grips giving a maximum depth of 132mm and a width of 48mm.

The Model 205 Amerikamodell of 1956–63 (confined to .22 Short) was identical mechanically with the 204, but had adjustable palm-rest grips for Free Pistol shooting. These gave the guns an overall length of 315mm, a depth of 155mm, and a width of 95mm. Maximum weight was 1,430gm (post-1958 system), and the magazines held eight rounds.

The 200 series of Hämmerli-Walthers were extremely successful, taking a gold medal in the 1954 world championship and the 1956 Olympic Games, but the emergence of rival designs, such as the US High Standards and the Soviet Margolins, gradually eroded the margin of superiority. Hämmerli embarked on a redesign programme, though initially confined largely to cosmetic issues, and the first Hämmerli Internationals, the Models 206 and 207, appeared in 1962.[12] The Hämmerli-Walthers were discontinued a year later, after only 2,916 had been made in .22 Short (numbered O-100 to O-3015) and 1,308 in .22 LR (O-5000 to O-6307).

The Walther designers, envious of the success of the Hämmerli derivatives of the pre-war Olympia-Pistole, had already embarked on a more radical design. The Olympia-Schnellfeuerpistole ('OSP') was completed in 1961, appearing on the commercial market a year later. Within a very short time – and, it has to be said, some effective product improvement – the OSP began to make a considerable name for itself in rapid-fire competitions. Though the Hämmerli-Internationals were still winning medals in standard pistol competition into the 1990s, their value for rapid-fire had declined rapidly towards the end of the 1960s. It was ironic that the Italian Giovanni Liverzani, firing an OSP, should smash his own world record (obtained with a Hämmerli-International) by posting an outstanding score of 598 × 600 in 1970.

Liverzani's new record stood for thirteen years – a very long time in shooting circles – before being broken by a single point, 599 × 600 being achieved by a Soviet marksman

---

12. A list of Hämmerli International pistols, and some of the championships gained with them, will be found in Douglas Robertson, 'Olympian Pistolen and Their Derivatives', in *Gun Collector's Digest*, fourth edition (1985), pp. 192–201.

with an IZh-31 pistol in 1983.[13] In the intervening period, however, the OSP won its fair share of glory: in the 1974 world championships, the individual gold and silver plus the rapid-fire team gold were won with it. In the 1978 championships, the first five positions in the rapid-fire competition (and the team gold) went to shooters with the OSP. At the 1984 Los Angeles Olympics, the Japanese marksman Takeo Kamachi took the individual rapid-fire gold.

A detailed examination of the Olympia-Schnellfeuerpistole shows something of the sophistication of this particular genre. The OSP is a very distinctive design, with the magazine ahead of the trigger aperture – a bad feature of combat pistol design, but ideally suited to a target gun, as it shifts a substantial part of the loaded weight ahead of the trigger finger. The greater the weight in front of the handgrip, the better the design; extra weight minimises the disturbance of aim caused by factors such as body tremors and trigger-snatch. Consequently, the OSP is markedly muzzle-heavy, especially fitted with its detachable muzzle weight.

There are only four basic components in the OSP: the frame, receiver, barrel, and detachable trigger/sear/hammer package. The first frames were machined from solid forgings, but a precision die-cast unit was perfected for production pistols. The back sight is carried on an extension of the frame, which runs backward over the top of the grip; the sight remains motionless during the firing cycle, owing to the enclosed reciprocating bolt, and is not prone to the inaccuracy that can arise from slide wear. The magazine housing is an integral part of the frame casting and lies directly ahead of the trigger aperture, which, on guns made prior to 1971, was virtually circular. It has since been a flattened oval.

The receiver is retained by a locking lever on the front side of the frame. This moved downward on the original prototype OSP, but has since been altered to move upward to unlock the receiver box. The barrel is retained by a locking screw in the front underside of the receiver. The breech block contains the spring-loaded inertia-pattern firing pin and, together with the main spring and the cocking piece, lies inside the hollow receiver housing. The packaged adjustable trigger is a masterful design, but contains an extraordinary number of parts to fulfil its multiple function.

The radial safety lever protrudes from the front left side of the grip, where it can be pushed down to the firing position. The letters 'F' and 'S' were struck into the frames of the pre-1971 OSP ahead of the lever, but are omitted from the later oval-aperture guns (where there is insufficient space). The magazine catch lies behind the magazine aperture, under the frame.

The first production guns were delivered in December 1961, differing from the prototype in many respects, although these were largely confined to unimportant details. The frame had become entirely slab-sided, but the barrel was cylindrical. So, too, was the supplementary barrel weight, which slid in a dovetailed slot under the

13. A tie-score of 598 × 600 had been achieved in 1976, by an Italian marksman firing an IGI-Domino pistol.

barrel and was locked in place with two bolts. The base of the magazine aperture was horizontal, rather than slanted, and the receiver-locking lever rotated upward instead of down. The back sight head had three large and one small transverse pins or screws visible on the left side, and the stippling design on the walnut palm-shelf thumb-rest grips had been revised. Only a single bolt held the grip to the frame casting.

These guns, which were made until 1971, had blued steel barrels and receivers, and matt-finish blue-grey diecast alloy frames. The company banner mark, the commercial marks of the Ulm proof house, and the calibre mark all appeared on the left side of the barrel ahead of its joint with the receiver. The serial numbers – for example O1064 – appeared on the left side of the frame in front of the rotary locking lever. The letters 'F' (*Feuer*, 'fire') and 'S' (*Sicher*, 'safe') were stamped into the left side of the frame ahead of the safety lever thumb-piece, which protruded from the leading edge of the grip behind the near-circular trigger aperture.

Early Olympia-Schnellfeuerpistolen were about 298mm long, had 115mm barrels, and weighed about 1,020gm without the supplementary barrel weight. They chambered the .22 Short rim-fire cartridge, having been specifically developed for rapid-fire shooting, and had five-round magazines. Shortly after volume production had commenced, in 1963, the OSP barrel was altered from eight- to six-groove rifling. At the same time, four holes were bored vertically through into the barrel from the top. Copied from an earlier Russian design, these were intended to leak some of the propellant gases upward as the bullet left the muzzle and act as a compensator to keep the muzzle down during rapid fire.[14]

The trigger system of the OSP underwent several minor changes in the late 1960s, and a special practice-firing trigger insert was introduced in 1967.[15] Sold with the OSP and its near-relation, the GSP, it is of much the same design as the standard trigger system and shares similar adjustments, but incorporates a 'ratchet hammer' to give five audible clicks as the trigger is pressed. This allows the pistol's owner to develop the rhythm that is so vital in rapid-fire shooting without expending ammunition.

In 1971, the OSP was altered to approximate to the GSP (introduced three years earlier) in an attempt to simplify production by rationalising the two differing sets of parts. The 'new' OSP, therefore, has an entirely angular receiver and barrel, and a modified receiver-locking lever with an auxiliary retaining spring. It can only be distinguished from a GSP chambering .22 Long Rifle rim-fire cartridges by the barrel designation/calibre marks, the position of the back sight, and the depth of the frame at the rear edge of the grip. The sight is shared by the OSP, the GSP and the later versions of the LP3 recoilless match air pistols. It lies on the rear of the OSP frame casting –

---

14. These ports are very effective, and the idea has been copied by many other manufacturers. Some writers have suggested that Walther introduced the ports in 1961–2; the autumn of 1963 seems a more accurate estimate.

15. Bundespatent 1453941, 'Trainingeinrichtung an Schnellfeuerwaffen', sought on 5 June 1965 by 'Carl Walther GmbH, Jagd- u. Sportwaffenfabrik'. Time elapsed before the design could be perfected.

above the back of the grip – or on the GSP receiver ahead of the grip, which provides a ready visual distinction between the two target-pistol designs.

The back sight is well protected and robust, alterations being effected through slotted-head bolts. The bolt on the top surface controls elevation, clockwise motion raising the point of impact on the target, while a bolt on the right side moves the point of impact laterally (clockwise motion moves impact to the right).

The rectangular back sight notches are cut into special replaceable inserts, which can be changed with the special sight-adjusting tool supplied with the guns. Post-1971 examples of the OSP are about 300mm long, 150mm deep and 50mm broad, have sight radii of about 260mm (compared with 220mm on the GSP), and 115mm barrels rifled with six grooves turning to the right. They weigh about 1,200gm, but do not accept supplementary weights. The detachable box magazines hold five .22 Short cartridges, and the trigger pull can be adjusted between 200gm and 300gm. Markings include the company's banner trademark, which appears on the left side of the barrel above OSP Cal. .22 Short; on the left side of the frame above the receiver-locking lever, Carl Walther lies above Waffenfabrik Ulm/Do. German commercial proof marks lie on the barrel and receiver, and the serial numbers are prefixed by the letter 'O'.

The guns have been sold with accessories including a spare magazine, a special short trigger, an Allen key, a special sight-adjusting tool, a cleaning rod, a wire brush, two additional back sight blades, a special wide front sight, a test card of five rounds at 25 metres, and an illustrated instruction manual. The result is an excellent purpose-built rapid-fire pistol that is still obtaining remarkable results.

### Single-Shot and Repeating Pistols

One of the fascinating aspects of late twentieth-century handgun shooting has been the rise and continued popularity of manually-operated pistols – often single-shot – drawing their inspiration from the designs of the past. The many copies and near-copies of the Remington Double Derringer are typical of the 'recreationalist' genre, together with copies of the rolling-block pistols of the 1870s.

Even the 'squeezer' principle employed by nineteenth-century pistols such as the Gaulois, the Lampo and the Protector has been resurrected in recent years. The MiniMax 9, developed in Hungary, has been marketed in 9mm Short, 9mm Makarov and 9mm Parabellum. The grip slides backward towards the palm, providing a surprisingly compact four-shot weapon measuring 96 × 68 × 24mm and weighing merely 360gm (9mm Short) or 420gm (9mm Parabellum). Even the larger five-shot 9mm Parabellum version is only 130mm long. Among the advantages claimed for guns of this type are small size in relation to barrel length or power, one-hand operation, permanent readiness to fire, and an absence of springs in the construction.

The American Derringer Corporation of Waco, Texas, has marketed a wide variety of single- and multi-shot pistols, including the Pen-Pistol (1993–7), alongside modernised versions of the High Standard Double Derringer, the COP gun, and the Semmerling

LM-4. The High Standard was a two-shot over/under with a double-action trigger; the COP had four barrels in a cluster, fired sequentially by a striker in the rear of the frame; and the double-action Semmerling (originally made by the Semmerling Corporation of Newton, Massachusetts), which looked like a small semi-automatic, is a manually-operated repeater loaded by pressing the slide forward for each of its four shots.

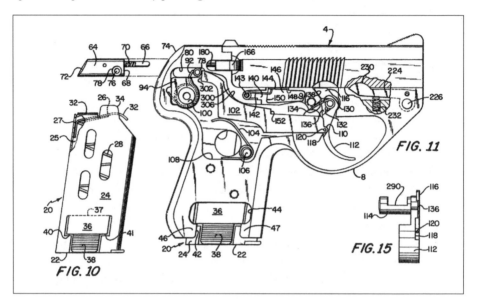

*Drawings of the Semmerling pistol, taken from US Patent 4155187, granted on 22 May 1979.*

There are many single-shot target pistols with electronic triggers and sophisticated sights, but even some of these are little more than adaptations of the Martini-type dropping block of the 1870s. Among the most interesting single-shot handguns, therefore, are those designed specifically for hunting. The most obvious disadvantages are the lack of a rapid second shot, though among the ranks of the shooters are some exceptionally disciplined men who make this perceived drawback into a positive test of their skills as trackers, stalkers and marksmen.

If the lack of a second shot is potentially a weakness, the ability to exchange barrels is a great asset. This can enable a single gun to convert from a .22 rim-fire 'plinker' to handle game cartridges as powerful as .30-30 Winchester in an instant. Among the best known of the guns of this type – a class that has its roots in the shotgun-like guns of the 1920s – are the MOA Maximum, marketed by MOA Corporation of Eaton, Ohio, in chamberings ranging from .22 LR rim-fire to .454 Casull; and the XL, developed by R&R Sporting Arms, Inc., of Brea, California, and now made by RPM in Tucson, Arizona, in chamberings from .22 LR to 45-70 Government. But perhaps the most widely distributed of these single-shot pistols is the Thompson/Center Contender, patented by Warren A. Center of Westminster, Massachusetts, on 9 February 1971 (US No. 3561149).

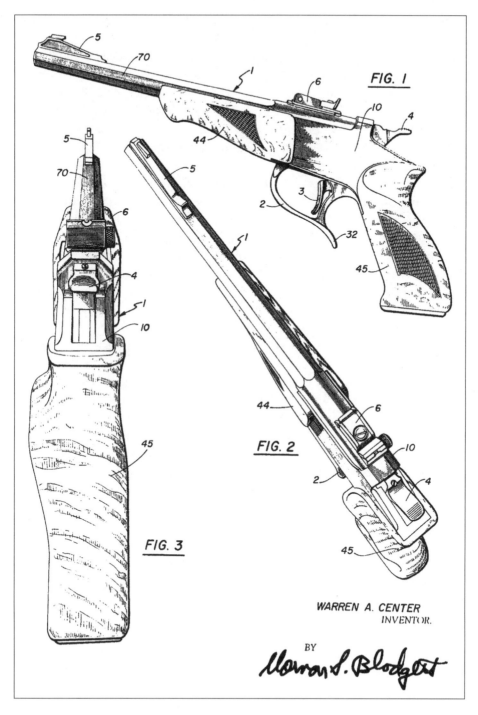

*The first page of drawings of the patent granted in the USA on 9 February 1971 (No. 3561149) to Warren Center, protecting the Contender pistol.*

Thompson/Center Arms, now owned by Smith & Wesson, has offered the Contender in more than forty chamberings from .17 Bumblebee to .45-70 Government; guns have also been regularly adapted to handle cartridges developed by individual experimenters.[16] Among these have been .30 and .357 Herrett, developed in the early 1970s by Steven Herrett and Bob Milek; the TCU series, developed for the Contender by Wes Ugalde at the beginning of the 1980s; the exceptionally wide range of JDJ rounds, designed by J. D. Jones for SSK Industries from 1978 onwards; and the IHMSA, or 'International Handgun Metallic Silhouette Association' rounds developed in the 1980s by Elgin Gates.

The JDJ handgun cartridges range from .226 to .475, often on the basis of re-worked commercially available cases (for example .270 or .307 Winchester, .444 Marlin or .45-70 Government). The power developed by the largest of these rounds is far in excess of what would have been considered desirable in a handgun prior to 1945, and it is sometimes hard to appreciate the benefits that are to be gained from extended range when the recoil is unmanageable by all but the physically strongest shooters. It could also be argued that there is no real need for excessive power in a handgun cartridge, owing to the limitations placed on accuracy by short barrels, but these arguments are rarely accepted by long-range pistol shooters!

The 100-grain bullet of the .257 Mini-Dreadnought leaves the muzzle at 3,000ft/sec, while the 140 grain bullet of the 7mm JDJ attains 2,145ft/sec. For the 9.3 JDJ (270-grain bullet) and 416-06 JDJ (300 grains) the muzzle velocities are 2,025 and 2,230ft/sec respectively. The muzzle energies of these rounds, therefore, are 2,000, 1,430, 2,460 and 3,315ft-lb. If these are compared with such pre-war benchmarks as the 9mm Parabellum, .357 Magnum, .455 Webley and .45 ACP bullets – with muzzle energies typically 345, 575, 220 and 355ft-lb respectively – the trend towards ever-increasing power is clearly evident. When the power of such pre-1945 European handgun standards as the ubiquitous 6.35mm Auto (66ft-lb) and the French 8mm Modèle d'Ordonnance or 'Lebel' revolver cartridge (104ft-lb) are included, the trend becomes even clearer.

The Contender is a 'break open' or tip-barrel design, with an external hammer and a barrel that can range from 8 to 21 inches long. The barrel is readily detachable, by removing the fore-end that restrains the lateral pivot pin, and a change from rim-fire to centre-fire ammunition can be made merely by rotating the firing pin. Mounting both sights on the barrel ensures that the 'zero' is maintained each time a barrel is changed.

The Encore, introduced in 1996, is a strengthened version of the basic Contender action designed to accommodate cartridges with higher power. The frame is larger – the side walls are noticeably higher – and can withstand the pressures generated by cartridges as large and powerful as .375 Holland & Holland Magnum: 4,000–4,500ft-lb,

---

16. The comparative lack of complexity in guns of the Contender class, allied with the strength of material, suits them to experiments with ammunition. Several modern handgun cartridges originated as 'wildcats' developed in single shot test-beds.

depending on bullet type and propellant loading. The Encore barrels, however, will interchange with the current Contender G2 patterns.

Periodicals such as *Guns and Ammo* or *Guns Digest* reveal the extent to which the North American market will support projects that can run from recreations of Civil War cap-lock revolvers and metallic-cartridge derringers to exceptionally sophisticated semi-automatic pistols and 'super size' revolvers firing cartridges that would normally chamber in a rifle.

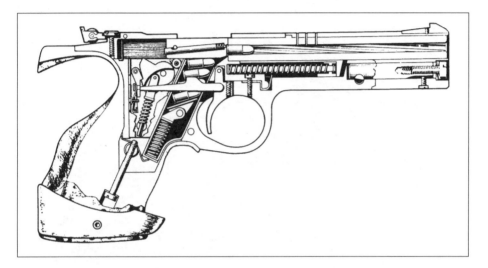

*The modern target pistol: a drawing of the Italian IGI-Domino OP 601, chambering the .22 Short rim-fire round for use in rapid-fire competitions. Note how the magazine has been accommodated in the grip.*

## Automatic Pistols: Research and Development

Though the products of major manufacturers have dominated the handgun market – Colt, Ruger and Smith & Wesson in the USA, Beretta, Fabrique Nationale and Heckler & Koch in Europe – there have always been groups of dedicated experimenters keen to provide 'something different'. In recent years, projects of this type have been most common in the USA This is due in part to the draconian restrictions that, in Britain at least, have largely stifled development. Less punitive regulations have nevertheless ensured that most of the work in European circles is confined to manufacturers, and only in the USA (and then only in the states that believe most strongly in the right to bear arms) does the individual have much chance of progressing his ideas to marketable product.

The 'New Products' sections of the gun magazines provide an interesting commentary on the state of a particular market at a particular time. For example, the 2004 *Guns Digest* featured a wide range of autoloading pistols. Among them were the products of the major manufacturers such as Beretta-USA, Colt, Glock, Heckler &

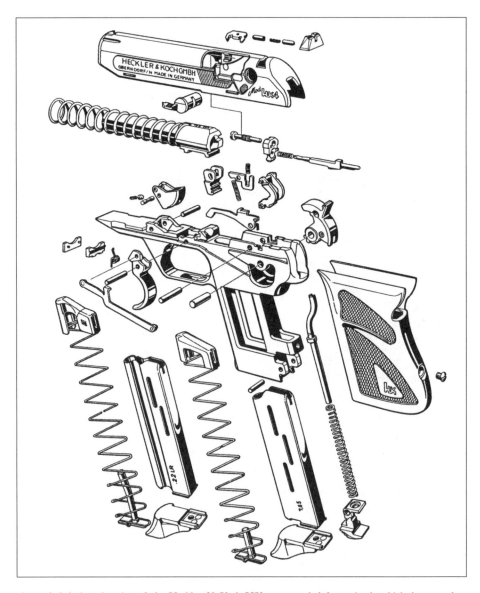

*An exploded-view drawing of the Heckler & Koch HK-4 personal-defence pistol, which drew much of its inspiration from the Mauser HSc.*

Koch, Ruger, Sigarms and Smith & Wesson; but the broad range of lesser-known guns, from Cobra Enterprises to Rohrbauch and Volquartsen, suggests fluidity. Cobra succeeded to the affairs of Davis, Republic and Talon, three lesser businesses which had failed – an illustration of the pitfalls that can confront efforts to raise the profile of guns made by individual inventors from niche-market status to mainstream mass production. Some designs do make the transition, but are comparatively rare.

A review of patents provides confirmation. Alongside specifications granted to Gaston Glock are many obtained by inventors who are further from the public eye – such as Martin Tuma of Solothurn, Switzerland, whose US Patent 5000075 of 19 March 1991 was assigned to International Technology & Machines AG and Sphinxwerke Muller AG of Solothurn; Alexander Kückens of Gross Sarau and Willi Korth of Ratzeburg, assignors of US Patent 4589326 of 20 May 1986 to Technica Entwicklungsgesellschaft mbH & Co. KG of Ratzeburg, Germany; or David Smith of Telscombe Cliffs, England, to whom US Patent 4589327 was granted on 20 May 1986. The Tuma and Kückens/Korth designs have both been successfully exploited commercially, by ITM/Sphinx Industries and Korth respectively, but the Smith pistol, marketed as the Victory Arms MC-5, has never been able to escape the straitjacket of its British origins.

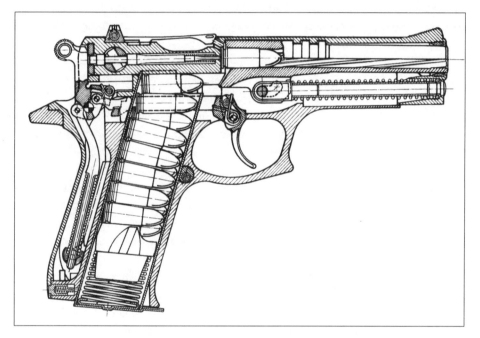

*A longitudinal section of the Star 28M, one of many adaptations of the proven Browning tipping-barrel operating system to have been made in recent years.*

Among the many guns of American origin have been the gas-operated pistol protected by US Patent 3069976, granted on 25 December 1962 to Frederick F. Stevens, Jr, of Brooklyn (but sought in December 1957); US Patent 3857325, granted to Frank S. Thomas of Los Angeles on 31 December 1974 to protect a form of delayed blowback; US Patent 3988964 of 2 November 1976, granted to Wildey J. Moore of Newburgh, New York, to protect a gas-operated pistol with a sliding radial piston concentric with the barrel; and US Patent 4275640 of 30 June 1981, granted to Gary Wilhelm of Hamden, Connecticut, to protect a pistol with a selectable single-/double-action trigger mechanism. The Stevens pistol, though illustrated and described in the relevant patent in great detail, was never made in quantity. Attempts were made to market the Thomas designs commercially, but never successfully. The Wildey was offered in some numbers, but the Wilhelm trigger mechanism was exploited not in the USA but instead in Spain, where it was embodied in the Llama Omni pistol.

The story of the Wildey encapsulates the problems that face even the most promising designs if they originate away from Colt, Ruger, Smith & Wesson or similar large-scale manufacturers with the ability to invest in research and then market the results aggressively. The first gas-operated Wildey pistols were chambered for the .45 Winchester Magnum cartridge and worked well enough to acquire not only a good reputation but also a dedicated band of followers. However, to raise the capital needed to widen the scale of production, Wildey Moore relinquished a controlling interest in his patents. His backers eventually elected to pursue their own course, firing Moore from his own business and going on to form Wildey, Inc., in January 1983. Deliveries became erratic and, as quality also declined, the reputation of the project was seriously compromised. After trading for less than eighteen months, Wildey, Inc., was liquidated. Legal complications prevented Moore regaining control of his patents for several years, delaying the recommencement of production until the late 1980s. By that time chambered for a new .475 Wildey Magnum cartridge, the much improved pistol finally gained some of the success it deserved.

A combination of a rise in pistol-making in developing countries and the increasing restrictions placed on the private ownership of handguns in all but a few traditional bastions has placed great strain on many established businesses. Colt and Smith & Wesson have both struggled at times since the 1970s, undergoing periodic changes of ownership, labour problems and, in the case of Smith & Wesson, a wholesale re-location of the factory.

Smith & Wesson ceased to be privately owned in 1963, when the business was acquired by the Bangor Punta Corporation, but Lear Siegler Group acquired Bangor Punta in 1984 and then sold out within two years to the Forstmann, Little Company. The new owners sought to dispose of unwanted assets, selling Smith & Wesson to the British F. H. Tomkins plc in 1988. Tomkins struggled for some years to reverse declining fortunes, with only limited success, and then sold Smith & Wesson to a group of US investors represented by the Saf-T-Hammer Corporation (since reconstituted as the 'Smith & Wesson Holding Corporation'). The new management embarked on an ambitious modernisation programme that will eventually see the abandonment of many well-established patterns and the introduction of new designs, including handguns with synthetic frames.

The problems have affected even Ruger, not only a relative newcomer but also firmly committed to new technology: manufacturing is expensive, and the improved efficiency made possible by better equipment is not always enough to offset the rock-bottom labour costs of businesses operating in, for example, the People's Republic of China.

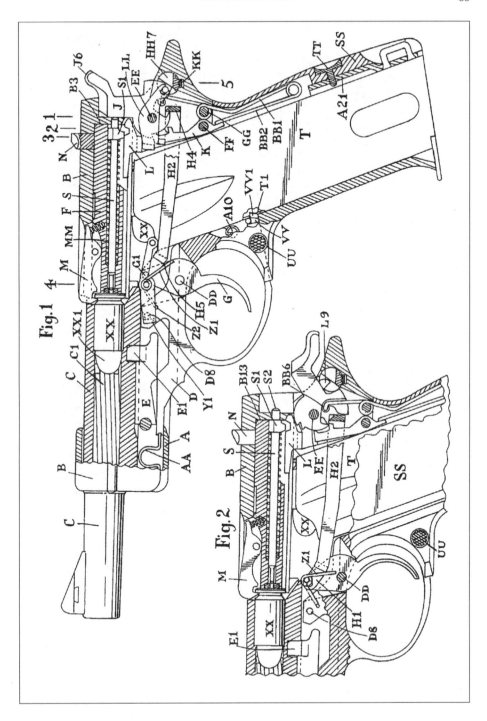

*US Patent 4589327 of 20 May 1986 was granted to Englishman David Smith to protect the design of what was to become the Victory Arms MC-5.*

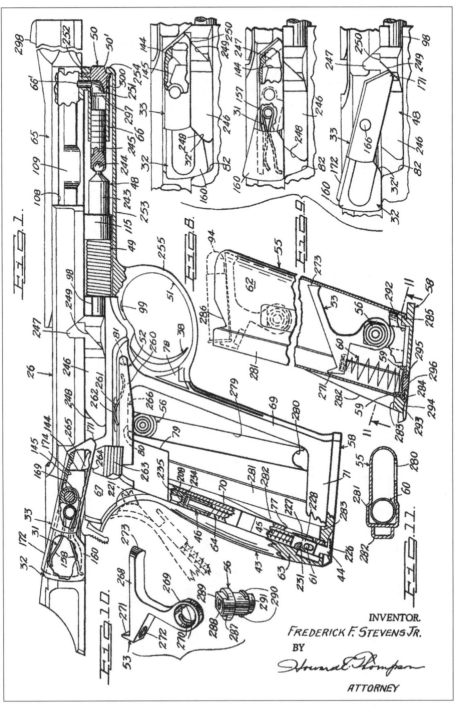

*Drawings of the gas-operated pistol protected by US Patent 3069976, granted to Frederick Stevens, Jr, on 25 December 1962.*

Casualties have included two of the large-volume revolver makers, Harrington & Richardson (which collapsed in 1987) and Charter Arms (reconstituted in 1999 as 'Charter 2000, Inc.'); in Britain, Webley & Scott has long since ceased production. Walther, with a lengthy history but probably persisting too long with the P1/P5 series, was unprepared for the collapse of its military/police pistol market and was acquired by Umarex. One immediate benefit of the change of ownership has been renewed investment in technology, leading, in particular, to the introduction in 1997 of the futuristic Walther P99.

Even Heckler & Koch was badly affected by the abandonment of the G11 caseless-cartridge rifle programme, and by the absence, until the recent advent of the USP, of a suitable replacement for the P7 series. FN Herstal SA, underpinned for so long by the success not only of the GP-35 ('High Power') but also by the FAL and the MAG, has not yet been able to find substantial enough markets for their replacements. The Five-seveN pistol, for example, has not yet been able to loosen the hold of the Glock and, to a lesser extent, the Beretta 92 series, on European military and police sales.

Consequently, it is hard to see how some of the leading manufacturers operating in 2007 can survive much longer, as the trials and tribulations of the handgun market can affect even the most powerful and the most diverse. Continued improvements in technology will undoubtedly allow some handgun gunmakers to make progress. In the USA, Smith & Wesson has already offered pistols embodying synthetic parts, though the commercial market, cautious and often conservative, tends to resist these advances: what else could explain the legions of US-made clones of a Colt-Browning patented before the First World War?

Some of the advances in technology are explained in detail in the closing chapter of *The Rifle Story*, and it is clear that there are areas in which great improvement can (and undoubtedly will) be made. One of the most obvious steps forward lies in the perfection, distribution and widespread acceptance of a caseless cartridge, which eases many design problems. Advances in precision die-casting, precision forming, investment casting, powder metallurgy and the chemistry of polymers will all influence the way in which guns are made. Particularly relevant to handguns is spray casting, which is already producing barrels by spraying molten metal over a rotating mandrel.

# Bibliography

Note: most manufacturers have websites, which are usually accessible through the best-known search engines or listings in periodicals such as *Guns Digest*.

Bady, Donald B., *Colt Automatic Pistols, 1896–1955*. Borden Publishing Company, Alhambra, CA, rev. (2nd) ed., 1973.

Barnes, Frank C. (Stan Skinner, ed.), *Cartridges of the World* . DBI Books, Northbrook, IL, 10th ed., 2003.

Boothroyd, Geoffrey, *The Handgun*. Safari Press, Huntington Beach, CA, 1999.

Breathed, John W., Jr, and Schroeder, Joseph J., Jr, *System Mauser*. Handgun Press, Chicago, IL, 1967.

Browning, John, and Gentry, Curt, *John M. Browning: American Gunmaker*. Doubleday, New York, 1964.

Bruce, Gordon, and Reinhart, Christian, *Webley Revolvers*. Verlag Stocker-Schmid, Dietikon-Zürich, 1988.

Derby, Harry, *The Hand Cannons of Imperial Japan*. Derby Publishing Company, Charlotte, NC, 1981.

Dowell, William C., *The Webley Story*. The Skyrac Press, Kirkgate, Leeds, 1962.

Erlmeier, Hans A., and Brandt, Jacob H., *Manual of Pistol & Revolver Cartridges*. Journal-Verlag Schwend GmbH, Schwäbisch Hall, Germany: Vol. 1 (centrefire, metric calibres), 1967, Vol. 2 (centrefire, Anglo-American calibres), 1980.

Ezell, Edward C., *Handguns of the World*. Stackpole Books, Harrisburg, PA, 1981.

——, *Small Arms Today*. Stackpole Books, Harrisburg, PA, 2nd ed., 1988.

Fors, William Barlow, *Collector's Handbook of U.S. Cartridge Revolvers, 1856–1899*. Adams Press, Chicago, IL, 1973.

Gangarosa, Gene, Jr., *Complete Guide to Compact Handguns*. Stoeger Publishing Co, Wayne, 1997.

——, *Complete Guide to Service Handguns*. Stoeger Publishing Co., Wayne, 1998.

——, *Spanish Handguns*. Stoeger Publishing Co., Wayne, 2001.

Gardner, Robert E., *Small Arm Makers*, Crown Publishers, New York, 1958.

Gluckman, Col Arcadi, *United States Martial Pistols & Revolvers*. The Stackpole Company, Harrisburg, PA, 1956.

Görtz, Joachim, *Die Pistole 08*. Verlag Stocker-Schmid, Dietikon-Zürich, Switzerland, and Motorbuch-Verlag, Stuttgart, 1985.

——, and Walter, John D., *The Navy Luger*. The Lyon Press, Eastbourne, and Handgun Press, Chicago, IL, 1988.

Grennell, Dean A., *The Gun Digest Book of the .45*. DBI Books, Northfield, IL, 1989.

Hackley, Frank W., Woodin, William H., and Scranton, Edward L., *History of Modern US Military Small Arms Ammunition*. The Macmillan Company, New York, Vol. 1 (1880–1939), 1976; The Gun Room Press, Aledo, IL, Vol. 2 (1940–45), 1978.

Hartnik, A. E., *Encyclopedia of Pistols and Revolvers*. Knickerbocker Press, New York, 1997.

Hatch, Alden, *Remington Arms in American History*. Remington Arms Company, Ilion, NY, rev. ed., 1972.

Hatcher, Maj.-Gen. Julian S., *Hatcher's Notebook*. The Stackpole Company, Harrisburg, PA, 3rd ed., 1962.

Häusler, Fritz: *Schweizer Fastfeuerwaffen – Armes de poing suisses – Swiss Handguns*. Verlag Häusler, Frauenfeld, 1975.

Haven, Charles T., and Belden, Frank A., *A History of the Colt Revolver*. William Morrow & Company, New York, 1940.

Heer, Eugen, *Die Faustfeuerwaffen von 1850 bis zur Gegenwart*. Part of *'Geschichte und Entwicklung der Militärhandfeuerwaffen in der Schweiz'*. Akademische Druck- und Verlagsanstalt, Graz, 1971.

Hogg, Ian V., *German Handguns, 1871–2001*. Greenhill Books; London, and Stackpole Books, Mechanicsburg, PA, 2001.

——, *Military Pistols & Revolvers*. Arms & Armour Press, London, 1988.

——, (John Walter, ed.) *Small Arms. Pistols and Rifles*. Greenhill Books, London, and Stackpole Books, Mechanicsburg, PA; rev. ed., 2003.

——, *The Greenhill Military Small Arms Data Book*. Greenhill Books, London, and Stackpole Books, Mechanicsburg, PA, 2000.

——, *The Cartridge Guide*. Arms & Armour Press, London, 1982.

——, and Walter, John, *Pistols of the World* . Krause Publications, Iola, WI, 4th ed., 2004. (Note: the first three editions were compiled with the assistance of John S. Weeks.)

——, and Weeks, John S., *Military Small Arms of the Twentieth Century*. Krause Publications, Iola, WI, 7th ed., 2000.

Honeycutt, Fred L., Jr, *Military Pistols of Japan*. Julin Books, Lake Park, FL, 1982.

Jinks, Roy G., *History of Smith & Wesson*. Beinfeld Publishing Company, North Hollywood, CA, 1977.

Kasler, Peter A., *Glock: The New Wave in Combat Handguns*. Paladin Press, Boulder, CO, 1993.

König, Klaus-Peter, *Faustfeuerwaffen*. Motorbuch Verlag GmbH, Stuttgart, 1980.

Kopec, John A., Graham, Ron, and Moore, Kenneth C., *A Study of the Colt Single Action Army Revolver*. La Puente, CA, 1976.

Law, Clive A., *Canadian Military Handguns, 1855–1985*. Museum Restoration Service, Bloomfield, Ontario, 1994.

Leithe, Frederick E., *Japanese Handguns*, Borden Publishing, Alhambra, CA, 1967.

Long, Duncan, *Combat Revolvers*. Paladin Press, Boulder, CO, 1999.

——, *Glock's Handguns*. Desert Publications, El Dorado, AZ, 1996.

——, *Hand Cannons: The World's Most Powerful Handguns*. Paladin Press, Boulder, CO, 1995.

Lugs, Jaroslav, *Rucní palne zbrane*, Naše Vojsko, Prague, Czechoslovakia, 2 vols, 1956. (An English translation, *Firearms Past and Present*, was published c.1976 by Ravenhill Publishing, London.)

Markham, George (John Walter), *Guns of the Empire*. Arms & Armour Press, London, 1990.

——, *Guns of the Reich*. Arms & Armour Press, London, 1989.

——, *Guns of the Wild West*. Arms & Armour Press, London, 1991.

Mathews, J. Howard, *Firearms Identification*. Charles C. Thomas, Springfield, IL, 3 vols, 1962–73.

Neal, Robert J., and Jinks, Roy G., *Smith & Wesson 1857–1945*. A. S. Barnes & Company, South Brunswick, NJ, 1966.

Nelson, Thomas B., and Musgrave, Daniel D., *The World's Machine Pistols & Submachine Guns*. TBN Enterprises, Alexandria, VA, 1980.

Parsons, John E., *Smith & Wesson Revolvers: The Pioneer Single Action Models*. William Morrow & Company, New York, 1957.

——, *The Peacemaker and its Rivals*. William Morrow & Company, New York, 1950.

Ramos, J. M., *The CZ-75 Family: The Ultimate Combat Handgun*. Paladin Press, Boulder, CO, 1990.

Reckendorf, Hans, *Die Militär-Faustfeuerwaffen des Königreiches Preussen und des Deutschen Reiches*. Published privately, Dortmund-Schönau, 1978.

——, *Die Handwaffen der Königlich Preussischen und der Kaiserliche Marine*. Published privately, Dortmund-Schönau, 1983.

Reinhart, Christian, *Pistolen und Revolver in der Schweiz*. Verlag Stocker-Schmid, Dietikon-Zürich, and Motor-Buch Verlag, Stuttgart, 1988.

——, and Am Rhyn, Michael, *Faustfeuerwaffen II. Selbstladepistolen*. The 6th volume of *Bewaffnung und Ausrüstung der Schweizer Armee seit 1817*. Verlag Stocker-Schmid, Dietikon-Zürich, 1976.

Rosa, Joseph G., *Guns of the American West (1776–1900)*. Arms & Armour Press, London, 1985.

Rubí, B. Barceló, *Armamento Portatil Español (1764–1939): una labora artillera*. Libreria Editorial San Martin, Madrid, 1976.

Schwing, Ned, *Standard Catalog of Firearms*. Krause Publications, Iola, WI, 14th ed., 2004.

——, *Standard Catalog of Military Firearms*. Krause Publications, Iola, WI, 2001.

Serven, James E., *Colt Firearms from 1836*. The Foundation Press, La Habra, CA, 7th printing, 1972.

Simpson, Layne, *The Custom Government Model Pistol*. Wolfe Publishing, Prescott, AZ, 1994.

Smith, Walter H. B., *Mauser, Walther & Mannlicher Firearms*. The Stackpole Company, Harrisburg, PA, 1971.

——, *The Book of Pistols & Revolvers*. The Stackpole Company, Harrisburg, PA, 7th ed., 1968.

—— (rev. by Joseph E. Smith and Edward C. Ezell), *Small Arms of the World*, Stackpole Books, Harrisburg PA, 11th ed.. 1977.

Stern, Daniel K., *10 Shots Quick*. Globe Printing Company, San Jose, CA, 1967.

Stevens, R. Blake, *The Browning High Power Automatic Pistol*. Collector Grade Publications, Toronto, Canada, 1996.

Still, Jan C., *The Pistols of Germany and Her Allies in Two World Wars*: Vol I *Military Pistols of Imperial Germany and Her World War I Allies, and Postwar Military, Para-military and Police Reworks*; Vol II *Axis Pistols*; Vol. III *Third Reich Lugers and Their Accessories*; Vol. IV *Imperial Lugers and Their Accessories*; Vol. V *Weimar and Early Nazi Lugers and Their Accessories*. Published privately, Douglas, AK, 1982, 1986, 1988, 1991, 1993.

Supica, Jim, and Nahas, Richard, *Standard Catalog of Smith & Wesson*. Krause Publications, Iola, WI, 2nd ed., 2001.

Taffin, John, *Big Bore Sixguns*. Krause Publications, Iola, WI, 1997.

Taylerson, Anthony W. F., *The Revolver, 1865–1888*. Herbert Jenkins, London; 1966.

——, *The Revolver, 1889–1914*. Barrie & Jenkins, London, 1970.

——, with Andrews, R. A. N., and Firth, J., *The Revolver, 1818–1865*. Herbert Jenkins, London, 1968.

Walter, John D., *Allied Small Arms of World War One*. The Crowood Press, Ramsbury, Wiltshire, 2000.

——, *Central Powers' Small Arms of World War One*. The Crowood Press, Ramsbury, Wiltshire, 1999.

——, *German Military Handguns, 1879–1918*. Arms & Armour Press, London, 1980.

——, *Military Handguns of Two World Wars*. Greenhill Books, London, and Stackpole Books, Mechanicsburg, PA, 2003.

——, *Secret Firearms*. Arms & Armour Press, London, 1997.

——, *The Greenhill Dictionary of Guns and Gunmakers*. Greenhill Books, London, and Stackpole Books, Mechanicsburg, PA, 2001.

——, *The Guns that Won the West*. Greenhill Books, London, and Stackpole Books, Mechanicsburg, PA, 1999.

——, *The Luger Book*. Arms & Armour Press, London, 1986.

——, *The Luger Story*. Greenhill Books, London, and Stackpole Books, Mechanicsburg, PA, 1995.

——, *The Pistol Book*. Arms & Armour Press, London, 2nd ed., 1988.

White, Henry P., Munhall, Barton D., and Bearse, Ray, *Centerfire Pistol & Revolver Cartridges*. A. S. Bames & Company, New York and South Brunswick, 1967.

Wilson, Lt-Col Robert K. (Ian V. Hogg, ed.), *Textbook of Automatic Pistols*. Arms & Armour Press, London, 1975.

Wilson, R. L., *The Colt Heritage*. Simon & Schuster, New York, undated (1979).

——, *Colt, An American Legend*. Blacksmith Corporation, Chino Valley, 1991.

Winant, Lewis, *Firearms Curiosa*. Ray Riling Arms Books, Philadelphia, PA, 1961.

Wood, J. B., *Beretta Automatic Pistols*. Stackpole Books, Harrisburg, PA, 1995.

Zhuk, A. B., *The Illustrated Encyclopedia of Handguns*. Greenhill Books, London, 1995.

# Index